AMERICAN INVESTMENT IN AUSTRALIAN INDUSTRY

American Investment in Australian Industry

Donald T. Brash, 1940 -

Department of Economics
Research School of Social Sciences
Australian National University

HARVARD UNIVERSITY PRESS
Cambridge, Massachusetts
1966

66-31366

Preface

By a rather remarkable turn of fate, my introduction to the subject of foreign investment in Australia, and the intense feelings which it generates, began on 22 December 1959. On that day, I was among a small group of people in the visitors' gallery of the Sydney Stock Exchange when it was announced that General Motors Corporation of the U.S. was making a bid for the Australian-held preference shares (the only Australian interest) in General Motors-Holden's Ltd.

Less than three years later, after writing a Master's thesis in New Zealand on the problems posed by international investment income for the balance of payments of that, my native, country, I was examining possible subjects for a Doctoral thesis at the Australian National University when Professor Sir John Crawford invited me to conduct a survey of American corporate investment in Australian manufacturing. The present book, with some revision and the omission of many referential footnotes, follows this thesis closely.

I have never held 'extremist' views on foreign investment, but it is fair to admit that, knowing something of the hostility generated by foreign capital both in this century and the last, I began this project very conscious of the disadvantages of foreign investment. The survey was therefore framed substantially in sympathy with Australian public sentiment. In particular, special attention was devoted to such matters as the quantitative importance of American capital in Australian industry, the extent to which American-affiliated companies share ownership with Australians, the dependence of such companies on the Australian capital market, the pricing of imports bought from affiliates, the importance of export franchise restrictions, and the effect on Australia's balance of payments of the growth of profits accruing abroad.

Data were gathered for the most part in a direct firm-by-firm study. As explained in the introduction, the response by the American-affiliated companies approached was good, particularly in view of the considerable quantity and sensitive nature of the information sought. Echoing Southard's comment made after a similar survey of American investment in Europe at the beginning of the thirties, 'I trust that the suspicious attitude of those other companies who refused to coöperate has not been justified by the contents of the book' (1931: viii).

As the survey progressed, I became increasingly conscious of the benefits Australia derives from foreign investment and this view was confirmed by a theoretical analysis of the factors involved. (Because Sir John Crawford had approached many American subsidiaries in Australia for their co-operation in the survey before I was asked to conduct it, the timetable of the project was to some extent 'exogenous'. For this reason, the theoretical analysis of foreign investment was carried out in large measure after the completion of the empirical work.) The conclusion eventually reached was that the most important question to be asked is not 'Does foreign investment benefit Australia?' but 'Is Australia maximizing the benefits from foreign investment?' In most circumstances, Australia must benefit from foreign investment.

It is no consolation that the conclusions of the study may well be unpopular with both Right and Left—in the context of Australian politics, with the Liberal and Country Parties on the one hand and with the Australian Labor Party on the other. The Left may be the more offended by what may appear a 'defence' of foreign investment, but those on both sides of the political fence may resent other criticisms, such as that of Australian tariff policy. But, since the publication of my own Master's thesis in 1964 (warning New Zealand against too much reliance on foreign capital), I can share at least some of the embarrassment.

The number of people who assisted in this project is far too large to permit individual mention of all of them. The survey would have been quite impossible without the time and effort which the executives of participating companies so generously donated, and, in response to an appeal by Professor Sir John Crawford, some companies even provided financial support for the project.[1] In addition to these, there were a great many companies, both American-affiliated and Australian-owned, which provided some information on their operations, not to mention countless people in all walks of life who offered comments and opinions on all aspects of American investment. Executives of six of the largest American subsidiaries provided not merely statistics on the operation of their own companies but also detailed advice on the wording of the questionnaires used in the survey and general advice on the conduct of the project.

[1] A list of companies which completed at least the first main questionnaire used in the survey and of those which contributed financially is given in Appendix D.

Contents

Tables

xi

I

Introduction

Private foreign investment has been of major importance in Australia's post-war industrial development. While it is impossible to compare what has actually happened in the Australian economy with what might have happened in the absence of a capital inflow, it seems clear that since 1945 private foreign investors have not only added substantially to the funds available for investment in the private sector, but have also provided access to much of the technical knowledge and managerial skill developed in the more industrially advanced countries of Europe and North America. The rapid growth of those sectors in which foreign capital and foreign skills are combined has been a vital force impelling growth throughout the economy.

The importance of the contribution made by foreign investment to Australia is widely recognized. Popular concern at the extent to which foreign-owned companies now appear to dominate the economy has nevertheless been growing throughout the fifties and sixties, aroused to a considerable extent by the well-publicized profitability of the largest foreign-owned company in Australia, General Motors-Holden's Pty Ltd. As Dr Penrose has observed, G.M.H. 'raised a hornet's nest of controversy about its corporate ears' with the publication of its Annual Report for 1954. Since that date, the annual profit of this company has frequently taken the record for the largest ever declared in Australia. Late in 1959, General Motors announced its intention to buy out the Australian holders of preference shares in the company: the purchase was widely felt to be a thinly disguised attempt to avoid the necessity of publishing profit figures and did little to improve the public relations either of G.M.H. or of foreign-owned companies in general. Indeed, one of the forces behind the enactment of legislation in 1961 which compelled many proprietary companies to publish their annual results

1

for the first time was just this determination to reveal the results of foreign-owned companies.

The official federal government attitude to foreign capital is one of welcome, particularly where that capital 'is of a kind likely to help in the balanced development of Australia's resources and brings with it the skills and "know-how" needed for the successful fulfilment of the project in which the investment is made' (Commonwealth Treasury 1960: 3). This is a policy which has been frequently reiterated by Sir Robert Menzies as Prime Minister and the Rt Hon. Harold Holt as Federal Treasurer in the House of Representatives and on other occasions. State governments, both Liberal and Labor, implicitly support the federal policy: the Premiers of both New South Wales and South Australia, for example, journeyed abroad in 1963 on tours which were confessedly designed in large measure to encourage foreign capital to their states.

But criticism of this 'open door' policy has been growing increasingly vociferous. On the government benches, the Deputy Prime Minister and Leader of the Country Party, the Rt Hon. J. McEwen, has kept up an almost constant stream of criticism of the present policy for some years. Addressing the annual meeting of the Australian Association of Advertising Agencies in 1962, he commented:

> Many of you here will realise how Australia has benefited from the establishment in this country of industries from overseas—the capital, the know-how, the marketing techniques and on some occasions the actual markets—all are a benefit from capital inflow. This is very good, but not very good if the whole nation becomes geared to a dependence upon capital inflow. . . . It has been perilously close to that on some recent occasions.

In 1963 he criticized excessive foreign investment in Australia at the annual conferences of the Country Party in both New South Wales and Victoria, commenting at the Victorian conference that 'we are selling a bit of our heritage each year'. He has often criticized the take-over of existing Australian companies by foreign capital and the restriction of the export franchise of foreign-affiliated companies.

Other recent indications of federal government concern are not hard to find. In 1964 the Minister for Territories indicated that there must be provision for Australian participation in any project to develop the bauxite deposits at Gove Peninsula, and later in the same year even the Prime Minister made a comment which was widely interpreted to be a hardening of the government's attitude: 'I would be much happier if all the [foreign investors] who came into Australia were willing to admit Australians to some share in the equity in the business. . . . But we haven't yet reached the point of time at which we can frown at a movement of investment [into] Australia.' There have also been stirrings of dissatisfaction with the present policy in the governing parties of several of the states.

The Federal Labor Party, the official Opposition, has been hostile to uncontrolled foreign investment for many years. It is hard to avoid the conclusion that some of the criticism levelled by Labor politicians—like that of some politicians in other parties—is more emotive than scientific: one Labor Member of Parliament has gone so far as to write of 'the Frankenstein that foreign investment has become'. But it was the Leader of the Federal Labor Party, the Hon. A. A. Calwell, who stated early in 1963 that Australia's 'reliance on the flow of capital from abroad to meet a substantial part of our annual imports bill is tantamount to mortgaging the house to pay the grocery bill'. In the federal election campaign later that year, the Labor Party committed itself to introduce legislation designed to give Australians a certain percentage in the ownership of foreign subsidiaries and to discourage the take-over of established Australian companies.

Among academic economists, attitudes to foreign investment differ widely. In recent years the most frequently quoted 'defence' of foreign investment has been that of J. O. N. Perkins (1960), while H. W. Arndt, at the end of an article in which he surveys post-war foreign investment in Australia in some detail, concludes: 'I think it is quite possible that the benefits, direct and indirect, of overseas investment during the past decade have greatly outweighed the costs, direct and indirect, and will continue to do so. My point is that I do not know and that I cannot see how anyone can find out.' (1957: 260.) Representing the more sceptical is E. L. Wheelwright, who feels that it 'is now possible to argue that Australia has less need of foreign capital than formerly, and that a little domestic innovation and ingenuity in the manipulation of our balance of payments could provide most of the necessary foreign exchange resources for future development' (1963: 160).

Editorial comment in Australian newspapers is almost uniformly critical, if not of foreign investment *per se*, of various aspects of the operation of foreign-controlled companies. In one important financial newspaper alone there were more than a dozen editorials critical of some aspect of foreign investment in the three years ending 1964. After the action of the British and New Zealand governments in mid-1964 to establish some control over foreign investment, the financial editorial of the *Sydney Morning Herald* called for similar action in Australia under the headline 'Australian Cast Needed for Third Act'.

OVERSEAS INVESTORS

"*ITS OUR STABILITY THAT ATTRACTS THEM.*"

Reproduced by courtesy of the *Australian*

Some Australians regard foreign investment with misgivings, as this reaction to a speech by the Prime Minister in 1964 indicates

The hostility of the press is also shown in the frequently irresponsible way in which the profits of foreign companies are reported: Dr Penrose (1956: 221) noted that the profits of G.M.H. in 1954 were reported as being equal to 560 per cent on the paid-up ordinary capital of the company, though return on shareholders' funds or net worth was only 39 per cent. Such distortion is not unusual. Under the headline 'Bonanza By Colgate', one paper reported that 'Colgate-Palmolive Pty. Ltd., the wholly-owned Australian subsidiary of Colgate-Palmolive Co., of the U.S., achieved a 447·6 per cent earning rate on capital' in the year ended December 1962 (*Australian Financial Review* [*A.F.R.*], 2 July 1963), while another described the earning rate on capital of Gilbert & Barker Manufacturing Co. (Aust.) Pty Ltd as '516 per cent' in 1963, failing to point out that the company's earning rate on shareholders' funds was only 10·1 per cent (*Australian*, 13 Aug. 1964).[1]

---

[1] In defence, of course, foreign-owned companies have sometimes resorted to their own misrepresentation of profitability. More than one, for example, has introduced royalty payments to its parent company since the enactment of legislation to compel profit disclosure, in order to reduce the published profit figure. One very profitable company makes a habit of including its dividend

(*Continued on facing page*)

Press opinion seems to reflect a remarkably widespread concern. Some of the comments of the man in the street, even the educated man in the street, border on the mercantilist in their preoccupation with foreign companies 'taking money out of the country'. But it is by no means only the man in the street who is concerned. At least one major Australian company, Australian Paper Manufacturers Ltd, has disfranchised non-Australians who acquired shares after a certain date. Statements urging foreign companies to accept a minimum percentage of Australian equity have become commonplace in recent years. Among those pressing for action of this kind are such highly respected leaders of the business community as Staniforth Ricketson, a leading Melbourne broker; M. John O'Neill, chairman of the City Mutual Life Assurance Society Ltd; C. G. Crane, chairman of the Australian Mutual Provident Society; Sir James Kirby, a prominent industrialist and chairman of the Manufacturing Industries Advisory Council; L. J. Hooker, a leading real estate agent; and P. L. Alroe, chairman of the Brisbane Stock Exchange. Sir Ian McLennan, chief general manager of the Broken Hill Proprietary Company Ltd, has expressed the view that it must be of some importance to any country that its basic resources and its basic industries 'have a substantial domestic content as to investment and as to direction' (*Australian*, 2 Oct. 1964). Sir John Crawford, deputy chairman of the government-appointed Committee of Economic Enquiry and Director of the Research School of Pacific Studies in the Australian National University, has urged Australians to 'pay more attention to the problem of overseas control of Australian industries —especially on the rights of local subsidiaries to compete in export markets against overseas parent companies' (*A.F.R.*, 4 Sept. 1962). This problem of the restriction of the right to export has been described by W. S. Johnston, manager of the Trade and Commerce Department of the International Division of the Bank of New South Wales, as 'the major hurdle facing Australia and without question . . . detrimental to the future development of our export trade' (*A.F.R.*, 27 Nov. 1962). Even Americans have urged modification of the present policy: J. S. Ewing of the Graduate Business School of Stanford University, California, stated that if Australia 'does not provide for some restriction on the flow of capital it will not be long before it finds itself in the same position as Canada—dominated by American interests. . . . Domination is not good for your economy

---

provision in its statement of shareholders' funds, probably to reduce 'apparent profitability'. And, in another case, the local company includes a loan to an affiliate in its statement of shareholders' funds when this is made available to the public but not when reporting to its parent company, again to reduce 'apparent profitability'.

no matter how great the capital inflow.' (*Age*, 19 Aug. 1963.) A similar comment has been made by Hoyt Ammidon, chairman of the United States Trust Company (*A.F.R.*, 7 Sept. 1964).

Enough has been said to indicate a very general feeling in Australia that some change should be made in the present policy of unqualified welcome for all private foreign capital. Even the most persistent critics of foreign investment rarely deny the benefits Australia has gained from this investment, though these benefits are usually alluded to in very general terms and it has become almost as fashionable to stress the strategic advantages of having a large body of investment from powerful political allies as it is to dwell on the more strictly economic advantages. Questions most often asked are: might not the admitted current benefits of foreign investment be more than outweighed by the long-term costs of this investment? Might not the 'great profitability of foreign investment', coupled with an alleged tendency for foreign companies to hold all the equity of their Australian subsidiaries, pose a mounting problem for the Australian balance of payments in future years? Might not restrictions on the right of foreign-affiliated companies to export hinder Australia's export drive in industrial goods? Many who would not question the desirability of foreign investment when it establishes new industries in Australia yet ask: should overseas companies be allowed to take over established Australian-owned companies? The sophisticated worry lest fluctuations in capital inflow make management of the economy more difficult, or lest foreign companies absorb local loan funds which would otherwise be available to locally-owned companies. Concern is expressed that foreign companies may do insufficient research locally, or that foreign oil companies may artificially maintain prices for crude oil purchased from their overseas affiliates at a level higher than the 'open market value'. Behind much of this concern lies a basic fear of being 'controlled by foreigners'.

In this situation surprisingly little is known of the operation of foreign-affiliated companies in Australia. The Commonwealth Bureau of Census and Statistics has published annual figures for private capital inflow into Australian companies only since 1947/8, and since no census of foreign capital already invested in the economy was made at that time (and none has been made since) no accurate estimate of the total of foreign capital invested in the economy is possible.[2] A reasonably satisfactory break-up of private overseas investment in Australian companies by country of origin has been

---

[2] E. L. Wheelwright (1963: 160) has estimated that the value of private overseas capital invested in Australian companies at 30 June 1947 was £300 million.

published by the Bureau for the whole period from 1947/8, but an industrial classification of this inflow is available only since 1956/7. The Department of Trade has periodically published lists of companies believed to have foreign affiliations and similar lists are available from some embassies. The results of a Department of Trade survey of export franchise restrictions have also been published (Arndt and Sherk 1959). Little else is available from official Australian sources.* R. O. Block has compiled lists of Australian companies having foreign affiliations, with an indication of the extent of the foreign equity interest in each, but apart from that there is little information even in unofficial Australian sources.[3]

A combination of strongly-held opinions and little factual information on which to base them is an explosive situation and there is a real danger in Australia of an otherwise insignificant occurrence triggering hasty or ill-considered action. The purpose of this study is to add to the meagre stock of information currently available on the subject of foreign investment and to attempt answers to at least some of the questions being asked in the field. The study was orientated to the Australian economy, but it is hoped that it may also be of some relevance in other countries faced with similar problems.

For reasons of time, the survey had to be limited to consideration of direct United States investment in Australian manufacturing industry.[4] The limitation of the survey to direct investment scarcely affects its usefulness since the greater part of capital inflow into the Australian economy since 1945 has been private capital and the larger part of that in turn has been direct investment.[5] To limit the

[3] Block's first list was published in the *A.F.R.*, 18 Nov. 1963. A subsequent list, published in the *Australian*, 26 Oct. 1964, showed that of the 50 largest companies (ranked by shareholders' funds) engaged in manufacturing, mining, or primary production in Australia in 1963 no fewer than 23 were 51 per cent or more foreign-owned.

[4] For the purpose of this study, investment is regarded as 'direct' when a foreign company or affiliated group of persons owns an interest of at least 25 per cent in the voting stock of a locally-incorporated company or an equivalent interest in a non-incorporated enterprise operating in Australia. With only one exception (where the foreign equity was very nearly 25 per cent and contact with the foreign company was known to be close), all other foreign investment has been regarded as 'portfolio' and is of no concern in the survey. For some information on corporate portfolio investment, see Appendix C.

[5] In the sixteen years 1948/9 to 1963/4, the total current account deficit in the Australian balance of payments was £1,772 million. Over the same period, the sum of the annual inflows of all private foreign investment in Australian companies was £1,929 million, and of direct investment £1,689 million (Commonwealth Bureau of Census and Statistics 1965a and b).

* Since going to press, however, the Department of Trade and Industry (formerly the Department of Trade) has made an important addition to official

(Continued on next page)

TABLE I-1 Annual Inflow of Private Overseas Investment in Companies in Australia,
by Domicile of Investor
£A(m.)

Year ended 30 June	U.S.A. and Canada	United Kingdom	Other	Total
1948	6·4	29·7	2·3	38·4
1949	4·1	35·2	3·2	42·5
1950	10·3	53·1	5·1	68·5
1951	20·3	43·3	4·9	68·5
1952	30·6	47·0	8·6	86·2
1953	2·0	21·1	2·3	25·4
1954	17·3	44·3	7·3	68·9
1955	39·5	57·0	8·6	105·1
1956	31·9	71·9	13·3	117·1
1957	27·5	61·5	15·7	104·7
1958	27·2	61·1	15·2	103·5
1959	46·8	66·0	12·5	125·3
1960	62·9	105·1	25·8	193·8
1961	87·7	112·0	35·0	234·7
1962	71·5	62·8	14·1	148·4
1963	92·1	103·4	26·0	221·5
1964	96·0	96·5	21·9	214·4

SOURCE: Commonwealth Bureau of Census and Statistics 1965b.

study to American investment is more serious, since in total British capital in Australia is still of significantly greater size than American. There are nevertheless good reasons for studying American rather than British companies.

Thanks to the U.S. Department of Commerce, considerably more published information is available on American investment in Australia than on that of any other nation. More important, American capital is already second only to British capital in level of annual inflow and, as Table I-1 shows, has been growing more rapidly than British investment. In the seventeen years after 1947/8, the sum of the annual inflows of private overseas investment in Australian companies, expressed in current prices and including both direct and portfolio investment, was £1,966·9 million, of which the North American share was £674·1 million, or 34·3 per cent.[6] But this aggre-

---

material on foreign investment by the publication of *Directory of Overseas Investment in Australian Manufacturing Industry—1966.* This not only lists those Australian companies in which there is a foreign equity interest, but specifies the size of that interest and the total assets of the company concerned.

[6] Throughout the study the symbol '£' should be taken to read 'pound Australian' or '£A'. Its par value in U.S. currency is $US2.24. This has been the par value since September 1949 when it fell from $US3.224 with the devaluation of sterling. Australia converted to decimal currency in February 1966 on the basis of £1 = $A2.

gate figure disguises the growth of the American share: whereas American investors provided only 18·9 per cent of the total private foreign investment in the four years 1947/8 to 1950/1, they provided 42·4 per cent in the four years ended 1963/4. (The capital inflow being referred to as 'American' actually represents capital from both the United States and Canada, though capital from the U.S. certainly represents the great bulk of the combined figures. Moreover, a considerable part of the inflow which is classified as 'Canadian' by the Commonwealth Bureau of Census and Statistics is, for the purpose of ultimate control, in reality American: one of the largest American companies in Australia, the Ford Motor Company of Australia Pty Ltd, is classified as a Canadian investment because the immediate parent company of the Australian subsidiary is resident in Canada. To the extent that the combined figures in the table still overstate the strictly American part of the inflow, this is almost certainly fully offset by other cases of 'indirectly American' investments, classified by the Bureau as 'British' or 'Other' investment. This is particularly likely in view of the tendency for quite a number of American-owned companies in Australia to have immediate parent companies resident in tax-haven countries.)

Not only has American capital become more important to Australia: Australia has also become relatively more important as a field of investment for American capital in the years since 1945. Between 1950 and 1962, total direct American investment abroad expanded by 216 per cent. The value of American direct investment in Australia, however, expanded by 446 per cent during that period (U.S. Dept. of Commerce 1964: 10). This, though not the fastest rate of growth recorded, was greater than the increase recorded for the United Kingdom (351 per cent) and substantially greater than the 239 per cent recorded by Canada, both areas of major American investment interest in the last decade. By 1962, only Canada, the United Kingdom, Venezuela, and West Germany had more American direct investment within their borders than did Australia. Brazil was on a par with Australia, but in that year France had less American direct investment than did Australia, and Japan had only one-third as much. On a *per capita* basis, corporate American investment in Australia was almost four times that in Germany and was substantially greater than that in the United Kingdom. Only Canada and Venezuela, of the major American investment fields, surpassed Australia.

There are as yet no indications that the rate of American investment in Australia will slacken. One leading American banker has been quoted as saying: 'There are so many fine potentials in Australia that they call for investment not by the millions of dollars, but by multiples of $100 million.' (*Newsweek*, 10 Aug. 1964.)[7]

There is a further reason for studying American rather than any other foreign investment in Australia: a very large part of the popular controversy on foreign investment has centred around American investment, not least, as already noted, because of the profitability of one particular company. E. T. Hamilton, president of the American Chamber of Commerce in Australia, could be excused a certain bitterness when he commented:

> A visitor to Australia might be pardoned for reaching the conclusion that overseas investment in this country is a synonym for American investment—for such a conclusion is to be drawn from editorials and letters from correspondents. . . . What is the peculiar ingredient that makes American investment suspect while investment capital emanating from Britain, France, Germany, Switzerland and other areas attracts unto itself no special nomenclature? Is U.S. money, then, some kind of monster? (*A.F.R.*, 2 May 1963.)

Not all American corporate investment in Australia is in manufacturing. In mining the American Smelting and Refining Company has a majority interest in the giant copper-silver-lead-zinc enterprise, Mount Isa Mines Ltd, while Cleveland Cliffs Iron Company and Kaiser Steel Corporation are just two of a number of American companies engaged in the development of vast iron ore deposits in Western Australia. It has been reported that, up to 1962, overseas investors had met 57 per cent of the cost of Australia's oil exploration programme, and a major part of this total would certainly have been from American sources. American capital is prominent in the development of Australia's bauxite deposits and there is growing American investment in the coal industry.

While American investment in Australian mining is of rapidly growing significance at present, perhaps the largest American investment outside manufacturing is still in distribution. There, American-owned oil companies have investments of many millions of dollars and other American firms engage in a wide variety of activities as diverse as the distribution of office equipment, the leasing of electronic computers, and the provision of after-sales service for industrial chemicals imported from the U.S. One of the biggest food retailers in the United States, Safeway Stores, has also begun operations in Australia, though direct retailing of consumer goods by American-owned companies is uncommon.

[7] This paragraph was written before the announcement by the American government early in 1965 of measures designed to reduce American investment abroad, but as of late 1965 there seems no reason to modify the conclusion in the text.

In many other fields, too, American capital is well represented. With the influx of American manufacturing companies have come companies accustomed to providing services to them in the U.S.: by early 1964, three of the estimated top four advertising agencies in Australia, for example, had substantial American investment in them, and in 1963 it was estimated that the eight largest American accounting firms all had some kind of partnership arrangement with counterparts in Australia. There are also quite a number of American companies engaged in engineering design or construction work, Utah Construction and Engineering Pty Ltd, Morrison-Knudsen of Australia Ltd, Austin-Anderson (Aust.) Pty Ltd (a division of the Austin Company of the U.S.), Bechtel Pacific Corporation Ltd, and the various subsidiaries of the Dillingham Corporation being among the best known. Investment in primary production by Americans is limited, though there are some significant individual projects such as that of the Chase Manhattan Bank, which is associated with the redevelopment of $1\frac{1}{2}$ million acres of land in Western Australia. In another example, an American syndicate is engaged in a large cotton-growing venture in the Narrabri district of New South Wales. American-owned firms even do some publishing in Australia: both *Time* and *Reader's Digest*, for example, are printed in Australia for part of the Asian area. Probably more important than many of these other activities is the very large number of licensing agreements which have been concluded between American and Australian companies, but these do not as such involve the investment of American capital.[8]

Australian official sources do not permit an estimate of the value of American capital in Australian manufacturing, and the U.S. Department of Commerce figure for 1962, which indicates that a total of $US582 million was invested in that sector, out of a total U.S. investment in Australia of $US1,097 million,[9] does not include investment in oil refining or metal smelting, both of which are taken here to be essentially 'manufacturing'. If American investment in both oil refining and metal smelting were included, it is certain that at least until 1962 the great bulk of U.S. investment in Australia was in manufacturing. It is probable indeed, though the figures necessary to prove it are lacking, that the proportion of American investment in manufacturing activities is much higher than the

[8] E. T. Hamilton, president of the American Chamber of Commerce in Australia, stated in 1963 that 'there are more than 800 Australian firms manufacturing American products under licensing agreements with U.S. firms' (*A.F.R.*, 4 April 1963).

[9] Revised figures supplied by the U.S. Department of Commerce.

corresponding proportion for British investment, which is heavily represented in banking, insurance, real estate, and pastoral trading.

It should be clear, then, that while direct American investment in manufacturing is but a part of total foreign investment in Australia, an examination of that part may serve as a fruitful case study. Most of the issues raised should apply to other direct investment, in manufacturing at least, though if the behaviour of American-owned companies does appear to diverge significantly from that of other foreign-owned companies, this will be noted wherever possible.

A total of 345 companies which were believed to be at least partially American-owned and to be engaged in manufacturing activities at 30 June 1962 were approached in the course of the survey. Their names were gathered from lists published by the Department of Trade and the American Consulates-General in Sydney and Melbourne, and from the financial press. Each company was initially sent a postal questionnaire designed to gain as much background, 'non-sensitive', information about the company as possible. (To those companies which were thought to be less than 25 per cent American in ownership an alternative questionnaire was also sent. Since the primary concern of the study was with companies more than 25 per cent American, this alternative questionnaire was quite short and the information gained therefrom is contained in Appendix C.) When companies had completed the first postal questionnaire they were sent a second and longer one, comprising questions which required a greater degree of executive discretion to answer. This second questionnaire was collected from each of the participating companies by the writer in person, a practice which permitted the clarification of points arising from replies to the first questionnaire, the detailed discussion of many of the questions in the second, and reference to other questions not included in either questionnaire. By using two questionnaires in this way it was hoped both to make the best possible use of executives' time by permitting the delegation of the work involved in the first, and to secure at least a minimum of information from companies which might be offended by some of the questions in the second. By collecting the second questionnaire in person, it was hoped to capitalize on the frequent willingness of executives to discuss verbally questions that they would not be prepared to answer in writing. Finally, companies which refused to answer either questionnaire were sent a very short list of questions designed to permit an estimate to be made of the response to the survey.

No scientific sample of American-owned manufacturing companies was attempted. It was felt that the very great industrial diversity, the considerable range of company size, and the relatively small number of companies eligible to participate in the survey precluded any such course. All manufacturing companies in which there was believed to be a corporate American investment in the ordinary (voting) capital at 30 June 1962 were approached. For the purpose of the study, 'American' was taken to include companies whose immediate parent was incorporated in the U.S. and also those whose immediate parent was incorporated in some third country but whose 'ultimate' affiliation was with an American company.

Even with the scope of the study confined to direct American investment in manufacturing, it is important to realize some additional limitations. To begin with, some questions which can be asked about foreign investment are not suitable for firm-by-firm study: most of these are discussed in the concluding chapter of the book. Further, though six large American companies provided detailed comments on drafts of the questionnaires, the importance of some questions which might have been asked in a micro-economic study was not fully realized at the outset. Perhaps surprisingly, the reliability of the answers provided by executives does not seem to set any serious limit to the usefulness of the survey. To a quite remarkable extent the attitudes of the executives interviewed (most of whom were Australian) mirrored the prevailing attitudes in the community at large. Comparatively few executives saw foreign investment as an unqualified good. One said he was 'categorically in favour of foreign investment' and another observed that 'overseas investment since the war has been the main factor in our current industrial status'. Much more general were comments like: 'We don't want the Canadian situation to develop here but their knowledge and experience help us a lot'; or, more coherently:

> I'm getting more and more nationalistic every year. I think there must be an incentive for foreign companies to come to Australia: we need foreign investment not merely for the economy—it's a question of survival. Our friends of today may not be those of to-morrow. But I don't like too much investment from one country. There is the danger of a large-scale liquidation of Australian investments if an economic calamity overtook the investing country. I think there should be some legislation and this should be restrictive.

The latter quotation was unusual only in its reference to legislation. In a small number of cases there was even open hostility to American investment: one executive commented that 'American companies are not doing us any good at all—only taking our money out of the country. They might have helped us years ago, but now we can turn out our own cars. . . . I've always voted Country Party but you can sympathize with Castro can't you?' And another described the company in which he held a senior position as 'an outstanding example of what American investment shouldn't be'. It was clear from most interviews that there was no reason whatsoever to suspect the reliability of the information provided. The great majority of companies that participated in the survey were unstintingly generous in their help.

Only in one special sense did it become apparent that some answers were generally unreliable: to a few questions executives gave answers which were not intentionally incorrect but which were so heavily conditioned by prevailing social attitudes that they had little meaning. To questions relating to 'Australian content' and company purchasing policy, for instance, the not very helpful answer, 'we buy locally-made materials wherever possible', was frequently given.

American companies held no ordinary shares in 27 of the 345 companies approached. Eight of these had once been partially American-owned but the others had been approached in error. (Three of them, however, did have preference shares held by an American company and another had an arrangement under which it anticipated that an American company would take up an equity interest subsequently.) Thirty-three companies approached had some corporate American investment in their equity but this amounted to less than 25 per cent. Seventy were found to be not engaged in manufacturing at all as of the middle of 1962, though at least 14 of these were preparing to commence production within two years of that date, and several others sub-contracted manufacturing operations to outside companies. The remaining 215 companies made up the total of those 'eligible' to participate in the survey.

Not all of the 215 were fully independent units. Some were 'secondary enterprises', or subsidiaries of companies incorporated in Australia which were themselves in turn controlled from the United States. Others were subsidiaries of the same U.S. parent company. The concern of this survey was primarily with the unit of control so that 'secondary enterprises' were in most cases amalgamated with the 'primary' units. It was not possible to be absolutely consistent in this: one secondary organization refused to participate in the survey despite the participation of the primary organization, possibly because of a slightly different ownership pattern in the secondary. In another case, the secondary organization not only had a different ownership pattern from the primary, but was also in a different industry, which further complicated the amalgamation process. Companies which were the direct affiliates of the same American company were in some cases part of the same managerial unit, and in these cases the separate entities were merged for the purpose of the survey. But in other cases the sister subsidiaries were quite clearly independent so far as management was concerned: in four cases of this kind, one company participated in the survey while the affiliate did not. When the process of amalgamation was complete, a total of 208 companies remained.

The response of these 208 companies to the survey is difficult to summarize. All but nine agreed to provide at least an employment figure for 1962, but at the other extreme very few were willing or able to provide comparative cost figures for American and Australian production. In Tables I-2 and I-3, as throughout the study, companies which answered all the first questionnaire (and usually most of the second) are described as 'participating', while those which answered only part of the first questionnaire (and usually none of the second), thirteen in all, and those which answered neither of the two main questionnaires, are indicated as 'non-participating' or 'other'. Whether or not a company answered the first questionnaire was in most cases a good measure of *willingness* to participate in the survey: with only one exception, answers to questions in it were readily accessible to all companies, but involved divulging confidential information on matters such as sales, wages, and gross manufacturing profit margins.

Reasons for non-participation varied greatly. In a minority of cases pressure of work appeared to be the genuinely determining factor. In a somewhat larger number there seemed to be a real fear of public reaction: one executive commented that 'if I give you anything, you will only use it to hit us', and with the background of public concern over foreign investment this fear may have been behind many refusals. In a few cases there was a desire to avoid publicizing the results of a very profitable operation, but in some others the motive may well have been a desire to conceal an unsuccessful operation. It is felt, however, that by far the largest number of non-participants refused to take part in the survey for reasons of company policy unconnected with this particular study. It is not surprising, for example, that one company which had a policy of concealing corporate sales figures even from its own divisional executives did not participate in the survey.

Table I-2 shows the response to the survey by industry. In total, slightly less than half the eligible companies actually participated, with particularly disappointing response rates in the agricultural equipment, gramophone record, sausage casing, inks and polishes, cosmetics, paper, and rubber industries. The motor vehicle, motor accessories, industrial chemicals, and electrical apparatus industries, however, were marked by very satisfying response rates. In terms of

TABLE I-2 Response to the Survey, by Industry

Industry	Companies				Employment in 1962[b]			
	Participating[a]	Other	Total	Response %	Participating[a]	Other	Total	Response %
Plant, equipment, machinery	20	12	32	63	4,293	2,756	7,049	61
Agricultural equipment	1	5	6	17	90	662	752	12[e]
Motor vehicles	5	2	7	71	34,609	96	34,705	100
Motor accessories	5	1	6	83	1,184	123	1,307	91
Metal manufactures, n.e.i.	7	11	18	39	5,205	1,600	6,805	76[e]
Electrical equipment, instruments, etc.	15	7	22	68	8,056	2,072	10,128	80
Gramophone records	..	3	3	..	..	389	389	..
Food and drink	8	9	17	47	5,164	3,633	8,797	59[e]
Sausage casings	1	3	4	25	61	387	448	14[e]
Industrial chemicals and plastics	11	6	17	65	3,582	733	4,315	83
Inks, polishes, adhesives, etc.	..	6	6	..	..	574	574	..
Pharmaceutical and toilet preparations	10	10	20	50	3,865	1,524	5,389	72[e]
Cosmetics	..	8	8	..	..	1,045	1,045	..
Oils, mineral	3	2	5	60	1,506	725	2,231	68
Paper products	2	7	9	22	815	761	1,576	52
Rubber products	..	2	2	..	..	3,671	3,671	..
Plastic products	1	2	3	33	54	126	180	30
Abrasives	2	2	4	50	420	987	1,407	30
Clothing and fabrics	3	3	6	50	1,067	455	1,522	70[e]
Furnishings	1	1	2	50	427	204	631	68
Writing instruments	2	1	3	67	52	86	138	38
Miscellaneous	3	5	8	38	2,797	637	3,434	81
Total, excluding 'Motor vehicles'	95	106	201	47	38,638	23,150	61,788	63[e]
Total, all industries	100	108	208	48	73,247	23,246	96,493	76[e]

[a] Participating companies are defined as those which completed virtually all of the first main questionnaire used in the survey. See text.

[b] Companies were asked to show their total employment at either 30 June 1962 or their 1962 balance date. Most companies provided figures for 30 June, but some large ones provided figures for later in 1962 and the figures presented thus form a somewhat composite picture. One company even gave figures for 1961.

In a few cases, companies gave employment figures inclusive of employees outside Australia, but these are insignificant in the total.

In the case of three companies judged to be not primarily manufacturing in intent—a difficult and therefore arbitrary criterion to apply—only the employees actually engaged in manufacturing have been included in the figures shown. Two of these companies were primarily engaged in marketing (of office equipment and oil products respectively), and one primarily in mining. Their total 1962 employment was 7,768, but only 1,802 of this has been included in the above figures. In all other cases the total employment of the companies concerned has been shown. See Appendix B for a warning against comparing these data with factory statistics published by the Commonwealth Bureau of Census and Statistics.

[e] Employment figures for nine companies, in the industries thus marked, were estimated in the absence of any information from the companies concerned.

TABLE I-3   Response to the Survey, by Employment in 1962[a]

Size of companies by employment	Participating No.	Participating Employment	Other No.	Other Employment	Total Companies	Total Employment	Response (%) Companies	Response (%) Employment
1–25	9	152	12	173	21	325	43	47
26–50	11	396	16	638	27	1,034	41	38
51–75	7	422	11	720	18	1,142	39	37
76–100	8	728	9	778	17	1,506	47	48
101–150	14	1,687	13	1,844	27	3,531	52	48
151–200	7	1,227	19	3,321	26	4,548	27	27
201–300	8	2,017	15	3,538	23	5,555	35	36
301–400	5	1,633	2	785	7	2,418	71	68
401–500	3	1,404	3	1,426	6	2,830	50	50
501–750	6	3,810	4	2,480	10	6,290	60	61
751–1000	8	7,066	1	965	9	8,031	89	88
1001–1500	5	6,312	..	..	5	6,312	100	100
1501–2000	1	1,627	2	3,297	3	4,924	33	33
Over 2000	8	44,766	1	3,281	9	48,047	89	93

[a] For explanatory comments on employment figures, see Notes [b] and [c] to Table I–2.

17

c

employment, the response rate was appreciably better: of the total employment, almost 76 per cent was in participating companies. Though the excellent co-operation of the motor vehicle industry was partly responsible for this very satisfactory result, the response rate of all companies apart from those in the motor vehicle industry was still almost 63 per cent in terms of employment.

From Table I-3 it may be seen that the participating companies cover a wide range of company size.[10] Though the number of medium-size companies participating in the survey was disappointing—only 15 of a total of 49 companies with employment in the 151-300 range took part—in most other size classifications the

TABLE I–4　Size of American-affiliated Companies Manufacturing in Australia in 1962, by Employment and Industry

Industry	Size of companies by employment[a]						
	1–50	51–100	101–200	201–500	501–1000	1001–2000	Over 2000
Plant, equipment, machinery	12	1	8	6	5	..	..
Agricultural equipment	2	1	1	2	..	..	..
Motor vehicles	2	1	..	..	..	..	4
Motor accessories	2	1	2	..	1	..	..
Metal manufactures, n.e.i.	2	4	7	2	1	1	1
Electrical equipment, instruments, etc.	5	5	5	1	2	3	1
Gramophone records	..	1	2	..	..	..	..
Food and drink	2	2	4	4	3	1	1
Sausage casings	..	2	2	..	..	..	..
Industrial chemicals and plastics	5	3	4	3	..	2	..
Inks, polishes, adhesives, etc.	1	3	2	..	..	..	..
Pharmaceutical and toilet preparations	2	2	9	5	1	1	..
Cosmetics	2	1	3	2	..	..	..
Oils, mineral	2	..	..	..	3	..	..
Paper products	2	2	2	2	1	..	..
Rubber products	..	..	..	1	..	..	1
Plastic products	1	2	..	..	..	..	..
Abrasives	..	..	1	2	1	..	..
Clothing and fabrics	2	1	1	1	1	..	..
Furnishings	..	..	..	2	..	..	..
Writing instruments	2	1	..	..	..	..	..
Miscellaneous	2	2	..	3	..	..	1
Total	48	35	53	36	19	8	9

[a] For explanatory comments on employment figures, see Notes [b] and [c] to Table I–2.

[10] Details of the response rate by ownership pattern are given in chapter IV.

response was satisfactory.[11] This is particularly true of the largest companies: of the 36 with employment in excess of 500, no fewer than 28 took part in the survey.

Both tables clearly show the importance of American-affiliated companies in terms of employment. In total, they employed almost 100,000 people in 1962. It is not possible to compare this figure directly with those published by the Commonwealth Bureau of Census and Statistics for factory employment, since it includes employees engaged in activities not classed as manufacturing by the Bureau. As a very approximate guide, however, total factory employment in Australia in 1961/2 was a little over 1·1 million, while the estimated total workforce was 4·3 million.

The vital significance of the motor vehicle industry in the total picture is brought out in Tables I-2 and I-4. No less than 36 per cent of the total employment of the companies approached was in that single industry—and this despite the impact of the 1961-2 recession on that industry. The impression is confirmed in Table I-5, which shows the sales and net fixed assets of participating companies only. The motor vehicle industry made up almost half the total sales of all participating companies, and its assets made up almost one-third those of the same group of companies. No accurate estimate can be made of the total sales and fixed assets in 1962 of all the companies approached, non-participating as well as participating, but it seems certain from information gathered in the survey that the total sales of the group amounted to between £680 million and £720 million, and the total book value of fixed assets to between £341 million and £349 million. The motor vehicle industry still remains the heaviest weight in the total.

The concentration of American investment in a few large companies is striking. The largest company, in the motor vehicle industry, employed more than 22 per cent of the total employed by all the companies approached and almost 30 per cent of the total employed by the participating companies. While the nine companies with employment of more than 2,000 employed 49·8 per cent of the total employment of all companies approached, 136 companies had employment of 200 or less and the median employment for the whole group was only 146·5. The five largest participating companies employed more than 51 per cent of the total employment of

---

[11] The causes of this relatively low response rate in the medium-size range are not clear. It may be that part of the explanation can be found in theories of business psychology but it is also possible that other factors (such as industry, length of experience in Australia, etc.) played a part. The character of the bias thus introduced into the figures is not obvious and is probably in any case of less importance than the bias introduced by differential industry response rates.

TABLE I–5   Sales and Fixed Assets of Participating
Companies in 1961/2, by Industry
£A('000)

Industry	Sales[a]	Fixed assets[b]
Plant, equipment, machinery	33,001	9,692
Motor vehicles	262,491	85,370
Motor accessories	5,598	3,179
Metal manufactures, n.e.i.	35,975	43,617
Electrical equipment, instruments, etc.	38,506	15,703
Food and drink	31,811	8,316
Industrial chemicals and plastics	26,723	34,598
Pharmaceutical and toilet preparations	28,092	7,963
Oils, mineral	42,535	38,828
Clothing and fabrics	3,696	1,221
Other industries	26,707	16,313
Total[c]	535,134	264,800

[a] Companies were asked to show their total sales for either the year ended 30 June 1962 or their own 1961/2 company year. Many companies gave figures for the year ended 30 June but many others used an alternative period ending in 1962. The figures shown thus present a somewhat composite picture. No correction was made to the figures of companies which operated for a part only of 1961/2: this results in an understatement of the import-ance of the 'Industrial chemicals and plastics' industry in particular, because of the establishment of a large number of American-affiliated companies in that industry during the year.

As with employment figures, a few companies gave sales figures inclusive of sales of manufacturing branches located outside Australia but these are insignificant in the total.

In the case of the three 'non-manufacturing companies' participating in the survey (see Note [b] to Table I–2), only 'manufacturing output' (as given to the Bureau of Census and Statistics) has been included in the sales figures. Total sales of the three companies in 1962 were £97·1 million but only £46·5 million of this has been included above. In all other cases the total sales of the companies concerned have been shown.

[b] Fixed asset figures (net of depreciation) have been taken from the 1961/2 balance sheets of the participating companies, except that figures for the three 'non-manufacturing companies' were based on those provided to the Bureau of Census and Statistics as assets employed in manufacturing. Total fixed assets of the three companies at the end of their 1962 financial year were £82·2 million but only £35·5 million of this has been included above. See Note [a] for parallel comments on the period to which data refer and the occasional inclusion of figures for operations outside Australia.

[c] Detail may not add to totals because of rounding.

the 100 participating companies. This comes as something of a surprise. It also makes the task of reporting on a study of the companies more difficult since to say that '20 companies' agreed with a certain proposition means little in the absence of some estimate of their total size.

With this background information on the conduct and limitations of the survey, it is possible to turn in detail to its results.

II

In Perspective

American direct investment in Australian industry is by no means a new phenomenon. Records are inadequate to determine when the flow first began but it was certainly before the turn of this century. Cleona Lewis, in her classic work on America's international investments, noted that 'at least one American company had established a manufacturing branch in Australia before 1897—the only one not in Canada or Europe concerning which we have information' (1938: 600). Unfortunately, she did not name the company in question though it is possible that she was in fact referring to the National Ammonia Company of Australia, which was established at Clyde in New South Wales in 1896 (Hunter and Webb 1963: 291). There may have been other isolated cases of this kind which have escaped the notice of historians.

Like American direct investment as a whole, however, that in Australia is predominantly of twentieth century origin. This is brought out clearly in Table II-1. The figures in that table require cautious interpretation: they represent book values of investment only and in no sense reflect the 'market value' of the companies concerned. The substantial rise in prices which has occurred over the period covered by the table introduces a further complication. But while it is not possible to be precise about the increase in the real value of American direct investment in Australia, it is certainly easy to see that the increase has been dramatic. Of the total, investment in manufacturing has not always been the largest part. Though it grew rapidly from small beginnings—the only setback to its growth apparently being during the depression of the thirties—it was not until near the end of the inter-war period that American capital in that sector overtook the American investment in petroleum (at that time almost entirely investment in marketing and distribution facilities). After World War II the value of American investment in the manufacturing sector soared, quickly becoming by far the largest single category of investment. This would be even more evident if to the figures shown for investment in manufacturing were added the investment in oil refining and metal smelting, both activities which are taken here to be essentially 'manufacturing' but which are included in Table II-1 under other classifications.

With the expansion in the value of American investment has gone a smaller expansion in the number of American direct investments in Australia. There is less published information available on this subject but it is reported that in 1936 the number of American-

TABLE II–1   Growth of American Direct Investment
in Australia, by Sector
$US(m.)

Year	Manu-facturing	Mining & smelting	Petroleum	Other[a]	Total
1897[b]	0·5	..	1	..	1·5
1908[b]	6	..	2	2	10
1914[b]	10	..	2	5	17
1919[b]	16	..	25	12	53
1924[b]	26	..	75	16	117
1929[b]	50	c	69	30[d]	149
1936	39	c	c	50[d]	89
1943	48	6	41	19	114
1950	98	11	70[e]	22[e]	201
1951	127	12	c	116[d]	255
1952	151	14	c	143[d]	308
1953	172	15	c	137[d]	324
1954	201	20	c	168[d]	389
1955	240	25	c	227[d]	492
1956	268	29	c	248[d]	545
1957	297	22	217[e]	47[e]	583
1958	350	22	231[e]	52[e]	655
1959	399	27	254[e]	62[e]	739
1960	476	33	c	347[d]	856
1961	506	36	c	415[d]	957
1962	582	46	c	469[d]	1,097

[a] Except for 1929, 1936, 1951–6, and 1960–2, most of the investment in this category was in distribution, though after 1943 small amounts of investment in public utilities, finance, and agriculture are included. See also Notes [c], [d], and [e].

[b] Figures in these years include investment in New Zealand.

[c] Included in 'Other'. American investment in 'Petroleum' in 1936 had fallen below $US40 million, investment in both the Australian and New Zealand petroleum industries together being only $US43 million.

[d] Figures include investment in 'Mining and smelting' and/or 'Petroleum'.

[e] Figures for 'Petroleum' are not separately published for these years, but since the figures for all other industries except 'Public utilities' are published for three of the four years thus marked, and the figure for 'Public utilities' is given as $US1 million in the fourth year, the figures shown are very close estimates.

SOURCES: 1897–1924, from Cleona Lewis 1938: 578–606.
1929–59, from U.S. Dept. of Commerce 1930, 1938, 1960, 1963b; and U.S. Treasury Dept. 1947.
1960–2, from information supplied directly by the U.S. Dept. of Commerce.

affiliated companies operating in this country was 94, of which 58 were engaged in manufacture and 20 in distribution other than petroleum marketing (U.S. Dept. of Commerce 1938: 16).[1] By 1957 the number had risen almost threefold to 271, though the number of those in manufacturing was not reported (U.S. Dept. of Commerce 1960: 99).[2]

Table II-2 shows the period during which 204 of the 208 companies approached during the course of the present survey commenced manufacture in Australia. Perhaps the most striking feature revealed is the very large number of companies which began operations in the period after 1955. Of the companies operating in 1962, the number established in the period 1955-9 was more than double that established in any previous five-year period, while the number commencing operations in the thirty-month period from the beginning of 1960 was higher than that in any ten-year period except the fifties. It is true, of course, that Table II-2 shows the dates at which manufacture began only for those companies still in operation at the middle of 1962. There were many companies set up in earlier years which had been liquidated or sold to other interests before 1962, and the figures shown cannot be used therefore to get an exact picture of the total number of companies in operation at any point except 1962. The same omission may lead to an exaggerated impression of the rate of growth of the number of individual direct investments. No comprehensive search was made for such 'deceased' American companies, but in the course of research for the survey a total of 26 were found. Of these, the dates at which 24 commenced manufacture are known: one, the National Ammonia Company of Australia, referred to above, began operations before 1900; one

---

[1] The accuracy of this figure is not absolutely certain. An earlier report of the U.S. Department of Commerce noted the establishment of 32 American-affiliated 'factories' in Australia to 1929: 'The number of factories started in Australia by Americans, by years, were as follows: 1892, 1; 1902, 2; 1903, 1; 1907, 1; 1908, 3; 1911, 1; 1914, 1; 1915, 3; 1917 and 1919 to 1925, 1 each year; 1926, 3; 1927, 2; 1928, 4; and 1929, 2.' (1930: 45.) Table II-2 alone notes the establishment of 33 companies by 1929, however, and that table takes no account of companies formed in that period but no longer in existence.

[2] D. M. Hocking (1955) has estimated, from files kept by the Division of Industrial Development of the Australian Department of National Development, that 69 firms with American affiliations were established in the Australian manufacturing sector in the period September 1945 to July 1953. This figure almost certainly overstates the number of American direct-investment enterprises established in this period, not only because it is known that in some cases the American interest in companies included in Hocking's list fell short of 25 per cent, but also because, as Hocking himself fully realized, some of the entries in the Division's files were based on announcements of intention rather than on actually verified establishments.

TABLE II-2   Manufacturing Commencement Dates of American-affiliated Companies Operating in mid-1962, by Industry[a]

Industry	1900–1909	1910–1919	1920–1929	1930–1939	1940–1949	1950–1954	1955–1959	1960–mid-1962	Not classifiable
Plant, equipment, machinery	..	..	3	4	3	..	13	8	1
Agricultural equipment	..	..	..	..	..	..	4	2	..
Motor vehicles	..	..	2	1	..	1	5	1	..
Motor accessories	..	..	..	..	..	..	5	1	..
Metal manufactures, n.e.i.	..	1	2	2	1	3	6	3	..
Electrical equipment, instruments, etc.	..	..	1	3	3	6	7	2	..
Gramophone records	..	1	1	3	1	3	..	2	..
Food and drink	..	..	3	3	..	..	1	5	..
Sausage casings	..	..	3b	1	..	1	..	..	..
Industrial chemicals and plastics	..	..	1	2	1	1	..	9	..
Inks, polishes, adhesives, etc.	..	..	..	2	2	1	..	..	..
Pharmaceutical and toilet preparations	1	3	3	2	1	1	3	4	2
Cosmetics	1	..	..	..	3	3	..	..	..
Oils, mineral	..	1	..	..	1	..	1	2	..
Paper products	..	..	1	3	2	1	1	1	..
Rubber products	..	..	1	..	..	..	1	1	..
Plastic products	..	..	..	..	1	..	1	1	..
Abrasives	..	..	..	..	2	1	1	..	..
Clothing and fabrics	..	..	1	..	..	1	2	..	1
Furnishings	..	..	..	..	..	..	2	..	..
Writing instruments	..	..	..	..	..	1	2	..	..
Miscellaneous	1	..	1	..	1	..	4	1	..
Total	3	6	25b	23	22	24	57	44	4
Total 1962 employment	2,929	4,597	42,855	14,874	5,596	8,241	9,286	7,155	960

[a] The year in which manufacture began is taken to be the year in which an American equity of at least 25 per cent was first acquired in the case of companies manufacturing previously as Australian-owned ventures.

[b] This figure includes the establishment of one company which has been counted as 'two' because it later 'divided' and had become two separate and distinct companies before 1962.

NOTES: (1) All companies have been classified according to what appears to have been their main activity in 1962.
(2) In a small minority of cases, the meaning attached to the word 'manufacturing' varied somewhat from that generally accepted, but almost always the interpretation adopted by the company concerned was used.

TABLE II-3 Manufacturing Commencement Dates of American-affiliated Companies Operating in mid-1962, by Employment in 1962[a]

Size of companies by employment	1900–1909	1910–1919	1920–1929	1930–1939	1940–1949	1950–1954	1955–1959	1960–mid-1962	Not classifiable
1–25	..	1	..	..	4	3	5	8	..
26–50	..	..	2	4	2	1	10	6	2
51–75	..	1	2	1	3	4	3	4	..
76–100	..	..	1	2	..	2	7	5	..
101–150	..	..	3	3	1	4	7	9	..
151–200	1	..	2	2	3	3	10	4	1
201–300	1	..	3	3	1	2	10	3	..
301–400	..	..	1	..	4	..	..	2	..
401–500	..	2	1	..	1	..	2	..	..
501–750	..	..	2	..	1	2	2	2	1
751–1000	..	1	1	4	1	1	1	..	..
1001–1500	..	..	2	1	1	..	..	1	..
1501–2000	..	..	1	1	..	1	..	..	..
Over 2000	1	1	4	2	..	1	..	..	..
Total	3	6	25[b]	23	22	24	57	44	4

[a] See Note ᵃ to Table II–2.
[b] See Note ᵇ to Table II–2.

began in the period 1910-19; two in the period 1920-9; seven in 1930-9; four in 1940-9; one in 1950-4; and eight in 1955-9. Both companies for which no date is known began operations before 1950. The inclusion of these companies and others like them modifies the picture somewhat but it is nevertheless clear that there has been a remarkable increase in the number of American direct investments established in the manufacturing sector.

On the other hand, Table II-2 also makes it clear that it was the old-established companies which formed the great bulk of total American investment in Australia in 1962. Of the total 1962 employment of the 204 companies whose commencement dates are known (95,533 in all), no fewer than 65,255 were employed by companies which began manufacturing before World War II. Of the 57 companies listed as being established before 1939, one in three had employment of more than 750 in 1962, while of the 147 listed as being established after that date only seven (of which five had been manufacturing prior to the acquisition of the American equity) exceeded 750 employees in size. (The 1962 size distribution of companies by the date at which they began manufacture in Australia is shown in Table II-3.)

Some idea of the growth of American investment in Australian industry can be gained from the very considerable expansion which has taken place in recent years in the total employment of American-affiliated companies. As far as is known, no reliable estimates have been published on this subject, though from figures published by the U.S. Department of Commerce it is possible to learn that employment was approximately 60,000 in 1957, excluding those employed in oil refining and metal smelting (1960: 122-3). From information derived from the present survey it appears that the total employment of American-affiliated manufacturing companies in Australia almost exactly doubled between 1950 and 1962, rising from about 48,000 in the former year to more than 96,000 in the latter. This compares with a growth of little more than 22 per cent for Australian manufacturing employment as a whole in the same period.[3] In part this was due to the fact that American-affiliated companies in operation in both 1950 and 1962 expanded their employment more quickly than the average for the whole economy: as Table II-4 shows, the

[3] The two sets of employment figures are not strictly comparable but their rates of growth may probably be contrasted to give an approximate picture. Figures for Australian manufacturing as a whole are from factory statistics published by the Commonwealth Bureau of Census and Statistics. While 1961/2 was a period of recession in the Australian economy, there is no reason to suppose that American-affiliated companies were affected any less by this than was the rest of the economy.

TABLE II–4   Employment of 81 American-affiliated Companies
Manufacturing in both 1950 and 1962, by Industry

Industry	No. companies covered	Employment in 1950	Employment in 1962
Plant, equipment, machinery	10	2,637	3,097
Motor vehicles	3	17,924	32,049
Metal manufactures, n.e.i.	6	1,751	3,927
Electrical equipment, instruments, etc.	7	3,642	6,659
Food and drink	8	4,867	6,260
Sausage casings	3	271	374
Industrial chemicals and plastics	6	1,720	3,296
Inks, polishes, adhesives, etc.	5	254	479
Pharmaceutical and toilet preparations	10	2,756	4,083
Cosmetics	5	270	636
Paper products	6	527	1,201
Other industries	12	6,603	9,762
Total	81	43,222	71,823

NOTES: (1) Employment figures for 1950 were only estimated by many companies. In
14 cases, with total 1962 employment of 5,951, employment for 1950 was
estimated by the writer.

(2) There is some understatement of the growth of four of these companies which
between 1950 and 1962 established other affiliates in Australia which have
been treated as separate units and therefore not included in the employment
of the 81 companies in 1962.

TABLE II–5   Growth in Employment Between 1950 and 1962
of 67 American-affiliated Companies

Change in employment between 1950 and 1962	Employment in 1950	Employment in 1962	Average increase or decrease(—) in employment (%)	No. companies covered
(i) Decrease	1,867	1,342	−28	9
(ii) Increase (%)—				
0–24	5,904	6,603	12	7
25–49	14,236	19,403	36	10
50–74	1,880	3,129	66	8
75–99	2,228	4,211	89	13
100–199	11,746	25,476	117	8
200 and over	1,424	5,708	301	12
Total	39,285	65,872	68	67

NOTE: The 67 companies included in this table are all those included in Table II–4 except
the 14 for which no company estimate of 1950 employment was available. See also
notes to Table II–4.

employment of 81 manufacturing companies in which there was direct American investment in both 1950 and 1962 expanded by more than 66 per cent between the two dates. (These companies appear to include all those which were both manufacturing and classifiable as American direct investment in the two years, with the possible exception of three firms—with total 1962 employment of about 800—which did not provide information on the date at which they began manufacture and which may have begun operations before 1950.) In part also the faster than average growth of American investment was due to the creation of new companies which together more than offset the 'loss' caused by the liquidation or sale of a number of American-affiliated companies operating in 1950. (Thirteen companies which had once been affiliated with an American company but which had terminated that association by 1962 are known to have been manufacturing in 1950. Their total employment in 1950 was approximately 4,200.)

Not surprisingly in view of the rise in prices since 1950, the sales of American-affiliated companies expanded by more than the expansion in their employment between 1950 and 1962. This increase in sales must be interpreted with considerable caution because of the possibility of a change in the degree of vertical integration of production over a period of this length. Such a change is especially likely to have occurred in these companies: many American-affiliated companies begin operations at a superficial level—assembling or packaging perhaps—and gradually 'deepen' their production by buying in materials at a progressively less developed stage of manufacture. For this reason the growth in the *production* of American-affiliated companies is considered in chapter VII. Suffice it to say for the moment, therefore, that the sales of the 81 companies known to have been manufacturing in both 1950 and 1962 expanded from £155-165 million in 1950 to £500-515 million in 1962.[4] The inclusion of an estimate for companies operating in 1950 but 'deceased' by 1962 yields a total estimate for sales in 1950 of £170-180 million, compared with the total estimate for 1962 given in chapter I of £680-720 million.

Growth has clearly been rapid. How large had American invest-

---

[4] A total of 44 companies gave precise figures for sales in company years ending in 1950 and 1962. A further two companies, both of medium size, gave an index of sales growth covering the two years. Of these 46 companies, three registered an absolute fall in sales between 1950 and 1962, four a gain of less than 50 per cent, four a gain of between 50 and 99 per cent, 18 a gain of between 100 and 299 per cent, 13 a gain of between 300 and 499 per cent, and four a gain of more than 500 per cent. The sales of the group as a whole rose by 212 per cent from £130 million to £405 million.

ment become by 1962 in relation to the Australian manufacturing sector as a whole? In an attempt to answer this question, all companies were asked to provide some of the data on their manufacturing activities which they had given to the Commonwealth Bureau of Census and Statistics for the year 1961/2. By its nature, a voluntary survey of this kind is ill-equipped to answer questions relating to 'industry shares', but the extent of the response to it, including about 76 per cent of the estimated total employment of American-affiliated companies in 1962, means that something of value can be said. Limitations of space preclude detailed examination of the findings here and most of the information collected is set out in tabular form in Appendix B. In summary, the participating companies employed approximately 5·1 per cent of the total number employed in Australian manufacturing industry in 1961/2; produced 7·0 per cent of the total value of production; owned 6·9 and 10·2 per cent of the total book value of land and buildings, and plant and machinery, respectively; and made 14·8 per cent of the additions and replacements to land and buildings and 13·1 per cent of those to plant and machinery. Perhaps the surprising thing about these figures is how low they are.

To digress briefly, these figures shed some light on the current controversy on the extent of all foreign ownership of Australian industry. Various estimates have been made of this 'foreign share'. E. L. Wheelwright (1963: 144), for example, estimated it as 'about one-third', using statistics both of new capital expenditure and of company profits. But at least to the extent that his estimate depends on figures for new capital expenditure it is unreliable: the statistics he used for the period 1945 to 1953, those published by the former Division of Industrial Development (also used by D. M. Hocking), appear seriously to overstate the importance of foreign capital.[5] E. J. Thomson (1962: 3-4) estimated that almost one-third of all investment in manufacturing in the years 1956/7 to 1959/60 was financed from abroad, but his method—the comparison of total foreign investment in the manufacturing sector with total 'additions and replacements' to land, buildings, plant, and machinery, as shown in factory statistics—is quite inadmissible. To compare total investment in *companies* of which the main activity is manufacturing, with addi-

[5] The figures published by the Division have been used as proof that, during the period 1945 to 1953, 45 per cent of all investment in manufacturing came from overseas. But it appears that all the announced investment expenditures of companies with even a minority of foreign equity were included in figures for investment financed from abroad, while the inclusion in the statistics of only the major investment projects of the period ensured the omission of very many small investments financed by Australians.

tions to the book value of the land, buildings, plant and machinery actually employed in manufacturing by *factories* is to invite a wide margin of error.

Part of the difficulty in making an estimate of the 'foreign share' lies in deciding whether it is the foreign share in profits, in production, in assets, or in employment that is of primary interest. If in employment, it is hard to see how the foreign share could exceed 20 per cent, for if companies participating in the present survey made up little more than 5 per cent of the total, it is likely that all American-affiliated companies in Australian manufacturing made up less than 7 per cent in 1961/2—and of course a number of these companies were jointly-owned and some were undoubtedly controlled in Australia. The importance of British investment, the largest part of the balance of foreign investment, is far from clear. More than a score of the companies considered here as 'American-affiliated' either have affiliations with the United Kingdom also or are entirely owned by an American-owned company based in the United Kingdom, and in both situations the foreign investment involved would appear in official statistics at least in part as 'British'. Further, much of the total of British investment in Australia is in banking, insurance, real estate, and stock and station agencies. Even if British direct investments in manufacturing employed twice the number employed by American-affiliated companies in 1961/2—and that seems unlikely—the total number of Australians employed in foreign direct-investment enterprises in the manufacturing sector could not have greatly exceeded 20 per cent of the workforce in that sector.

If value of production is taken as the relevant measuring-stick, it is possible indeed that the figure of one-third could be attained, especially in view of the likelihood of there being some understatement in the value of production attributed to the motor vehicle industry (see Appendix B). But it would still be necessary to assume that British manufacturing investment in Australia produced twice as much, in value terms, as did American, and that seems at least open to question.[6] *

[6] The government-appointed Committee of Economic Enquiry, however, accepted that about one-third of Australian manufacturing industry was directly owned abroad in the early sixties, basing its estimate on the proportion of total after-tax company income accruing to overseas residents.

* Since going to press, the *Directory of Overseas Investment in Australian Manufacturing Industry—1966*, published by the Department of Trade and Industry, has revealed that British investment in the Australian manufacturing sector may (after allowing for substantial indirect American investments through Canada) be less than 25 per cent greater than American.

A low figure for overall foreign ownership of Australian industry does not conflict, of course, with evidence of very high percentages of foreign ownership in particular industries. Unfortunately, the attempt to gain some idea of the market shares enjoyed by American-affiliated companies was among the least successful objects of the survey. All participating companies were asked: 'What is your estimate of the share of the market for the products of your industry held by your Australian company in 1961/2?' To this question 65 companies, with total employment of 53,041, gave a single-number answer. Sixteen firms (with employment of 11,591) estimated their market share at less than 20 per cent; fourteen (with employment of 7,799) at between 20 and 39 per cent; fifteen (with employment of 26,493) at between 40 and 59 per cent; twelve (with employment of 5,006) at between 60 and 79 per cent; and eight (with employment of 2,152) at between 80 and 100 per cent. (Perhaps obviously, the total employment of the group of companies claiming to hold between 40 and 59 per cent of their respective markets is heavily inflated by one very large company.)

But though the impression is interesting, in detail the figures are of little significance. Two large companies gave a figure which was simply the arithmetic average of market shares held by widely different products and in a number of other cases companies found difficulty in interpreting the phrase 'the market for the products of your industry'. The difficulty can be illustrated by the case of a company which supplied electric time systems, electronic computers, and electric typewriters. Not only was its share of the market for each of these products different but also there was a considerable problem involved in defining each of the markets concerned. It is common knowledge that the company supplied a relatively small part of the total Australian demand for, say, typewriters, but a significant part of the demand for electric typewriters.

Many of the large multi-product companies dominated at least one market but were insignificant in others. This can be seen most clearly in the chemical industry. Union Carbide Australia, for example, was the sole Australian producer of 57 per cent of its product range in 1962 but was one of at least four producers for 18 per cent of its range. Monsanto Chemicals (Australia) was the sole producer of 25 per cent of its range and one of only two producers for a further 17 per cent, but shared the market with at least four other producers in 38 per cent of its range (Hunter and Webb 1963: 311).

Regrettably, U.S. Department of Commerce figures do not help the problem of assessing the share of particular Australian industries held by American-affiliated companies. The most recently published

TABLE II–6   Sales of, and American Investment in, American-affiliated
Manufacturing Companies in 1957, by Industry[a]
$US(m.)

Industry	Book value of investment	Sales
Food products	24	92
Paper and allied products	2[b]	12[b]
Chemicals and allied products	25	52
Rubber products	14[b]	36[b]
Primary and fabricated metals	8	27
Machinery, except electrical	26	52
Electrical machinery	33	68
Transportation equipment	139	390
Other manufacturing	26	58
Total	297	787

[a] As noted previously, the U.S. Department of Commerce does not classify the smelting activities of mining companies or the refining operations of oil companies as 'manufacturing'.

[b] Estimates based on figures published by the U.S. Department of Commerce for Oceania.

Source: U.S. Dept. of Commerce 1960.

figures showing book value of investment and total sales, by industry, are for 1957, and in the absence of comparable data for Australian companies they indicate only the relative importance of various Australian industries to American investment (Table II-6).[7]

The factory statistics to which reference has already been made are somewhat more useful. In four of the industries enumerated in Table B-7—'Industrial chemicals', 'Pharmaceuticals and toilet preparations', 'Motor vehicle construction and assembly, and motor bodies', and 'Foundation garments'—the share of production supplied by participating American-affiliated companies exceeded 20 per cent, and in two of these industries their share exceeded 50 per cent. In the large-scale section of Australian industry, too, American investment was particularly important, as Tables B-2 and B-3 show. Of the sixty-six plants throughout Australian industry which employed more than 1,000 persons during 1961/2, participating companies owned ten. But even these figures must be treated with caution, and the industrial classification used was, of necessity, too broad to permit really meaningful conclusions.

If precise statistics *were* available, it is beyond doubt that they would reveal that some Australian manufacturing industries are almost the exclusive province of foreign-owned companies. The

[7] F. N. Bennett (1961: 10) has compared the sales figures shown in Table II-6 with figures for the value of Australian factory output. Such a comparison is not valid, however, since the two sets of figures are collected on quite different bases, as explained in detail in Appendix B, especially Note 2.

federal Minister for Works, Senator Gorton, is reported as estimating the foreign share of the Australian motor vehicle industry in the early sixties at 95 per cent, of motor parts and accessories at 55 per cent, of telecommunications at 83 per cent, of pharmaceutical and toilet preparations at 97 per cent, of soap and detergents at 80 per cent, and of petroleum refining and distribution at 95 per cent (*A.F.R.*, 18 Feb. 1965). Figures relating to American investment only would be somewhat less dramatic than these, but they would tend to confirm the popular impression that most American capital is concentrated in relatively few industries.

To conclude from the low percentage of total Australian manufacturing output produced by American-affiliated companies that such companies are of relatively minor importance in Australia's industrial development, therefore, is to ignore the quite crucial role being played by American companies in some of Australia's most vital industries. The motor vehicle industry is perhaps the most striking example: it is not only dominated by American-owned companies, it was to an important extent the *creation* of those companies. Many other examples could be cited, and it is probably fair to say that most Australians would have difficulty naming a breakfast food, a cosmetic, or a toilet article *not* produced by the local subsidiary of some American company. There is no short way to describe this aspect of American investment in Australian industry —its seminal influence on particular industries and its kaleidoscopic diversity—and a detailed description of American-affiliated companies in their industrial setting must be deferred to Appendix A. For the moment it is enough to stress that, because of its dominant position in certain key industries and its often catalytic effect on the economy as a whole, American investment is of considerably greater importance to this country than any aggregate figure for the 'American share' would suggest.

D

III

Why Do They Invest?

Essentially, the factors bearing on a decision to invest abroad fall into two categories: those concerning the general investment climate in the recipient economy, and the immediate or proximate causes. The present survey asked no questions about the part that the Australian investment climate played in inducing investment here, mainly because the evidence of other surveys indicates that, from the point of view of American companies, the Australian 'climate' is one of the most favourable in the world.[1] The country is politically stable, and for nearly two decades the party in power on the federal level has been a conservative one with a basic economic philosophy closely akin to the American. On the international plane, Australia and the United States are linked in the ANZUS and SEATO defence pacts. There is no discrimination of any kind against foreign companies, except in the ownership of television stations, and there is no limitation on the proportion of a company's share capital which may be held abroad. Taxation on company income is somewhat lighter than that in the U.S., and since the United States-Australia Income Tax Convention came into force in 1953 there has been a limit of 15 per cent placed on the tax on dividends paid by a company incorporated in Australia to its American shareholders. Though no guarantee has been given on the freedom of companies at all times to remit profits or repatriate capital, the government has indicated that under present policy 'all current net income (after taxation) accruing to firms or individuals resident overseas may be remitted overseas without restriction'. Further, while 'advance commitments to allow repatriation are not entered into . . . approval would be withheld only in cases where the circumstances were excep-

---

[1] In recent years, a number of studies have been devoted exclusively to an examination of the factors which lead companies to engage in foreign investment. Among the best of these are: Barlow and Wender (1955); Robinson (1961); and U.S. Department of Commerce (1953).

34

tional' (Commonwealth Treasury 1960: 4-5). The very modesty of these claims bears witness to their reliability.

That American business executives see Australia in a most favourable light is amply confirmed not merely by the rapid growth of American investment in Australia but also by repeated statements to this effect. Only slightly more extravagant than usual were the reported comments of Boon Gross, president of the Gillette Company of America, in 1961: 'Australia is the promised land, of all the countries I have visited. Its stable economy, its sound political atmosphere and its people add up to an excellent guarantee for the future.' (*A.F.R.*, 31 Oct. 1961.)

But the existence of a favourable 'climate' in Australia does not in itself explain American investment here, though it does form an important pre-condition for such investment.[2] Companies in the present survey were asked to indicate their American associates' main reasons for deciding to undertake manufacturing operations in Australia, and the one hundred answers received to the question are presented in Table III-1. Companies were requested to use a ranking procedure to indicate the order of importance of each factor mentioned, and while some companies marked more factors than others, the overwhelming significance of two or three factors is clearly brought out. The possible factors were listed on the questionnaire in the order in which they appear in the table.

By far the most important single reason given for the decision to invest in Australian manufacturing facilities was 'to take advantage of the expected growth of the Australian market'. No fewer than 54 per cent of all respondents gave that as the primary motive of their American parent in investing here, while 86 per cent mentioned it among the first three reasons. One executive explained that 'we feel Australia is beginning a period of industrial expansion similar to that which occurred in the U.S. after the First World War', and the sentiment was common. While the small number of respondent companies in each industry prevents detailed analysis of the importance attached to this factor in different industries, it may also be of significance that eleven of the twelve respondents in the chemical industry and all of the seven respondents in the pharmaceutical and toilet preparations industry gave market growth as the primary reason for investment in Australia.

It is nevertheless hard to see how market growth in itself could be the cause of American investment in Australia. In the absence of

[2] There is no discussion here on why some companies prefer licensing Australian companies to establishing their own equity investment in manufacturing facilities. For treatment of this topic, see Behrman (1962b: 130-1); and Enid Baird Lovell (1958: 20-1).

TABLE III–1   Motives of 100 American Companies for Investing in
Manufacturing Facilities in Australia

| Motive for investment | Number of times factor ranked— | | | | |
	First	Second	Third	As additional factor	Total
To overcome tariff barriers	13	21	15	1	50
To overcome import restrictions	9	10	4	5	28
To take advantage of the expected growth of the Australian market	54	19	13	3	89
To take advantage of lower Australian unit cost conditions	1	4	4	2	11
To take advantage of consumer preference for 'made in Australia' goods	2	8	6	8	24
To gain access to Asian markets	..	1	4	6	11
To gain access to the New Zealand and other Pacific markets	..	6	3	10	19
To take advantage of specific encouragement by state or federal government	2	2	8	1	13
To avoid unfavourable conditions for expansion in the U.S.	..	2	1	..	3
To avoid freight charges	..	9	4	9	22
To meet a need caused by the break-down of a previous licensing agreement with a local manufacturer	1	..	..	2	3
Other	18	2	7	4	31
Total	100	84	69	51	304

NOTE: The 100 companies included in the table are basically the 'participating companies'
referred to in chapter I. A small number of the latter, however, were unable to
answer the question and some 'non-participating companies' (so called because
they completed only a small part of Questionnaire I) supplied the balance of the
answers. That there were 100 companies that completed this question is quite
fortuitous.

any obstacle to trade, there would be no reason why an expanding
market in Australia should not be served by exports from the United
States, possibly in conjunction with a local company engaged in
selling and in the provision of after-sales service. Therein lies the
importance of the other factors listed in Table III-1, almost all of
which are concerned in one form or another with obstacles to trade.

Tariff barriers stand out as by far the most important of these
obstacles. One-half of all respondent companies mentioned the desire
to bypass tariff barriers as a motive in their establishment in Australia, and such companies were widely dispersed through industry.

An executive of one company producing a specialized type of machinery stated that the Australian subsidiary became the first foreign affiliate of the American company to produce this machinery because of an Australian tariff of 60 per cent *ad valorem* on the American product. Had the Canadian affiliate been in production at the time, Australian manufacture would not have been started because of the lower Australian tariff on goods of Canadian origin. Another company engaged only in the assembly of imported parts explained that, though a tariff of 42½ per cent was paid on both parts and assembled units imported from the U.S., local assembly permitted the company to obtain some parts at lower rates of duty by importing from the Canadian affiliate and avoided the payment of duty on American assembly costs, overhead, and profit. Since the tariff is usually levied on the current domestic value of the imported article, there is often a further stimulus to local assembly. One firm commented that while nominally a 45 per cent tariff is levied on both parts and assembled units, the Customs Department actually levies a 73 per cent duty on the invoice value of the fully assembled article, estimating the current domestic value to be considerably higher than the invoice value. Since it is harder to estimate the current domestic value of a component, the 45 per cent tariff on parts is levied on invoice value only, and the tariff thus provides a significant incentive to import components rather than the assembled product.

Attention may be drawn to a number of specific cases where already published material makes it possible to illustrate the importance of tariffs in causing the influx of foreign companies. In the motor vehicle industry, very high tariffs protected the Australian body-building industry from 1920 on.[3] Soon after 1920, the tariff preference in favour of the unassembled chassis, as against the fully assembled unit, was increased, while a parallel movement increased the preference in favour of British cars. George Maxcy connects this change in tariff structure closely with two major American investments:

> Convinced that the only way to retain a hold on the Australian market in the long run in the face of high tariffs (and especially tariffs discriminating heavily in favour of British producers) was to get behind the trade barriers, Ford and General Motors made the decision to invest substantial amounts in production and assembly facilities in Australia. (1963: 503.)

[3] In 1935, the Tariff Board stated that 'the existing duties on sets of motor panels represent ad valorem equivalents of from about 200 per cent to about 600 per cent, and are, in effect, prohibitive'.

The Goodyear Tire and Rubber Company of Ohio is another company which, after more than a decade of exporting tyres to Australia, decided to establish Australian manufacturing facilities in 1926 'because of the Commonwealth Government's well-defined tariff policy' (Forster 1964: 55).

Forster (ibid.: 97) believes that the Australian tariff was the factor which more than any other compelled Julius Kayser & Company and the Holeproof Hosiery Company, both of the U.S., to establish manufacturing ventures in Australia at the end of the twenties and, in view of the opposition of both companies to the Australian tariff on silk stockings in 1925, this seems very likely. Even earlier than this, the Australian tariff had played a vital role in encouraging the Eastman Kodak Company to form a joint venture with an Australian firm to manufacture photographic film. This case has been described in such detail by Thomas Baker, first managing director of Kodak (Australasia) Ltd, in evidence submitted to a tariff inquiry in 1914, that it merits quoting at length:

> Prior to 1908 the duty imposed upon films was 15 per cent, and a similar duty was then also imposed upon dry plates. Upon the introduction of the Tariff Bill in 1907, showing the increased duty upon the films, I went to America for the purpose of consulting with the Eastman Kodak Company, whose agents we then were, who manufacture about 80 per cent of the photographic films used in the world, to see if any arrangement could be made by which the films could be manufactured in Australia. They pointed out to me the difficult nature of the undertaking, which I think is evidenced by the fact that throughout the world only about six factories are engaged in it, of which three are Kodak factories, viz., one at Rochester, N.Y.; one at Toronto, Canada; and the factory of the Australian company here. Other factories are—one in England, one in the United States of America, and one in France; but, with the exception of the Kodak manufacture, the success achieved has not been at all striking . . . They also pointed out the large amount of capital which would be necessary to provide a suitable factory and machinery; but in the end, the imposition of the new duty having been ratified by Parliament, it was agreed that the attempt should be made. (*Inter-State Commission of Australia, Tariff Investigation: Report*, p. 66.)

Even the existence of a tariff barrier shielding a rapidly growing market may not be sufficient inducement for a foreign company to establish manufacturing facilities. If the market is still very small in relation to the most economic plant size, there is little likelihood of domestic competition for the imported product and so no need to invest in the market concerned. As the market grows, however, the risk of competition substantially increases, and with it the incentive to invest. This can be well illustrated from Australian experience. Despite a 35 per cent British Preferential Tariff and a 45 per cent General Tariff on domestic irons in Australia throughout the twenties, it was not until late in that decade, and the entry into the local industry of several other companies, that Australian General Electric began the local production of the Hotpoint irons it had previously imported from the U.S. (Forster 1964: 108-9). The particularly frank statement of the general manager of a recently established chemical company provides an even better example:

> Personally, I don't think any U.S. chemical company would establish operations in Australia if it could continue to supply the Australian market from the U.S. But import controls and tariffs, and particularly the fear that a competitor will establish himself before you in the Australian market and then secure heavy tariff protection, compel U.S. companies to invest here.

This attitude was by no means uncommon.

Import controls were mentioned by respondent companies as the second most important obstacle to trade. The number of companies which mentioned this factor as the primary reason for investment in Australia is too small to permit meaningful comment on their number by industry, and no special significance appears to attach to the fact that five of the nine were in the electrical products industry. One particularly graphic illustration of the effect of import restrictions may be taken from that industry, however. After the suspension of import controls on electric shavers in February 1960, the local production of shavers by two foreign companies, Ronson of the U.S. and Philips of Holland, ceased almost entirely. Ronson did not explain at the tariff inquiry of 1962 why it began the production of shavers in Australia but from its subsequent action it may be surmised that its reason was parallel to that of Philips. The latter company admitted that 'during 1959, 1960 and part of 1961, part of its electric shaver requirements were made locally, mainly because import restrictions prevented it from obtaining its total needs from overseas' (*Tariff Board Report* [*T.B.R.*] 1962i: 5).

Other examples of the importance of import restrictions are not hard to find. Their importance in the decision to build at least two of the plants in the Altona petrochemical complex (and therefore probably in the decision to build the complex as a whole) has been noted by the Tariff Board (1962j; 1963c). Two American pharmaceutical companies which began manufacturing in Australia in the late fifties expressed in almost identical terms the view that 'manufacture might not have been started in Australia but for import licences. The import licences restricted the *value* of imports and it was cheaper to import the bulk raw materials than the finished pills.' Though Maxcy believes that it was tariffs which caused the initial investment in Australian assembly facilities by Ford and General Motors, he yet feels that it was the skilful use made of the dollar shortage by the federal government immediately after World War II which caused four companies, all of them American, to embark on extensive investment programmes involving a progressive increase in the Australian content of their vehicles (1963: 505).

Writing of American investment in South America in the twenties and thirties, Phelps observed that 'upward revision of tariffs has been more important than any other single cause in bringing the question of migration [of industry] to the fore' (1936: 63). It appears that tariffs have played the decisive role in Australia too, though since World War II import restrictions have also been important. Both may pose a threat to an existing market. There appears to be much to be said for the view of Barlow and Wender, reached after very extensive empirical investigations, that, far from objectively weighing up the differential profit prospects in various countries, 'manufacturing companies invest abroad primarily to maintain a market that has been established by export but which is in danger of being lost' (1955: 160).

Very few companies in the present survey indicated that their American parents had invested in Australia in the expectation of receiving a differentially higher profit rate here than in the U.S., though it is possible that the structure of this section of the questionnaire was partly to blame for this. One firm mentioned that foreign subsidiaries are expected to show a return 'commensurate with the risk involved', and another that, while a U.S. company might require only a 5 per cent profit on turnover at home, it would require a profit of 'at least 20 per cent' in a 'real risk market'. But both of these firms gave 'tariffs' and 'expected market growth' as the main reasons for their own investment in Australia. Only one company stated explicitly that 'the big reason a company decides to invest abroad is because it believes it can get a better return on its investment abroad than at home'. In answer to a question on the size of differential profit rate needed to induce an American company to invest in Australia, the executive stated:

> About 25 per cent probably. In the U.S. we might be happy with a net profit of 6 per cent on sales and 13-14 per cent on net worth. We might expect 7-8 per cent on sales in Australia, 16-17 per cent on net worth, and of course higher rates of return in less stable countries.

But even this company felt that an important motive behind its own investment in Australia was the fear that an American competitor 'would get too big internationally'.

If the approach of Barlow and Wender be accepted, it is not surprising to find that of the seventy-one companies which provided information on the connection which their American parent had had with the Australian market *before* its investment in the manu-facturing facilities of the company concerned, only six had parent companies which had had no prior contact with Australia—and in at least four of these cases the primary initiative for investment was not American. None of the six was a wholly American venture in 1962 (though one of them had been at the time of establishment here), a fact which tends to support the view that it was not American initiative that was responsible for the decision to invest in Australia. Thirty-three parent companies had confined their operations to exporting to Australia, leaving distribution in local hands. A further ten had established their own sales subsidiaries in Australia, while as many as eighteen had made arrangements with a local firm for the manufacture of at least some products under licence. In practice such an arrangement often went hand in hand with a considerable export from the U.S. company.[4]

In view of the widely held opinion that the sudden cancellation of an agreement of this kind by a foreign licenser is a frequent cause of loss to Australian licensees, it is interesting to note in passing that only three of these eighteen licensing agreements had been cancelled and the link between licenser and licensee severed. At the time the survey was conducted, it was anticipated that one more licensing agreement would not be renewed on its expiry. Of the others, one licensee went bankrupt (which was a potent factor in the American company's decision to invest in Australia); one was acquired by the American firm; one sold its assets to the American licenser after declining an offer of a shareholding in the new subsidiary; one held a licence not affected by the American investment; and ten retained an equity interest in the local manufacture after the American investment. Of these latter, eight still retained an equity interest in 1963, an interest which ranged from 31 to 75 per cent.

In some cases, even companies which have only been engaged in the distribution of American products are affected by the establish-ment of local manufacturing facilities by the American firm. It is

[4] Three of the four remaining local companies were affiliates of other American-owned companies operating in Australia before their own establish-ment, while the fourth was the newly established subsidiary of a company which, after many years of manufacturing experience in Australia, had been compelled to withdraw from this market for some years.

well known, for example, that Pfizer's decision to handle the distribution of its own products in Australia following its investment here had a considerable impact on the local firm F. H. Faulding & Co. Ltd. But though the evidence is insufficient to be dogmatic, it would appear that for the most part dealers do not suffer greatly as a result of American investment in manufacturing. Of the eight cases uncovered by the survey in which the 'fate' of the previous dealer is known, four were acquired by the American firm (at least one of them at a price which later proved to be far too high), and four initially held substantial shareholdings in the newly formed companies. Two of these local shareholdings, of 15 and 25 per cent, still remain. A familiar case, though one which fell outside the scope of the survey, was the cancellation by Cyanamid of the distribution rights of Drug Houses of Australia Ltd: the latter was able to acquire a 20 per cent interest in the new manufacturing company Cyanamid-D.H.A. Pty Ltd. In another case, when an American firm terminated the distribution rights of a local firm, the American company bought back the local firm's existing stock of American-made goods at a price above that paid originally by the local company, and agreed to pay the latter 5 per cent of total Australian sales for the first year after the termination of the agency, 3 per cent for the second year, and 1 per cent for the third.

Turning to the other reasons given for the establishment of manufacturing facilities in Australia, it is somewhat surprising to see that relatively few companies rated the avoidance of freight charges as significant in their decision. Twenty-two companies made some mention of freight charges, but none reckoned them as of primary importance.[5]

Only slightly more significant was the desire to take advantage of consumer preference for goods made in Australia. Two companies mentioned this as their primary reason for investing in Australia and a further twenty-two firms mentioned this as a supplementary reason. But it will bring little cheer to those who spend considerable sums promoting the 'Buy Australian' concept to learn that even these figures exaggerate the importance of this factor, as usually understood. Certainly, one company explained that preference for Australian goods 'is quite important because our main customers are tradesmen subject to union pressure'; and another company, producing household appliances, felt that while consumer preference for 'made in Australia' products was not significant when manufac-

---

[5] Forster (1964: 45), however, believes freight charges were of greater importance in inducing Ford and General Motors to invest in Australian assembly plants in the twenties than was the tariff.

ture was begun in the fifties, such preference 'is significant now'. But even the former of these two companies felt that it was the threat posed to the Australian market of the American company by a sudden increase in tariff protection that was the primary reason for Australian investment.

Only seven of the twenty-four companies which mentioned consumer preference for Australian-made products sold a significant fraction of their output directly to domestic consumers. None of the eight companies which mentioned this factor in the electrical products industry, and only two of the six in the industrial chemicals industry, sold any of their output to domestic consumers. Most companies were in fact not thinking of domestic consumers when they mentioned this motive. Four of them were almost certainly referring to government preference that certain strategically important products be locally manufactured, while a number of the balance had in mind the preference of their industrial consumers for the flexibility which only a local source of supply confers. This was probably the factor prompting two companies producing motor vehicle components to mention 'consumer' preference for Australian-made goods, though the ability of the motor vehicle company itself to advertise a high Australian content may also have been relevant. Two companies supplying parts to firms operating in the highly volatile home appliance market did not have the Australian content of the end product in mind, however. One of these contended that Australian manufacturers of household appliances would sooner buy an inferior Australian-made article than a better American one because of the greater availability of local supplies in a market typified by sharp fluctuations in demand. Indeed, an offer of a more or less guaranteed market by one of the Australian appliance manufacturers, at prices initially above those of imports, was one important reason for this company's Australian investment. The other company stated that it had been told by one of its chief customers that it was worth a $12\frac{1}{2}$ per cent Australian price disadvantage to have a local source of supply because of the greater flexibility of delivery and the closer contact made possible between customer and supplier. A company in the chemicals industry, with 1962 sales of less than £2 million, estimated that savings made by customers because of local production exceeded £100,000. This was a result of the substantial reduction in inventories made possible.

There is little in the above to suggest that the preference of domestic consumers for Australian-made goods was a significant factor in encouraging American investment in Australia. On the contrary, prejudice *against* Australian-made products was encountered on several occasions. A complaint by Kodak (Australasia) in

1914 about 'the prejudice existing against the local product' (*Inter-State Commission of Australia, Tariff Investigation: Report*, p. 66) is perhaps not surprising, but the following statement made in 1963 by the general manager of a company in the metal-working industry is in a different category:

> Nobody has a preference for 'made in Australia' even today—that is certainly not one reason for manufacturing here. This might be a factor in goods where quality isn't important but not in our line. We considered stamping our boxes with the 'made in Australia' sign but decided against it. Last week we got a consignment returned from one of Australia's biggest companies with a complaint that was so trivial that we knew it was only an excuse and didn't even bother arguing with them.

A total of thirteen companies mentioned 'government encouragement' as a significant factor in their decision to invest in Australia. Two companies referred specifically to encouragement received from the Department of Trade, one stating that during a period of acute foreign exchange shortage it had been offered an assurance of import licences for all components if the total cost of importing the components could be reduced to 55 per cent of the previous cost of importing the fully assembled article. Another three firms mentioned encouragement from the Department of Supply, one being promised duty-free admission for imported materials and another a premium above the price of imported goods. The encouragement given by the Postmaster-General's Department to the two American-affiliated manufacturers of telecommunications equipment is well known. Even in the twenties, that department assisted Standard Telephones and Cables Pty Ltd through the payment of a 15 per cent price premium (Forster 1964: 112-13). World War II, and the drastic reduction in the availability of imports which it caused, convinced the government of the need to foster the local manufacture of this equipment, and both S.T.C. and its affiliate, Austral Standard Cables Pty Ltd, secured major benefit as a result.

The government's encouragement of the motor vehicle industry after 1945 has been noted in Appendix A. It is public knowledge that the government provided tariff concessions on imported machinery, assistance in the acquisition of government wartime machinery, freedom to import equipment without exchange restrictions, tax concessions to visiting foreign experts, and even, in the case of G.M.H., assistance in the securing of a local bank overdraft of more than £2 million. It may be less widely known that government interest in the car industry, in addition to that reflected in tariff policy, had its genesis as far as American companies are concerned in the twenties, when representatives were sent to North America in what proved to be a successful attempt to persuade Ford to invest in the Australian industry (Forster 1964: 38).

Perhaps surprisingly, only two companies felt that *state* government encouragement had been a contributing factor in their decision to come to Australia, though a number indicated that inducements extended by state governments had been an important consideration in the location of their Australian plants. One of the more unfortunate aspects of the Australian federal system in its present form is that it gives rise to totally unplanned competition by state governments for industries of every kind. An illuminating example of this was provided by the president of the Gillette Company in 1962 on the occasion of the official opening of the new plant of Gillette (Aust.) Pty Ltd. He commented that since Gillette had been trading in Australia for more than fifty years and had its headquarters in Sydney, that city appeared the natural choice for the site of Gillette's new Australian plant. But the 'real personal interest shown in our problems' by the Victorian government had induced the company to invest near Melbourne instead (*A.F.R.*, 13 Dec. 1962). It is widely known that the South Australian government has a highly developed system of 'Buy South Australian', and the policy of extending inducements to prospective investors is so common there that the policy is becoming nationally known as 'Playfordism', after a former South Australian Premier. When Mobil Oil decided to build its second Australian oil refinery, the South Australian government encouraged the company to build in that state by agreeing to provide not only access roads and railway line but also housing, water, and electricity. This was in addition to an undertaking that state preferences would be given to the products of the new refinery (Grant 1963: 260). It is scarcely to be wondered at that both companies that mentioned state government encouragement as significant in their decision to invest in Australia are located in South Australia, though since even these two mentioned such encouragement as the third factor in their decision to invest in Australia, it is quite possible that both were thinking more in terms of location than of whether to invest in Australia as such.

The desire to gain access to the markets of Asia on the one hand and New Zealand and the Pacific on the other by establishing operations in Australia was mentioned by twenty-two companies (eight firms mentioned that the desire to serve both the Asian and Pacific areas had been significant in their decision to invest), but none ranked this motive as of primary importance and only seven mentioned it as of secondary significance. Twelve of the twenty-two were in the metal-working industries, three produced food or drink, two industrial chemicals, three pharmaceuticals, one plastic products, and one was in the 'Miscellaneous' classification.

Very few companies indeed mentioned either a desire 'to avoid unfavourable conditions for expansion in the U.S.' or 'a need caused by the break-down of a previous licensing agreement with a local manufacturer'. Both motives for investment would be meaningless without the presence also of some other factor such as freight charges, tariffs, or quotas. The only firm which mentioned 'the break-down of a licensing agreement' as of first importance in its decision to invest in Australia was engaged in the production of an item on which freight charges are prohibitively high: when the licensee was taken over by a major competitor, the American company had little choice but to invest if it were to retain its market share. In another case, the Australian licensee went bankrupt and fell back to being an import agent for the American firm. Tariff barriers made this increasingly difficult and so, after encouragement from no fewer than five American subsidiaries already in Australia, the decision to invest was taken.

Only eleven companies gave 'lower Australian unit costs' as a motive in their decision to invest in Australia, and only one of these felt that this had been the main motive. Eight of the eleven were in one or other of the metal-working industries. The smallness of the number of companies which sought lower costs by manufacturing in Australia is not, perhaps, surprising: a cost study made by the American National Industrial Conference Board indicated that Australian unit costs were lower than American in only four of the nineteen cases available to them, and that the median Australian cost, at 25 per cent above the American cost, was the highest in any of the five major areas examined by them (Gates and Linden 1961: 11, 19). The conclusions of the present survey seem to show that this picture may be slightly too pessimistic but the general impression is confirmed.[6]

A significant number of companies felt that the reasons offered in the questionnaire were inadequate as an explanation of their investment in Australia. Thirty-one mentioned some reason for investment other than those already discussed. Seven spoke of the establishment of some American customer in Australia, and no fewer than three

[6] Comparative costs are discussed at greater length in chapter VII. For the moment it may be noted that of the 82 cost comparisons provided by 70 companies, 23 indicated that Australian costs were lower than American, 12 that they were about the same, and 47 that they were higher. Many of the companies indicating that Australian costs were lower than American, however, confine their operations to assembly or to the production of a part only of the finished article.

of these companies commented on the investment of one company, G.M.H. While for some the establishment of a major American customer in Australia meant the automatic creation of a growth market in this country, in other cases the investment was undertaken at a loss in order to preserve the goodwill of the American parent company. One firm explained that 'it'll be many years before the Australian market is really big enough to support economic production but they are our best customer and we supply them all over the world'.

Three companies mentioned that a large part of the reason for their investment in Australia was a desire to speed the sale of American-made products. One of these acquired its previous Australian dealer because of the inability of the latter to keep pace with the overall growth pattern set by the U.S. company and then almost drifted into assembling the imported product. Another felt that the establishment of a limited Australian assembly operation would increase consumer acceptance of the whole range of parent company products.

Some companies invested in Australia for reasons not directly related to Australian economic conditions. It is well known that Alcoa and Kaiser Aluminium invested in Australia at least partly in order to secure access to large bauxite deposits in a politically stable country, while the investment of Asarco in the Mining Trust Ltd of London, whence it acquired its holding in Mount Isa Mines, was scarcely related to Australian economic growth. Similarly, the establishment of Swift Australian and the four American companies producing sausage casings for the American market was clearly motivated by growth in American demand and by the size of Australia's farming sector. Reasons for American investment in Australian oil refining capacity are many: tariffs played some part, as also did the political security of the area and an increase in the number of refined products (Grant 1963: 257, 260). But none of these motives means a great deal without the overriding desire on the part of international oil companies to find market outlets for their crude oil.

Other motives were varied. One company stated that one of its most important reasons for investing in Australia was a desire to play a part in Australia's economic development. Since this country is hardly one of the world's poorest, however, one may be forgiven for being a little suspicious of the apparent altruism. One firm mentioned the protection of a weak patent position as its primary reason for investment, while the shareholding of another American company had been acquired as an income investment in support of a licensing agreement. Two companies spoke of a general policy favouring the decentralization of production, and two more of the improvement in servicing facilities made possible by local manufacture. Only one firm mentioned the relatively low rates of company taxation in Australia as a reason for initial investment, and even in this case it was but a contributing factor. The personal whim of executives also played a part in some investment decisions. The managing director of one local subsidiary stated that 'we are really in Australia because I wanted to come to Australia', and exporting from the U.S. without a local manufacturing operation was not possible because of the great importance of after-sales service. A senior executive in another firm felt that the liking which parent company executives had for international travel was a factor in the establishment of his own firm in Australia.

Only four firms, apart from those subject to government encouragement, specifically mentioned the receipt of an invitation from an Australian firm as a significant reason for investment. This is, perhaps, not unnatural since most questions were designed to discover why invitations were accepted rather than how many were received. Australian initiative of this kind has certainly been important.[7] In the case of at least twenty-two participating companies, private Australian initiative played an important role in the decision to invest here. (It is interesting to note that all but four of these remained joint Australian-American ventures for at least a period after the initial American investment.) In some cases, the Australian initiative was taken only to gain access to American technical know-how. In some others the motive was access to cheap finance. In one case, for example, an Australian firm issued convertible notes to an American company at 5 per cent; the Australian firm benefited by avoiding the necessity of paying 8 per cent for local funds and the American firm benefited by being able to convert the notes into ordinary shares at substantially below the market price. In this way, the Australian firm became predominantly American-owned within six years of the initial issue. In a variation on the shortage-of-funds theme, an Australian company asked an American firm to establish a local operation because the British subsidiary of the American company, which had previously been supplying the Australian firm with materials, refused to grant the Australian company thirty days' credit on its imports and the local company was experiencing difficulty in obtaining letters of credit from its bank. In several cases the Australian firm lacked both capital and know-how, while one company, already partly owned by an American firm, successfully sought

---

[7] Arthur Denning, Commissioner for New South Wales in North America, reported in 1962 that his New York office had 200 specific inquiries from Australian firms seeking investments from American companies (*A.F.R.*, 6 Sept. 1962).

a doubling of the American shareholding as an insurance against the American firm's entering the Australian market in competition with the local firm after the latter had spent considerable resources developing consumer acceptance of the American products.

It was disturbing to find that at least two Australian-American companies felt that the 'real benefit' of their American association was not access to know-how or capital but freedom to use 'an American name'. One of these firms was using the brand name of its American associate on some products not even produced by the American firm. The other stated: 'We could get by without the U.S. company, but it is very useful to have the U.S. name behind us.' The executive went on to name one large Australian retailing firm which does not use the products of this industry unless they bear an American name.

In some cases, soliciting a take-over offer from an American firm is the simplest and most profitable way to dispose of a large personal shareholding, especially if this is in a proprietary company. At least two participating companies had become American in ownership after their founders had hawked their personal holdings in them around a number of American firms in search of the highest bidder.

Before concluding this section of the chapter, it should be stressed that the whole discussion has been confined to the reasons given by companies for their *initial* investment in Australia. The contention of Dr Penrose (1956: 224-9)—that the local subsidiaries of foreign companies develop a life of their own which leads investment in them to continue long after a strictly objective consideration of the return to be earned would justify this—has been deliberately left to one side. Her thesis is discussed in the following chapter when the dividend policies of American companies in Australia are under examination.

It is interesting to compare the above evidence with present theories of why capital moves between nations, and to see in general terms what these theories suggest about the future importance of foreign capital in Australian development. With few exceptions, such theories are little more than three decades old, the first detailed examination of the causes of international capital movement being that of Ohlin (1933).[8] Probably influenced to some extent by the great importance of the international bond market in the nineteenth century, Ohlin placed primary emphasis on the role of international interest rate differentials as giving rise to foreign investment.

[8] Earlier writers, such as J. S. Mill, E. G. Wakefield, and J. A. Hobson, had elements of a theory, however.

E

Further, by adopting the classical assumption that the rate of interest is a reflection of the supply of capital relative to other productive factors, he could believe that international capital movements exercise an essentially equilibrating function: 'Since factors move from countries where their prices are low to those where they are dear, their scarcity and reward in the former is increased, while their prices in the latter fall, unless there is some counteracting tendency.' Ohlin qualified this by stating that 'foreign investments may . . . be largely independent of differences in interest levels when there is a chance of profit', and dealt also with the importance of tariffs, the desire to guarantee the supply of vital raw materials, the urge to secure marketing outlets, the desire to avoid high domestic taxation, and the need to extend credit to promote the sale of exports. Even the equilibrating function of international capital movements he qualified by noting the case where the 'quantity of certain productive factors in a country may be so small that an increased supply of them will not reduce, but increase their prices'.

After the publication of Ohlin's book, however, what had been for him merely the most important of many forces leading to foreign investment was developed by some writers into the only 'normal' reason for international capital movement. Fanno (1939) provided perhaps the most complete statement of this point of view but, as Arndt (1954) has noted, it was accepted by a much wider circle of economists.

This view was inadequate in several respects. Above all, it failed to explain the actual movements of capital—often from countries with high rates of interest to those with low, rarely from capital-rich countries to capital-poor. Gradually an awareness grew up that, in the case of *direct* foreign investment, it is the marginal efficiency (or profitability) of capital which is of primary relevance and that this is rarely higher in capital-poor countries than in capital-rich (Rosenstein-Rodan 1943; Balogh 1945; Abramovitz 1952: 155; Nurkse 1953: 83-5; Arndt 1954). Far from flowing *into* countries with little capital in relation to other factors, capital might be expected to flow in the *reverse* direction (Myrdal 1956).

But the explanation was still incomplete, for even granted that it is the relationship between the return on investment and the cost of investible funds—the relationship between the marginal efficiency of capital and the rate of interest—which determines the level of investment, why should *foreign* investment take place? If the return on investment were greater than the cost of investible funds in Australia, Australian entrepreneurs might be expected to seize the investment opportunity and drive the rate of profit down towards the rate of interest. Only in the short term can the rate of profit exceed the rate of interest, and *Australian* businessmen, being closer to the domestic scene than those of other nations, might be expected to seize investment opportunities created by short-term divergences between the two rates. Only if relatively cheap funds are available abroad will *foreign* investment take place—and the explanation of foreign investment is once more interest rate differentials.[9]

In the third edition of his *International Economics*, Kindleberger cites a thesis by Stephen Hymer which appears to provide the missing link. Hymer has suggested that direct investment only occurs when a firm has some 'major advantage over its competitors at home and those abroad or can obtain a peculiar advantage from the international co-ordination of economic action' (Kindleberger 1963: 411). While this advantage may in some cases be access to capital, it may equally well be superior technology, command over patents, access to a market, consumer familiarity with an internationally advertised product, etc. From Kindleberger's brief summary, this appears to be one of the most useful contributions yet made to the theory of direct foreign investment.

If company executives could be quite confident that no obstacles to trade—whether in the form of tariffs, quotas, freight charges, consumer preference for local goods, or government bias in favour of the products of local industry—would ever arise to interfere with their export trade, it is hard to see why many *manufacturing* companies would embark on foreign investment. There might be a few which would invest abroad to take advantage of lower foreign costs of production, but not many of these would come to Australia. It is the fear of being cut off from a rapidly expanding export market which so often *raises the question* of foreign investment; it is the relatively low marginal cost of investing in avenues already familiar to the parent company—in avenues where its name is widely known and its techniques highly developed—which makes foreign investment appear attractive. To the foreign company, the marginal cost of extending operations to Australia is not only low absolutely, it is also substantially lower than the cost which a domestic company would incur—in terms of research expenditure, costly experimentation, and even advertising—if it attempted to enter the same industry. This gives the experienced foreign company a considerable competitive advantage over the domestic firm, and the more advanced the technology of the foreign firm or the better known its products, the greater its competitive advantage. This advantage is still further enhanced by the greater ease with which the large,

9 If Australian entrepreneurs can themselves secure access to the cheaper funds abroad, foreign investment may well take the form of fixed interest borrowing rather than direct investment.

internationally-known corporation can draw on funds, both local and foreign. In other words, trade barriers are important in raising the question of whether to invest abroad or face the prospect of losing a market. Direct investment *may* result because foreign companies can secure access to funds more cheaply than can Australian companies, but is most likely to occur in practice because foreign companies face higher marginal efficiency of capital curves than do Australian companies in the 'same' market situation—because the value of a given quantum of investment in Australia is higher to the foreign companies than to the Australian. A corollary of this approach is that for the most part companies with no export trade and no special advantages of technology or reputation are those which do not invest abroad.

Superior technology is almost certainly the main advantage which foreign manufacturing companies enjoy *vis-à-vis* their Australian counterparts. The general level of skills in a community tends to be positively correlated with the community's capital stock, but the amount of original research and development done, which may be expected to influence substantially the competitive advantage enjoyed by that society's companies, tends to depend also on other factors. Since it may be assumed that the economies of scale available to companies operating in the very large nations of North America, Europe, and Japan are very much greater than those available to firms operating in the small and fragmented Australian market, it seems likely that the scope for original research in this country will be not only absolutely but also proportionally smaller than in larger countries, unless some differentially large stimulus is given to research in this country.

The view has sometimes been expressed that Australia's dependence on foreign capital will fall as the economy matures. But if the primary pre-condition for international direct investment in manufacturing is differential rates of technical progress, there seems no reason why foreign ownership of capital in Australian industry should not continue to increase as long as foreign countries do more research in all sectors of manufacturing than this country and trade barriers prevent their enjoying the fruits of this effort through exporting. Since Australia is a much smaller economy than the main capital-exporting economies, there would appear to be no way of halting this trend except by legislative action, unless Australia is prepared to concentrate research effort in particular sectors and thus secure a technical advantage over foreign companies in those areas. In this way it is conceivable that Australia might not only protect domestic ownership of these sectors but also secure ownership of corresponding sectors abroad.

IV

Ownership Patterns and Source of Funds

The first decision an American executive has to make after deciding to invest in Australia is whether to establish a totally new operation or to buy an interest in an existing firm. The outcome of this decision will depend on a number of factors, including the speed with which the foreign company desires to establish its local beachhead, the funds available to it, and the attitude of any previous licensee. Certainly, many American companies have decided in favour of making their initial investment in the stock of an Australian firm. Of the 208 companies covered in the present survey, at least 48, with 1962 employment of 20,690, began their American association when an American company acquired all the assets of, or a share interest of at least 25 per cent in, a firm already operating in Australia. All but four of these investments have taken place since 1945, which indicates either that the practice has grown in popularity or that the executives of long-established companies were unaware of the origins of their company.[1]

The acquisition of Australian firms by large foreign corporations is one of the most controversial aspects of overseas investment. Yet popular concern is largely unconnected with dislike of acquisitions *per se*: the American practice of vetting acquisitions and mergers to prevent undue restriction of competition is totally unknown in Aus-

[1] Similarly there may be a bias in figures gathered for acquisitions and mergers made between the date of local establishment and 1962. Eighty companies denied making any acquisitions since they first set up manufacturing operations in Australia, while 19 companies admitted acquiring between them 20 local companies *in toto* and at least part of the assets of 6 others. Two more local firms were 'merged'. All but 9 of these 28 acquisitions occurred between 1958 and 1962. It should be noted that the 28 acquisitions referred to include those by companies, like Ducon and Boral, in which the American shareholding was only a minority in 1962.

tralia.[2] It is the *foreign* element that arouses public anger.[3] But it seems that the reasons for this are largely emotional. To begin with, some Australian equity frequently remains in the company in which the foreign corporation makes its investment, and indeed the invest-ment is often made at the invitation of a local company desirous of a partnership with an overseas firm. Of the forty-eight cases referred to above in which the acquisition was part of the initial investment, twenty-six still retained a substantial element of Australian equity in 1962. At least another five were partly Australian-owned for a period of years after the initial American investment, while two more had been entirely British-owned before the American investment. In some of the cases in which an American firm acquired all the out-standing shares, the previous Australian shareholders had declined an invitation to retain a portion of their equity. The Australian executive of one large food company which has recently been acquired by an American firm expressed regret that some Australian shareholding had not been retained. On being asked why this had not been done in view of the frequency with which the American parent embarked on joint ventures in European countries, he replied that the original shareholders 'wanted to get rid of the company and the price was right'. Similar comments were made by executives in two other companies. When Hunter Douglas acquired control over the local firm of Mello-Lite Ltd in 1961 in a share exchange which left the original shareholders of Mello-Lite with a substantial minority interest in the enlarged company, a writer in a financial newspaper stated that 'there will probably be some disappointment that the deal is not a direct takeover'.

Whether the acquisition is complete or not, foreign investment by take-over still adds to the resources available to the Australian economy. Indeed, it is strange that those who most object to foreign companies' financing their local growth from internally-generated funds and not 'new capital from overseas' should also object to foreign investment by take-over, for in many cases companies making their initial investment in an existing company have to 'bring in' substantially larger dollar funds than those needed by firms planning

[2] For an interesting discussion of Australian mergers and American antitrust laws, see J. A. Bushnell (1961: 166-75).

[3] This was graphically illustrated during a prolonged take-over battle between the American-owned Nabisco company and the locally-owned Australian Biscuit Company Pty Ltd for control of Swallow & Ariell Ltd in 1964. Though the failure of the Nabisco bid meant that the privately-owned Australian Biscuit Company increased its estimated share of the Australian biscuit market from 70 to 80 per cent, public sentiment during the conflict was strongly against the American firm.

to grow from small beginnings. This is not invariably true. It is known that one American firm used local bank overdraft facilities to purchase a majority shareholding in a medium-sized Australian company, and it appears that occasionally American companies pay for their acquisitions over a period of time from the profits of the local operation itself. But by and large, the acquisition of a local firm initially requires more 'new capital' than setting up a small operation from the beginning.

There is another obvious reason why popular concern at foreign take-overs is misplaced: the firm in which the initial investment is made is often in economic difficulties before the change of ownership. Asarco's acquisition of an interest in Mount Isa Mines is a vivid example of this. Without the injection of funds which Asarco provided in 1930, Blainey estimates that the Mining Trust, which then owned a majority of Mount Isa's share capital, 'would have faced liquidation, a thousand workmen at Mount Isa would have been suddenly dismissed, and millions of pounds worth of machinery would have lain idle and unused' (1960: 143). The American company continued to pour money into Mount Isa but did not receive its first dividend until 1947. Borg-Warner is another firm which began life in Australia by acquiring a majority holding in a local firm which was on the point of collapse: Coote & Jorgensen Ltd had an accumulated deficit in profit and loss account of £987,332 by mid-1956, shortly before the American investment. Holden's Motor Body Builders was also facing a difficult period when it was acquired by General Motors (Australia) in 1931, and Swallow & Ariell Ltd, which Nabisco attempted to acquire in 1964, had declared no ordinary dividend since 1960/1, with losses in 1961/2, 1962/3, and the first half of 1963/4.

The initial acquisition of an interest in an Australian company is often only the vehicle for further investment of the 'conventional' type. The expansion of Coote & Jorgensen since the acquisition of Borg-Warner's interest, for example, has been dramatic. Another case is that of Comalco: when it acquired the interest of the Commonwealth government in the aluminium smelter at Bell Bay in 1961, it entered into an agreement to increase its capacity from 12,000 to 28,000 tons per annum. It was originally expected that this would take about four years. In the event, capacity reached 52,000 tons by July 1963. In the food industry also, where foreign take-overs are most criticized, investment in several companies since acquisition has been considerable. Parsons General Foods embarked on the construction of a large new plant at Liverpool shortly after General Foods entered Australia by acquiring Parsons Foods Pty Ltd in 1961, and Campbell's Soups opened a plant reported to have cost well in excess of £1 million at Shepparton in 1962 after its initial acquisition of the food division of Kia Ora Industries in 1959.

In some industries there may even be good reasons for *encouraging* take-overs if the alternative is the construction of considerable excess capacity and consequent pressure for increased protection against imports. The possibility that in some situations take-overs should be encouraged is taken up again in chapter XI, but for the moment there appears little justification for the frequently unquestioning condemnation of all foreign take-overs common in Australia today.

If an American company decides to set up a completely new operation in Australia—and even if it decides to acquire a local firm in its entirety—it must decide whether to run the operation as a branch of the parent concern or to establish a separately incorporated company structure. The significant factors to be taken into account in making this decision mainly concern company taxation.[4] American tax authorities regard the income of foreign branches as an integral part of the income of their parent corporations, but ignore the income of subsidiaries incorporated abroad (except those in tax-haven countries) until they remit dividends to their parent companies. This has a number of important effects. First, where the rate of company income tax in the capital-importing country is below that in the U.S., as in Australia in the early sixties, there is an incentive for American companies to establish unincorporated branches initially, to permit foreign establishment losses to be written off against the relatively high rates of U.S. taxation. When the foreign operation becomes profitable, however, there is, other things being equal, a strong incentive to incorporate locally.[5] An example may illustrate this. If an Australian branch makes a pre-tax profit of £100,000, the U.S. parent company is subject to tax on all this amount, although a credit is allowed to the extent of taxes paid in Australia provided this does not exceed the effective rate of company taxation in America. Assuming that Australian taxation is at the rate of 40 per cent (as it was in 1962), and so takes £40,000, and the effective U.S. tax is 50 per cent, the American parent has to pay a further £10,000 in tax, irrespective of whether the profit remains in Australia or is remitted to the U.S. This leaves a net income from Australian operations of only £50,000. If the Australian operation

[4] The following section is a necessarily simplified version of information gleaned from two sources: a confidential booklet describing the tax situation in 1959, lent to the writer by an international firm of chartered accountants; and a booklet published by the Commerce Clearing House, Inc., of Chicago, *Revenue Act of 1962 with explanation,* for which the writer is grateful to Hunter Douglas Ltd.

[5] This practice, of course, benefits total Australian tax revenue.

had been incorporated locally, however, and no dividend were paid, total taxation would have been only £40,000 to the Australian government and total after-tax income £60,000.

The U.S. tax position with regard to dividends received from a foreign subsidiary has recently undergone a change. The situation before the American Revenue Act of 1962 was passed can be illustrated by continuing the above example. (It is assumed for the moment that there is no Australian tax levied on the dividend itself.) If, instead of reinvesting all its £60,000 net income, the American-owned subsidiary operating in Australia had declared a dividend of £30,000, the American parent company would have been liable to taxation on that dividend only and could have claimed a taxation credit of £12,000 (being the product of the rate of Australian taxation and the size of the dividend). Total American tax payable on Australian operations, therefore, would have been £3,000 (still assuming a U.S. tax rate of 50 per cent) and total income after Australian and U.S. taxes would have been £57,000. Even had a dividend equal to £60,000 been declared, total income after both Australian and American taxes would have been £54,000, or £4,000 higher than the situation where the Australian operation was unincorporated. The Revenue Act of 1962 introduced the principle which has come to be known as 'grossing-up'. This implies that taxes paid in Australia by incorporated subsidiaries—which could previously be used as both a tax deduction and a tax credit—can now be used as a tax credit only. This provision has no effect on companies not declaring dividends but increases the American taxation payable on dividends remitted to the U.S. Thus, in the above example, if the Australian subsidiary were to declare a dividend of £60,000, the American tax would be applied to the dividend *plus* the equivalent amount of Australian company taxation already levied, that is £40,000. The application of the American rate of tax to the full £100,000 means that subsidiaries with a high rate of dividend remittance are in no better position as subsidiaries than as unincorporated branches.

The existence of a withholding tax in the capital-importing country—on dividends declared by subsidiaries but not on profits remitted by branches, as in Australia—further complicates the issue. This may, in certain circumstances, make it more profitable for companies with a high rate of profit remittance to be branches rather than subsidiaries. If withholding tax is only 15 per cent (which is its maximum at present on dividends remitted to the U.S. from Australia), Australian tax on a dividend of £60,000 is £9,000, for which a credit is available against U.S. taxation. Before the Revenue Act of 1962, this meant that an American company would receive only £51,000 of a £60,000 Australian dividend but, because of tax credits up to the maximum American tax liability of £30,000 (for the £9,000 paid in withholding tax could not be claimed as a tax *deduction*), retained the full £51,000. This still left it in a marginally better position than if the Australian operation had been unincorporated. Since the Revenue Act of 1962, a parent receiving a dividend of £60,000, gross of withholding tax, from a subsidiary in Australia is liable to a 50 per cent tax on £100,000—and has tax credits for only £49,000. After payment of a further £1,000 American tax, the net profit is neither more nor less than had the Australian operation remained a branch. If the Australian tax on dividends had been appreciably higher than 15 per cent, however, as it was prior to the tax agreement between the U.S. and Australia in 1953, or if the Australian rate of company tax had been significantly higher than the 40 per cent assumed, as it has become since 1962, the income eventually accruing to the American parent of an Australian subsidiary declaring all its profits in dividends would actually have been less than if the Australian operation had not been incorporated. Clearly, what is relevant is not the level of Australian *company* tax merely but that of *total* Australian tax, including withholding tax, in relation to the American rate.

There is only one other important consideration confronting a manufacturing venture from a tax point of view. If a long established foreign branch is incorporated in the country of operation, a prohibitive U.S. tax might apply to the book-keeping profit made by the 'sale' of the assets of the branch to the newly incorporated company.

It appears, in summary, that companies setting up an operation in Australia at present have a short-term advantage to be gained in setting up a branch structure if the venture is expected to be unprofitable initially. When the operation becomes profitable, the decision on whether or not to incorporate will depend largely on the policy to be adopted towards profit repatriation. Companies remitting all (or almost all) after-tax profits have, since the change in U.S. tax laws in 1962, no incentive to incorporate in Australia and, since the increase in Australian tax rates, some positive incentive to remain unincorporated. Those with lower rates of profit repatriation have every incentive to incorporate locally, unless they have been operating for a long period as a branch and now face a heavy tax penalty if they incorporate, or unless they see very positive advantages in retaining the cloak of secrecy which non-incorporation still provides.

It is no accident that the fourteen American companies manufacturing in Australia under a branch structure in 1962 fell for the most part into one of three categories: those established in Australia for a long period, those established very recently, and those which might be expected to have a high rate of profit repatriation. The companies concerned were Parke Davis, Coca-Cola, Watkins Products, Coty, Max Factor, Chesebrough-Pond's, American Flange & Manufacturing, Corning Glass Works, Smith Kline & French, Cummins Diesel, Pepsi-Cola Metropolitan Bottling Company, Pfizer, Lubrizol International, and Lily Cups. One other firm which recently changed from a branch operation to a subsidiary did so at the same time that the Australian operation changed from being merely a sales organization to being a manufacturing venture, and this presumably coincided with a change in the company's profit remittance policy. Only one of the companies interviewed mentioned a disadvantage of the branch form not associated with taxation, namely, the vulnerability of the U.S. parent to legal attack through a foreign branch.

Even after choosing the form of corporate structure to be adopted, the American company contemplating investment still has to decide whether to be the sole owner of its venture or to share ownership with others. In making this decision, it must recognize that one of the most potent causes of popular suspicion of American investment in Australia is the widespread belief that American companies almost invariably deny Australians an opportunity to participate in the ownership of their local subsidiaries. This popular hostility is not diminished by the belief that British subsidiaries in Australia more often tend to share ownership with Australians than do American subsidiaries.[6] The Commonwealth government has announced that

[6] The foundations for this belief are only moderately secure. Dr Penrose stated in 1956 that 'on the average American companies hold 85% and British companies 40% of the Ordinary Shares of their subsidiaries in Australia' (1956: 227), though she gave no source for her statement. A survey of 666 companies conducted in 1958 by E. L. Wheelwright (1963: 170) indicated that while only 46 per cent of the total value of paid-up capital held by British companies in Australia was in wholly-owned subsidiaries, the corresponding American figure was 60 per cent. On the other hand, the Australian British Trade Association (1964: 1) found Australian equity participation in only about one-third of the 222 British-affiliated companies it surveyed in 1964. Further, E. T. Hamilton, president of the American Chamber of Commerce in Australia, contended in 1963 that 'recent studies by the Chamber reveal that of 215 American companies operating in [New South Wales], 115 or 53 per cent have Australian participation. By contrast, of a total of 85 British companies surveyed, 38 or only 44 per cent have Australian shareholders.' (*A.F.R.*, 4 April 1963.) In fact, none of these calculations is very meaningful since Wheelwright had to use the unsatisfactory weight of paid-up capital in his estimates and neither the Australian British Trade Association nor the American Chamber of Commerce in Australia used any weighting technique at all. There *are* many British subsidiaries in which Australians can buy an interest—such as I.C.I.A.N.Z., John Lysaghts, and Commonwealth Industrial Gases—but there are others in which British owner-

(Continued on next page)

TABLE IV–1   American Equity in American-affiliated Companies
Manufacturing in mid-1962, by Industry[a]

Industry	Companies incorporated in Australia in which American interest at 30 June 1962 was				Branches	Total
	25–49%	50–74%	75–99%	100%[b]		
Plant, equipment, machinery	4	6	3	18	1	32
Agricultural equipment	2	1	..	3	..	6
Motor vehicles	..	2	..	5	..	7
Motor accessories	2	2	..	2	..	6
Metal manufactures, n.e.i.	6	5	1	5	1	18
Electrical equipment, instruments, etc.	5	4	..	13	..	22
Gramophone records	..	1	..	2	..	3
Food and drink	..	3	..	12	2	17
Sausage casings	..	1	..	3	..	4
Industrial chemicals and plastics	..	9	..	8	..	17
Inks, polishes, adhesives, etc.	1	1	..	4	..	6
Pharmaceutical and toilet preparations	..	..	1	15	4	20
Cosmetics	2	1	..	2	3	8
Oils, mineral	1	..	..	3	1	5
Paper products	1	3	..	4	1	9
Rubber products	..	1	..	1	..	2
Plastic products	1	1	..	1	..	3
Abrasives	..	1	..	3	..	4
Clothing and fabrics	2	3	..	1	..	6
Furnishings	..	1	..	1	..	2
Writing instruments	..	..	..	3	..	3
Miscellaneous	1	..	..	2	1	8
Total	28	50	5	111	14	208

[a] 'American equity' refers only to 'direct investment', as earlier defined. It includes ownership by way of a controlled company in a third country. More than 20 of the above companies had some or all of their 'American' shares held in some country other than the U.S., usually the U.K. or Canada.

[b] In a few cases, the actual American equity in '100% companies' was less than 100 per cent because an intermediate parent company had some non-American shareholding. Thus, Hoover (Aust.) Pty Ltd is included as a '100% company' because it was wholly-owned by Hoover Ltd of the U.K. The latter company, though controlled in the U.S., has a substantial British shareholding. For the purpose of the table, directors' qualifying shares have been ignored, as also has one 'genuine' Australian shareholding of about 0·2 per cent.

ship is complete. Among these are such giants as Unilever, British Motor Corporation, British Petroleum, Thos. Borthwicks, and Cadbury-Fry-Pascall. [Since going to press, the *Directory of Overseas Investment in Australian Manufacturing Industry—1966*, published by the Department of Trade and Industry, has revealed that British affiliates in Australian industry are in fact more often wholly owned abroad than are American affiliates. On the other hand, because of the very large size of the wholly American affiliates, a greater proportion of total American investment is in wholly-owned affiliates than of British.]

'it is in general considered desirable that there be Australian participation in ownership and management' (Commonwealth Treasury
1960: 4), and even the senior executives of many wholly American
subsidiaries have expressed fear that the growth and proliferation
of American companies in which Australians are denied a share
interest might lead to undesirable domination of the economy.
Again and again during the present survey the view was expressed
that 'we don't want to become like Canada'.

What in fact was the actual situation with regard to the ownership
of American-affiliated firms manufacturing in Australia in 1962?
The data gathered in the survey are presented in Tables IV-1 to
IV-5. These show that 125 out of 208 operations were either
branches or wholly-owned subsidiaries of American companies; 5
had between 75 and 99 per cent of their voting shares held in the
U.S.; 50 between 50 and 74 per cent; and 28 between 25 and 49 per
cent. Since 22 of the companies in the 50-74 per cent category were
only 50 per cent American, there were exactly 50 companies, or 24
per cent of the total, in which the American share interest fell short
of a majority. And this, of course, with one exception, takes into
account only American interests of at least 25 per cent.

Table IV-1 reveals that there were significant differences in ownership patterns between different industries. Almost all American-
affiliated firms in 'Pharmaceutical and toilet preparations' were
entirely American in ownership, and high ratios of wholly-American
companies also prevailed in 'Motor vehicles', 'Food and drink', 'Oils,
mineral', 'Abrasives', and 'Writing instruments'. On the other hand,
only one of six companies in 'Clothing and fabrics' was wholly
American, and the proportion of wholly-owned firms in 'Industrial
chemicals and plastics' and 'Metal manufactures, n.e.i.' was not high.

Considerable caution must be exercised in the interpretation of
Table IV-2. At first glance it appears to indicate a fairly steady
change in the ownership preferences of American firms. All three of
the American-affiliated firms still in existence in 1962 which began
manufacturing in Australia between 1900 and 1909 were wholly
American in 1962. Corresponding ratios for the successive periods
shown in the table, expressed in percentages, are: 100, 84, 78, 36, 67,
54, 41. Apart from the period 1940 to 1949, when the existence of a
Federal Labor government keen to encourage joint ventures was
probably responsible for the apparently very low proportion of
wholly-owned companies established, the figures evince a most pro-
nounced tendency in favour of the jointly-owned company.[7] There

---

[7] Fifty-one American-affiliated companies are known to have begun manufacturing (or to have made plans to do so) in the 30 months from 1 July 1962 to the
end of December 1964. Of these, thirty had a substantial Australian equity in them.

TABLE IV–2   American Equity in American-affiliated Companies
Manufacturing in mid-1962, by Date at which Manufacture Began[a]

Period in which Australian manufacture began[b]	Companies incorporated in Australia in which American interest at 30 June 1962 was				Branches	Total
	25–49%	50–74%	75–99%	100%[c]		
1900–09	..	..	..	3	..	3
1910–19	..	..	..	5	1	6
1920–29	..	3	1	21	..	25
1930–39	..	5	..	16	2	23
1940–49	7	6	1	6	2	22
1950–54	6	2	..	15	1	24
1955–59	10	15	1	28	3	57
1960–mid '62	5	19	2	13	5	44
Not classifiable	..	..	..	4	..	4
Total	28	50	5	111	14	208

[a] See Note [a] to Table IV–1.
[b] The year in which manufacture began is taken to be the year in which an American equity of at least 25 per cent was first acquired in the case of companies manufacturing previously as Australian-owned ventures.
[c] See Note [b] to Table IV–1.

has almost certainly been a tendency of that kind operating but this conclusion cannot be reached with certainty from a consideration of Table IV-2 alone. It is possible, for example, that companies which begin as joint ventures become wholly American after a period and Table IV-2, therefore, may merely reflect the different ages of the companies covered.

The information available on changes in ownership pattern is not great. Of 104 firms that gave the American interest in their company at the commencement of manufacture in Australia, 21 had experienced an increase in that percentage interest by 1962 and 8 had experienced a decrease. Between 1962 and the end of 1964, it is known that at least another 5 firms experienced an increase in American shareholding, while 4 American companies sold out their interest entirely and 4 more allowed their holding to decrease. Of the 26 firms in which the American interest is known to have been increased, 12 previously jointly-owned companies have become wholly American ventures. One of these began operations in the period 1900-9, three in 1920-9, two in 1940-9, two in 1950-4, and four in 1955-9. Their number includes such companies as Chrysler, Kraft, Monsanto Chemicals, P. & H. Power Cranes & Shovels, and Revlon. In another three cases, the increase in the American interest was from a minority position to one of majority shareholder, while in two more the American interest moved from a minority one to a 50 per cent holding. Of the 12 firms in which the American interest is known to have been reduced (leaving out of account those in

TABLE IV–3 American Equity in American-affiliated Companies
Manufacturing in mid-1962, by Employment in 1962[a]

Size of companies by employment	Companies incorporated in Australia in which American interest at 30 June 1962 was				Branches	Total
	25–49%	50–74%	75–99%	100%[b]		
1–25	4	8	..	7	2	21
26–50	4	4	2	15	2	27
51–75	1	8	..	8	1	18
76–100	1	5	..	9	2	17
101–150	4	1	2	17	3	27
151–200	5	6	..	13	2	26
201–300	3	7	..	12	1	23
301–400	1	4	1	1	..	7
401–500	..	1	..	4	1	6
501–750	2	1	..	7	..	10
751–1000	1	2	..	6	..	9
1001–1500	1	2	..	2	..	5
1501–2000	1	..	..	2	..	3
Over 2000	..	1	..	8	..	9
Total	28	50	5	111	14	208
Total 1962 employment	7,606	13,401	665	73,038	1,783	96,493

[a] See Note [a] to Table IV–1.
[b] See Note [b] to Table IV–1.

which the American interest has been entirely withdrawn), 6 were
formed as wholly American ventures. In 4 of the 6, the American
interest remains a majority one, but in the 2 others only 50 per cent.
Four of them established manufacturing operations in Australia in
the period 1930-9 and two in the period 1955-9. All but one, however, remained wholly American till after 1955. They include such
well-known firms as Rheem, Union Carbide, Hunter Douglas, and
Kimberly-Clark.

When allowance is made for these known changes, the ratio of
wholly-owned firms established in the period 1930-9 increases sharply
while the ratio in 1940-9 falls sharply, both movements which are
not unexpected. The incompleteness of the data still prevents
dogmatism on the subject, but it does appear very likely that there
has been a marked shift in the ownership preferences of American
firms operating in Australia in favour of sharing ownership.

Table IV-3 shows that not all wholly American firms operating
here are large. Forty-six such firms had employment of 100 or less
in 1962. But at the other extreme, the origins of the public belief
that American firms almost always hold all the ordinary shares in
their Australian subsidiaries may be seen from the fact that eight of
the nine firms with employment of over 2,000 in 1962 were wholly-
owned.

The importance of the large wholly-owned firms in the total picture is brought out in another way in Table IV-4. In this table, the 1962 employment of each of the 208 companies covered was used to weight the percentage of the ordinary shares (or equivalent equity in an unincorporated operation) held by the ten types of shareholder shown.[8] Thus, if a company had 60 per cent of its shares held in the U.S. and a 1962 employment of 1,000, the figure of '600' was allocated to the 'American ownership' column in the row for companies having an American equity of 50-74 per cent. Similarly, '400' was allocated to one of the 'Non-American ownership' columns. When all companies in that row had been treated in this manner, the 'employment' in each category of ownership was calculated as a percentage of the total employment of all the companies in that row. The resulting figures permit a number of interesting observations.

First, the importance of the wholly American firms is clearly demonstrated by the fact that, despite 83 of the total of 208 firms covered being jointly-owned ventures, more than 88 per cent of the total 'weighted average ownership' of the whole group was American in 1962. Secondly, not even all of the non-American ownership was Australian. Small interests were also held by other foreign firms, by Australian proprietary companies in which the majority of the shares were held abroad, and by firms listed on Australian stock exchanges in which the majority of the shares were held abroad. Of the total *Australian* ownership of somewhat less than 10 per cent of the total, individual Australians and Australian-owned proprietary companies unconnected with any listed company held a significant share, but by far the largest part was accessible, directly or indirectly, to the ordinary Australian investor. No fewer than thirty-four companies were partly owned by listed companies which were predominantly Australian owned, while shares in another twelve firms—Borg-Warner, Union Carbide, Boral, Formfit, Sporting Arms, Ducon (in 1962), Mount Isa Mines, F.M.C., Ralph McKay, Australian Controls, Hunter Douglas, and Philip Morris—could be directly purchased on an Australian stock exchange.

Table IV-5 presents the same information as does Table IV-4, except that it does so by industry instead of by the percentage of American shareholding. It is self-explanatory.

---

[8] It must be admitted that employment is not an entirely satisfactory weight, but its use was dictated both by the absence of any other weight which could be used for all the 208 companies concerned and by its probable superiority over any other weight in a survey of this kind. The use of sales figures, for example, was impossible not only because of the lack of data but also because of the number of companies which conduct substantial sales operations unconnected with their manufacturing activities.

TABLE IV-4 Weighted Average Ownership of American-affiliated Companies Manufacturing in mid-1962, by Percentage of American Ownership

Percentage U.S. ownership[a]	Employment in 1962	Non-American ownership at 30 June 1962 (%)										American ownership at 30 June 1962 (%)
		A	B	C	D	E	F	G	H	I	Total	
25–49%	7,606	27·70	9·34	..	8·48	6·75	2·07	1·33	5·64	4·53	65·84	34·16
50–74%	13,401	13·39	18·82	1·97	2·16	0·52	5·70	..	..	2·05	44·61	55·39
75–99%	665	..	16·54	..	4·18	..	..	..	..	..	20·72	79·28
100%[b]	74,821	..	..	..	..	..	..	..	..	..	..	100·00
Total	96,493	4·04	3·46	0·27	1·00	0·60	0·96	0·11	0·44	0·64	11·53	88·47

A Shares directly listed, and mainly held, in Australia.
B Shares held by a company listed, and mainly owned, in Australia.
C Shares held by an Australian proprietary company which, by virtue of its being a subsidiary of a listed Australian company, is 'indirectly listed'. More than 50 per cent of its equity is held in Australia.
D Shares held by a small number of private shareholders in Australia.
E Shares held by an Australian proprietary company unconnected with a listed company. More than 50 per cent of its equity is held in Australia.
F Shares held by a company listed in Australia, but mainly owned abroad.
G Shares held by an Australian proprietary company in which a listed Australian company holds a share but which is mainly owned abroad.
H Shares held by an Australian proprietary company unconnected with a listed Australian company. Though there is some Australian equity in the company, it is mainly owned abroad.
I Shares held directly by a foreign (usually British) company.

ª See Note ª to Table IV–1.
ᵇ Includes branches. See also Note ᵇ to Table IV–1.

NOTE: In each of the four categories of American ownership shown in the first column, the 1962 employment of the companies concerned was used to weight the percentage of the ordinary shares held by the ten categories of shareholder shown *across* the table. See text.

F

TABLE IV-5 Weighted Average Ownership of American-affiliated Companies Manufacturing in mid-1962, by Industry

Industry	Employment in 1962	Non-American ownership at 30 June 1962 (%)										American ownership at 30 June 1962 (%)
		A	B	C	D	E	F	G	H	I	Total[a]	
Plant, equipment, machinery	7,049	1·50	7·33	..	1·43	6·04	..	..	..	0·64	16·94	83·06
Agricultural equipment	752	14·08	..	..	4·34	..	..	..	..	..	18·42	81·58
Motor vehicles	34,705	..	0·07	0·07	0·02	0·02	..	..	..	..	0·17	99·83
Motor accessories	1,307	28·38	..	..	..	2·26	6·40	..	0·54	3·08	40·64	59·36
Metal manufactures, n.e.i.	6,805	8·59	22·33	..	0·96	..	10·97	1·49	..	..	44·34	55·66
Electrical equipment, instruments, etc.	10,128	13·20	0·35	..	0·60	..	0·73	..	4·16	2·08	21·12	78·88
Gramophone records	389	..	7·71	..	..	..	..	..	..	..	7·71	92·29
Food and drink	8,797	..	1·94	..	0·91	..	..	..	..	..	2·85	97·15
Sausage casings	448	..	..	..	10·29	..	..	..	..	..	10·29	89·71
Industrial chemicals and plastics	4,315	13·90	1·11	3·03	0·40	..	0·41	..	..	2·10	20·95	79·05
Inks, polishes, adhesives, etc.	574	..	23·75	..	..	..	..	..	..	..	23·75	76·25
Pharmaceutical and toilet preparations	5,389	..	..	..	0·28	..	..	..	..	..	0·28	99·72
Cosmetics	1,045	..	..	10·53	3·00	..	..	..	..	..	13·52	86·48
Oils, mineral	2,231	24·15	..	..	..	..	..	..	..	..	24·15	75·85
Paper products	1,576	..	16·85	..	..	5·46	..	..	..	10·98	33·28	66·72
Rubber products	3,671	..	4·46	..	0·21	..	..	..	..	..	4·67	95·33
Plastic products	180	..	..	..	20·56	7·50	..	..	..	11·28	39·33	60·67
Abrasives	1,407	..	3·35	..	..	..	..	..	..	2·79	6·14	93·86
Clothing and fabrics	1,522	5·85	11·94	..	30·33	..	..	..	..	..	48·12	51·88
Furnishings	631	18·34	..	..	..	..	..	..	..	..	18·34	81·66
Writing instruments	138	..	..	..	..	..	..	..	..	..	0·00	100·00
Miscellaneous	3,434	1·57	5·97	..	..	0·64	..	..	..	..	8·18	91·82

[a] Detail may not add to totals because of rounding. See also Notes to Table IV-4.

Before turning to a discussion of the reasons why American firms choose particular ownership patterns, it is interesting to note the somewhat better response accorded to the survey by jointly-owned companies than by wholly-owned. While 60 per cent of all the companies approached were wholly American, only 55 per cent of the 100 participants were so. The assessment of the answers to most survey questions by the percentage of American shareholding helps to reduce the practical impact of any resulting bias.

TABLE IV–6   Response to the Survey, by Percentage of American Ownership[a]

| Response | Companies incorporated in Australia in which American interest at 30 June 1962 was | | | | Branches | Total |
	25–49%	50–74%	75–99%	100%[b]		
Participating companies	16	26	3	47	8	100
Other companies	12	24	2	64	6	108
Total	28	50	5	111	14	208
Response (%)	57	52	60	42	57	48

[a] See Note [a] to Table IV–1.
[b] See Note [b] to Table IV–1.

Why do most American firms prefer to retain for themselves all the shares in their Australian subsidiaries?[9] A great many answers to this question were offered to the writer during the course of the present survey. To begin with it was stated that 'any overseas entrepreneur that owns an Australian enterprise that is realizing or holds potential for good earnings and substantial growth is unlikely to be enthusiastic about sharing good fortune with others'. This motive, so unambiguously expressed by the managing director of one wholly American concern, undoubtedly lies behind the reluctance of many such firms to sell part of their equity to local investors. The motive may be expected to be especially strong if the task of breaking into the Australian market was particularly expensive and fraught with above average risks: having borne the costs of establishment, wholly American firms are not likely to be eager to share later harvests. (It is no doubt significant that of all the Australian-American ventures studied only two are known to have resulted from the yielding to local investors of an interest in a previously all-American firm, except where this was done to acquire another Australian firm.)

Secondly, many executives in wholly American companies expressed the fear that Australian shareholders would exercise considerable pressure for dividends in conflict with the frequent desire

[9] For a particularly full discussion of the advantages and disadvantages of different ownership patterns, see E. R. Barlow (1953: 114-47).

of parent companies to reinvest profits for a considerable period. Dividend policy is discussed in some detail in the second half of this chapter but for the moment it may be noted that wholly American firms do often adopt extremely conservative dividend policies. Not only may dividends be abjured for many years after the initial investment, they may also be discontinued for several years at a later period to finance further investment. This is a situation which most Australian shareholders, whether corporate or individual, accept only with reluctance. Several of the jointly-owned companies visited were keenly aware of the pressure for dividends from local shareholders and in the case of at least two 50/50 joint ventures this pressure had been so acute as to end the partnership and compel the American shareholder to buy out the Australian. In one of these cases, no dividend had been remitted to the American company for over a decade (though dividends had been declared and paid to the Australian shareholder until the dissolution of the arrangement), while in the other the Australian shareholder was accused of being 'after a quick quid'.

A conservative dividend policy may be due only in part to a desire to build up the local investment rapidly. The desire to avoid Australian tax on dividends remitted to the U.S. is also an important factor encouraging their reinvestment. Here is found a reason for preferring 100 per cent ownership which is logically distinct from considerations of dividend policy alone, for it is sometimes possible for wholly American companies which *are* keen to receive some return on their Australian investment to secure this without incurring Australian dividend tax. One way of doing this involves manipulation of the balance sheet (as will be explained later) in a manner which is rarely attractive if ownership is shared with local investors.

There are other important areas of possible disagreement. When a subsidiary is entirely owned by its parent company, the problem of ordering inter-company relations is in fact not a problem at all. Technical information and know-how of all kinds can be freely transmitted without concern for a strict accounting. Exports to the subsidiary may be invoiced at prices determined by questions of taxation and convenience. Production may be allocated between parent and subsidiary and between various foreign subsidiaries without regard to the profitability of any one operation. But if the ownership of the subsidiary is shared with local investors, the problem of parent-subsidiary relations can give rise to innumerable conflicts.

These points bear elaboration. If direct international investment in manufacturing is essentially the process of applying abroad techniques learnt at great cost at home, it is not surprising that the firms concerned are not prepared to hand over part of the fruits of this effort to local investors at the marginal cost of transmitting the know-how to the foreign company. This points to a need for some kind of formalization of relationships, and this in turn may cause considerable ill-feeling on the part of both American shareholder and local investor; for who can place an objective value on the knowledge gained from fifty years of manufacturing experience? One management consultant commented to the writer that G.M.H. initially invested not only a few million pounds in the production of the Holden car but also $US1,000 million worth of experience in the production of motor vehicles. It was not to be expected that the company would have been willing to grant local investors a cheap equity in this experience, even had local investors been willing to invest in the company when it first commenced Holden production. A number of wholly American firms mentioned that difficulties of this kind were important in their decision not to invite Australian participation. Several felt that Australian equity participation would inhibit the free flow of information between parent and subsidiary.

Other companies were worried about potential conflicts in the pricing of commodity transactions between parent and subsidiary. One of the several oil companies interviewed commented that Australian shareholders might bring pressure 'to buy crude from the cheapest source of supply, forgetting that the cheapest source in the short run may not be the cheapest source over the long-term'. For another firm the problem was the reverse: though the executive of this wholly American company was in favour of some Australian share participation, he saw that there could be some difficulty about import pricing policy:

> We have a pricing policy which leaves most of the profit where we want to expand facilities. Some years ago, it was decided that the U.K. subsidiary would sell us components at a price which only left the U.K. company a very small margin and let us make a big profit here. This was mainly because of the low tax rates in Australia compared with rates in the U.K.

Obviously, such a policy would be out of the question if Australian shareholders owned part of the local operation.

At least two major companies whose parents had adopted a policy of international specialization of production saw that this policy would lead to serious conflict if pursued in a situation where Australian investors had a share in the local firm. One stated that, being in an industry where technology changes rapidly,

> we must make frequent changes in our production programme in assigning new products to plants and in re-assigning old ones. It

will often be the case that a re-assignment of this kind reduces the manufacturing profitability of one subsidiary although overall benefit accrues to the parent company.

The other felt that while it might not be to the Australian company's advantage to import certain components, it might be to the whole company's advantage if the supplying subsidiary had considerable excess capacity.

Other reasons for preferring the '100 per cent pattern' were noted only occasionally. Several executives commented on the extent to which complete ownership simplifies the problem of management at all levels: it permits complete control over quality (of very great importance in some products); it reduces the risk of dissemination of technical information; it permits complete control of marketing policies; it even simplifies the consolidation of accounts in the U.S. While a majority holding is in theory sufficient to permit the American parent to exercise absolute authority in management, in practice the need to preserve an atmosphere of harmony with the Australian shareholder sometimes prevents this, particularly in cases where the Australian holding is actively represented in management.

One firm which began operations in Australia during the thirties mentioned that the American parent had adopted a 100 per cent pattern here because at that time 'nobody in Australia had any money to spare'. No company indicated that complete ownership had been chosen for fear that the local investor might not be able to provide sufficient funds in the event of a later expansion of facilities (except to the extent that dividend policy was at issue), but the Australian shareholder of at least one joint venture *was* concerned lest the American partner desire to develop the company more rapidly than he would have funds available. One company mentioned that an important advantage of not having Australian shareholders was that until 1961 this permitted annual results to be kept secret, but the firm was presumably confusing proprietary status with complete American ownership and, of course, the two are frequently not identical.

Interestingly, two factors sometimes mentioned in connection with a preference for 100 per cent ownership were not mentioned by any of the companies interviewed, though that is not to say they were not operative in some cases. One is the fear of creating a body of dissatisfied potential customers and a bad public image if local shareholders suffer share market losses during the period of establishment. It has been said, for example, that Phillips Oil Products Ltd regretted issuing a 50 per cent holding in its newly established marketing operation to Australian shareholders in 1961. Certainly, late in 1963 the company offered to buy back the publicly-held shares at par (which was then more than 17 per cent above market price) after a series of trading losses. Secondly, the more complete the American ownership of an Australian subsidiary, the less likely it is that the parent company will be charged with conspiracy in restraint of trade under American antitrust law if the freedom of that subsidiary to export is restricted in any way. (Indeed, the surest way of avoiding antitrust action in a situation where it is desired to restrict the export activities of a foreign operation appears to be to operate the foreign concern as a branch rather than as an incorporated entity.) It is doubtful, however, whether particular importance should be attached to this factor since, as will be seen later, there appears to be no great hesitation on the part of American companies to impose export restrictions on their jointly-owned affiliates in Australia.[10]

That many American firms see very strong advantages in having complete ownership of their foreign subsidiaries is confirmed not only by the predominance of wholly-owned American subsidiaries in Australia but also by similar patterns in other countries. Of the 3,481 manufacturing concerns in which there was a 'direct' American investment in 1957, 2,455, or more than 70 per cent, were 95 per cent or more owned in the U.S. (U.S. Dept. of Commerce 1960: 102).[11] But while some American parent companies owning all the shares in their Australian subsidiaries maintain a policy of complete ownership throughout the world, this is not by any means true of all of them. Ford, for example, has joint ventures in more than one country, and so also do the parents of Merck Sharp & Dohme, Mobil Oil, Parsons General Foods, and Corning Glass. Dunning (1958: 70, 101) noted in his survey of American investment in Britain that the British Hoover and Singer affiliates were both

[10] For a full discussion of American antitrust law and the ownership of foreign subsidiaries, see K. Brewster, jr (1960).

[11] It is interesting to note that, like the data gathered in this survey, U.S. Department of Commerce figures show a declining percentage of '95 per cent or more' companies as the date of their establishment approaches the census year, 1957. American figures also make possible a comparison of the ownership patterns of American direct investments in various areas. Their interpretation, however, is not easy. F. N. Bennett (1961: 9) has noted that while 80 per cent of the total value of American direct investments established in Oceania (mainly Australia and New Zealand) in the period 1951-7 was in companies owned to the extent of at least 95 per cent in the U.S., the corresponding figure for Europe was only 73 per cent and for Canada only 57 per cent. If the *number* of such ventures be taken, however, the Australasian percentage is 68, the European 72, and the Canadian 80 (U.S. Dept. of Commerce 1960: 101).

Anglo-American companies, and General Milk shares the ownership of its subsidiary in the Philippines. Sometimes local equity is yielded only under duress: at least four firms known to the writer which appear to follow a general practice of retaining sole ownership have recently announced the establishment of joint ventures in Japan, presumably as a result of Japanese government pressure. An important pharmaceutical firm, which owns all the shares in its foreign subsidiaries throughout the world, indicated that pressure from a government department controlling import licences in New Zealand was on the verge of breaking the company's policy in that country. It does not follow, of course, that pressure from the Australian government would automatically ensure that companies which had intended to set up wholly-owned subsidiaries would in fact establish joint ventures. The necessity to share ownership is, as seen above, undoubtedly regarded as a 'con' by many companies and some would certainly decide not to invest in Australia rather than accept local shareholders. Moreover, Australian shareholders would be very hard to find for some ventures. But it does seem likely that Australian pressure would have some effect in the direction of increased joint ventures, and has indeed already done so.[12]

A number of companies which hold most strongly to the principle of complete ownership of their subsidiaries have advocated that Australian investors, instead of pressing for the right to buy shares in the local subsidiary, should purchase the shares of the American parent corporation. F. G. Donner, chairman of General Motors Corporation, has been one of the most outspoken advocates of this policy. Apart from the obvious drawback that such purchases are not allowed under Australian foreign exchange regulations at present, it is doubtful if buying American shares would be regarded by most Australian investors as a genuine alternative to buying stock in the local subsidiary. Few Australian buyers are able to follow the progress of the American firm as easily as they can that of the local offshoot, and the American withholding tax on dividends is another deterrent. For those who believe an equity in the local operation would permit significant influence to be exercised over it, the alternative offered is naturally quite inadequate. It is probable also that most Australian investors expect a somewhat higher dividend yield on their shares than can be obtained from investment in top quality American stocks with long established reputations, and it may be significant that the only American share listed on Aus-

[12] Late in 1964 the Federal Treasurer stated that 'there have already been instances where the influence of the Government has been directly exerted to protect the national interests in oversea take-over bids, [and] to encourage a degree of Australian participation' (*A.F.R.*, 15 Oct. 1964).

tralian stock exchanges, National Dairy, appears to have been too highly priced for Australian investors.[13]

Obviously, not all American companies are wedded to the idea of complete ownership of their foreign affiliates. Many have a policy of inviting local participation in all their foreign operations, and it has already been seen that American ownership was incomplete in eighty-three of the manufacturing ventures under study in Australia. Several large wholly American companies—notably Amoco and S.T.C.—have been reported as stating that some Australian participation would eventually be appropriate. It has also been noted that more than one American firm, on acquiring an Australian company with which to commence local operations, offered an equity in the now wholly American venture to the previous owners in vain. The Australian executive of one wholly American firm indicated that, since he did not approve of the wholly American pattern, his company had attempted to form a jointly-owned operation with one of Australia's largest companies—but the offer had been repulsed. In yet another case, the senior executive of one of the largest American subsidiaries in the chemical industry explained that his company began Australian operations in a 50/50 partnership with an Australian firm. The company is now wholly American because of the failure of the Australian partner to take up the frequent cash issues made. It is common knowledge that the present American owners of Australian Synthetic Rubber tried hard to persuade Australian tyre companies to form the company.

American firms often see very positive advantages in joint ownership. In these cases, executives tend to deprecate the importance of conflicts of interest between American and Australian shareholders: as one American said, 'Nobody says in General Motors in the U.S. that only one person must hold all the shares in case a conflict of interest develops. We have disagreements with *our* partners, but by and large we get on very well together.' Some companies emphasized the importance of tapping Australian management's knowledge of local conditions. One explained in this connection that a jointly-owned firm had been established because of the difficulty of managing a plant so far from the U.S., its being 'too expensive to send out

[13] National Dairy shares were first issued in Australia in 1959 in exchange for the Australian shareholding in Kraft Holdings Ltd. This was permitted because the deal involved no cost to foreign exchange reserves. Originally, 100,164 National Dairy shares were issued to Australian shareholders, and up to 26 August 1963 755 more had been issued under stock option schemes to senior employees, and 200 had been transferred from the New York to the Melbourne register. However, only 47,650 shares remained on the Melbourne register on 26 August 1963 and it is probable that the great bulk of the remainder, transferred to the New York register, had been sold to Americans.

a special U.S. administration', and another said that 'the U.S. company wanted Australians to manage the company and feels that a 50/50 partnership establishes a mutual trust'.[14] One American firm has in Australia its only jointly-owned foreign subsidiary because of its need for management with knowledge of local labour and local conditions. Other firms established joint ventures to conserve limited funds for foreign investment, and in at least one case the executives of a wholly American subsidiary wished they could invite Australian participation because the parent company's shortage of funds was hampering expansion of the local operation. In the extreme case the American parent may contribute no capital at all—the cash needed to start the operation can be supplied by a local investor and the American company be issued shares in exchange for technical assistance, brand name, and marketing rights.

There was disagreement among the executives interviewed about the value of some Australian ownership as an aid to sales. An executive of a wholly American company in the food industry felt that Australian participation 'would certainly make promotion easier and consumer acceptance greater', and executives in several other wholly American firms felt the same. One firm felt that there might be some disadvantage in being wholly American but for the fact that all the other firms in the industry were also entirely foreign-owned. The only joint venture to mention the connection between sales and Australian participation, however, had had a most indifferent record in Australia to date and commented that: 'Australian participation in the ownership and on the board of directors of this company has not been of any real value.' Another executive questioned on this point contrasted the highly successful sales performance of the wholly American firm G.M.H. with the relative failure of a predominantly Australian-owned company in the same industry. And since even the food company quoted above dominates the market for most of the products it manufactures, it might reasonably be doubted if Australian participation has any appreciably beneficial

14 The number of 50/50 ventures encountered was rather surprising. Some companies having such arrangements were dissatisfied with them because of the uncertainty about who is final master, and several 51/49 ventures expressed strong distaste for the 50/50 pattern. The reasons for the adoption of that pattern appear to be a desire 'to establish the partnership principle', to avoid the necessity of consolidating the venture's results with those of either shareholder, and to avoid the risk of one shareholder manipulating the results of the venture to his own advantage. This last motive was mentioned by one company in particular whose Australian shareholder had had a 49 per cent interest in a British subsidiary. The British parent of the latter had established a separate sales company and, having effective control of the manufacturing subsidiary, had contrived to appropriate most of the profits itself.

influence on sales. It might also be doubted whether American firms establishing operations in Australia really take this factor into account at all.

This is not to say that American firms in Australia are indifferent to their public image or to the widespread sentiment in favour of some Australian shareholding in American subsidiaries. Several companies mentioned that one reason for establishing a joint venture was the desire to avoid the odium incurred by some of the wholly-owned companies, and more than one referred to encouragement from the American Chamber of Commerce in Australia to retain local equity. But it does appear that very few companies establish an Australian-American operation for fear of *customer* discrimination against them as wholly American ventures.

It would be an exaggeration to leave the impression that the American parents of all the 83 operations in which American ownership was incomplete in 1962 consciously chose to invite others to share the ownership of their Australian ventures. Many American companies almost drifted into a partnership arrangement, while some were compelled to seek the assistance of local shareholders. One of the most common ways in which American companies find themselves with a joint venture in Australia is through an approach for technical or marketing assistance from an Australian firm. Or an Australian distributor may draw the attention of the American firm to the fact that an import quota or an increase in tariff is making importing increasingly difficult. In both these cases, the American firm is quite likely to invest in facilities in Australia, and it is more than possible, judging by past experience, that an Australian-American partnership is the result. In this situation, the percentage of the shares held in the Australian operation by the American shareholder is in part a function of the attitude of the Australian partner. In at least two of the joint ventures studied, the American company could not have entered the Australian market without raw materials to which only Australian companies had access, and in another case establishment would have been impossible without the import licences which the Australian partner was able to provide.[15] Again, when previously wholly American companies issue

[15] This particular venture provided an interesting illustration of the kind of bargain which Australian companies can drive. Initially, the Australian firm demanded a 45 per cent equity in the new operation but eventually settled for 25 per cent since this was the first foreign subsidiary of the American company in which it did not have complete ownership. The Australian partner protected its own interests, however, by compelling the American parent to agree to buy out the holding of the Australian partner at the net asset backing of the shares if the venture was not a success.

shares to acquire a local company, this may have little to do with a desire to share ownership with Australians: rather it may be made necessary by the reluctance of the American parent to invest 'new dollar funds' in Australia. That was certainly the motive behind at least one such move in recent years.

Is the widespread hostility towards wholly American firms justified? In large measure, it springs from very basic emotions—national pride, the fear of being 'controlled', distrust of foreigners. These emotions are easily aroused and it is hard to avoid the impression that they have been aroused by some for not altogether disinterested motives. But it remains true that many thoughtful Australians feel that an Australian share in the ownership of American subsidiaries would have some important national advantages. What these advantages are is not always specified very clearly but it is probably fair to say that many feel that a partly Australian company is more likely to act in Australia's interests than is a wholly American one, and that, since some of the profits of a jointly-owned firm accrue to Australians, such ventures pose less of a problem for the nation's balance of payments.

Before attempting to analyse these arguments, it should be repeated that any really serious attempt by government to compel foreign investors to accept local share participation would encounter two difficulties. First, some foreign firms would decide against investing in Australia. Those who minimize the importance of this factor are probably justified in doing so because of the admittedly strong attraction which Australia has for foreign capital, but that some firms would cancel investment programmes there can be no doubt. Secondly, a few foreign firms would find it very difficult, if not impossible, to attract local investors for their project.

Even if it be granted that these objections are probably of relatively minor importance, there must remain serious doubt that any likely level of Australian equity participation, whether it be 25 or 49 per cent, could achieve what its proponents hope of it. To begin with, any minority Australian share participation would leave ultimate control in the hands of the foreign majority shareholder. Certainly it seems likely that Australian shareholders could have *some* influence on policy in some companies, particularly if Australian ownership was concentrated in a few hands: an executive of one wholly American company, a man who believed strongly in Australian participation, said that even a minority shareholding would have some effect on policy

> because all companies are vain to some degree. If an Australian executive were being directed to adopt a policy at variance with

the interests of Australia or the Australian shareholders, he could always invite the U.S. executive out to Australia—and let *him* face the dissatisfied locals!

On the other hand, an executive of another wholly American firm felt that a minority Australian holding would only lead to a 'meaningless Board'. A senior executive of a large Anglo-Australian company felt that 'Australian shareholders have no control over the company at all. All the directors are appointed by the British company'—and this was a firm in which the Australian interest is substantial. If, as seems most likely, a minority Australian shareholding achieves relatively little control over the vital aspects of company policy, Australian participation just becomes a means whereby the resources controlled by the foreign firm are increased at a lower cost to the foreign firm itself. (Indeed, even a majority Australian shareholding is likely to leave control with the foreign shareholder if the Australian holding is widely dispersed, or if the company is heavily dependent on its foreign affiliate for technical know-how.)

It is also probable that the Australian investor would gain access to a smaller share of the 'profits' of the local operation than he imagined, for wholly-owned firms which now neglect to pay their parents fees for much of the technical information received from them, and often interest for very considerable advances received from them, would naturally introduce such payments if the firm became jointly owned. Some parent companies would also increase the price of goods sold to the Australian subsidiary. Both tendencies would not only reduce the apparent profitability of the local operation but would also reduce Australian taxation revenue. (To some extent this loss of tax revenue would be offset by increased revenue from withholding tax on dividends, a tax which American shareholders of jointly-owned companies find it more difficult to avoid than do the shareholders of some wholly American subsidiaries, as explained below.)

Whether American parents would be more reluctant to pass on technical information to a jointly-owned company than to a wholly-owned company probably depends to a large extent on the size of the Australian equity. Other things being equal, it would seem that there would be some decrease in the American company's desire to assist the Australian venture, but this decrease might not be significant as long as the American holding were in the majority. One 60/40 venture indicated this ratio of American-Australian ownership to be 'a very desirable, if not the optimum, ratio to gain maximum benefits. . . . A higher Australian participation may have tended to weaken the American interest in developing our company at a high rate.' One wholly-owned company felt there would be no reluctance to impart technical know-how to a jointly-owned firm in which the American company still held a majority of the shares, and cited as an illustration a jointly-owned sister subsidiary in Venezuela. Confirming this impression is an interesting comparison between the assistance granted one local firm in which the American equity was 50 per cent and another in the same industry in which the American equity was substantially less than this. The firm which was 50 per cent American maintained very amicable relations with its parent, but the firm which was mainly Australian complained bitterly about the lack of American assistance.

There could be more specific disadvantages of Australian ownership. If it succeeded in influencing subsidiary dividend policy, local ownership would probably have the effect of slowing down the rate of investment of the company concerned. This would have dampening effects on the growth of industry. It is also likely (as contended in chapter IX) that jointly-owned firms are more often restricted in their freedom to export than are wholly American firms; in fact wholly Australian firms operating under licence are probably more restricted in this regard than are firms which have some American equity participation.

As for the balance of payments, Perkins has drawn attention to the fact that if shares in the American subsidiary were obtained at a fair market price,

> this would presumably reflect the accepted current expectation about the future earnings of the shares. If so, the capital outflow involved in their purchase would merely be a reflection of the present value of the expected future stream of earnings, and there would therefore in the long run be neither loss nor gain to the Australian balance of payments from the transfer of ownership. (1960: 79.)

This conclusion follows, of course, only if expectations about the future are in fact fulfilled. It is possible that, if Australian investors underestimate the future stream of earnings in calculating the price they are prepared to pay, there could be some gain to the Australian balance of payments. But because a small number of highly profitable American subsidiaries have received such considerable publicity, it is at least as likely that Australian investors would overestimate future profits and in this way cause positive harm to the balance of payments.

It appears, therefore, that local equity participation would have few advantages from Australia's point of view. Moreover, the immediate costs of providing for such participation would be high.

To purchase an equity in existing wholly-owned subsidiaries would require a very considerable diversion of capital resources from other investment projects. The cost of a 25 per cent equity in General Motors-Holden's, for example, would have been in the vicinity of £100 million in 1963 (on the assumption of an earnings yield of about 5 per cent). A capital outflow on such a scale would have seriously disruptive effects on the Australian domestic economy. If only newly-established companies were to be compelled to share their ownership with Australians, the provision would almost certainly serve to reduce the total capital flow to Australia because foreign companies would be able to raise locally an increased proportion of their funds for investment.

Even if dependence on foreign investment has disadvantages, and these are examined in later chapters, especially chapter XI, there is no reason to suppose that compelling foreign investors to accept local partners is the most desirable way to reduce the inflow. Australian minority participation could at best secure only limited control over the decisions of the joint venture: it seems doubtful if it could have any appreciably beneficial effect on the balance of payments. The cost of minority participation would, at the least, be an increase in the Australian resources under the ultimate control of the majority American shareholder. There is ample evidence also that had there been compulsion to accept local shareholders in the years since 1945, some of the most economically beneficial American investments would never have been made. Of course, if an American company prefers to find an Australian partner for its venture than to provide all the funds itself, it should not be discouraged simply because it is not prepared to finance the *whole* venture—half a loaf is better than no bread! And from a public relations point of view, American companies might be well advised to invite Australian share participation. But it would hardly seem desirable that they should be *encouraged* to share ownership.

Closely associated with popular resentment at being unable to buy shares in many of the local subsidiaries of American companies is the belief that many of these companies finance their operations in Australia without hazarding 'one dollar of American capital'. American-owned companies, it is asserted, not only rely heavily on locally generated funds for their expansion but even draw on Australian fixed-interest funds to supplement their investment. There is some truth in this contention.

Table IV-7 presents data taken from the 1962 balance sheets of 101 American-affiliated companies. At first sight it appears to confirm

TABLE IV–7   Source of Funds Employed in 1962 by
101 American-affiliated Companies[a]
£A('000)

Type of investment	U.S.	Aust.	Other	Total[b]
Ordinary shares issued	96,624	19,379	4,086	120,088
Preference shares issued	2,668[c]	2,865	..	5,534
Profit and loss, and other similar reserves	163,750	24,941	1,035	189,725
Home office value of branch assets	6,873	..	..	6,873
Interest of outside shareholders on consolidation	4,696	3,239	87	8,022
Total shareholders' funds[b]	274,611	50,424	5,208	330,243
Debt to U.S. parent and its affiliates	95,711	..	..	95,711
Other long-term liabilities	270	43,586	8,034	51,890
Other short-term liabilities	354	119,817	661	120,832
Total liabilities[b]	96,334	163,403	8,695	268,433
Total funds employed[b]	370,945	213,827	13,903	598,676

[a] The above figures were taken from balance sheets for company years ending in 1962.

[b] Detail may not add to totals because of rounding.

[c] Includes some participating preference shares.

NOTES: (1) In contrast to previous practice, the *complete* balance sheets of the three 'non-manufacturing companies' in the survey (see Note [b] to Table I–2) were incorporated in the above table. This was done because it is ratios and percentages that are of primary importance here and not absolute magnitudes.

(2) The allocation of funds employed by country presented several problems. The following are the main principles adopted:

(i) All shares owned by the U.S. parent company or any of its controlled affiliates, whether in the U.S. or not, were treated as being held in the U.S. itself. The same rule was applied to all other items of ownership and liability. (See also notes to Table IV–1.)

(ii) All shares owned by companies incorporated in Australia were treated as being wholly owned by the country having the majority holding in the shareholding company. Thus, 50 per cent of the equity of Comalco would be indicated as being held in 'Other' countries, though a company listed on Australian Stock Exchanges holds this portion of Comalco's shares. This rule tends to understate the Australian shareholding in a number of companies.

(iii) On the other hand, all the shares of listed Australian-American companies *not* owned by the U.S. parent company were treated as being owned in Australia. This probably results in some overstatement of the Australian shareholding in such companies as Mount Isa Mines, Union Carbide Australia, and Borg-Warner (Aust.).

(3) Directors' qualifying shares have been ignored, as also has one 'genuine' Australian shareholding of about 0·2 per cent.

(4) It is believed that all 'double-counting', which could arise because of investment by one American-owned company in another treated separately in this survey, has been eliminated with the following exceptions:

(i) The minority shareholding of one company in the electrical equipment industry in another in the same industry has not been eliminated. The total overstatement on this account is £1 million.

(ii) Obviously, no consolidation has been possible to take account of the fact that some American-owned companies have trade debts to other American-owned companies. This factor may be significant in 'Industrial chemicals and plastics' where it is known that one company alone had a trade debt to another American-owned company in excess of £3 million in 1962.

TABLE IV-8   Source of Funds Employed in 1962 by 101 American-affiliated Companies, by Industry[a]
£A('000)

Industry	Australia					United States and Other					Total[b]
	Ordinary and preference shares	Profit and loss, and other similar reserves[c]	Long-term liabilities	Short-term liabilities	Total, incl. interest of outside shareholders on consolidation	Ordinary and preference shares	Profit and loss, other similar reserves, and home office value of branch assets	Debt to U.S. parent and its affiliates	Other liabilities	Total, incl. interest of outside shareholders on consolidation	
Plant, equipment, machinery	2,254	946	1,482	5,207	9,889	5,141	7,922	6,250	722	20,034	29,923
Motor vehicles	847	(119)	4,731	43,431	48,890	34,020	80,560	20,367	..	134,948	183,838
Motor accessories	790	357	..	859	2,006	2,273	578	168	14	3,033	5,038
Metal manufactures, n.e.i.	6,333	16,124	13,000	14,871	51,401	11,237	18,352	7,091	6,675	43,356	94,757
Electrical equipment, instruments, etc.	1,522	818	4,186	8,967	15,493	9,924	7,790	2,996	217	21,014	36,508
Food and drink	376	39	5,239	6,610	12,270	6,866	9,661	2,348	..	18,875	31,145
Industrial chemicals and plastics	3,891	251	5,875	13,630	23,646	14,177	1,116	12,709	260	28,261	51,907
Pharmaceutical and toilet preparations	..	..	494	4,275	4,770	3,157	11,865	771	..	15,793	20,563
Other industries	6,231	6,525	8,578	21,968	45,462	16,584	33,815	43,010	1,430	99,535	144,997
Total[b]	22,244	24,941	43,586	119,817	213,827	103,378	171,658	95,711	9,319	384,849	598,676

[a] See notes to Table IV-7.
[b] Detail may not add to totals because of rounding.
[c] Parentheses denote an accumulated loss.

G

the importance both of reinvested profits and of locally borrowed funds. In fact the former are far more significant. The figures in the table, which show that no less than 60 per cent of the American equity in these companies in 1962 was in the form of undistributed profits, actually understate the importance of profit reinvestment. This is partly because the unremitted profits of American branches operating in Australia are not separately distinguished, but more significantly because the figures shown for both issued ordinary shares and profit reserves are misleading. In the case of most long-established companies, figures for profit reserves understate the true 'worth' of the assets they represent because of the considerable conservatism of many American companies in their attitude towards depreciation and asset revaluation. Where assets *have* been revalued, as has frequently happened in recent years, the increased valuation has usually been 'capitalized' by the issue of bonus shares to the parent corporation.[16] This means that the ratio of undistributed profits to total shareholders' funds is arbitrarily reduced.

Concerning the use of Australian credit facilities, the table appears to show that no less than 27 per cent of the total assets of the whole group were financed by Australian creditors. Moreover, while the United States owned 83 per cent of the shareholders' funds of the group, it provided only 36 per cent of the liabilities.[17] In assessing the relative importance of the U.S. and Australia as sources of funds, however, several points must be borne in mind. To begin with, all figures shown are book values. In older firms which have not revalued their assets recently, this leads not only to an important understatement of the total value of funds employed but also to understatement of the ratio of shareholders' funds to liabilities. Secondly, a not inconsiderable part of the current liabilities shown as being owed to Australian creditors is accounted for by taxation provision. Some firms had made considerable provision also for employee long-service leave, and neither provision could with

[16] The reasons for this are not hard to find: the Australian Uniform Companies Act of 1961 exposed many American subsidiaries for the first time to the misleading Australian habit of relating after-tax profits to the par value of the company's issued ordinary capital. If a bonus issue is made from accumulated profits, the issue attracts a substantial Australian tax and so companies sensitive to their public image have chosen for the most part to increase capital by way of asset revaluation. Some very substantial revaluations and bonus issues have taken place. Goodyear and Bristol-Myers, for example, have both increased issued capital more than threefold since 1961, while Ford and G.M.H. have increased issued capital more than sixfold.

[17] The U.S. Department of Commerce (1960: 108) census of 1957 indicated that American companies held 84 per cent of the equity of their direct investments in Australia in that year, but provided only 24 per cent of the liabilities.

justice be termed 'Australian borrowing'. Thirdly, it is thought that many firms did not include provision for unpaid dividends in 'Debt to U.S. parent and its affiliates', so that this item, too, often appears as a liability to Australia. In addition, as noted at the foot of the table, there is some double-counting of the current liabilities owed to 'Australian' creditors because some liabilities were actually owed to other American-owned companies in Australia. This factor is believed to be of particular significance in the chemicals industry. Of the balance of current liabilities owed to Australians, a further large part is ordinary trade credit, and as such can hardly be a cause of Australian resentment.

When attention is confined to long-term Australian liabilities, it is found that little more than 7 per cent of the total book value of the funds employed in 1962 was accounted for by this item. Indeed, only 4·5 per cent of the book value of the funds used by the 56 wholly American companies in the group was represented by long-term liabilities to Australia (Table IV-9). Certainly, the figure of 4·5 per cent probably underestimates the importance of long-term borrowing on the Australian market by foreign firms. A number of foreign subsidiaries have become public companies (though still entirely owned abroad) since the Uniform Companies Act of 1961 removed the advantage of secrecy from proprietary status, and their avowed purpose in doing so has been to increase access to local loan funds. Several have made substantial issues of debenture stock to the Australian public in recent years, though by no means all the firms doing so have been American. General Motors Acceptance Corporation, Australia, a firm specializing in the provision of hire purchase finance for the sale of General Motors-Holden's products, had borrowings of £28 million at the end of 1960, equivalent to more than eighteen times shareholders' funds. At that time, this was the highest ratio of borrowing to shareholders' funds enjoyed by any major hire purchase firm in Australia. (Since these borrowings carry the unconditional guarantee of the parent corporation in New York, it is hardly surprising that the local company is sometimes able to attract funds at lower rates of interest than Australian firms must pay.)

But granted that the situation may now be changing, it nevertheless seems significant that only eighteen of the fifty-six wholly American firms covered in the table had any long-term liability to Australia at all in 1962. Only fourteen of these exceeded £100,000 and only five exceeded £1 million. In only five cases did long-term liabilities to Australia exceed 50 per cent of shareholders' funds, and the weighted average ratio of long-term Australian liabilities to the shareholders' funds of the eighteen companies concerned was only

18·3 per cent. By contrast, twenty-four of the forty-five jointly-owned enterprises reported a long-term liability to Australian creditors. Fifteen of these exceeded £100,000 and seven exceeded £1 million. In eight cases, the long-term liabilities to Australia exceeded 50 per cent of shareholders' funds, and the weighted average figure for the twenty-four companies was 28·3 per cent. Because of one very large debt owed by a jointly-owned company to the federal government, it is perhaps misleading to compare directly the average use of Australian long-term funds by all jointly-owned companies (13·6 per cent of the total book value of funds employed) with their use by wholly American companies. It does seem, however, that at least in the case of the wholly American firms surveyed in 1962, long-term Australian borrowings were of relatively minor importance. Indeed, the very fact that so many foreign subsidiaries in Australia are substantially independent of the local capital market has given rise to the fear that foreign subsidiaries may be at an unfair advantage *vis-à-vis* local companies, particularly in times of monetary stringency. This seems to be an unavoidable corollary of foreign investment.[18] (To examine the borrowing policies of companies of different ownership patterns in detail, Tables IV-9, IV-13, and IV-14 may be compared.)

Table IV-8 presents an industrial classification of the information that appears in Table IV-7. It is largely self-explanatory. Care must be exercised in comparing Tables IV-5 and IV-8, however. Not only do the two tables use quite different weights, they also cover different numbers of companies. Two further points should be noted. First, more than half the long-term liabilities owed to Australian creditors in 'Metal manufactures, n.e.i.' was owed by one jointly-owned firm to the Australian government. (The long-term liabilities of this company also account for more than half of the total long-term liabilities of the companies covered in Table IV-13, and almost half the Australian long-term liabilities of the companies in that table.) Secondly, by far the largest part of the 'Debt to U.S. parent and its affiliates' in the industrial category 'Other industries' was on account of one wholly American oil company.

Particular interest focuses on the use of borrowed funds by foreign firms in first becoming established in Australia. The executives of several of the firms interviewed felt strongly that American companies too often tend to borrow heavily in Australia to become established, committing the minimum necessary dollar capital. The view that this is common practice with many firms investing abroad

---

[18] This may point to the need to make increasing use of fiscal rather than monetary measures to control the economy's progress.

TABLE IV–9   Source of Funds Employed in 1962 by 56 Wholly American Companies[a]
£A('000)

Type of investment	U.S.	Aust.	Other	Total[b]
Ordinary shares issued	73,485	..	..	73,485
Preference shares issued	1,177	1,223	..	2,400
Profit and loss, and other similar reserves	138,452	..	..	138,452
Home office value of branch assets	6,873	..	..	6,873
Interest of outside shareholders on consolidation	4,696	53	..	4,749
Total shareholders' funds[b]	224,683	1,277	..	225,960
Debt to U.S. parent and its affiliates	83,988	..	..	83,988
Other long-term liabilities	20	18,923	1,300	20,243
Other short-term liabilities	10	86,996	100	87,106
Total liabilities[b]	84,018	105,918	1,400	191,337
Total funds employed[b]	308,701	107,195	1,400	417,296

[a] See notes to Table IV–7.
[b] Detail may not add to totals because of rounding.

has been expressed by several writers on foreign investment. Barlow and Wender, for example, noted that American firms investing abroad are frequently 'willing to pay exceedingly high rates of interest in foreign countries for local funds, in preference to investing dollars in the operation' (1955: 162).

In an attempt to shed some light on this issue in the Australian context, wholly American companies were classified under three headings: those which began manufacturing here before 1957,

TABLE IV–10   Source of Funds Employed in 1962 by 32 Wholly American Companies which Began Manufacturing in Australia Before 1957[a]
£A('000)

Type of investment	U.S.	Aust.	Other	Total[b]
Ordinary shares issued	61,026	..	..	61,026
Preference shares issued	1,074	1,223	..	2,297
Profit and loss, and other similar reserves	138,515	..	..	138,515
Home office value of branch assets	3,638	..	..	3,638
Interest of outside shareholders on consolidation	4,696	53	..	4,749
Total shareholders' funds[b]	208,948	1,277	..	210,225
Debt to U.S. parent and its affiliates	68,254	..	..	68,254
Other long-term liabilities	..	18,282	1,300	19,582
Other short-term liabilities	10	76,857	100	76,967
Total liabilities[b]	68,264	95,139	1,400	164,803
Total funds employed[b]	277,212	96,416	1,400	375,028

[a] See notes to Table IV–7. Also note that the year in which manufacture began is taken to be the year in which an American equity of at least 25 per cent was first acquired in the case of companies manufacturing previously as Australian-owned ventures.
[b] Detail may not add to totals because of rounding.

those which began manufacturing in the years 1957 to 1959, and those which began manufacturing (or became American in ownership) in 1960 or subsequently. The funds employed by each group of companies were then analysed and are presented in Tables IV-10, IV-11, and IV-12. The results of this exercise, though distorted somewhat by the very heavy establishment losses incurred by two wholly American members of the Altona petrochemical complex, provide little confirmation for the view that it is the newly-established firms which draw heavily on Australian resources. (This conclusion is reinforced by the fact that by far the largest single item in the category of short-term liabilities owed to Australian creditors in Table IV-12 was a trade debt to another American-owned subsidiary in Australia.) In so far as it is long-term liabilities which are of primary interest, it appears, in fact, to be rather the long-established subsidiaries which borrow from Australian sources.

It is instructive, however, to examine the behaviour of individual companies in this regard. It is certainly true that some American-owned firms have drawn on Australian funds for a substantial part of the resources needed to commence local operations. In some cases this has taken the form of the issue of preference shares in the local company: Goodyear and Jantzen, for example, both raised considerable sums in this way in the twenties, and the issue of preference shares by General Motors (Aust.) Pty Ltd to acquire Holden's Motor Body Builders soon after its commencement in Australia is well known.[19] In other cases, American-affiliated companies have made substantial borrowings from Australian banks to help finance initial development. It is known that at least two chemical companies commencing operations in Australia raised loans equivalent to their issued capital, while a firm in the pharmaceuticals industry borrowed locally a sum equal to more than twice its issued capital. Another firm in the same industry stated that though its parent had paid for its initial share issue in cash, this was supplemented by 'a very considerable bank overdraft because of the reluctance of the U.S. company to send cash overseas'. Two firms stated specifically that premises had been leased in Australia because of the determination of their American parents to avoid sinking dollar capital overseas, and one of these mentioned that it was parent company policy never to invest in a factory overseas unless profit remittance became impossible. It is likely that both companies initially used Australian credit facilities to a significant degree. Two particularly striking cases were uncovered in which local funds had been used to finance the initial investment entirely. In one of these cases the American

---

[19] Actually the acquisition was achieved by the issue of 561,600 20s. 6 per cent preference shares and by a cash payment of £550,000.

TABLE IV–11 Source of Funds Employed in 1962 by 13 Wholly American Companies which Began Manufacturing in Australia Between 1957 and 1959 Inclusive[a]
£A('000)

Type of investment	U.S.	Aust.	Other	Total[b]
Ordinary shares issued	2,457	..	..	2,457
Preference shares issued	3	..	..	3
Profit and loss, and other similar reserves	2,792	..	..	2,792
Home office value of branch assets	250	..	..	250
Interest of outside shareholders on consolidation	..	..	..	..
Total shareholders' funds[b]	5,501	..	..	5,501
Debt to U.S. parent and its affiliates	4,200	..	..	4,200
Other long-term liabilities	20	551	..	571
Other short-term liabilities	..	2,024	..	2,024
Total liabilities[b]	4,220	2,575	..	6,795
Total funds employed[b]	9,721	2,575	..	12,296

[a] See notes to Table IV–7, and Note [a] to Table IV–10.
[b] Detail may not add to totals because of rounding.

company established a holding company in Australia, borrowed a sum from an Australian bank, and with the proceeds purchased a majority holding in an Australian company. For a number of years afterwards the dividends received from this shareholding were used to pay off the local overdraft. In the other case it was stated that the American firm paid for the shares in its newly-established Australian operation from the proceeds of a local overdraft, 'except about £2 which the American over here arranging the deal had in his pocket'.

TABLE IV–12 Source of Funds Employed in 1962 by 11 Wholly American Companies which Began Manufacturing in Australia in or after 1960[a]
£A('000)

Type of investment	U.S.	Aust.	Other	Total[b]
Ordinary shares issued	10,003	..	..	10,003
Preference shares issued	100	..	..	100
Profit and loss, and other similar reserves[c]	(2,855)	..	..	(2,855)
Home office value of branch assets	2,985	..	..	2,985
Interest of outside shareholders on consolidation	..	..	..	..
Total shareholders' funds[b]	10,234	..	..	10,234
Debt to U.S. parent and its affiliates	11,534	..	..	11,534
Other long-term liabilities	..	89	..	89
Other short-term liabilities	..	8,115	..	8,115
Total liabilities[b]	11,534	8,204	..	19,738
Total funds employed[b]	21,768	8,204	..	29,972

[a] See notes to Table IV–7, and Note [a] to Table IV–10.
[b] Detail may not add to totals because of rounding.
[c] Parentheses denote an accumulated loss.

It is not unusual, either, especially where the American firm does not insist on complete ownership, for the parent company to be issued shares in exchange for technical information or market rights. It has been reported, for example, that the Aluminium Company of America acquired almost half of its 51 per cent interest in Alcoa of Australia in exchange for its processes and technical knowledge, and on a much smaller scale Ralph McKay Ltd issued shares sufficient to give Borg-Warner a 25 per cent holding in the company in exchange for technical information. One local firm issued 20 per cent of its shares in exchange for marketing rights in Australia, New Zealand, Malaya, and Indonesia. A number of cases of this kind were uncovered, though only one involved a large company.

Shares are often issued to the American parent for goods sent out to establish the local operation. Sometimes the goods involved are ready for sale and form the initial stock of the subsidiary. In other cases the products received in Australia are raw materials: one company commented that its American parent 'was very reluctant to put any money into Australia—they only paid up the minimum allowable capital and we bought furniture for the office after the sale of our first production in Australia!' In yet other cases, and this is one of the most common practices, shares are issued in payment for plant and equipment from the U.S. company. (This practice may be a way in which the American company can dispose of its obsolete machinery in a relatively profitable manner: both Dunning and Phelps, in their studies of American investment, found that foreign subsidiaries frequently have to make do with second-hand equipment from their parents, but in only a few instances was this behaviour detected with certainty in the present survey.)

Despite the various ways in which American parents can avoid remitting dollars to Australia, however, it remains true that a great number of American subsidiaries are established here with an allowance of American cash. This is almost always true if American companies make their initial Australian investment in the shares of an already existing company, but it is also true in many other cases. The very large dollar sums initially subscribed by Asarco for the support of Mount Isa Mines have already been mentioned. The Aluminium Company of America subscribed in cash for 6,500,000 £1 shares in Alcoa of Australia shortly after the local firm was formed. Two firms mentioned that, in addition to funds from their parents, they had also used loans from American banks during their establishment period, both because of the greater ease of securing credit in the United States at that period and because of lower American rates of interest. The most spectacular example of the use of American credit facilities is the recent borrowing of more than

TABLE IV–13   Source of Funds Employed in 1962 by 28 Companies in which the American Shareholding was Between 50 and 99 per cent[a]

£A('000)

Type of investment	U.S.	Aust.	Other	Total[b]
Ordinary shares issued	19,378	13,587	2,075	35,040
Preference shares issued	1,081[c]	100	..	1,181
Profit and loss, and other similar reserves[d]	21,389	17,352	(85)	38,656
Home office value of branch assets	..	..	..	..
Interest of outside shareholders on consolidation	..	1,074	..	1,074
Total shareholders' funds[b]	41,848	32,113	1,990	75,951
Debt to U.S. parent and its affiliates	10,306	..	..	10,306
Other long-term liabilities	250	19,595	6,675	26,520
Other short-term liabilities	344	24,234	63	24,640
Total liabilities[b]	10,899	43,828	6,738	61,466
Total funds employed[b]	52,748	75,941	8,728	137,417

[a] See notes to Table IV–7.
[b] Detail may not add to totals because of rounding.
[c] Participating preference shares.
[d] Parentheses denote an accumulated loss.

£50 million for the construction of an alumina refinery at Gladstone by Queensland Alumina Ltd, a firm in which the largest single shareholder is the Kaiser Aluminium and Chemical Corporation of the U.S. While several of these examples concern mining as much as manufacturing, they dramatically illustrate that not all borrowing is in one direction.

TABLE IV–14   Source of Funds Employed in 1962 by 17 Companies in which the American Shareholding was Between 25 and 49 per cent[a]

£A('000)

Type of investment	U.S.	Aust.	Other	Total[b]
Ordinary shares issued	3,760	5,792	2,011	11,563
Preference shares issued	410	1,542	..	1,952
Profit and loss, and other similar reserves	3,909	7,589	1,120	12,617
Home office value of branch assets	..	..	..	..
Interest of outside shareholders on consolidation	..	2,112	87	2,199
Total shareholders' funds[b]	8,079	17,034	3,218	28,332
Debt to U.S. parent and its affiliates	1,417	..	..	1,417
Other long-term liabilities	..	5,069	59	5,128
Other short-term liabilities	..	8,588	498	9,086
Total liabilities[b]	1,417	13,657	557	15,631
Total funds employed[b]	9,496	30,691	3,775	43,962

[a] See notes to Table IV–7.
[b] Detail may not add to totals because of rounding.

At the commencement of the present survey it was hoped that it would be possible to gain some quantitative estimate of the importance of the various alternative methods of financing a foreign investment at its establishment. Unfortunately this proved impossible. This was partly because executives in old-established firms seemed to have no recollection of the method used to finance the initial investment but, more important, failure was due to the different interpretations placed upon the questions asked and, perhaps, failure to ask the right questions.

Companies were asked to indicate how their initial liability (including shareholding in the case of incorporated companies) to their American parent had been incurred—for the provision of cash, technical information, plant and machinery, etc. A fundamental difficulty was quickly encountered, however: it proved impossible for many companies to decide what the 'initial liability' to their parent was, for American companies do not, for the most part, establish a subsidiary with a fixed issue of shares and then leave it to its own devices. In the case of many wholly American subsidiaries, the initial share capital is only a fraction of the American company's 'initial investment'. The typical pattern is for quite a small part of the American investment to be 'capitalized' and the rest to be in the form of a rather flexible inter-company loan. This pattern may be seen clearly in Tables IV-11 and IV-12. In the latter, showing the funds of wholly American companies which began operations in Australia in 1960 or subsequently, advances from parent companies and their affiliates are larger than the total shareholders' funds of the companies concerned, while even in Table IV-11 such advances are substantially larger than the paid-up capital of the group.

It appears in fact that, while American subsidiaries setting up operations in Australia frequently do use credit facilities to supplement their own equity capital, the creditors are more often their parent companies than Australians.[20] Some striking examples of this behaviour were encountered. Firms which had inter-company debts as large as their paid-up capital were by no means unusual. Goodyear, for example, a firm which has been noted as utilizing Australian funds for part of its investment, was also employing an advance from its parent company of £618,000 two years after it commenced operations in 1927.[21] One of the companies cited as using Australian overdraft accommodation to purchase the shares

[20] Barlow and Wender (1955: 163) have also observed a marked tendency on the part of American companies to avoid 'capitalizing' funds invested abroad.

[21] This compares with the company's paid-up ordinary capital of only £500,000 at that time (Forster 1964: 56).

of the Australian operation was employing an advance equal to nearly forty times its issued capital four years after manufacturing commenced. Another firm with a paid-up capital of only £2,000 operated for its first years with a loan from its parent of £250,000. The most dramatic example of all was the company with a paid-up capital of substantially less than £1,000 and a deficit in shareholders' funds of more than £100,000—the company was operating almost entirely on advances from affiliates totalling £164,000. In very many cases, it is clearly in serious error to speak of an American subsidiary's paid-up capital as being the dollar funds 'initially brought in'.

The reasons for this reluctance to 'capitalize' the funds invested are fairly obvious. Some companies may feel that in the event of exchange difficulties there would be a greater chance of withdrawing loans than of remitting dividends. Also, were the Australian currency to be devalued the fact that the American investment was in loan form would probably ensure that the exchange loss would be incurred by the subsidiary rather than the parent. But almost certainly the main reason for adopting this pattern of financing is the desire to avoid payment of withholding tax on dividends, for in this manner a large part of the American investment can be returned to the American company without the payment of any tax on dividends.

This is the pattern of financing which makes it difficult to share ownership with Australian partners. It is a pattern that is mainly of use in the early years of a subsidiary's life but is on occasions used even with long-established firms. One firm, for example, manufacturing in Australia for more than twenty years, operated for most of this time as an unincorporated entity and remitted its entire annual profit to its parent company every year. When it was incorporated recently, its issued capital was set at a figure equal to only about 10 per cent of its parent's total investment in Australia. The executive interviewed explained that he was puzzled that at the time of incorporation his parent company had requested no dividends for the near future. It was only further questioning that revealed that the local firm was instead engaged in the repayment of the very large inter-company loan. Another firm which has been operating in Australia for an even longer period financed a major expansion by parent company credit of more than three times issued capital. When the investment programme was completed, these loans were reduced and in fact even larger credit was extended to another affiliate of the parent company. The company had declared no dividends for fifteen years at the time of the survey.

Once the foreign subsidiary has been established, most American parents are even more reluctant to invest 'dollars' in the operation.

Many American firms, in announcing overseas investment programmes to their shareholders, stress that no dollars from the U.S.
will be involved. Henry Ford II stated late in 1962, for example,
that Ford planned to spend $US270 million on capital expansion
abroad in 1963, but he emphasized that the foreign expenditures
would come from foreign earnings, depreciation, and borrowings
from abroad. Similar comments could be quoted from the annual
reports of almost any of the major American foreign investors.

It has already been seen that some finance for the expansion of
American subsidiaries in Australia is derived from local borrowing.
Often such borrowings are made under parent company guarantee,
and one executive commented that in this situation local banks 'fall
over each other to lend us money'. The best known example of an
established American subsidiary drawing on Australian loan funds
for expansion is that of General Motors-Holden's. This company
borrowed about £3 million from Australian banks—with the assistance of the Commonwealth government and under a guarantee
from General Motors Corporation—at the time when the Holden
project was first planned at the end of World War II.[22] A number
of other cases of a similar, if less spectacular, kind could be cited.

Sometimes the international connections of the foreign subsidiary
permit it to raise loan funds more cheaply in other capital markets.
Union Carbide Australia, for example, a firm which also has large
local borrowings, raised £1 million in London late in 1962, and
another large chemical company has in past years done the same.
Swift Australian announced that the finance to acquire Mayfair
Hams Ltd in 1963 was secured through a loan raised by its parent
company from a group of American lending institutions, and at least
one of the major oil companies has borrowed substantial sums in
European capital markets.

On the other hand, there appears to be no policy to use Australian
(or other non-American) funds to the utmost at every opportunity.
While many recent increases of paid-up capital have been bonus
issues made from asset revaluation, many companies have in past
years made cash issues to their parents, often long before the
Uniform Companies Act of 1961 provided any incentive for this.
At least two American companies, moreover, have bought out the

[22] This loan is a major factor in popular resentment at the company's current
profitability; it has led to the notion that it was actually Australia that financed
the development of the Holden car. But the overdraft seems never to have
exceeded about 27 per cent of the book value of the funds employed by the
company and it appears to have been completely repaid before the end of 1950.
Moreover, if it were merely £3 million which was required, one wonders why
no Australian-owned company accepted the government's challenge to build a
car locally at that time.

Australian holders of preference shares, though the motive for one of these moves appears to have been primarily to take shelter behind the secrecy then available in proprietary status. Two jointly-owned firms were encountered where the only preference shares issued were held by the American parent, while one large wholly American firm had made an issue of one million preference shares to its parent to finance local expansion. Inter-company credit is also used substantially by long-established companies. Both the major American-owned oil companies, for example, have very considerable debts to affiliated companies and the extent to which these advances are made may be seen in Table IV-7. One Australian-American firm, a company in which the American holding was in a minority, owed its American affiliate an amount very much larger than the total of all its Australian liabilities: the executive simply explained that the Australian market was unable to cater for his company's need for capital. One wholly American firm even stated that its American parent had advanced it money for which no need was felt, while another had difficulty persuading its parent that further advances were not needed.

It is beyond doubt, however, that the most important sources of the funds required for expansion are undistributed profits and depreciation allowances. The importance of undistributed profits has been noted in Table IV-7. The importance of depreciation allowances is not clear from that table and may only be inferred from Table IV-15. Their significance may perhaps be grasped from the

TABLE IV–15   Asset Structure in 1962 of 101 American-affiliated Companies, by Percentage of American Ownership
£A('000)

Percentage U.S. ownership and period in which Australian manufacture began[a]	Current assets	Fixed assets (net)	Other assets	Total[b]
25–49%	15,500	24,131	4,331	43,962
50–99%	39,782	93,784	3,851	137,417
100%—				
(i) Manufacture began before 1957	170,695	180,876	23,458	375,028
(ii) Manufacture began 1957–1959	7,323	4,653	319	12,296
(iii) Manufacture began 1960–1962	7,445	19,628	2,898	29,972
Total[b]	240,746	323,073	34,857	598,676

[a] The year in which manufacture began is taken to be the year in which an American equity of at least 25 per cent was first acquired in the case of companies manufacturing previously as Australian-owned ventures.

[b] Detail may not add to totals because of rounding.

NOTE: The rather unusual classification used in this table was adopted to permit comparison with Tables IV–10 to IV–14.

fact that the 93 firms which provided figures for depreciation reserves had total reserves of £93 million at their 1962 balance dates. Their net fixed assets were valued at £267 million. Figures published by the U.S. Department of Commerce (1960: 140-1) give the same impression. Of the funds absorbed by all American direct-investment enterprises in Australia in 1957—a total of $US129 million after payment of dividends and remitted branch profits—$US46 million came from undistributed profits, $US46 million from depreciation allowances, $US35 million from 'Funds obtained abroad' (mainly Australia), and $US2 million from 'Other' sources. Less than $US500,000 came from the U.S. Unfortunately, no separate figures are given for the Australian manufacturing sector, but figures for manufacturing are available for 'Oceania' as a whole. Since American investment in Australia comprised approximately 86 per cent of the total for this area in that year, figures for Oceania may be taken as a reasonable approximation. These show that of the funds available —a total of $US69 million, excluding funds used in the petroleum industry—$US31 million came from undistributed profits, $US24 million from depreciation allowances, $US7 million from the U.S., and $US7 million from 'Funds obtained abroad'.

Many individual companies were encountered in the present survey which, because of a policy of profit reinvestment, had almost no liabilities in Australia at all. A number had substantial bank balances, with no overdraft accommodation of any kind. All companies were asked to indicate how they financed their growth during the fifties and, though most of the answers provided were unsuitable for use because of an ambiguity in the wording of the question, fourteen useful answers were tendered. Generalizations based on such a small number of responses must inevitably be tentative, but three conclusions appear warranted. First, in almost every case the percentage of American ownership somewhat exceeded the proportion of funds supplied from the U.S. or by the American shareholder (including the latter's share of depreciation and reinvested profits). Secondly, in most cases credit extended by the American affiliate was considerably more important to wholly American subsidiaries than to joint ventures. And thirdly, internally generated funds were of greater importance for wholly American companies than for joint ventures.

The dividend policies of most American-affiliated companies in Australia tend to be conservative. Many firms were encountered which had declared no dividend at all for at least the first five or six years of operation in Australia. One company commented that 'the decision on how much to remit to our parent is taken here, in the light of how much we need for expansion. We have been instructed to maintain a minimum cash balance of £50,000 at all times.' This attitude was not uncommon. Even General Motors-Holden's, a company often criticized for the absolute size of its dividends, appears to be no exception to this conservatism. There is no published information available for the company's results in 1960 and 1961 (though published figures for shareholders' funds in 1959 and 1962 make it seem likely that dividend remittances were particularly high in those years) but, excepting those two years, the company's annual dividend on ordinary shares fell short of 50 per cent of net profit (itself conservatively arrived at) in every post-war year to 1964 except 1956, 1959, and 1962. Companies which are compelled to declare dividends, either because of their status as private companies for taxation purposes or because of pressure from local shareholders, often hold in Australia the dividend accruing to the U.S. shareholder. Sometimes this is done to avoid dividend withholding tax but in other cases this tax is paid even though the dividend is left on deposit with the local subsidiary.

It appears that wholly American companies are more conservative in their dividend policies than jointly-owned ventures. There are exceptions to this generalization: most Australian investors are familiar with the caution exercised by Mount Isa Mines, Borg-Warner, and Philip Morris, for example. Wiltshire File declared its first dividend, of 5 per cent, in 1952, twelve years after manufacturing began. Two joint ventures told the writer that it had been agreed that no dividends would be withdrawn from the companies concerned for at least ten years. But for the most part the only Australian-American ventures not declaring dividends in 1962 were firms in which the Australian shares were held by a large company, firms which had just been established, or firms in which the Australian shares were held by the manager of the venture who was deriving an income from the company in his executive capacity. Even medium-sized Australian firms do not like to receive no return on a portion of their invested capital for a lengthy period, and two 50/50 ventures mentioned that all the pressure for dividends comes from the Australian shareholding company. The smaller of these joint ventures, a company with a total employment in 1962 of far less than one hundred, was compelled by the Australian shareholder to declare a dividend in 1961 substantially greater not only than after-tax profit in that year but also than the total of all dividends declared in the previous four years. The violent disagreement between the shareholders on this issue caused the resignation of the company's general manager. When the Australian shares are held publicly, dividend policy may be conservative, but it can hardly be subjected to the kind of sudden changes which are often the rule in wholly American ventures. Goodyear, for example, declared a dividend on its ordinary shares in 1953, 1954, 1959, 1962, and 1963, but despite profitable operation throughout, the American shareholder received no dividend at all in the other years of the fourteen-year period from 1950.

Table IV-16 gives in aggregate form some information about the dividend policies of 66 American-affiliated companies. The column showing after-tax profit in 1962 needs some explanation. In an attempt to gain consistent figures from all participating companies, firms were requested to give figures for 'taxable income (before taxation)' rather than after-tax profits. It was hoped to gain some idea of after-tax profits from these figures. The hope may well have been vain in any case, but in fact firms often provided 'pre-tax profit' figures, as they understood them, rather than figures for 'taxable income'. When it was known, from published taxation provision, that a company had provided conservatively stated figures for pre-tax profit, the after-tax profit figure used in the table was 150 per cent of the taxation provision.[23] When it was known, again from published figures, that the figure provided was heavily influenced by recent establishment losses or other similar factors, the published after-tax profit figure was adopted. In all remaining cases, the majority of the total, the after-tax profit figures embodied in the table merely represent 60 per cent of the 'taxable income (before taxation)' figures provided. It is certain that in some cases the figures accepted as 'taxable income' were in fact 'pre-tax profit', and therefore the after-tax profit figures shown tend to understate the 'true' picture somewhat.[24]

These figures for the average ratio of dividend to after-tax profit tend to confirm the view that wholly American subsidiaries do have a more conservative attitude to dividends than do jointly-owned ventures. Actually, three of the most crucial figures for comparative purposes are significantly 'distorted', and with the removal of these 'distortions' the picture is made even clearer. The ratio of 53·4 per cent, for wholly American firms which commenced manufacture in Australia before 1957, falls to 27·0 per cent on the exclusion of the

[23] Rates of company taxation in 1962 were, for most companies in the survey, 7s. in the pound on the first £5,000 of assessable income, and 8s. in the pound on income above £5,000.

[24] In case a comparison of the total figure for after-tax profits in the table with the figure for income accruing to U.S. parent companies from their operations in Australia in 1962 published by the Commonwealth Bureau of Census and Statistics leads to the conclusion that Table IV-16 covers the great majority of American investment in Australia, it should be stressed that the table *excludes* all companies operating unprofitably. (Losses are offset against profits in the Bureau's figures.)

TABLE IV-16 Dividends Declared in 1961/2 by 66 American-affiliated Companies, by Percentage of American Ownership and Period in which Manufacture Began[a]

Percentage U.S. ownership and period in which Australian manufacture began[b]	No. companies covered	After-tax profit in 1962[a] £A('000)	Total gross dividend[c] £A('000)	Average ratio of dividend to profit (%)	Ratio of dividend to profit (%), by company					
					Nil	1–24	25–49	50–74	75–99	100 and over
25–49%: Manufacture began—										
before 1957	7	1,986	1,199	60·4	1	..	3	3	..	..
in or after 1957	4	105	16	14·7	2	..	..	1	1	..
50–99%: Manufacture began—										
before 1957	11	6,114	3,836	62·7	..	..	2	6	2	1
in or after 1957	6	515	165	32·0	1	..	4	..	1	..
100%: Manufacture began—										
before 1957	25	29,345	15,659	53·4	9	3	5	6	..	2
in or after 1957	13	1,211	328	27·1	8	2	1	1	..	1
Total[d]	66	39,277	21,202	54·0	21	5	15	17	4	4

[a] Only companies which both operated at a profit in 1961/2 and provided to the survey what appeared to be a 'reliable' profit figure are included in this table. See text for further explanation.
[b] See Note [a] to Table IV–15.
[c] For the purpose of the table, 'dividend' includes branch profits remitted. Not all dividends, as usually understood, were actually remitted abroad.
[d] Detail may not add to totals because of rounding.

97

H

results of one very large company, one large stock dividend, and preference dividends paid to Australian shareholders by four companies in the group. Ratios for joint ventures manufacturing in Australia before 1957 also fall when the results of single large companies are left out of consideration, those for '50-99% companies' and '25-49% companies' falling from 62·7 and 60·4 to 53·4 and 50·2 respectively. The difference between wholly American firms and joint ventures appears even more striking.

Of the sixty-six companies covered, wholly American firms make up about 58 per cent of the total, but they comprise no less than 81 per cent of those not declaring dividends in 1962. The figure is slightly higher still if one firm declaring only a preference dividend to Australian shareholders is excluded. The impression is only partially modified if twenty-eight more companies—not included in the table either because they were operating at a loss in 1962 (eighteen of them) or because the figures they provided seemed to bear no relation to published after-tax profit figures—are taken into consideration. Fourteen of them (nine operating at a loss) were wholly American, and fourteen (including another nine operating at a loss) were joint ventures. None declared a dividend in 1962.

Seventy-nine firms (of which forty-three were wholly American) provided full details of their dividends since 1950 (or since they began manufacturing in Australia, if this was after 1950). Though it is not possible to present all this evidence here, the conclusion emerging from it confirms the impression gained from the study of 1962, namely that wholly American companies are significantly more cautious in their dividend policies than are Australian-American companies.

American direct-investment enterprises in general tend to be more conservative in their dividend policies than British-owned enterprises. The relevant facts are presented in Table IV-17.[25] Whereas 55·3 per cent of the total net profits of American ventures in Australia were reinvested over the seventeen-year period, the corresponding British percentage was only 41·9 per cent. Whereas undistributed profits made up 41·0 per cent of the total American direct investment in Australia over the period, the British proportion was only 28·9 per cent. Indeed, if the last three years of the table be excluded, the contrast is even more apparent. American enterprises reinvested 63·0 per cent of their total profits for the period to 1960/1, compared with a British figure of 39·5 per cent, and while 56·0 per cent of all American investment in Australia during that

[25] Actually data in Table IV-17 include dividends declared on the shares of foreign portfolio investors in Australia, but these are relatively small.

TABLE IV-17 Comparison of 'North American' and 'British' Profit Remittance Policies

Year ended 30 June	Investments of U.S.A. and Canada in Australian companies					Investments of U.K. in Australian companies				
	Distributed profits[a] £A(m.)	Undist. profits £A(m.)	Investment other than undist. profits £A(m.)	Ratio of undist. to total profits (%)	Ratio of undist. profits to total investment (%)	Distributed profits[a] £A(m.)	Undist. profits £A(m.)	Investment other than undist. profits £A(m.)	Ratio of undist. to total profits (%)	Ratio of undist. profits to total investment (%)
1948b	2·3	2·1	4·3	47·7	32·8	14·1	4·7	25·0	25·0	15·8
1949b	2·6	2·0	2·1	43·5	48·8	12·4	3·1	32·1	20·0	8·8
1950b	2·4	4·2	6·1	63·6	40·8	14·8	10·6	42·5	41·7	20·0
1951b	3·1	8·1	12·2	72·3	39·9	18·1	12·9	30·4	41·6	29·8
1952b	2·6	12·1	18·5	82·3	39·5	18·1	10·2	36·8	36·0	21·7
1953b	3·0	12·4	−10·4	80·5	620·0	24·5	5·2	15·9	17·5	24·6
1954a	13·5	17·0	0·3	55·7	98·3	22·8	12·4	31·9	35·2	28·0
1955b	12·5	15·8	23·7	55·8	40·0	25·7	13·9	43·1	35·1	24·4
1956b	11·9	20·1	11·8	62·8	63·0	28·6	19·5	52·4	40·5	27·1
1957	12·3	20·6	6·9	62·6	74·9	25·5	24·1	37·4	48·6	39·2
1958	17·4	20·6	6·6	54·2	75·7	29·1	19·8	41·3	40·5	32·4
1959	16·5	31·5	15·3	65·6	67·3	28·4	27·6	38·4	49·3	41·8
1960	17·0	34·8	28·1	67·2	55·3	31·3	30·6	74·5	49·4	29·1
1961	19·0	30·7	57·0	61·8	35·0	35·1	19·6	92·4	35·8	17·5
1962	29·1	8·0	63·5	21·6	11·2	29·3	21·5	41·3	42·3	34·2
1963	31·6	13·3	78·8	29·6	14·4	34·9	35·3	68·1	50·3	34·1
1964	26·3	22·8	73·2	46·4	23·8	36·2	38·7	57·8	51·7	40·1

a Net of withholding tax on dividends.
b For these years a relatively small proportion of 'Undistributed profits' would have been classified as 'Investment other than undistributed profits'. The difference in basis would mainly affect particulars for the United Kingdom.

NOTE: The table covers both direct and portfolio investment, except for undistributed profits on shares held by portfolio investors.
SOURCE: Commonwealth Bureau of Census and Statistics 1965b.

period was made up of profit reinvestment, the British figure was only 26·5 per cent.

With the exception of 1947/8 and 1948/9, American direct-investment enterprises in Australia consistently reinvested more than 50 per cent of their total after-tax profits until 1961/2. In that year the policy of profit reinvestment seemed to come to an end, and figures for 1962/3 seemed to confirm the impression. Figures for these two years led some Australians to believe that such a change in policy had been adopted by at least a number of large American subsidiaries. It is certainly true that changes of this kind do appear to occur from time to time. A similar change in American reinvestment policy, albeit on a much smaller scale, was observed by the writer in New Zealand about the mid-fifties (1964: 30-1). But on this occasion the explanation seems to lie rather in the change in U.S. tax legislation outlined at the beginning of this chapter. Under the Revenue Act of 1962, American subsidiaries operating abroad had a very definite tax incentive to remit substantial dividends to their parent companies before either 1 January 1963 or 1 January 1965, depending on circumstances. It seems probable that this is the explanation of the sudden decrease in profit reinvestment, and at the same time the increase in capital inflow in other forms, witnessed in 1961/2. It is known that a number of the companies covered in the survey sharply increased their dividends during that period (though this does not for the most part affect Table IV-16), some declaring dividends of substantially greater sums than their total after-tax profit in the relevant year. There seems little doubt that, at least for the near future, the policy of reinvestment by American-affiliated enterprises in Australia will be resumed.

The explanation of the policy of heavy reinvestment itself is not absolutely clear. To some extent, the policy is illusory, as has been noted. It may be merely a manoeuvre to avoid dividend withholding tax while the parent firm receives its 'reward' by the repayment of outstanding advances making up the greater part of the American investment. There is nevertheless some reality to the policy. The contrast in the behaviour of American-controlled subsidiaries with that of companies in which Australians have an influence on dividend policy probably stems in part from differences in business philosophy—undoubtedly some American executives believe this to be the principal factor—but almost certainly more important are differences in the relative value of the Australian operation to American and Australian shareholders.

It is revealing in this connection to compare the size of American-affiliated companies in Australia with that of their American parents. If employment be used as a rough index of size, it appears that in

105 cases (of the 137 where availability of data made comparison possible) the Australian venture was less than 3 per cent of the size of its American affiliate in 1962. In only five cases (four of them joint ventures) did the employment of the local enterprise exceed 10 per cent of the parent company's employment. Clearly, in most cases the receipt of a dividend from the Australian operation can have little effect on the results of the parent.

That British subsidiaries reinvest a significantly smaller proportion of their after-tax profit than do American subsidiaries probably in part reflects the same forces: the results of the British-owned subsidiary are likely to be much more important to many British parent companies than are those of American subsidiaries to their parents. In part, it may also be the result of a different industry distribution of British investment in Australia, away from investment in manufacturing where the policy of profit reinvestment may well be most prevalent. If British subsidiaries share ownership with Australians to a greater extent than do American, this could also be a significant factor.

Increasing attention is currently being devoted to the implications of the policy of profit reinvestment. One theory, evolved primarily by John Knapp (1957), argues that reinvested profits do not constitute a genuine addition to the capital resources available to the capital-importing country, and this view has been supported implicitly by E. L. Wheelwright (1963: 145) in Australia. A corollary of this theory is that the net 'increase in our access to foreign resources' can be calculated by subtracting remitted profits from capital inflow excluding undistributed profits. But the theory is clearly based on a fallacy: the profits of foreign subsidiaries operating in Australia, whether remitted or not, are the property of foreign shareholders, and if these profits are reinvested in Australia this constitutes a genuine addition to the savings available to the Australian economy. The only point which must be conceded to the modern statement of this theory is that profit reinvestment constitutes an addition to Australia's capital resources only to the extent of 85 per cent of the amount reinvested, since up to 15 per cent of that profit would have accrued to Australia in dividend withholding tax in the event of a dividend being declared. To compare remitted profits with capital inflow, whether net of undistributed profits or not, is to confuse in a quite unwarranted manner the current and capital accounts of the nation's balance of payments and 'conclusions' based on such exercises, often quoted in the popular press, must be regarded as without foundation.

A theory with much more plausibility is that evolved by Dr Penrose. She argued in 1956 that after a foreign subsidiary is established it acquires to some extent a life of its own and develops in the same way as other firms—expanding, diversifying into the production of new products, and so on. In this situation,

> It seems highly probable . . . that there will be a strong tendency for the parent company to take its 'cut' of the profits and to permit the subsidiary to retain a part long after a comparison of rates of return on capital would attract new investments in the absence of the existing subsidiaries. In other words, even if increasing investment reduces, or even eliminates, the original differential between foreign and domestic rates of return on capital, foreign investment will still increase because foreign-owned firms will continue to grow through their own earnings. (1956: 229.)

Dr Penrose did not make it clear whether she expected foreign subsidiaries to expand into fields new even to the parent corporation or only into fields already well explored by the latter. If she expected expansion into fields new even to the parent company, the evidence of the present survey would seem to contradict her thesis. It is true that some American subsidiaries, even wholly American ones, have branched out into fields unfamiliar to their American parent. One firm, established to produce asphalt roofing, has developed principally as a producer of adhesives for floor coverings, an industry in which the parent company has almost no interest. Another firm, jointly owned by American and Australian interests, has embarked on the manufacture of 'cricketing machines', a field quite unknown to the American parent. Other cases could be quoted, but it seems that, at least up to the present, they are exceptions rather than the general rule. Subsidiaries certainly tend to expand and diversify, but usually into product lines well tried by the parent corporation. General Motors-Holden's, cited by Dr Penrose as an example of a foreign subsidiary expanding into ever new fields, produces no major product line not also produced by General Motors Corporation.

In the absence of any information on marginal rates of profit in the U.S. and Australia, it is not possible to judge whether profits are really reinvested in Australia after 'the original differential between foreign and domestic rates of return on capital' has been eliminated. There are some American operations in Australia which contradict the Penrose thesis by remitting all their after-tax profit, presumably because investment in other areas does prove more attractive than further investment in Australia. The former manager of one company commented that the Australian company remitted 'every penny of after-tax profit. This remittance often posed a problem of liquidity but our parent treated it very seriously and laxness in this regard was an important reason for the dismissal of my predecessor.' Another firm stated that 'sometimes we get a reminder to remit the profit before we have our accounts completed—nothing is retained here'. A third asserted that its parent 'doesn't seem to understand that you have to invest in advertising to keep sales high. They want every last pound we earn.'[26] All three firms had been operating in Australia for more than ten years.

Some companies reinvest profits primarily to protect the profitability of existing investments. One firm was encountered which had invested in costly facilities to produce a previously imported raw material to avoid the necessity of purchasing the commodity in question from an American competitor, then thought to be about to invest in Australia. Another firm was fearful of the consequences of failing to take this action.

But there is certainly some basis for the Penrose view, and the extent to which the local subsidiary does develop its own separate existence is well illustrated by a quotation from the manager of an American subsidiary in the Australian chemical industry. Asked whether the initiative for major capital expenditure came from the American parent or from the local firm in Australia, he commented that 'generally the initiative is ours—it has to be since there are a lot of other countries competing for U.S. capital'. This attitude, combined with the small size of the Australian operation in relation to the American, is probably an important part of the explanation of the profit reinvestment policy of American firms in Australia. It implies that even if no new foreign affiliates were established, a significant amount of foreign investment would continue almost 'automatically'.

[26] It is significant that two of the three firms cited operated as branches in Australia.

V

The Management of American-affiliated Companies in Australia

The extent of American ownership of a direct-investment enterprise is not always a good reflection of the extent of American control over the behaviour of that enterprise. For most purposes, control of a company may be thought to reside with the shareholder having an absolute majority of the voting shares. In the present survey a broader definition has been used: an enterprise is considered to constitute a direct or controlled investment when a single foreign shareholder (or affiliated group of shareholders) holds at least 25 per cent of the voting shares in a locally incorporated company or an equivalent interest in an unincorporated enterprise. Several companies were encountered, however, in which the foreign shareholding was more than 25 per cent and was substantially the largest single shareholding, which felt themselves to be completely free of American 'control', while almost all firms felt themselves to be independent in at least some areas of policy. American control of the management of the local affiliate may be greater than consideration of the American shareholding alone would imply if the local firm is heavily dependent on the American parent company for technical know-how, patents, trademarks, etc. On the other hand, American control may be substantially unexercised even in the case of a wholly American subsidiary if the parent actively pursues a policy of decentralization of decision-making, if it has lost interest in the local operation, or if the executives of the local operation are of particularly independent disposition.

The present chapter discusses in general terms the extent of American control on the policies of affiliated companies in Australia and the importance of American influence on the management techniques of these companies even when their decisions are free from control. Two special aspects of this subject—the freedom of American affiliates to conduct research in Australia, and their freedom to buy and sell in markets of their own choosing—are discussed in chapters VI and IX respectively.

There appears to be no infallible standard by which 'control' can be measured. Though none of the various items of evidence to be adduced constitutes a reliable guide in itself, taken together they do present an interesting impression.

To begin with, the composition of the boards of ninety-seven of the respondent companies was examined. In all, these companies had 590 board members in 1962, of whom 224 were American.[1] Only a small proportion of this number lived in Australia, however, and most of them were on the boards of the wholly American firms in the group. The seventeen companies with less than 50 per cent of their ordinary shares held in the U.S. had 95 board members, but only 16 were American and only 3 of these lived in Australia. The twenty-nine companies in which the American holding was between 50 and 99 per cent had 180 board members, 67 of them American, but only 7 of these Americans (2 of them managing directors) lived in Australia. The fifty-one wholly American subsidiaries, on the other hand, had 141 Americans in a total board membership of 315: no fewer than 40 of these (including 14 managing directors) lived in Australia. It is noteworthy that even among wholly American companies Australian directors were in the majority.

It was clear, however, that the boards of many American subsidiaries are purely nominal entities, in existence to comply with Australian company law. Of greater interest is the nationality of the executive personnel of these companies. There are obvious reasons why an American parent may wish to employ men from its own operation in the top management of the foreign subsidiary. If an executive with long experience of the ways of the parent company is in command of the subsidiary, it may greatly facilitate the problem of communication between the two members of the corporate family. It may be very much quicker to despatch an American to commence operations than to wait until a local has been trained in the ways of the parent company. In some cases the reason for preferring an American in top management stems from the belief that Americans have a better 'attitude' to business than locals, though this factor

[1] The term 'American' here includes not only citizens of the U.S. but also in a few cases citizens of Canada, and any other person who has spent a prolonged period of years employed by the American parent company. Not included, however, are two American nationals who had never been employed by the American parent company and who had become directors of a local subsidiary without reference to their nationality, and a few directors (mainly British) who had been associated with a sister affiliate in another country. The latter category of director was excluded on the grounds that British directors resident in Australia often settle here permanently.

TABLE V-1   American Employees in 105 American-affiliated Companies, by Percentage of American Ownership and Period in which Manufacture Began[a]

Percentage U.S. ownership and period in which Australian manufacture began[b]	No. companies covered	No. American employees in—			Employment in 1962
		1950	1955	1962	
25-49%: Manufacture began—					
before 1950	4	..	..	..	2,912
1951–1955	3	n.a.	..	..	1,920
1956–1962	10	n.a.	n.a.	..	1,773
50-99%: Manufacture began—					
before 1950	7	5	1	2	5,707
1951–1955	5	n.a.	1	..	949
1956–1962	17	n.a.	n.a.	24	4,162
100%: Manufacture began—					
before 1950	24	36	56	86	50,454
1951–1955	7	n.a.	2	12	4,119
1956–1962	28	n.a.	n.a.	22	3,601
1962 total	105	n.a.	n.a.	146	75,597

[a] The term 'American employees' includes not only citizens of the U.S, but also citizens of Canada and any other person who had spent a prolonged period of years employed by the U.S. parent company. To be included in the above table, however, an employee must have been employed at some time by the American parent or its Canadian subsidiary—Americans hired independently of the American parent company by the Australian subsidiary are not included. Also excluded for the purpose of this table are American directors living in Australia.

[b] The year in which manufacture began is taken to be the year in which an American equity of at least 25 per cent was first acquired in the case of companies manufacturing previously as Australian-owned ventures.

appears to operate more in dealings with underdeveloped countries than with Australia.[2]

But there are in fact very few Americans employed by American affiliates in Australia, if the evidence of the present survey is typical. Table V-1 shows that in 105 companies[3] with total 1962 employment of 75,597,[4] there were in 1962 only 146 Americans associated with the American parent company. To be sure, that figure does not include any of the American directors referred to earlier, though most of the fifty living in Australia were indeed working directors. Moreover, personnel previously associated with other affiliates of the American parent are not included in the figure (except those from Canada and those who had spent many years working in the U.S. company). With the inclusion of the American directors, however, the importance of personnel from the parent company is at least fully stated because personnel from other affiliates often settle permanently in Australia (especially those from a sister affiliate in the United Kingdom) and even some Americans become 'Australianized'. The writer met several 'Americans' who had lived in Australia for more than a quarter of a century and others who, after living here for a very much shorter time, were rapidly adopting an Australian point of view. The Australian executive of one firm described the American executives of another as 'more Australian than the Australians'. Because the performance of an American executive in

[2] The American manager of one joint venture reported, however, that one of the main reasons he was employed in the Australian subsidiary was: 'Australians don't always look ahead far enough—they are too interested in making quick returns.' He wished strongly that his company were wholly American because, though the American parent had nominal voting control, it did not exercise this authority for fear of offending the Australian partner. This meant that he was compelled to adopt many 'short-term policies' which conflicted violently with his own views. He complained that his company had no fire protection system in the office because the Australian partner 'doesn't seem to appreciate all the intangibles that would be lost if a fire destroyed the building. The same attitude prevails towards mechanization. A forklift truck might cost £3,600. In the U.S. this may be equivalent to only one man-year in cost, whereas in Australia it might cost three and a half man-years. But an American feels its purchase is still worthwhile, not on grounds of direct cost but because of the intangible benefits. Without the forklift, men with few brains and little initiative must be hired to lift heavy loads, with high risk of injury. With the forklift, the company can attract skilled labour with initiative and intelligence which will be loyal to the company and help build company morale.'

[3] The 105 companies referred to include the 97 firms referred to earlier and 8 unincorporated branches.

[4] For the sake of consistency, employment figures are quoted on the same basis as elsewhere in the survey. Had the *total* employment of the three 'non-manufacturing companies', referred to in Note (b) to Table I-2, been included, however, the 'total employment' of the group of 105 companies would have been 5,966 higher than shown.

charge of a foreign subsidiary is naturally judged on the growth and development of that subsidiary, American executives were found not infrequently who adopted an aggressively 'Australian' attitude.[5]

By no means all of the 196 Americans, 50 directors and 146 other employees, were of executive status. Nineteen Americans in one company were assisting in the construction of an oil refinery and most of the eighteen in another company were helping in a technical capacity on a temporary basis. One firm in the motor vehicle industry employed nearly fifty Americans from its parent company in 1962, but the majority of these were technicians in Australia for the launching of a new vehicle rather than managers. Unfortunately, the precise proportion of the total who were in executive positions is not known, though if outside directors are also excluded it was certainly somewhat less than half the total of 196. The relatively small number of American executives in American affiliates in Australia is brought out by a consideration of the nationality of the executives interviewed during the course of the present survey. This information, presented in Table V-2, shows that, even in the case of wholly American companies, most of the senior executives interviewed were Australian.

American employees were well spread through the industries in which American capital is represented, as shown in Table V-3. Nevertheless, the impression conveyed by this table is rather deceptive, because in some industries almost all of the Americans in that industry were in one company. Indeed the concentration of the 196 Americans in a small number of companies was striking. Sixty-three companies, or 60 per cent of the present sample, employed no Americans at all and had no American directors living in Australia. Though only one of these companies had total employment in 1962 of over 2,000, the group included some very substantial firms. Seventeen firms either employed only one American or had only one American director living in Australia. Seven companies shared between them no less than 124 Americans.

Most commonly, American managers and technicians are employed in the early months of a subsidiary's life in Australia but are 'repatriated' as the local operation becomes established. Again and again

[5] The writer met one American managing director who was not only chief executive of the Australian subsidiary but was also in charge of all sales of the parent company in the Asian area. He was vigorously intent on proving to the American company that Australia was the 'logical' source of supply for the Asian area and had prepared a quite extraordinarily detailed multi-page report to document his case. This included not only comparison of distances between all Asian capitals and Sydney with distances between the same capitals and the home city of the parent corporation, but also data on everything from Asian political prospects to Asian climatic conditions.

TABLE V-2 Nationality of Executives Interviewed in 105 American-affiliated Companies, by Percentage of American Ownership

Status of person interviewed	Companies in which U.S. equity was 25–49%			Companies in which U.S. equity was 50–99%			Companies in which U.S. equity was 100%		
	Executive's nationality			Executive's nationality			Executive's nationality		
	U.S.	Aust.	Other	U.S.	Aust.	Other	U.S.	Aust.	Other
Managing director	..	3	..	1	3	..	3	10	1
Assistant managing director	..	..	..	..	1	..	..	1	..
Secretary and Controller-secretary	..	10	..	1	9	..	..	25	..
Assistant secretary	..	..	..	..	1	..	..	3	..
Secretary-treasurer and Treasurer	..	..	..	..	2	..	1	2	..
Controller	..	2	..	..	..	..	2	2	..
General manager	..	2	1	2	5	..	1	7	5
Finance manager and Finance director	..	..	..	..	2	..	2	5	..
Other executives	..	4	..	..	4	..	1	20	1
Total	..	21	1	4	27	..	10	75	7

TABLE V-3   Americans in 105 American-affiliated Companies in 1962, by Industry[a]

Industry	No. companies covered	Employment	American managing directors in Aust.	Other American directors in Aust.	Other Americans employed
Plant, equipment, machinery	21	4,191	6	4	11
Motor vehicles	5	34,609	4	11	56
Motor accessories	5	1,184	1	..	2
Metal manufactures, n.e.i.	8	5,374	..	1	19
Electrical equipment, instruments, etc.	15	8,056	..	..	8
Food and drink	9	6,870	1	3	12
Industrial chemicals and plastics	11	3,738	1	7	14
Pharmaceutical and toilet preparations	11	4,083	1	..	2
Clothing and fabrics	3	1,067	..	..	..
Other industries	17	6,425	2	8	22
Total	105	75,597	16	34	146

[a] See Note [a] to Table V-1 for use of the term 'American' in this table.

this policy was encountered and its results are discernible in Table V-1, though this table does not include American working directors. While it is true that the number of American employees in all companies that began manufacture before 1950 appears to have grown more quickly than their total employment (total employment of the group of thirty-five companies grew from 35,316 to 59,073 between 1950 and 1962, while American employment of the same companies grew from 41 to 88), this result is heavily influenced by two large firms which together had only one American employee (excluding a small number of working directors) in 1950 but employed sixty-three on a short-term basis in 1962.

The reasons for this frequent 'repatriation' require little explanation. Many companies stressed the importance their American parents attach to having subsidiaries staffed by local personnel 'on principle'. The 'principle' involved is probably a mixture of a desire to achieve better public relations by manning subsidiaries with nationals and a recognition that nationals often have a more detailed comprehension of the local business situation than is possible for expatriate Americans. Certainly not all American executives in Australia have been resoundingly successful in their achievements. Some are geared in their thinking to a market very much larger than the Australian, and several companies complained that their initially poor performance in Australia was the result of a grossly over-optimistic market assessment by an American executive. Other Americans, with experience of being a specialist in a whole company of specialists, find it difficult to adjust to a situation where initiative in broad areas of policy is required. One company secretary asserted that his company would never again request the assistance of an American to install equipment because 'they're too narrow in their experience'. The same man resented the fact that he had to write reports for his American managing director 'in words of one syllable' because the man had never been beyond the confines of one specialized department in the U.S. company.

There is also a cost element involved. Several companies noted this aspect of the policy of repatriation as a reason why Americans were *not* employed in Australia. Others which did employ Americans were, in some cases, resentful of their cost. The Australian secretary of one company was very bitter that Americans sent out to advise for periods of six to twelve months not only had to be paid salaries equal to more than twice those earned by the Australian general manager, but also expected the Australian company to meet all their living expenses in the most expensive motels. The comment of another Australian secretary illustrates the point so clearly that it is worth quoting at length:

Americans are employed out here with a cavalier disregard for cost—which is all charged to the local company. The average cost of each American to our company (and we employ a significant number) is about £10,000 per annum. Americans seem to regard living in a foreign country as a kind of punishment, so in addition to their basic American salary they receive a special salary for living overseas, *plus* a substantial allowance based on the alleged extra cost of living in Australia. We pay the school fees of any children they may have, and cover a number of other costs as well. Furthermore, at periodic intervals the company pays the first class air fares of the American and his whole family back to the States, whereas other company executives on business trips travel second class. All in all, American executives out here do very well: they are much better off than Australian executives and from the financial point of view are considerably better off than executives of similar rank in the U.S. company.

The very high cost of employing Americans to some extent reflects the fact that many Americans *do* regard being sent to a foreign subsidiary as a serious threat to their chances of promotion within the American company and substantial 'fringe benefits' must be paid as an inducement to the reluctant.[6]

Undoubtedly there are a few American companies in Australia which persist in employing American executives in most of their top management positions despite the cost. The Australian executive interviewed in one firm commented that his company had several Americans in senior posts, and there was no policy to replace these by Australians. He felt that this was not because American executives were better than Australian but just because 'we have adopted a policy of not seeking high-grade Australians. We have tended to take young, inexperienced people and when they fail to measure up to the standard of a senior executive, the Americans assume that this is just because they're Australian.' By and large, however, the number of Americans employed in direct-investment enterprises in Australia is extremely small, and there is even an increasing tendency to use Australians in the higher echelons of the American company itself.[7]

[6] Because foreign posting may interfere with an American executive's prospects in the American company, it has been observed by some that only when the local subsidiary becomes large enough for the parent company to notice an executive's performance in it does it attract the most competent American executives. There is some truth in this observation, though there are certainly exceptions to it, and it probably explains why, as one management consultant explained to the writer, American executives in Australia tend to be either very good or very poor. See also J. N. Behrman (1962b: 115, 118).

[7] The president of at least one American company is an Australian who worked up through the ranks of the Australian subsidiary and the international division of the American firm. Several Australians are known to be in senior positions in the international division of American parent companies.

It is beyond question that in many companies American control is tightly exercised even when all local management is Australian. In an attempt to shed further light on the question of control, companies were asked to indicate to what authority in the American company they were finally responsible. In none of the 104 companies examined did there exist a separate department of the American company responsible solely for Australian operations. Forty-six companies indicated that they were responsible to a division of the parent company dealing with all overseas operations of the company, and eleven said they were responsible to a division dealing with overseas investments alone. Thirty-four firms were responsible to one of the directors of their American parent, and ten of these were directly responsible to the chairman of directors himself. Of the other thirteen companies, about half were jointly-owned ventures which contended that all authority was vested in the local board, and most of the rest were responsible to various regional controllers in the U.S. The classification is not very helpful, however, because varying degrees of control were found in each category. The only exception to this is that most of the firms responsible only to the chairman of directors of the U.S. company appeared to be little subject to direct American interference in management.

Differences in the amount of information sent by American affiliates to their parent companies are striking. At one end of the spectrum was the branch enterprise which sent its parent six copies of every invoice and every letter handled by the local operation.[8] Another firm forwarded two copies of every invoice, while a third despatched to the parent company a duplicate of every letter written by the manager of the subsidiary. It is interesting that none of these three companies employed any Americans in Australia. At the other extreme was the Australian-American venture (in which the American shareholding was only a minority) which commented that 'we don't do any reporting—except annually when we tell them what dividend we're going to declare'. Another firm in which the American shareholding was a minority one said that quarterly sales reports are 'normally sent but we haven't worried about this lately'. Even a wholly American firm, which now sends very brief monthly reports (of about six figures, covering such main aggregates as total sales, total profits, etc.), 'didn't even send annual accounts sometimes' at one stage of its history in Australia.

Between these extremes lie the great majority of the American direct-investment enterprises in Australia. An attempt has been made

[8] This company sent the questionnaires used in the present survey to its parent company, not to seek permission to answer them, but to have them actually answered completely.

I

to classify companies by the frequency and detail of their reporting, and it has been found that of the 94 companies which provided sufficient information to make classification possible, 43 reported frequently and in considerable detail, 28 reported fairly often but in less detail, and 23 reported only infrequently or in very brief terms. It is significant that while 33 of the 43 reporting frequently and in great detail were wholly American, only 3 of the 23 reporting infrequently or in very brief terms were wholly American. The classification is necessarily subject to a wide margin of error but some illustrative comments received in answer to the question seeking information on the methods used to keep in contact with the parent company may be helpful. One rather small firm which kept particularly close contact with its parent stated:

> We send one page sales reports to the U.S. fortnightly and very detailed reports on all financial and production matters monthly. Almost every single item of expenditure, sales, etc. is documented each month in these reports, which are about 50 to 60 pages long. And they must reach the U.S. by the fourteenth day of the following month.

Another company of medium size reports in similar detail. Within five days after the end of each month, a preliminary statement of the month's results is forwarded to the U.S. parent. Within ten days of the end of the month, a summary report of final results for the month is cabled and at the same time a very detailed financial report is despatched by air mail. This latter is a multi-page document and includes statements on total sales, sales by product source, sales by product type, orders (in similar detail), profits, commissions from the sale of American products, etc.—each compared with figures for the previous month and the same two months of the previous year. Finally, by mid-month a general statement of about fifteen pages is posted covering such topics as labour relations, state of the Australian economy, and litigation. Annual statements are sent in even greater detail and an audited financial statement must be in the U.S. three weeks after the end of the financial year.

Not all the forty-three firms classified as being in very close contact with their parent company report as fully as these two examples, but many of them certainly do. The Australian secretary of one food company which had recently been acquired by an American firm believed that his company 'generated more figures' in its first twelve months under American control than in all the several decades of previous Australian ownership. It was not uncommon for executives to preface their answers to this question with comments such as 'we send them information three times daily after meals', or 'our monthly reports include everything but the colour of our executives' hair'.

Typical of companies in the group of firms reporting in less detail was the firm which, though it sent a monthly report on a standardized form, confined its reporting to this one-page document and a statement of sales in twenty-eight product categories. The reports sent by companies in this group are often copies of those prepared for use by the board or management committee of the local firm, and sometimes the forms used for forwarding information are not the 'standardized' reporting forms almost invariably used by firms in very close contact with their parent.

Almost all firms in the group having only infrequent contact with their parent were either very small or principally Australian in ownership. Only one of the twenty-three firms in this group was a large wholly American firm, and in only three other cases was the American shareholding in a majority. In some cases in this group, the American parent only secures copies of monthly reports through its representative on the local board, while in other cases the Australian firm itself does not prepare monthly statements. One executive of a firm in which the American shareholding was in a minority stated that he had been asked to complete standardized reporting forms monthly for consolidation with parent company figures, but he had resisted this pressure. Though this company currently prepares production figures daily, sales and production figures are only sent to the U.S. firm 'occasionally'.

The preceding discussion sheds some light on the question of control. Clearly it is not possible for a parent company to exercise detailed management control on a subsidiary which transmits very little information on its activities. On the other hand, it does not follow that all companies which send very detailed reports on their operations are strictly controlled in all aspects of their life. Several companies indicated that their parent company never queries the information forwarded. Others added that no American executive had visited the Australian operation for a number of years, which obviously made a full understanding of the local situation difficult even in cases where large amounts of information were sent monthly.[9]

Perhaps the most satisfactory way to assess the actual extent of American parental control on the activities of Australian affiliates is to examine the importance of American control over particular areas of management policy. Certainly some firms are controlled in all

[9] By contrast, some subsidiaries regularly receive visits from parent company personnel several times annually, and if any important decision is contemplated visits may be very frequent.

major areas: one firm indicated that, though initiative is often taken in Australia, all decisions of any importance in whatever field must be reviewed by the American company. Another stated that since its biggest asset was its world-wide reputation for quality, Australian management must be 'directly derivative'. The managing director of one large firm was so strictly controlled that he was unable even to decide whether to submit sales figures to an independent firm of accountants for the sake of obtaining useful data on industry sales. Other firms, while carefully controlled in certain crucial decisions, are allowed considerable independence in many other areas. E. R. Barlow (1953: 91-7) has noted that General Motors pursues a policy of requiring considerable information from its foreign subsidiaries while allowing much discretion to the local management. The evidence of L. J. Hartnett (1964: e.g. 69, 77), a former managing director of General Motors-Holden's Pty Ltd in Australia, substantially bears this out. Still others, even some which report to their parent company in great detail, seem to be allowed almost complete freedom. Typical of this group was the small company, in which the American interest was only 50 per cent, which contended that

> even when building a new factory, it is not necessary to seek permission from the U.S. company unless they actually have to put up some additional capital . . . The vice-president in charge of international operations, when asked his opinion on a decision being made, gives advice but always adds that he can't make the decision 12,000 miles away.

Another company, this time of considerable size and with a majority American shareholding, contended that on principle its parent company 'only gives suggestions'. Even some wholly American companies are in this group: an executive of one such company stated that 'if we are planning a very major expansion here, we send a very full report of the planned expansion and its justification. But it is more to keep them in the picture and to get their advice than to get their approval.'

Capital expenditure is substantially the most carefully controlled aspect of the operation of Australian affiliates of American firms, as Table V-4 illustrates.[10] Of the ninety-five firms that answered the section of Questionnaire II dealing with this subject, seventy-five stated that U.S. approval had to be obtained before embarking on any major capital expenditure (though in some cases it was clear that seeking parental approval was almost as much a matter of courtesy as a matter of necessity). At least three of those which felt themselves

---

[10] Control over the sale of exports, however, is also exercised in some detail in many cases. Discussion of this aspect is deferred till chapter IX.

TABLE V–4   Parent Company Control Over Four Aspects of the Management of 95 American-affiliated Companies, by Percentage of American Ownership

Policy decision	Companies which had an American equity of			Total
	25–49%	50–99%	100%	
Major capital expenditure				
(i) Companies which must seek U.S. approval	3	19	53	75
(ii) Companies which may act independently	11	8	1	20
Product innovation and development				
(i) Companies which must seek U.S. approval	2	11	45	58
(ii) Companies which may act independently	12	16	9	37
Production planning				
(i) Companies which must seek U.S. approval	..	1	9	10
(ii) Companies which may act independently	14	26	45	85
Wages policy and labour relations				
(i) Companies which must seek U.S. approval	..	..	5	5
(ii) Companies which may act independently	14	27	49	90

to be free of American control, moreover, qualified this, either by saying that this freedom was subject to the internal generation of funds for the purpose, or by admitting that beyond a certain high figure permission would be required. There were wide differences in the freedom of different companies to spend money on capital expansion, even among those which felt themselves controlled. One fairly small firm said that 'all capital projects, even expenditure of £10 on a permanent article, must be approved in the U.S.' Another firm of comparable size indicated a maximum discretionary limit of $US500, except for annual authorizations which the U.S. company approved in general terms in advance, and the same firm stressed that this limit applied whether the funds involved reinvested profits or 'new capital' from the parent company. But these two firms were the most strictly controlled in this regard of any encountered. Of the twenty firms that specified a limit above which capital expenditure must be approved by the U.S. parent, three mentioned a figure of £1,000 or less, ten mentioned a figure above £1,000 but not more than £5,000, four mentioned a figure of above £5,000 but not more than £20,000, one firm mentioned £25,000, one £50,000, and one £150,000. Another firm indicated that it can spend without restriction on plant and machinery, provided more cash is not required from the U.S., but has to seek U.S. approval for the purchase of any new land or the construction of any new buildings. Of course, a limit which may be very restrictive for a large company may be very liberal for a small one, and the figures quoted above do in fact cover a wide range of company sizes. To illustrate the point, the five companies that mentioned a discretionary limit of $US5,000 had employment in 1962 of 106, 116, 146, 314, and more than 2,000 respectively.

In other areas of policy, U.S. control is not so close. Most wholly American companies must seek parental approval before embarking on the production of a new product or substantially altering an old one, though at least one firm mentioned that this control applied only to products initially designed by the U.S. company. The great majority of firms are independent of American control in planning production, and very few indeed must seek parental approval of decisions in the field of wages and labour relations.

While the areas of management decision-making surveyed are too few to permit of dogmatic conclusions, the impression is one of strict control in particular areas of policy, combined with considerable freedom in others.[11] Obviously there are some American affiliates which are free from American control in all areas of policy. These are mainly firms in which the American shareholding is less than 50 per cent, some of which made it very plain that their U.S. affiliate is quite unable to block any move which the Australian management wish to take. Of the eight firms in the '50-99%' category which indicated that they could take decisions with regard to capital expenditure without recourse to their American affiliate, six firms were only 50 per cent American, and the other two were very small. The only wholly American firm which felt itself able to embark on capital expenditure without parental approval appeared to be granted a very substantial measure of freedom in all respects.

In the great majority of companies examined, the initiative for a major capital outlay, or major management decision of any kind, comes from the local management, wherever the locus of final authority. Of seventy-four firms which commented on the source of

[11] Information was sought on the freedom of local management in some areas of policy other than those mentioned in the text, but because of ambiguities and misunderstandings the answers received were unsuitable for tabulation. Very few companies made specific mention of parent company control over the pricing of final products. Of three which did, one mentioned that all pricing decisions involving materials imported from the U.S. company are very strictly controlled in the U.S.; another mentioned an international pricing agreement on the sale of its output; and the third stated that while at one time the U.S. company had urged all foreign subsidiaries to price their products to yield an operating income of 20 per cent on sales, this policy had been dropped because of pressure from the Australian subsidiary for a lower price.

initiative for a major decision, sixty-eight felt that initiative almost invariably stems from local management in Australia, five felt that management in both Australia and the U.S. take initiative about equally, and one felt that almost all initiative comes from the U.S. company.

J. H. Dunning (1958: 112) observed in Britain that American-affiliated companies tend to become more loosely controlled as the years go by. Such a tendency was not apparent among the companies examined in the present survey. When the companies included in Table V-4 were classified by ownership and date at which manufacture began, the proportion of 'controlled' companies was almost identical among companies which began manufacture before 1957 as among companies which began manufacture in 1957 or subsequently, within each ownership category. This conclusion was reached in all four areas of management decision-making. The problem was approached in a different way by asking companies directly how they felt the control exercised over them now compares with that exercised immediately after manufacturing was begun in Australia. The answers to this question, from fifty-two firms which began manufacturing in Australia before 1957, produce a result which may be more meaningful than that achieved by comparing control in particular areas of policy by date at which manufacture began. Seventeen of the fifty-two firms felt the control now exercised over them to be stronger than that exercised in the years immediately after manufacture began here, seventeen felt the control to be about the same, and eighteen felt it to be weaker. But there is an interesting variation in the pattern of responses which is concealed by these aggregate figures. Among the twenty-one firms in which American equity in 1962 was less than 100 per cent, only three indicated that control in 1962 was stronger than in earlier years (and in the case of all three firms the U.S. shareholding exceeded 70 per cent), eight indicated control to be about the same, and ten indicated that control had become weaker. Among the thirty-one wholly American firms, on the other hand, the pattern was reversed: only eight firms felt that control is now weaker than in the establishment period, nine felt it to be about the same, and fourteen felt that control had become stronger.

Various reasons were suggested to explain the increase in parental control experienced by such a significant fraction of wholly American subsidiaries. Some executives felt it was the effect of developments in air transport and the growth of relatively cheap long-distance telecommunications. Others felt that growth in scientific management in the U.S. had been an important factor. Undoubtedly important also is the fact that as foreign operations generally become a more significant part of the total activity of more and more American corporations, an increasing number of firms establish international divisions within their corporate structure to permit a closer watch to be kept on foreign subsidiaries. A further increase in control in the case of some companies may therefore be the prospect for the future.

Some of the independence enjoyed by so many American affiliates in Australia is certainly a result of their satisfactory performance. One company controller stated that the executives of his company 'have bags of independence—till something goes wrong. Then the boot really goes in!' Several others expressed a similar sentiment. The writer visited one long-established company which was actually in the process of being 'renovated' by a number of Americans sent out to discover why it had begun to operate unprofitably. The company had experienced a sharp fall in sales and the problem was to reduce overhead costs commensurately. The four Americans detailed to solve the problem—one budgeting and costing expert, one administrative and sales expert, and two production experts— helped in the installation of a new electronic computer, advised on data processing systems, amalgamated five previously almost independent divisions into one, and secured the dismissal of more than two hundred employees. To keep things running smoothly, an American was appointed assistant to the Australian managing director for two years.

When attention is turned from the question of American control to that of American influence over the *techniques* used by the management of Australian affiliates, the problem of assessing the true situation is just as difficult as before. Because of the wide dissemination of advanced management techniques throughout the industrialized world, many of them having their origin in the United States, the executives of progressive companies in Australia as elsewhere would in many cases be using 'American techniques' whether or not their companies were American in ownership.

To gain a general impression, companies were asked whether the management techniques employed by them had, as a whole, benefited strongly, moderately, or negligibly from their association with an American company. Ninety-eight companies answered the question, and of these 38 felt they had benefited strongly, 38 moderately, and 22 negligibly. There are significant differences in the answers received by companies of different ownership pattern. None of the firms in which the American equity was in a minority felt that it had benefited strongly from the management techniques of its American affiliate, and only 6 of the 14 in this category felt that the benefit had been moderate. Wholly American firms, on the other hand, believed they had received much greater benefit in the field of management, 28 of 57 feeling the benefit to be strong and another 22 feeling it to be moderate. The 27 firms in which the American equity was between 50 and 99 per cent occupied an intermediate position, 10 feeling they had benefited strongly, 10 moderately, and 7 negligibly.

It is possible that these answers exaggerate the importance of American management techniques to the companies studied. Companies were also asked to indicate to what extent specific areas of

TABLE V–5   Parent Company Influence on Management Techniques and Methods in 95 American-affiliated Companies, by Percentage of American Ownership

Field of management	Companies which had an American equity of			
	25–49%	50–99%	100%	Total
Production planning				
Techniques influenced by U.S. company				
(i) Strongly	3	4	10	17
(ii) Moderately	..	8	16	24
(iii) Negligibly	11	15	28	54
Budgetary planning and costing				
Techniques influenced by U.S. company				
(i) Strongly	..	6	23	29
(ii) Moderately	2	10	20	32
(iii) Negligibly	12	11	11	34
Plant supervision and manufacturing methods				
Techniques influenced by U.S. company				
(i) Strongly	4	9	14	27
(ii) Moderately	4	5	21	30
(iii) Negligibly	6	13	19	38
Sales and distribution				
Techniques influenced by U.S. company				
(i) Strongly	..	2	14	16
(ii) Moderately	3	11	21	35
(iii) Negligibly	11	14	19	44
Wages policy and labour relations				
Influenced by U.S. company				
(i) Strongly	..	1	3	4
(ii) Moderately	..	3	12	15
(iii) Negligibly	14	23	39	76
Purchasing techniques				
Influenced by U.S. company				
(i) Strongly	..	2	3	5
(ii) Moderately	..	4	14	18
(iii) Negligibly	14	21	37	72
Administrative techniques				
Influenced by U.S. company				
(i) Strongly	..	1	11	12
(ii) Moderately	3	10	24	37
(iii) Negligibly	11	16	19	46

management were influenced by the techniques and attitudes of their American parent. The answers to this question provided by ninety-five companies are shown in Table V-5, which shows the importance of American influence in each of seven separate fields. The seven fields are, rather obviously, not mutually exclusive. Moreover, the category designated 'plant supervision and manufacturing methods' was interpreted by some companies to mean the techniques of production rather than the organization of production, as intended, a misinterpretation which leads to some overstatement of the importance of American influence in that field. Even with these qualifications the impression is interesting, however. As before, firms in which the American shareholding was in the minority appear to have been influenced to only a slight degree by American techniques of management. Even in the case of wholly American firms, however, the proportion of companies which felt that American techniques of management had influenced them strongly was in no area higher than twenty-three out of fifty-four firms, in the field of budgetary planning and costing. In most other fields, the number which felt themselves strongly influenced by American management techniques was substantially less than this. While companies which are strongly influenced by American techniques may or may not feel benefit from them, it is certainly not possible for companies that are negligibly affected by American techniques to receive benefit from them, and a surprising number of the companies covered in the table did not feel themselves influenced by American techniques of management in more than a few areas.

All companies were asked whether Australians are sent to the U.S. company for training and, if so, whether this is primarily for training in management techniques or technical aspects of the firm's work. As Table V-6 shows, only 6 of the 110 respondents to this question send employees to the U.S. primarily for training in management techniques, though a further 32 firms felt unable to distinguish the 'primary' purpose of their training visits. It is probable, of course, that many of the firms sending employees primarily for training in technical subjects also send men for training in management techniques. On the other hand, the interpretation placed on the phrase 'period of training' by some companies tended to be liberal and included in a few cases brief visits by company executives once in two or three years. It appears beyond doubt that training in American techniques of management plays a smaller part than training in technical aspects in the programme of most American affiliates in Australia. (It is interesting that five of the six firms sending employees to the U.S. for training primarily in management techniques were wholly American in ownership, as also

TABLE V–6   Training of Australian Personnel in the United States by 110 American-affiliated Companies, by Percentage of American Ownership

	Companies which had an American equity of			
	25–49%	50–99%	100%	Total
Companies sending no personnel to U.S. for training	7	7	12	26
Companies sending personnel to U.S. for training				
(i) Primarily in management techniques	..	1	5	6
(ii) Primarily in scientific or technical fields	10	16	20	46
(iii) Equally in both management techniques and scientific or technical fields	..	6	26	32
Total	17	30	63	110

were twenty-six of the thirty-two firms sending employees for training equally in both management techniques and technical areas.)

Many American-affiliated firms have not been influenced at all by American management techniques. In some cases this is because the techniques evolved in the American affiliate for control of a vast corporate structure are quite unsuited to the management of a relatively tiny operation in Australia. In a number of cases the contact between parent and affiliate is too slight to permit the Australian operation to derive any real benefit on the management level. One quite substantial wholly American firm, which indicated on the survey questionnaire that American techniques have benefited it 'moderately', confessed that the only real benefit it derived from the U.S. company in the field of 'management' was cheap access to American advertising material and radio and television programmes! In fifteen years only six Americans had visited the company, and the only movement in the opposite direction was a visit every two or three years by the Australian managing director. One small wholly American firm stated that in more than thirty years of production in Australia only two Americans from the parent company had visited the subsidiary, and in the last fifteen years only two Australians had visited the parent company. This firm, however, frankly admitted that the benefit derived from its parent company in the field of management techniques was negligible.

There were other reasons why some firms felt they were little influenced by American management techniques. Several companies (in none of which the American equity exceeded 50 per cent) stated that though they did produce monthly reports in considerable detail this practice was quite unrelated to their association with an American company. In most of these cases the Australian shareholder was a large company accustomed to producing such reports for its own operations. No fewer than eight more firms, four of them wholly American, felt that their American affiliates had nothing to teach them in the field of management. One of these stated that its parent company was making a profit of $US50 million only because it was too inefficient to make a profit of $US100 million. An executive in another firm complained that it took the parent company three weeks to despatch an order to the Australian subsidiary, while in yet another subsidiary a senior executive resented the fact that the parent company preferred to do all its 'correspondence' on recording tapes, which permitted parent company executives to be very verbose.

In the case of some jointly-owned firms, American techniques of management are not introduced because of a desire on the part of the American shareholder to preserve the co-operation of the Australian management, particularly when the American company has acquired an interest in an already existing firm. Among the firms visited there were certainly some which gave the impression of such inefficiency that it was difficult to believe that 'American techniques' as usually understood had had any impact on them at all.

In many companies American techniques are adopted in a few selected areas but are ignored in others. Thus, the American manager of one joint venture was able to convince other executives of the desirability of 'technical services selling' as a sales technique but was quite unable to change their attitudes in most other areas. The managing director of another firm who felt that U.S. marketing expertise had been perhaps the most important single factor in the growth of his company in Australia also felt that 'the aura of American competency [in management] is often in the imagination —many suggestions on improving managerial efficiency have gone from this company to the U.S.' Several firms mentioned in particular the American approach to quality control: one previously wholly Australian firm commented that

> by Australian standards the U.S. company goes to quite extreme lengths. We first discovered this when we exported some of our products to them and had them rejected all the time. As a result we had to install procedures which in fact have improved *all* our production. Ten years ago we would have regarded their approach as involving intolerable paper work.

The manager of a newly-established branch concern was told, on requesting from the parent company a procedural manual for his guidance, to sort out his own methods: only techniques of quality

control and of production were specified. In another field of management, a jointly-owned firm whose methods are mainly those of the
non-American shareholder has adopted the practice evolved by the
American shareholder of sending blank cheques with small orders
as a means of reducing paper work and securing maximum discounts
for cash payment. On the other hand, a large wholly American firm
which is substantially influenced in its techniques by those of its
parent turned to an independent firm of management consultants
when it wanted to reduce its transportation costs.

One Australian-American firm which felt that the American
shareholder had not been of great use in modernizing its accounting
methods nevertheless felt that it was because of an impending issue
of shares to an American firm that the previously wholly Australian
firm had been forced to reorganize its methods.

Despite some evidence to the contrary, it is nevertheless beyond
doubt that very many of the large wholly American subsidiaries
operating in Australia have been substantially influenced by American management techniques. In a limited number of cases, executives
of these firms regard the American influence as one designed
primarily to standardize the procedures used by affiliates throughout
the world, and not of great benefit in itself. A few companies even
resent the amount of detail which American techniques compel
them to evaluate, but for the most part the benefit is both real and
appreciated. A number of companies said that it was the necessity
to meet reporting deadlines imposed in the U.S. which had forced
them to improve efficiency. A comment from the company secretary
of quite a small firm was typical:

> The U.S. company sent us a very detailed operating manual on
> the financial side. It caused a lot of heart-burning to begin with
> but we are now reaping the benefit. We now compile complete
> and final monthly accounts (even down to the calculation of
> depreciation), and we are aiming to get these to the U.S. by the
> seventh working day of the following month. This gets progres-
> sively easier and enables much better production planning and
> financial forecasting.

The chief accountant of another firm felt that the U.S. company had
not directly helped to improve efficiency in the Australian subsidiary, though the local firm had the use of two very large procedural manuals covering every aspect of accounting, but the very
detailed budgetary planning which the local firm was compelled to
do had made it conscious of cost and efficiency in a new way.

A senior Australian executive of one large company felt that,
though he had spent a period training in the American company

some years ago, it was the 'atmosphere' of the company rather than any particular techniques that were of especial benefit. He had recently conducted an inventory study, using advanced exponential functions, and had discovered that whereas stocks equal to nine months' sales were then being kept to give a 'probability coverage' of 82 per cent, by readjusting the composition of the stocks somewhat a coverage of more than 90 per cent could be obtained with stock equivalent to less than three months' sales. He commented that 'in total management technology, we're so far ahead of Australian companies that it worries me. In the techniques of management control, the average Australian company is twenty years behind— they know almost nothing about it.'

The benefit received by another Australian subsidiary from management techniques developed by its parent company was outlined in the following terms:

> Management procedures for control of all aspects of our business are constantly being strengthened and improved by our International Accounting Systems Department in the United States. The benefit of studies and experience in mechanization and automation of manual and clerical procedures is constantly being passed on to us, avoiding the necessity for us to adopt the even more costly 'trial and error' method. Company consulting teams visit all subsidiaries, reviewing systems and procedures, enabling us to reduce costs and improve control procedures.
>
> Latest cash-flow analysis techniques are developed and used by the Australian subsidiary to evaluate the economics of capital investment proposals, enabling us to continually up-grade production processes and lower production costs.

How much more efficient than their Australian competitors this assistance makes some American firms was noted in another case by the Tariff Board. Evaluating the need of local tractor manufacturers for assistance in 1955, the Board recommended in favour of some assistance for the main locally-owned firm in the industry, even though it was obviously not as efficient as the main foreign manufacturer, International Harvester Co. of Australia Pty Ltd. The Board made the comment that it

> does not interpret its requirement of efficiency in the sense that every industry seeking protection should have the high standard set by International Harvester Company of Australia Pty. Ltd. There are few industries in Australia that would qualify for protection or assistance under such an interpretation. And while it is comforting to know that there is in Australia an engineering industry capable of producing an intricate piece of machinery without protection or assistance—an industry setting a standard

for other industries—the Board takes the sensible view that an industry or a unit of an industry is not necessarily inefficient because it fails to reach that high standard. (*T.B.R.* 1955b: 10.)

Though it appears that the larger the Australian subsidiary and the higher the proportion of American equity in it the more important is American influence on local management techniques likely to be, there are numerous exceptions to this generalization. One very small firm was encountered which, though too small to make use of American purchasing techniques (which presupposed a large purchasing department), made use of American techniques in most other fields. The general manager had two volumes of instructions, each four inches thick, about all aspects of management. These covered such matters as the correct method of filing letters and orders, when quality inspections should be conducted in the manufacturing process and when 'batch cards' should be initialled, the best way of running an employee suggestions scheme, and the way to establish a purchasing department. Though having employment in 1962 of less than forty, the company took very seriously its responsibility to educate customers in the various uses of its products. On another occasion, a small jointly-owned firm was encountered, in which the American equity was in a minority moreover, which had adopted the accounting procedures of its American affiliate in their entirety. Indeed, such adoption had been a condition imposed by the American firm for the establishment of the joint venture.

The effect of American ownership on management techniques is perhaps most graphically seen where a previously Australian company is acquired by an American firm. One firm which now prepares detailed sales and financial reports monthly for comparison with predetermined targets never produced a sales budget before it was acquired by an American company, and only produced a very small manufacturing budget. Another firm of moderate size, in the food industry, used to budget on an annual basis before acquisition by an American company, but now budgets twice yearly—and revises the budget quarterly. Moreover, every quarter a cash forecast covering a period of two years is prepared. In the field of sales the company has dropped a number of lines on which profit margin was very low in order to concentrate on a smaller number of more profitable items.

The impression that emerges from this varied evidence seems to be that something like half the American-affiliated subsidiaries manufacturing in Australia have derived very substantial benefit from the adoption of techniques of management evolved by their American parents. Most, though by no means all, of this fraction are wholly

American firms, and many of them are very large. For the other firms, American management techniques are either not important at all or are important only within a very limited area.[12]

As an addendum to this chapter on management, it is interesting to examine the attitude of American-affiliated firms in Australia to the payment of wages and salaries. It is important to recognize that most companies in the survey felt that U.S. influence is weaker in this area than in almost any other (as can be seen in Table V-5), so that evidence produced here must not be regarded as typical of American influence in other areas of management. On the other hand, a number of writers (Behrman 1962c: 147; Blyth and Carty 1956: 452; Dunning 1958: 254) have presented very definite views on this subject, and it is important to portray the situation as it was found here. Most writers have contended that American direct-investment enterprises tend to pay a higher total remuneration per employee than do locally-owned companies, and some have even asserted that the wage *rates* paid by American enterprises are higher than those paid by local firms. F. N. Bennett (1961: 15-16), however, has argued that the higher than average income which employees in American direct-investment enterprises in Australia receive, according to U.S. Department of Commerce figures, is a result of the concentration of American-owned firms in industries where the

---

[12] In chapter I it was mentioned that wherever possible attention would be drawn to ways in which American affiliates differ significantly from other foreign subsidiaries. On the evidence available it would be presumptuous for the writer to make any definite judgment on the relative contributions of American and other foreign subsidiaries in the field of management techniques. It should perhaps be noted, however, that a significant number of executives spontaneously voiced dissatisfaction with the management of United Kingdom companies (even British-managed subsidiaries of American companies) with which they had dealings—complaining in particular about unreliability of deliveries. Australian executives in several firms indicated that they prefer to pay a higher price for an American product than depend on the punctual delivery of a British-made product. One man who had previously been employed by a British subsidiary in Australia and is now a senior executive with an American subsidiary felt that Australia is learning far more about the techniques of mass production from American firms here than from British. A management consultant quoted earlier as believing that American executives employed in Australia tend to be either very good or very poor indicated that even if they are poor they are more competent than British executives in Australia. The writer met one American manager who was particularly critical of the methods of British management, even including in his criticism the British executives of some American-owned companies in Australia. In fairness it should be added that during the course of the survey the writer also met several British managers who were obviously efficient.

average income received by employees in all companies is higher than the national average.

Relevant evidence derived from the present survey is presented for the most part in Table V-7. This shows that the average income received by an employee in the factory of one of the ninety-nine American-affiliated companies covered was almost 16 per cent higher in 1961/2 than the average income received by employees in all Australian manufacturing industry. An important part of the explanation of this figure is the greater than average 'maleness' of the employment of American-affiliated companies, but even in the individual categories of the table employees in the American-affiliated firms received a significantly higher total income than did those in Australian industry as a whole.

The industrial classification of the table shows that Bennett was correct in his belief that American-affiliated firms tend to cluster in those industries where the average wage for the whole industry is higher than that for manufacturing as a whole, though of course in some cases the presence of American companies may itself play a part in raising the industry average. But it also appears beyond doubt that even within each industry American-affiliated firms on average pay higher total incomes to their employees than do firms without American connections. This is the case in all the main industries except 'Food, drink, tobacco'. Moreover, because the figures for each industry include those for American-affiliated firms, the difference between the latter and Australian or other non-American firms is even greater than is shown. This bias is only significant in industries where American capital is particularly important, and the greatest error is in the industry designated 'Motor vehicle construction and assembly, and motor bodies'. Here the exclusion of the American firms from the total reduces the average payment for 1961/2 from £1,191 to £1,070, compared with an average payment by American firms of £1,291.

A number of factors could explain this phenomenon. Being larger than Australian firms on average, American firms might employ more specialized—and so more highly paid—labour than Australian-owned firms. This appears a likely possibility, but unfortunately the evidence to prove it is lacking. It may be that within each of the industries covered in Table V-7 there are sub-industries in which the American firms operate, and in which the total wage payments of American firms are only typical of the non-American firms; but this does not seem likely.

In an attempt to shed more light on the wage policies of American-affiliated firms, most companies were questioned on the subject. Only three companies felt that, because of American influence, they paid

K

TABLE V-7 Wage and Salary Payments Per Employee in Australian and American-affiliated Factories in 1961/2, by Industry, Category of Employee, and Sex[a]

£A

Industry	Managerial and clerical staff, chemists, draftsmen, etc.		Wages staff		Total		
	Male	Female	Male	Female	Male	Female	Persons
Industrial chemicals	1,968 (1,773)	855 (778)	1,452 (1,286)	863 (595)	1,593 (1,398)	859 (712)	1,477 (1,314)
Pharmaceuticals and toilet preparations	1,766 (2,089)	847 (914)	1,164 (1,072)	674 (619)	1,339 (1,396)	734 (681)	1,049 (1,000)
Plant, equipment, and machinery	1,638 (1,597)	774 (732)	1,189 (1,111)	688 (645)	1,301 (1,190)	753 (694)	1,229 (1,137)
Electrical machinery, cables, and apparatus	1,839 (1,563)	754 (757)	1,148 (1,133)	728 (681)	1,292 (1,208)	733 (703)	1,099 (1,089)
Motor vehicle construction and assembly, and motor bodies	1,754 (1,667)	880 (771)	1,239 (1,148)	752 (745)	1,316 (1,216)	827 (764)	1,291 (1,191)
Motor accessories	1,987 (1,580)	830 (751)	1,303 (1,154)	650 (678)	1,414 (1,243)	697 (698)	1,276 (1,095)
Other metal products	1,664 (1,555)	811 (700)	1,164 (1,099)	712 (686)	1,242 (1,150)	755 (692)	1,199 (1,105)
Foundation garments	1,663 (1,934)	788 (798)	1,033 (1,030)	580 (581)	1,270 (1,325)	606 (598)	713 (675)
Food, drink, tobacco	1,574 (1,552)	751 (715)	1,103 (1,110)	603 (672)	1,165 (1,169)	630 (682)	1,008 (1,033)
Paper, stationery, printing, etc.	2,640 (1,689)	741 (761)	1,130 (1,238)	685 (638)	1,404 (1,300)	698 (671)	1,170 (1,135)
Other products	1,937	761	1,215	658	1,357	692	1,222
Total	1,779	813	1,217	685	1,317	728	1,220
Total manufacturing	(1,605)	(741)	(1,112)	(651)	(1,176)	(671)	(1,054)

[a] Figures not in parentheses refer to wage and salary payments per employee in the factories of 99 American-affiliated companies. Those in parentheses relate to payments for the whole of the Australian industry concerned, including the American-affiliated companies. For further explanatory notes, see Appendix B.

substantially more to wages staff than other companies in their industry. One of these companies, the Lincoln Electric Co. (Aust.) Pty Ltd, has become known throughout business circles in Australia for its revolutionary approach to wages. The company, which is by no means among the giants of Australian industry, operates a system of job evaluation and merit rating which, it claims, makes its workers the highest paid in its industry in Australia. In its first twenty-four years of operation in Australia (to 1964) the company distributed more than £900,000 in annual bonuses based on profit sharing (in addition to substantial fortnightly production bonuses), and in 1963 the lowest annual bonus paid is reported to have been £125. Two other firms provided somewhat similar, if rather less spectacular, examples. The manager of another company contended that 'we pay our workers more than any other shop in town', though this was because of the manager's personal dislike of trade unions, not because of American influence.

There are in fact quite a number of American-affiliated firms which, though not paying substantially above average wages, do try to keep their wages a little above the average in their industry. One large firm said that parent company policy throughout the world is to pay wages '*at least* equal to the going rate in the local community —we don't have to be the leader, but we would certainly never lag behind'. Several firms made comments of a similar kind. One executive described his company's wage policy as 'probably a little more liberal than the wage policies of most Australian companies. All wages and salaries are reviewed twice yearly and if everybody's doing well there is a 5 per cent annual increase across the board.'

Probably more common than companies which consciously pay their workers above average wages are companies which maintain better than average 'fringe benefit' schemes or, in a few cases, profit sharing schemes. One firm which indicated that 'our approach [to wages] is strongly influenced by Australian conditions' also said that it had operated an 'employee superannuation scheme long before they became general in Australia', while another making a similar comment on its wages had a very generous system of Christmas bonuses. In one newly-established company, the secretary said that the American company 'has a very parental attitude to its employees and the same attitude is being introduced here. At the moment we haven't got any more social amenities for employees than the typical Australian company but we're working to change that in line with our world-wide policy.' One large company has a scheme whereby employees may purchase parent company shares at 85 per cent of market value with up to 10 per cent of their annual salary, and another operates a bonus system which results in the annual distribution of a fixed percentage (currently $1\frac{3}{4}$ per cent) of each employee's total five-yearly income.

The majority of American-affiliated firms contacted, however, felt that wage payments are entirely governed by Australian factors. One American executive commented that 'flat award rates are paid' and went on to add that only trade unions advocate bonus or incentive schemes. Another wholly American company, defending its efficiency before the Tariff Board, explained that 'it had become necessary to pay above award rates to skilled employees such as fitters, carpenters and electricans, in order to obtain their services in competition with other industries in the area. It did not consider that these payments were greater than those made by other industries in the locality.' (*T.B.R.* 1962a: 8.) An executive in one large branch operation queried the meaning of the question on wages policy since 'that is all covered by awards'. When asked whether the singularly good employee amenity block—a building so impressive that the writer cannot have been the first to mistake it for the main administrative offices—was built as a result of American influence, the Australian executive quite frankly admitted it had been built during the early fifties to attract labour at a time of acute labour shortage.

A surprising number of companies (at least eight) said that though wages staff are paid at the general level prevailing in the industry, executive staff are paid according to 'American principles'. In some cases this means merely the use of some management incentive or bonus scheme, but in at least one case Australian executives are paid the Australian currency equivalent of the salaries received by executives of similar status in the U.S. company, plus the bonuses to which American executives are entitled. (Interestingly, this is despite the fact that there are no Americans in the Australian subsidiary to generate tension on relative salary levels.)

In only one case was an American-owned firm encountered which openly admitted that until recently its wages staff had been paid less than employees in other parts of the industry. The executive explained that some American executives had built an argument for fixing wages on the most poorly paid firms they could find and that it was only when the company began to lose too many of its employees that the situation was remedied. The same company still retains a salary structure for its Australian executives which compares most unfavourably at every level with the salary of comparable executives in Australian-owned companies. The executive interviewed, a man who gave an impression of competency surpassed by none and equalled by few of all the executives interviewed, had been told by a firm of chartered accountants that in any large Australian company he could be expected to receive an annual salary of from

£4,750 to £5,250. 'Allowing for some exaggeration on their part, you could say that £4,500 is a reasonable figure. Till a few months ago, I was on £3,200.' At the time of the survey he was still receiving a salary of less than £4,000.

How common it is for American-affiliated firms to pay their employees less than the 'going rate' is not known. It would appear that the firm quoted above is not an isolated example, though its experience does not seem to have been common. One long-established engineering firm, in which the American shareholding was 75 per cent in 1962, has been accused by a trade union organizer of being 'the lowest-paid shop in the area' (*Sydney Morning Herald*, 7 Mar. 1964), and the writer was told that in at least one of the very large wholly American firms executives are paid salaries below those typical in Australian-owned firms of comparable size and status. Indeed one Australian executive contended that he had been told by a firm of chartered accountants that, with a few notable exceptions, American subsidiaries in Australia tend in general to pay their top Australian executives rather poorly. But the admittedly limited evidence of this survey does not seem to support this conclusion, and for every executive who felt that salaries paid by American firms are generally low there was another who felt that they are generally rather high.

The remaining data gathered on the subject of wages and salaries are also inconclusive. Because a number of companies seemed to pay their salaried staff 'above average' incomes but their wages staff only 'the going rate', an examination was made of the relative incomes received by 'Managerial and clerical staff, chemists, draftsmen, etc.' and by 'Wages staff'. If attention be confined to male employees, it appears that salaried staff in American-affiliated factories were paid on average 10·8 per cent more than salaried staff in Australian industry as a whole in 1961/2. In the same year, wages staff in American-affiliated factories received 9·4 per cent more than average. When the figures for individual factories are examined the picture is the same. Of the 152 comparisons possible,[13] 90 paid salaried staff more than the average for their industry and 62 paid them less. On the other hand, 86 paid wages staff more than average for their industry and 66 paid them less. Clearly the difference in the approach to the payment of salaried and wages staff in American-affiliated firms is negligible. If there is any 'American influence', it either applies to both groups equally or to only a very small number of executive personnel.

---

[13] In some cases companies gave consolidated data for all their factories. Here the comparisons were taken on a company basis. In other cases there were no salaried males employed in the factory, and in these cases no comparison was possible.

Though the wages and salaries paid by American-affiliated firms in Australia are higher than those ruling in Australian industry as a whole, the rate of growth of wage and salary payments per employee in American-affiliated firms has been almost identical with that in Australian industry. Twenty-one companies, with total employment in 1962 of 47,864, provided information on total manufacturing employment and total wage and salary payments for each year from 1952/3 to 1961/2. The average payment to employees in this group rose from £831·3 in 1952/3 to £1,253·4 in 1961/2, a growth of 50·8 per cent. At the same time, the average payment for all Australian manufacturing industry grew from £707 to £1,054, a growth of 49·1 per cent. The slightly faster rate of growth of income payments in American-affiliated firms in fact entirely reflects the influence of the motor vehicle factories of four large companies: wage and salary payments per employee in these factories grew by 53·6 per cent over the period, and with their exclusion the rate of growth of other American-affiliated firms falls to only 46·2 per cent. Twenty-five more firms, making a total of forty-six firms, with total 1962 employment of 59,199, provided the data necessary to calculate wage and salary per employee figures for the five years 1957/8 to 1961/2. The average income paid per employee by this group of forty-six firms rose from £1,004·1 in 1957/8 to £1,225·2 in 1961/2, a growth of 22·0 per cent. Over the same years, the average payment for all Australian manufacturing industry grew from £898 to £1,054, a growth of only 17·4 per cent, but again, most of the explanation of the faster than average growth in payments by American-affiliated firms is to be found in the motor vehicle industry, where payments per employee in American-owned plants grew by 25·4 per cent. When this industry is excluded from the American figures, the rate of growth of their wage and salary payments falls to little above the Australian average, at 18·8 per cent.

Finally, it is interesting to compare the rate of growth of wage and salary payments per employee in wholly American firms with that in jointly-owned firms. If American firms do tend to carry abroad the high wage policies some of them adopt in the U.S., it might be expected that wages and salaries per employee would rise more rapidly in wholly American firms, where American influence would be stronger, than in jointly-owned ventures. Examination of the twenty-one firms that provided data on wages for the decade 1952/3 to 1961/2 does seem to provide some support for this thesis. Of the fourteen wholly American firms, wages per employee grew more rapidly than the relevant industry average in ten cases and fell short of the relevant industry average in four cases. By contrast, in only one of the seven jointly-owned firms did payments per employee rise more rapidly than the relevant industry average. In total, wages and salaries per employee rose by 52·2 per cent in the wholly American firms, but only 40·1 per cent in the jointly-owned firms (compared with a national average of 49·1 per cent). Even with the exclusion of factories in the motor vehicle industry, wages and salaries per employee in the remaining wholly American plants rose by 49·7 per cent, substantially above the growth experienced in the jointly-owned firms. But the evidence afforded by the forty-six firms that provided data for the period 1957/8 to 1961/2 (including, of course, the twenty-one which provided data for the full decade) is not so clear. In seventeen of the twenty-nine wholly American firms, payments per employee grew more rapidly than the relevant industry average, and in twelve cases they grew more slowly. By contrast, in eight of the seventeen jointly-owned firms payments per employee grew more rapidly than the industry average, and in nine cases they grew more slowly. In total, wages per employee rose by 22·4 per cent in the wholly American firms, compared with a national rise of 17·4 per cent, but the rise in jointly-owned firms was 20·2 per cent, little short of the rise in wholly American firms. When plants in the motor vehicle industry are excluded from the wholly American group, the average rate of growth of income payments in this group falls to only 17·7 per cent, below the average growth in the jointly-owned firms and only marginally above the average growth for all Australian manufacturing.

Dogmatic conclusions appear inappropriate. Some American subsidiaries in Australia do make a policy of rewarding their employees at least marginally more highly than do Australian-owned firms, and among firms that adopt this policy are some of the largest. But these cases aside, there is little doubt that most American subsidiaries, like most Australian companies, pay wages which are no higher than necessary.

VI

Technical Benefits

It has been widely recognized in Australia that the technical and scientific know-how transferred by foreign companies to their affiliates in this country is one of the most important benefits of foreign investment. Surveying Australia's post-war industrial development in 1955, D. M. Hocking contended that 'it is hardly an exaggeration to say that in every rapidly changing industry practically every major innovation was introduced by a firm wholly or part owned by one or more overseas firms'. He went on to argue that,

> whatever basis of evaluation is adopted, overseas companies must be given the credit for most of Australia's technological progress in the post-war period . . . I have estimated that about one third of the American and one quarter of the U.K. firms which have commenced manufacturing in this country since the end of the [Second World] war have done so with the specific purpose of introducing a new product or process. (1955: 8, 9.)

Writing three years later (1958: 28-9), he observed that Australian subsidiaries or licensees of foreign companies, comprising just over 21 per cent of his sample of 903 companies operating in Australia, were responsible for 54 per cent of all the innovations introduced by this group of companies over the period 1939 to 1953. Of firms responsible for major innovations (those leading to an investment of more than £1 million), 83 per cent had overseas affiliations (64 per cent by an equity link and 19 per cent by a technical agreement).

The purpose of this chapter is to assess the importance attached to American technical know-how by executives in the group of companies covered in the present survey, and to examine some of the costs of Australia's considerable dependence on the fruits of foreign scientific endeavour.

There is no doubt that most American-affiliated companies operating in Australia believe their access to American technology to be of vital importance to their continued growth, and indeed their continued existence, in the Australian market. Table VI-1 shows that

TABLE VI-1   Assessment of Importance of Technical Information Received from Parent Companies by 75 American-affiliated Companies, by Percentage of American Ownership and Period in which Manufacture Began

Percentage U.S. ownership and period in which Australian manufacture began[a]	Companies assessing access to parent company technology as			
	Of vital importance to all Australian operations	Of vital importance in only one major area of production	Of only moderate importance	Of negligible importance
25–49%: Manufacture began—				
before 1957	4	..	2	1
in or after 1957	4	1	1	..
50–99%: Manufacture began—				
before 1957	6	..	4	..
in or after 1957	10	..	2	..
100%: Manufacture began—				
before 1957	19	1	3	..
in or after 1957	14	2	1	..
Total	57	4	13	1

[a] The year in which manufacture began is taken to be the year in which an American equity of at least 25 per cent was first acquired in the case of companies manufacturing previously as Australian-owned ventures.

fifty-seven of the seventy-five companies that answered the question seeking to clarify the importance attached to American technical know-how indicated that this was vital to their total operation, while another four firms felt that it was vital in one major area of production. Thirteen companies indicated that access to American technical know-how was of moderate benefit, and only one, a firm in which the American equity in 1962 was little more than 25 per cent, regarded the benefit it derived from the know-how of its American affiliate as negligible. (It is significant that this company had a technical know-how agreement with another American firm.) It appears that executives of wholly American firms feel that access to American technology has been more important than do executives of jointly-owned ventures, but the number of companies in the sample is insufficient to draw dogmatic conclusions from this evidence.[1]

Almost always the transfer of American technical know-how involves the provision of detailed designs and blueprints, of formulae, patents, and work methods. Frequently, as seen in Table V-6, personnel from the Australian company are sent to the U.S. parent for a period of training in American production methods. The most comprehensive scheme of this kind encountered is operated by one of the large motor vehicle manufacturers. This company sends about six young men each year to a two-year training course in engineering in the parent company, and in addition Australians are sent for periods ranging from one to six months for training in specific fields when the local company contemplates the introduction of a new or improved product. Each department of the local company also sends one or two men to the parent company annually for a period of 'familiarization', and the manufacturing department may send as many as five for this purpose. Though a training scheme of such dimensions appears exceptional, most of the large firms have some procedure for training local personnel in the U.S. company. A company in the chemical industry, to take another example, sent eight of its senior production men to the United States for a special course associated with the introduction of a new product, and at the time of the survey had just sent two engineers for a period of more than two years on a study tour of parent company plants throughout the U.S.

---

[1] It does seem significant, however, that wholly American companies, in contrast to jointly-owned ones, generally seem to have 'automatic' access to the know-how of their parents. Fifteen companies out of sixteen in which the American equity was complete contended that their access to the technology of their parent companies is 'automatic', but only five of ten companies in which the American equity was between 50 and 99 per cent and only five of eleven companies in which the American equity was less than 50 per cent could make the same contention.

It is impossible to describe in short compass the technical benefit derived by the local affiliates of American firms, and so the following quotations may help to provide some useful impressions. Executives of all the firms quoted felt that American technical know-how had been 'vital' to the growth of their firm. By chance, none of the firms quoted was wholly American in ownership (though similar remarks could have been quoted from a number of such firms), and none exceeded a total employment of two hundred in 1962:

(a) The Americans are very generous people with technical information. We have had about 1,000 blueprints on the design of [a motor vehicle component] from the U.S. since we began its production four years ago. We write to them about four times a week on technical problems, and as far as we are aware the U.S. company has never withheld technical information from us, and normally is very forthcoming in giving us information.

(b) Technical information from the U.S. company is vital—we get access to all information in our own field automatically and usually can negotiate the transfer of information in other fields also. Technical reports are always going back and forth. When we started up initially, they sent two men out here for several months to help on the technical side, and at the same time we sent two people over for training, one on the technical side and the other a salesman. Since then, one of these has been back to the U.S. again and another technical man has been over there for three months. Also, last year there was a world-wide symposium of all affiliates held in Paris to which we sent two men.

(c) When we want to produce a new product, we first secure a licence from our parent company and then send from one to three people over there for two or three months. There they have discussions with their U.S. counterparts, going right through the methods of production, ironing out difficulties and learning from the American company's experience. The U.S. company then supplies us with full specifications on materials, full tooling drawings and break-up drawings of components—everything required to plan production in Australia.

(d) Most of our senior production men have been in the States— and if we get into a difficulty we can't solve here, the best man on the problem from our parent company is rushed out here to help, no matter where he is.

(e) We sent two people—the factory manager and the works supervisor—to the U.S. to study their operating methods, which are peculiarly American, for a period of ten months when we first began here. These two now run training schools lasting five or six weeks for all our new staff. . . . Also the research department of the U.S. company issues a monthly bulletin on how to improve manufacturing methods and materials—this is circulated to all affiliates throughout the world.

The implications of this kind of assistance were outlined in some detail by another jointly-owned firm. This company, with employment in 1962 of little more than two hundred, receives regular monthly bulletins giving information on all products manufactured by the parent company, and executives of the local firm are thus able to select products of special interest and request further details. The American company provides precise manufacturing instructions and, wherever possible, blueprints for all the machines required. If no prints are available, photographs of the machines in question are provided instead, or an engineer from the Australian company visits the U.S. to inspect them personally. The managing director made the following comment:

> Over the last five or six years, since our affiliation with a U.S. firm, we have reduced direct labour cost from 22 per cent to about 11 per cent of total unit cost. . . . This is partly due to the introduction of an incentive scheme for labour, which has permitted a considerable increase in wages at the same time. The incentive scheme was our own idea, but for it to be any good we have to employ the correct manufacturing methods. This is where our overseas connection is important. . . . The flow of technical information has also been important in reducing the percentage of rejects at final inspection. We used to get about 25 per cent of finished articles returned for further work. This is now almost always under 5 per cent, with an average rejection of probably $2\frac{1}{2}$ per cent. Moreover, if 25 per cent were having to be rejected at final inspection, chances are that there were some faulty articles getting through. Under our eighteen months' guarantee, we used to have an average return of about 8 per cent four years ago. This is now down to $0 \cdot 6$ per cent, and this fall is definitely attributable to the flow of technical information from the U.S. . . . We pay a 5 per cent royalty for this information—but it is the cheapest thing we buy.

Not all American-affiliated firms receive technical benefit of this magnitude from their American associates. In some cases this is because the American company is not geared to the dissemination of information, and in other cases local executives are not sufficiently familiar with the workings of the parent company to know what to request and how to request it. Where an American shareholding has been acquired in a local company, or where a local firm has been completely acquired by an American company, American technical know-how may not be relevant to all fields in which the local firm operates. If the local company is engaged only in assembly or in packaging operations, again little of the American company's know-how will be of value. Even if the local firm is engaged in full production, it is unlikely to be concerned with more than a fraction of the products occupying the attention of the American company, and more than one firm indicated that only a very small proportion of its parent's technology was relevant to Australian operations. There was a small number of firms which doubted if parent company technology had been of any appreciable importance, but without exception these companies were either small or substantially Australian in ownership. In general, American technical know-how has been of considerable importance to direct-investment enterprises in Australia, whether wholly or only partly American in ownership.

There are, of course, offsetting costs. The most obvious of these is the need to pay for much of this know-how. Table VI-2 classifies one hundred companies which provided information on this question by the main kind of 'service fee'[2] they pay to their American parent. The table gives some interesting information. To begin with, it is perhaps surprising to see that no fewer than thirty-one companies were paying no charge of any kind in 1962. Twelve of these, moreover, were firms in which the American equity fell short of 100 per cent, and indeed in six cases the American shareholding was not even 50 per cent. In eight of the thirty-one cases, however, six of them wholly American, the company concerned anticipated the introduction of a charge of some kind 'when we get on our feet'. In one more case, a long-established firm expected the parent company to press for the payment of a technical assistance fee following American government concern at the U.S. balance of payments position.

Six firms paid a fixed fee annually, though in at least two cases this fee was subject to periodic negotiation. In two other cases the Australian company had acquired an obligation to pay a fixed sum, of substantial proportions, when the American firm first extended its technical assistance, and was paying this off over a period of ten years. At the end of the decade their obligation was expected to cease. Four companies made their principal payment for technical know-how by a contribution to parent company expenses based on the proportion which the sales of the Australian operation bear to the sales of all affiliated companies throughout the world. Only wholly American companies appear to use this method.

---

[2] Included under the heading of 'service fee' are payments going by many different names, often only for taxation reasons. The table includes such charges as engineering fees, management fees, technical assistance fees, and contributions to parent company research and development expenditure.

TABLE VI-2 Type of Payment Made to Parent Companies for Technical and Managerial Assistance by 100 American-affiliated Companies in 1962, by Percentage of American Ownership and Period in which Manufacture Began

Percentage U.S. ownership and period in which Australian manufacture began[a]	Companies which paid—				
	No special charge	Fixed annual charge	Charge based on proportion of Aust. sales of other affiliates	Charge based on sales of Aust. company only	Other[b]
25–49%: Manufacture began—					
before 1957	2	2	..	2	2
in or after 1957	4	..	..	4	1
50–99%: Manufacture began—					
before 1957	2	1	..	8	1
in or after 1957	4	1	..	10	..
100%: Manufacture began—					
before 1957	6	2	3	11	10
in or after 1957	13	..	1	7	3
Total	31	6	4	42	17

[a] See Note [a] to Table VI-1.

[b] Throughout the table, companies have been classified by the *main* type of payment made. Companies in this category, however, either did not specify the basis on which they pay their technical assistance fee, or make payment in such a variety of ways that classification was not possible.

By far the most common basis for rewarding the parent company for its contribution to the technical know-how of the subsidiary is by a payment which varies with the sales of the subsidiary. In many cases this is a flat percentage levy on the total sales of the Australian operation, but in other cases the charge may be levied on a part of local sales only: the charge may be only on goods of Australian manufacture, for example, or it may be only on American-designed goods. In some cases the charge may vary inversely with the American content of the final product, reflecting the fact that the American company makes some profit on the sale of components or materials to the Australian subsidiary.[3] Sometimes a small fixed charge is payable in addition to the fee based on sales. Some companies have 'multiple rate' systems: one previously wholly Australian firm, for example, pays a royalty of $1\frac{1}{4}$ per cent on all sales of products which know-how from the American company merely improves, and this rate reduces to 1 per cent after five years. On a completely new product, introduced with the help of the American company, the rate is 1 per cent on sales up to £900,000, but 2 per cent on sales above £900,000. This rate also reduces to 1 per cent after five years. Another company pays a royalty of 3 per cent till the total annual royalty reaches $US10,000, 2 per cent till it reaches $US20,000, and 1 per cent till it reaches $40,000. The maximum payable in any one year, however, is $US40,000.

Some of the companies in the 'Other' classification pay only a small management fee, others pay a special technical and administrative charge based on a formula applied to the overheads of their parent company and in addition pay for all engineering costs incurred specifically for the Australian company. The variety is almost infinite.[4]

A few companies were encountered which felt they were paying too much for access to parent company technology, but on the other hand there were many which felt they were receiving a very cheap bargain. One large jointly-owned company indicated that its agreement with its parent company provided for the transfer of technical information at cost—'which frequently means that they charge us only for the time it takes them to write it up'. Most companies expressed no particular opinion on the level of service fee paid, so

---

[3] A technical service fee which varies inversely with the American content of sales may be at its highest when the American contribution to know-how is at its lowest, since products with a high Australian content may be those on which most *Australian* design work has been done. If the fee is based on the Australian content of American-designed goods only, however, this would not be the case.

[4] For comment on the great variety of royalties and other payments made to U.S. licensers, see Enid Baird Lovell (1959: 42-54). See also chapter X below for discussion of the importance of all such fees in relation to profits.

it is probably safe to assume that most were at least content with their arrangement.

But though interesting, Table VI-2 is not very useful. Above all, it does not permit a comparison between payments made by wholly American and jointly-owned companies, and no table can adequately do this. Even if it could be shown that all firms pay a uniform royalty, or that all wholly American companies pay a royalty above that paid by jointly-owned companies, no meaningful conclusions could be drawn. The writer has found it impossible, even with knowledge of the individual companies involved, to reach a definite impression in this area.

Six of the seventeen companies in which the American share-holding fell short of 50 per cent paid no special technical assistance or management fee. Those in this category which did make special payment frequently paid quite a small charge, and the highest charge appeared to be a 5 per cent charge on the sale of American-designed products. Royalties of 4 or 5 per cent appeared rather more common among the companies in which the American shareholding in 1962 was between 50 and 99 per cent—and one company paid almost 8 per cent—but again there were a number of companies paying charges of less than 3 per cent, and some even less than 1 per cent. Six of the twenty-seven companies in this group made no special payment of any kind. Among wholly American firms the picture was again one of diversity. Nineteen firms were making no payment in 1962 and many of those which were making a special payment were paying only a very small fee. One firm with sales of nearly £9 million, for example, paid a management fee in 1962 of only £50,000, and another firm with sales of more than £6 million paid a management fee of less than £24,000 in the same year. But at the other extreme was the highly profitable pharmaceutical firm paying a royalty on all sales of 5 per cent, in addition to a management fee equivalent to 8 per cent on all sales. Another firm paid a negligible engineering fee but a management fee of more than 9 per cent on sales, while a third paid a charge of $7\frac{1}{2}$ per cent on the sale of all products of U.S. design. These payments were among the highest encountered, but payments of 5 per cent were not uncommon.

Even if some 'general impression' emerged, it could mean little. It is not the absolute rate of royalty or technical assistance fee that is relevant but the total payment related in some way to the amount of technical information made available. It is simply not possible to say that a company in the metal-working industry is paying less for know-how because it pays of royalty of 2 per cent than a pharma-ceutical firm which pays 10 per cent: the technical information made available to the metal-working firm may be of much smaller value than that made available to the pharmaceutical firm. Moreover, a technical assistance fee or royalty is only one way in which the American parent company can receive a reward for the technical information it supplies. In many cases, especially where ownership of the Australian affiliate is shared by others, at least a part of the Australian shareholding has been acquired not for cash but in exchange for technical know-how. While it might be possible to make some estimate of the value of this share issue if the shares of the local firm were listed on a stock exchange, many of the companies concerned are proprietary ventures, and assessment of the 'disguised cost' of know-how is quite impossible. It may be relatively simple to assess the cost of technical information in the case of the jointly-owned venture in which the Australian partner initially paid a ten shilling share premium on each twenty shilling share to 'offset' the contribution of the American company in terms of know-how—this was one of the firms in Table VI-2 which made no regular payment for know-how—but what of the cost involved when an American company takes up nearly half of its entitlement to shares in each new issue made by a proprietary company in return for the supply of technical information? Another complication, as noted above, is that American companies sometimes receive payment for technical information by making a profit on the sale of components and materials to the Australian firm, and payments that take this form are quite impossible to estimate.

Wholly American companies often make no distinction between payments for technical information and ordinary profits, and when distinction is made it often appears arbitrary. Some companies make payment of a 'technical assistance fee' only to avoid Australian taxation. One firm commented that

> up till the end of 1962 a technical assistance fee was paid, based on sales. This was not taxable in Australia, though since it was taxable at 52 per cent in the U.S. it was channelled to a tax-haven country. Since the change in U.S. tax laws relating to tax-haven countries, our parent company has changed the arrangement. Now we pay a 2 per cent royalty, which is taxable at 26 per cent in Australia, and a 3 per cent engineering fee, which is taxable in the U.S. only, and both sums are sent to the U.S.

Other companies use technical assistance fees only as an insurance against times of foreign exchange shortage, reasoning that the more avenues available for the remittance of 'profits' the more chance there is of being able to remit at least some return from the Australian investment. More than one company commented that royalty payments are 'just another way for the American company to get a

L

return on its investment'. One reason why some wholly American firms pay technical assistance fees of substantial proportions appears to be a desire to improve their public image in a society tradition- ally suspicious of 'exorbitant profits'. The writer is aware of at least two companies which commenced payment of a substantial service fee in 1962 after the Australian Uniform Companies Act compelled many foreign companies to disclose their profits for the first time, and payment of large service fees is certainly one reason why American-owned companies can sometimes appear to pursue conser- vative dividend policies. One firm, for example, with an admittedly conservative dividend policy, pays 'engineering fees' equal to $7\frac{1}{2}$ per cent on the sale of all American-designed products, and these fees are 'annually more than five times the size of the biggest dividend ever remitted by us to the U.S.' Another firm refrained from declar- ing any dividend for more than a decade after it commenced manu- facture in Australia, but has paid a service fee, now equivalent to about 7 per cent of sales revenue, since establishment. In 1962 the American parent of this company received substantially more from this fee than it did from the dividend of the Australian firm.

A priori, one would expect to find jointly-owned enterprises making a higher 'special payment' for technical assistance than do wholly American concerns, and Australian-owned licensees making a higher payment than jointly-owned firms. Certainly the evidence does seem to show a slight tendency in that direction and companies paying royalties of above 5 per cent, which were said by some to be common among Australian-owned licensees, were not typical of the companies covered in the survey. To the extent that this is the case, pressure for Australian equity in American direct-investment enter- prises might be expected to reduce Australian taxation revenue since, by a variety of devices, many companies contrive to avoid Australian taxation on their technical assistance payments. But regrettably the evidence, as so often in economics, does not lend itself to dogmatic conclusion.[5]

Though the most obvious, the direct cost of dependence on foreign technology may not be the most important cost, for at least when a jointly-owned firm contracts to pay a certain level of royalty or other fee it has calculated that the benefit of receiving the American technical information exceeds the level of payment. And in the case of wholly American companies, it is rarely possible for the combined total of profits earned and technical assistance fees paid to exceed

---

[5] Interestingly, the writer was told by the managing director of one large Australian firm, holding licences from many foreign companies, that British companies are much more exacting in their demands for payment for technical information than are American firms.

the increment of production which takes place as a result of the foreign investment.[6] It is possible, however, though there seems no way to test the hypothesis on the basis of data gathered in the present survey, that Australia's dependence on the technology of other countries results in the introduction here of production methods unsuited to either the relative or absolute endowment of Australia in terms of productive factors. While Australia's relative endowment of capital and labour may not be too dissimilar from that in the United States, its absolute endowment, or total size, is obviously very different. If Australia is using methods of production unsuited to a small market (as, perhaps, in parts of the chemical and petrochemical industry) and if there is a genuine alternative to this in the development of a more suitable technology, misallocation of resources and unnecessarily high prices are important costs of dependence on foreign technology.[7] Australia still receives full benefit from foreign *product* research but may pay a considerable penalty in some industries in its dependence on foreign *process* research.

There may be a further cost, the possibility of which has worried several previous writers on foreign investment: the free access to parent company technology which many American-affiliated companies in Australia enjoy may inhibit the conduct of research within the Australian economy. Certainly of the ninety-six participating companies that answered questions on research in the present survey, fifty-five said they did no research of any kind, other than market research, in 1962. Some difficulty attaches to the interpretation of the word 'research'. A small number of the fifty-five firms which said they did no research in 1962 nevertheless did do some basic design or product development work. One company in the food industry, for example, runs experimental farms and nurseries in close co-operation with its U.S. parent and the Australian Department of Agriculture. Its research department works both on the modification of American recipes to suit the Australian taste and on the discovery of new recipes. Yet because it does no 'basic research', in the opinion of its treasurer, it is listed as one of the firms not conducting research. Another large firm indicated that 'by using our brains here in Australia, we are developing ingeniously automatic machinery which is much cheaper than machinery imported from the U.S.', but the company secretary considered this 'adaptive

[6] The profitability of American companies in Australia and the 'cost' which this profitability entails are discussed in chapters X and XI.

[7] If the use of unsuitable technology is to be sustained, of course, the companies using it must be able to operate profitably. This suggests that part of the blame for the undesirable situation outlined must be attributed to domestic policy towards tariffs, etc. See also chapter XI.

engineering' rather than research. At least six other firms, four of them (like the two quoted) wholly American in ownership, were doing some product development of this kind in 1962, though they declined to call it 'research'. One more set up its own product development department in 1963, staffed with three engineers and two tool makers. Most of the remaining firms which indicated that no research was conducted in 1962, however, appeared to be attempting no real product development of any kind. Most contented themselves with modifying U.S. designs and formulae to meet Australian safety regulations, voltages, etc. Some companies did not even have facilities for testing their output in Australia, and several were encountered, particularly in the pharmaceutical industry, which sent samples of all their local production to the U.S. parent for testing. It is reported that some companies in the cosmetics industry do likewise, while a large metal-working firm whose immediate parent company is British is required to send an article to the United Kingdom for testing by British engineers every three months.

Of the forty-one companies that claimed to be conducting some research in Australia in 1962, six (including one very large motor vehicle manufacturer which was undoubtedly conducting not only substantial design work in Australia but also some fairly basic research on motor oil and steel) felt unable to estimate their research expenditure in 1962. In several cases this was because they felt unable to distinguish between expenditure on 'design', which they felt does not constitute 'research', and expenditure on 'research proper'. Expenditures by the other thirty-five companies in 1962 are shown in aggregate in Table VI-3. It should be noted that some firms interpreted 'research' very widely, and the research activities of at least ten seemed to be almost entirely the adaptation and modification of American designs and formulae. But a number of companies, some of them quite small, were doing some original product development. Two food companies, for example, which had recently been acquired by American firms, both maintained small research and development departments engaged in product improvement because so much of their manufacture in 1962 was concerned with commodities not produced by their parent concerns. Another firm in the food industry had been accustomed to paying £10,000 annually to the Australian company of which it was a subsidiary, but when the American interest was acquired the company appointed its own research director with the encouragement of the American parent. One company in the earth-moving equipment industry boasted that it had recently developed a new type of front-end loader, and that this had proved so successful that the parent company was contemplating making it in the U.S. Several companies had diversified away

TABLE VI–3   Research Conducted in Australia in 1962 by 90 American-affiliated Companies, by Percentage of American Ownership and Period in which Manufacture Began

Percentage U.S. ownership and period in which Australian manufacture began[a]	Companies conducting research					Companies not conducting research		
	No.	Total employment	Employees engaged in research	Total sales in 1962 £A('000)	Expenditure on research in 1962 £A('000)	No.	Total employment	Total sales in 1962 £A('000)
25–49%: Manufacture began—								
before 1957	5	3,511	20	22,630	58	2	1,362	9,067
in or after 1957	1	b	9	b	34	7	1,137	7,520
50–99%: Manufacture began—								
before 1957	8	6,721	99	49,731	417	4	575	2,725
in or after 1957	1	b	5	b	10	13	1,260	9,030
100%: Manufacture began—								
before 1957	14	18,297	292	153,546	999	12	6,078	51,503
in or after 1957	6	1,420	12	8,973	31	17	1,579	14,815
Total	35	30,418	437	238,457	1,549	55	11,991	94,660

[a] See Note [a] to Table VI–1.
[b] Not available for separate disclosure. Figures included in total.

NOTE: The definition of 'research' adopted by some respondent companies was broad (see text). In all cases, the definition used by the respondent company has been used. Market research is excluded. Figures for employment and sales do not include the non-manufacturing activities of the three 'non-manufacturing companies' (as defined in Note [b] to Table I–2).

from the products manufactured by their parent companies, and in most cases these firms did some 'research' of their own. One small wholly American firm, for example, stated that 'we have four chemists and spend a fair bit of money on research. This is necessary because in type of production we have grown right away from the U.S. company.' The company is not included in Table VI-3, however, because the managing director said that he never calculates an exact figure for research done by his company in Australia because he feels the American company might not understand why so much is spent here.

One company in which the American shareholding was substantially more than half had developed a new product which it believed to be the best of its type in the world: the company had, in fact, taken out patents on it in most industrialized countries. Another company, small by any standards, had developed a special type of electrical connection used in rocketry which it believed to be very much better than similar articles produced by its parent company, while the production manager of the same firm had designed an unusual piece of machinery which, in 1963, the parent company was seriously thinking of adopting itself. Not many firms claimed to have developed better production *methods* than their parent company but one large firm did assert that its production line was the 'most modern of its type in the world'; it had been entirely designed in Australia and was in 1963 being copied by the American parent.

The general picture that emerges shows that only a very small amount of basic research is conducted in Australia by American-affiliated firms. On the other hand, effort in the field of product development, though small, is not entirely insignificant. Moreover, as Table VI-3 makes clear, the longer companies are established in Australia the greater is the likelihood that they will establish at least a rudimentary research and development department. While only 18 per cent of companies in the table which began manufacturing in 1957 or subsequently claimed to conduct research in Australia in 1962, 60 per cent of those established before 1957 felt they did some research in 1962.[8] Several of the recently established firms which conducted no research in 1962 indicated that they expected to engage in some research activities as they expanded and became more highly integrated. One executive felt particularly strongly on this point and

[8] As elsewhere in the survey, the expression 'began manufacturing' refers to the date at which an American equity interest of at least 25 per cent was acquired in the case of companies which were operating previously as Australian-owned enterprises. In fact, half of those which 'began manufacturing in or after 1957' and are listed in Table VI-3 as conducting research in 1962 were operating before 1957 as Australian-owned companies.

stated that 'you can be a parrot for just so long—to get real growth
in a company you have to get people thinking'.

There is no clear indication, either in Table VI-3 or in Table
VI-5, that jointly-owned companies conduct any more research
locally than do wholly American firms. The data are subject to a
wide margin of error because of the different interpretations placed
on 'research', but the main determinants of whether a company was
conducting research seem to have been the size of the company (as
shown in Table VI-4) and the date at which it commenced operation
in Australia, factors which, of course, tend to go together. Some
wholly American firms receive specific encouragement from their
parents to engage in original product development. One firm in the
chemical industry, for example, is responsible for conducting research
for sister affiliates in Japan, New Zealand, and South Africa. Two
wholly American companies were encountered, one in the pharmaceutical industry and another producing electrical equipment, which
actually receive finance from the U.S. on a regular basis specifically
for the conduct of local research. The electrical equipment firm
indicated that until recently no research other than the adaptation
of U.S. designs to local conditions had been done locally. Now,
however, the U.S. company is keen for all subsidiaries to do research
work if they can justify their project, and the Australian firm has
been assigned primary responsibility for research in three distinct
fields. For these 'general development' projects, the Australian
company is entitled to a portion of the parent company's allocation
for research and development, and in 1963 the Australian company
received a very considerable sum from this source. Sharp increases
of this kind in local research expenditure were, incidentally, found
on several occasions: one wholly American firm had increased its
Australian expenditure on research from £12,000 in 1948/9 to
£253,000 in 1961/2, while two more wholly American firms were
constructing large development departments—one costing £250,000
and the other £500,000—at the time the survey was conducted in
1963. Among wholly American subsidiaries well known in Australia
for their conduct of design work (and even in some cases basic
research) locally are General Motors-Holden's, Monsanto Chemicals,
Standard Telephone & Cables, Kraft Holdings, Kodak, and International Harvester.

Granted that relatively few American-affiliated companies do
conduct research in Australia, however, there are two questions
which must be answered before passing judgment on them. First,
are American-affiliated companies unusual in their neglect of research in Australia? Here all the evidence points to the fact that
they are not. Solomon Encel (1961: 265) estimated the total expen-

TABLE VI-4   Research Conducted in Australia in 1962 by 90 American-affiliated Companies, by Sales[a]

Total sales in 1962 £A	Research expenditure in 1962								No. companies covered
	Nil	£5,000 and under	£5,001–£10,000	£10,001–£25,000	£25,001–£50,000	£50,001–£75,000	£75,001–£100,000	Over £100,000	
500,000 and under	24	4	1	..	..	..	..	..	29
Over 500,000 and not above 1,000,000	10	1	1	..	1	..	..	..	13
Over 1,000,000 and not above 3,000,000	13	3	4	..	2	..	..	..	22
Over 3,000,000 and not above 5,000,000	1	..	2	2	2	..	1	..	8
Over 5,000,000 and not above 7,500,000	4	..	..	..	..	..	1	..	5
Over 7,500,000 and not above 10,000,000	2	..	..	..	..	2	2	1	7
Over 10,000,000	1	..	..	2	..	..	1	2	6
Total	55	8	8	4	5	2	5	3	90

[a] See note to Table VI-3.

TABLE VI–5 Ninety American-affiliated Companies Classified by Research Conducted in Australia in 1962, by Sales and Percentage of American Ownership[a]

Total sales in 1962 £A	Companies conducting no research			Companies conducting research			All companies		
	25–49% Amer.	50–99% Amer.	100% Amer.	25–49% Amer.	50–99% Amer.	100% Amer.	25–49% Amer.	50–99% Amer.	100% Amer.
500,000 and under	5	7	12	1	1	3	6	8	15
Over 500,000 and not above 1,000,000	2	4	4	2	..	1	4	4	5
Over 1,000,000 and not above 3,000,000	..	6	7	1	2	6	1	8	13
Over 3,000,000 and not above 5,000,000	..	..	1	1	3	3	1	3	4
Over 5,000,000 and not above 7,500,000	1	..	3	..	..	1	1	..	4
Over 7,500,000 and not above 10,000,000	1	..	1	..	2	3	1	2	4
Over 10,000,000	..	..	1	1	1	3	1	1	4
Total	9	17	29	6	9	20	15	26	49

[a] See note to Table VI–3.

diture on research by Australian industry in 1958/9 at between £3 million and £5 million, only about one-quarter of 1 per cent of net industrial output, while B. R. Williams (1962: 8), making an estimate in 1962, did not put the total figure much above £9 million. In the same year, P. H. Karmel and Maureen Brunt commented that 'research remains almost wholly in non-private hands' (1962: 108), and after an extensive survey of Australian industrial research in the early sixties, S. H. Bastow commented that the 'typical Australian director, on hearing the words "scientific research" will cough politely, take a quick look at the length of your hair, and change the subject' (*A.F.R.*, 15 April 1964). Actually, it is possible that American-affiliated firms devote a higher percentage of their resources to 'research' than do other firms in the Australian economy, though whether this conclusion would hold true if the comparison were between firms of the same size is uncertain. Table B-5 in Appendix B indicates that the ninety-nine American-affiliated firms covered in that table employed on average more than twice as many chemists, draftsmen, and other laboratory and research staff in their factories as did Australian industry as a whole in 1961/2: whereas the total manufacturing employment of these factories was only 5·1 per cent of the Australian total in that year, their employment of chemists and draftsmen amounted to 11·1 per cent of the Australian total. Care must be exercised in basing conclusions on these data: in part, they are the result of the importance of the motor vehicle industry in the total picture, and in fact in only six of the ten industries where comparison is possible in the table did American-affiliated firms employ proportionally more chemists and draftsmen than did the Australian industry in question.[9] But the six industries are among the most important of the ten. About one-quarter of participating firms provided details of the income earned by their chemists and draftsmen in 1961/2, and though the figures (an average of £1,594 for each of 309 males and £903 for each of 22 females) do not indicate the employment of great numbers of highly qualified scientific personnel, nor do they indicate that most of those involved were entirely unskilled.

There is a second and perhaps more important question: should American-affiliated companies be encouraged to do more research than they do currently? It has been generally assumed, both in

[9] Care must be exercised for another reason. It appears that most companies include all their 'research personnel' on their statutory 'Factory Returns', from which aggregate figures for Australian industry in Table B-5 are derived. It is probable, however, that some companies having large research and development departments quite separate physically from their factories do not include personnel in these departments on their 'Factory Returns'.

Australia and in Canada (where the same situation seems to exist), that a great increase in the research done by the local subsidiaries of foreign companies is to be desired. Often foreign subsidiaries incur much of the blame for the small amount of research done locally. The argument that foreign subsidiaries should do more research locally must rest, however, on the belief that conducting research in Australia yields significant benefits to Australians which the mere importation of foreign technology by these companies does not. There are indeed some ways in which these benefits could accrue. If foreign subsidiaries, by conducting research locally, were able to produce an article more suited to Australian needs than one developed abroad, or if they were able to produce an existing article more cheaply (perhaps by adapting their method of production more appropriately to the size of the Australian market), this could benefit Australian consumers, Australian shareholders (if any), and Australian tax revenue (unless of course tax concessions designed to stimulate research more than offset this gain). If foreign subsidiaries were to make discoveries suitable for use by their affiliates overseas, Australian tax revenue (and Australian shareholders, if any) would benefit if the local subsidiary were able to charge affiliates for the use of these discoveries.[10] Increased local research would also increase the demand, and so the reward (in the short term at least), for Australian scientists. But probably the greatest benefit of any measures to encourage local research in foreign-owned companies would accrue to the foreign shareholders. The situation is in no way parallel to the employment of Australians in the management of foreign subsidiaries: this practice may yield benefits both in the modification of policies which might otherwise be detrimental to Australia and in the training of Australians in modern management techniques, techniques which the men concerned take with them thereafter. In contrast, Australians employed in the research and development

---

[10] The idea of locally-based foreign subsidiaries charging affiliated companies for the use of information discovered in Australia was first suggested to the writer by E. Barraclough, assistant managing director of Monsanto Chemicals (Aust.) Ltd, during an address he gave to a symposium of the Melbourne University Chemical Society in August 1963. It seems likely, however, that the number of foreign subsidiaries which would be able to charge their affiliates for technical information discovered in Australia would be very small indeed, at least where there is an Australian shareholding in the subsidiary. As the managing director of one jointly-owned company (which had recently developed a new product in Australia) explained when questioned on the possibility of charging affiliates for the design, 'there are some rivers which flow in only one direction'. Of fourteen companies questioned on the return of information to their U.S. affiliate, eleven indicated that technical information of value is occasionally (though rarely in most cases) returned to the U.S. None of these eleven received payment for this information.

departments of foreign subsidiaries are rarely in a position to influence the policies of their employers, and most of their training has been done previously at the expense of the Australian community.

If important technical developments occurred randomly, therefore, there would appear to be much in favour of confining tax concessions designed to stimulate research to companies of predominantly Australian ownership. But such developments have a tendency to occur in particular industries—such as the industrial chemicals and plastics industry—and at present those industries where technical developments appear likely to occur most rapidly in the future are also those in which foreign companies occupy dominant positions. As long as there is some net gain to Australians from research conducted by foreign affiliates in this country, therefore, measures to encourage research must be instituted on a non-discriminatory basis.

VII

Of Productivity and Costs

In view of the considerable technical benefit which most American-affiliated enterprises in Australia undoubtedly derive from their American association, it is interesting to examine the operating performance of these companies, measured in terms of productivity and unit costs, compared both to that of their parent companies and to that of other firms in the Australian economy. The data on this subject gathered in the present survey are inadequate in many respects: to make them more adequate would have required not only a better response to this section of the questionnaire than was in fact forthcoming but also the devotion of a much greater section of the total survey to this aspect than was felt to be warranted. Some points of value nevertheless emerge.

If the operation of American-affiliated firms in Australia is compared first with that of their parent companies, it is evident that physical productivity, or physical output per man-year, is substantially lower in Australia than in the United States. Of thirty-five companies asked to comment on the physical productivity achieved in Australia, eight felt Australian productivity to be 'considerably lower' than American, nine felt it to be 'lower', three felt it to be 'about the same', one felt it to be 'higher', one felt that it was 'considerably lower' in one major area of production but 'higher' in another, and thirteen were unable to answer the question or felt it was meaningless because the local operation was so different from that in the U.S. Only five companies were able to be more precise than this: three in the 'considerably lower' category felt Australian production per man to be less than half the American figure (one company put the Australian figure as low as 39 per cent of the American), and two in the 'lower' category estimated Australian productivity at 85 and 65 per cent of the American respectively. The number of respondents was too small to discern any clear industry pattern.

There was general agreement on the reasons for the relatively poor

Australian productivity. All but one of the companies which felt
Australian productivity to be low in relation to that in America
attributed this primarily to the relatively small volume of production
in the Australian company and the effect of this volume difference
on the methods of production. The secretary of a firm in the electrical equipment industry, comparing the methods used in the Australian plant with those used by a sister affiliate in the United Kingdom, made a comment which was typical of those received from
executives in metal-working industries:

> Where we use a two- or three-cavity die, the U.K. company uses
> a twenty-four-cavity die. . . . And where we have a machine on
> which we do five different processes consecutively, stripping down
> the machine between each process, the U.K. company does the
> five processes simultaneously on the one machine—but their
> machine costs about £400,000.

Another firm, with a major shareholder in both the U.S. and the
U.K., commented that 'where we use an ordinary turret lathe, the
U.K. company uses a multi-station loading lathe, and the U.S.
company uses a twelve spindle machine which performs twelve operations simultaneously'. A third company stated that 'where the U.S.
company can set up a machine in eight hours to run for weeks, we
take the same time to set it up but only run it for two hours'. On
the relatively small production runs typical of Australian industry
(and few companies have annual production equivalent to more than
5 per cent of that of their parent companies), the purchase of expensive special-purpose machines and dies is rarely justified and output
per man is almost inevitably lower than in the U.S. In the chemical
industry the methods used in both Australian and American plants
may be similar but, as one executive commented, 'the same workforce which we employ could run a plant of five times our capacity'.

Differences in production volume would lead to a smaller use of
machinery relative to labour (and hence lower output per man) in
Australia than in the U.S. even if the price of labour were identical
in the two countries. The fact that wage rates are considerably lower
in Australia than in the U.S. tends in the same direction.

The small number of companies which felt their productivity
to be comparable with or above that in the U.S. were all operating
in industries where economies of scale are exhausted at low volume.
Two of the three which felt Australian productivity to be 'about
the same' as that in the U.S. operated in the foundation garment
industry, where beyond a comparatively low volume existing machines
are duplicated rather than replaced with more automatic ones. The
only firm which felt that throughout its range its productivity

exceeded that of its parent produced only two simple metal products for which it dominated the whole Australian market. The machinery it used was identical with that in the U.S., and higher physical productivity was achieved in Australia, it was claimed, because of superior plant layout.

The company which felt that in one major area productivity fell far short of that achieved by its American parent explained that in this field U.S. sales volume was about twenty-five times that of the Australian company. In its other major area of production, in which Australian productivity exceeded American, Australian volume was almost one-third of the American. Moreover, while the Australian company dominated the local market for products in this field, and so was able to secure relatively large orders, the American company, in a much more competitive market, was compelled to cater for the more frequent but relatively smaller orders of American customers.

Only one firm of those which could estimate Australian productivity in relation to American felt that a difference in the diligence with which labour works in the two countries was the primary reason for lower Australian productivity. The secretary of this firm commented that 'the vicious piece-work system used in the U.S. and their system of instantaneous lay-offs whenever demand slackens temporarily' combine to result in Australian productivity being only about two-thirds of the American, despite the use of almost identical equipment.

There were other companies which felt that Australian labour does not work as well as American, though not all of them were in a position to estimate the overall productivity difference between the two countries. One engineering firm indicated that the hourly output of American workers in the parent company tends to be about 90-95 per cent of 'possible', whereas 'we in Australia have a hard job to get above 70 per cent'. The firm felt that this was partly due to severe fluctuations in demand, which mean a high rate of labour turnover (the company was working at only 20 per cent of capacity at one period during the recession of 1961-2, but was operating at 87 per cent late in 1963), but also important was the different attitude towards productivity on the part of American workers. An Australian executive in another engineering firm commented:

> Australian workers are far more versatile than American workers. But in attitude Australian workers fall by the wayside. On a recent visit I made to the U.S. I was impressed with how keen the ordinary workers on the floor were to explain how they had thought up some scheme to save money and man-hours. Of the eight factories I visited, I was volunteered this kind of information in five of them.

A firm in the Altona petrochemical complex felt that the physical productivity of Australian construction labour is only about 60 per cent of construction labour on America's Gulf Coast. The executive admitted that this is partly because particular skills, unknown to Australians until now, are required in the building of petrochemical plants, but he felt that part of the reason is 'the very full employment in the Australian economy'.

Comments from other executives, however, differed from those quoted. Of twenty-four firms which specifically compared the quality of Australian labour with that of American, only eight (four of them wholly American) felt that Australian labour is not as productive as American. Five (three of them wholly American) actually felt that Australian labour is better than American. One of these companies (one which was wholly American in ownership) commented:

> You wouldn't get better female staff in the world than we've got —and the two machine operators who came out from America in the early stages couldn't give us the same output as our first Australian operator. The Australian tradesman has a lot more initiative than his American counterpart because he has to make do with a lot less outside help.

Most of the other firms which felt Australian workers to be superior to American stressed the greater versatility of Australians.

While relatively few firms went so far as to contend that Australians actually work better than Americans, eleven out of twenty-four firms felt that Australians work just as well as Americans. The comment of one of the three wholly American firms which held this view is quoted in illustration:

> We have just had an industrial engineering team out from the U.S. and they concluded that there is no 'man productivity' difference between the two countries—the only difference is in the extent to which machinery is used. We work on the same labour times as the U.S. plants where equipment used is comparable. Decrying the quality of Australian labour in comparison with that in the U.S. is a popular drum to beat, but in my view the 'slack work' of Australian workers is a result of poor management.

The same executive went on to explain how he had recently avoided the need to employ two clerks by rearranging an office to cut down walking distance. It is interesting to note also that the American firm Bechtel Pacific Corporation, which based its estimates for the construction time of a Brisbane oil refinery on the assumption that Australian workmen achieve something like two-thirds the output of American workmen (possibly on a knowledge of labour performance at Altona), found the construction of the refinery running ahead of schedule because 'Australians are doing as much or even more than Americans would' (*A.F.R.*, 14 Sept. 1964).

A number of companies complained about the great difficulty of securing skilled labour in Australia and some also lamented the difficulty of securing adequate labour for shift work. A few complained of high labour absenteeism and one felt that high labour turnover was a factor in the low productivity of the Australian operation. Offsetting these complaints, however, were frequent words of praise for Australian trade unions. There were some notable exceptions to this, but in general executives who commented on industrial relations in Australia felt that they are better than in the U.S.[1] One said:

> Americans are convinced that Australia is a hot-bed of labour troubles. They can hardly believe me when I say that I have never met a union representative in my life, except in the pub. We have far less labour trouble in Australia than our parent does in the U.S.—they have a four or five week strike every two years when their wage settlement comes up for review. . . . We never have complaints from employees about facilities—and of course if I did get a justifiable complaint I would fire the factory manager.

Inefficient management of the Australian subsidiary was a factor not mentioned by any of the executives interviewed as an explanation for low Australian productivity. Nor did any executive offer the view that the use of an outdated production method is the main reason for low Australian productivity. This is, perhaps, not surprising, but it does not mean that neither factor played a part in causing low Australian productivity. As mentioned in chapter V, the writer gained the impression that several of the smaller American-affiliated enterprises in Australia are inefficiently managed. The Tariff Board (1963c: 9) also observed of the two Australian producers of polyvinyl chloride resins (one of them affiliated with an American firm and the other with a British) in 1963 that differences between the proportion of total unit costs attributable to overheads in the Australian industry and in the Japanese industry were greater than could be explained by differences in labour costs, plant capacities, and accounting procedures. Another American-affiliated company in the chemical industry was accused before the Tariff Board early in 1965 of employing methods of production which are 'as old as the hills' and of operating inefficient means of transportation and supply. Such cases appear to be relatively isolated examples, however.

---

[1] The U.S. Department of Commerce shares the view that labour disputes are less disruptive in Australia than in the U.S. In a recent publication it concluded that in most industries 'time lost through industrial disputes is considerably less than in the American experience' (1963a: 12).

M

It is quite possible, of course, for Australian unit costs to be lower than American despite relatively low output per man in Australia, provided wages and other costs are sufficiently low to offset the effects of poor productivity. Australian wages at least are very much lower than American. Of twenty-five companies which felt able to estimate the level of employee remuneration in their Australian operation in comparison with that prevailing in the factories of their parent, two firms felt that the Australian level would be less than 40 per cent of the American, eighteen that it would be between 40 and 50 per cent of the American, and only five that it would exceed 50 per cent.

Some difficulty was encountered in the collection of unit cost statistics: a large number of foreign subsidiaries appear to be genuinely ignorant of the costs of their parent company, and some of those which are better informed are not prepared to share their secret. Nevertheless enough information was forthcoming to permit certain general principles to be discerned. Table VII-1 shows a total of 82 unit cost comparisons supplied by seventy companies. In all, 23 of the comparisons showed Australian costs to be below American, 12 showed them to be 'about the same', and 47 showed them to be higher. Though the number of comparisons within each industry is not large enough in most cases to warrant detailed analysis of unit costs by industry, it does seem safe to conclude that a disproportionate share of the cases where Australian costs were lower or 'about the same' belonged to one or other of the metal-working industries, while in all the cost comparisons provided by companies in the

TABLE VII–1   Unit Costs of 70 American-affiliated Companies Compared with Those of Their Parent Companies, by Industry[a]

| Industry | Cases in which Australian unit cost was | | | Total |
	Lower than American	About the same as American	Higher than American	
Plant, equipment, machinery	8	3	13	24
Motor vehicles	1	..	3	4
Motor accessories	2	..	2	4
Metal manufactures, n.e.i.	3	1	5	9
Electrical equipment, instruments, etc.	4	2	7	13
Food and drink	2	1	2	5
Industrial chemicals and plastics	..	..	7	7
Pharmaceutical and toilet preparations	..	2	5	7
Other industries	3	3	3	9
Total	23	12	47	82

[a] The 70 companies supplied a total of 82 cost comparisons.

industrial chemical industry Australian unit costs exceeded those in the U.S.[2]

Thirty-eight of the 82 comparisons, provided by thirty-five companies, were given more exactly than is shown in the table. In two cases Australian unit cost actually fell short of 55 per cent of American cost; in one case Australian cost was between 56 and 75 per cent of American; in four cases between 76 and 95 per cent; in four cases between 96 and 105 per cent; in ten cases between 106 and 125 per cent; in ten cases between 126 and 150 per cent; and in seven cases more than 150 per cent. It is not possible to calculate any kind of average of these estimates because in several cases the figures given were in the form of a range rather than a single figure, but the tendency for Australian unit cost to be higher (and in many cases much higher) than American is clearly brought out. As noted in chapter III, the same general conclusion was reached by the American National Industrial Conference Board in its study published in 1961.[3]

In only one case was the cheapness of an Australian raw material mentioned as an important factor in relatively low Australian unit cost—and in this case 70 per cent of the cost of the product was raw steel. This was one of the few cases, however, in which the physical productivity of the Australian plant was higher than the American, so that cheap raw material was only one of the factors involved in the low Australian unit cost. By far the most important reason for low Australian cost was the relative cheapness of Australian labour. This became a relevant factor whenever the product involved was one which neither the American nor the Australian firm supplied in large volume, or whenever the volume supplied by the Australian firm was sufficient to warrant the installation of equipment similar to that used by the American firm. Where volume was small in both countries, expensive special-purpose machinery was not justified in the American plant and 'jobbing' methods had

[2] No break-down of these responses by ownership is shown because no pattern appeared obvious, and indeed none would be expected. There may be a significant pattern by date of establishment of manufacturing operations: of those involving companies manufacturing before 1957, 14 comparisons showed Australian costs to be lower than American, 10 to be 'about the same', and 21 to be higher; of those involving companies which began manufacture in or after 1957, 9 comparisons showed Australian costs to be lower than American, 2 to be 'about the same', and 26 to be higher. Part of the explanation of this distribution, however, is in the industry pattern.

[3] Gates and Linden (the authors of the National Industrial Conference Board study) concluded that 'between Latin America and Australia . . . there was little to choose; their average total costs put them unmistakably well into the higher-cost zone' (1961: 18).

to be adopted. This gave maximum advantage to the Australian operation with its low labour cost, and in one case a company was encountered producing an item for $US31·4 which cost the American firm $US64 to produce. Where volume was considerable in both plants, but where Australian volume was sufficient to justify the same kind of machinery as that used in the American plant, the same result obtained. One firm, holding most of the Australian market for a particular product, indicated that its production cost was 81 per cent of the American and would have been lower but for the need to pay overseas freight on a significant fraction of the raw materials needed. (The Australian cost compared with a figure of 69 per cent for the British affiliate, and 66 per cent for the French, both countries where wage rates below those in Australia prevail. On the other hand, South African costs were 94 per cent of the American, and Mexican 172 per cent, showing that volume of production is also important up to a certain level.)

In some cases, it should be stressed, Australian costs are lower than American only when the scope of the Australian operation is strictly confined to a small part of the production process. Thus several firms indicated that Australian costs are below American because the local operation is engaged only in the assembly of imported parts. Because of the importance of labour costs in this operation, the Australian firm has a marked advantage over the American. Several companies also emphasized the advantage which the Australian operation enjoys in having to bear almost no part of the research and development costs of the parent, and one company indicated that, in addition to designs, the American company had supplied free of charge even the machinery needed to manufacture one product.

Two of the case studies shown in Table VII-2 deal with products which are cheaper to manufacture in the Australian subsidiary than in the American parent. In Case A, despite the comparatively small volume of production of the Australian plant, the manufacturing methods used in both countries are substantially similar. The only important difference is the greater use of mechanized methods of conveying the product from one stage of production to another in the American plant. The result of this is that the physical productivity of labour in the Australian plant is lower, but not greatly so, than in the American. The relative cheapness of Australian labour gives the Australian operation a decisive advantage in the categories 'manufacturing labour cost' and 'other overheads', but because of the high cost of raw materials to the Australian operation, Australian unit cost is only 20 per cent less than American. The same general picture emerges from an examination of Case B, though with somewhat less clarity because cost categories adopted by the American and Australian plants differed. The Australian executive explained that Australian unit expenditure on materials is higher than the American figure entirely because of the higher price of materials in Australia: if anything, the American plant buys in its materials at a more advanced stage of manufacture than the Australian because of the absence of satisfactory suppliers in Australia.

Most of the companies which felt Australian unit cost to be about the same as American indicated that though the American company had an advantage in being able to secure cheaper materials this was adequately compensated for by lower Australian labour costs. Most of these comparisons involved products for which the Australian market is sufficiently large to permit the maximum benefit from economies of scale: one company even contended that its affiliate in New Zealand has lower costs for some products than does the Australian company because both markets are large enough for 'economic production' and the price of plastic (an important raw material) is substantially cheaper in New Zealand than in Australia.

The only detailed comparison available of a product whose cost is the same in Australia as in America appears as Case C in Table VII-2. From the relatively high share of labour in unit cost (despite very much lower Australian wages and the contention of the company that Australian workers are just as satisfactory as American) and the relatively low share of depreciation and other overheads, it is evident that the American plant employs substantially more mechanized methods of production than the Australian. Offsetting the Australian net advantage on these items, however, is the higher cost of raw materials in Australia. Actually a classification of raw material costs provided by the company indicated that the Australian disadvantage is entirely in the area of packaging materials, where Australian costs in 1961 were more than 50 per cent above those incurred by the American plant.

Among reasons offered as explanation by the large number of companies which felt Australian unit costs to be higher than American, relatively low volume of production in Australia received by far the greatest number of mentions. Again and again companies explained that low volume results in under-utilization of machinery and high unit costs on expensive dies. One firm in the engineering industry indicated that at its operating level in 1962 manufacturing overhead in Australia was 622 per cent of productive labour cost, but that this would fall drastically with higher operating levels. Several firms felt that a doubling of Australian volume would suffice to reduce costs to a par with American but one firm felt that an expansion of 500 per cent would be required. Others felt that at no

TABLE VII-2　American and Australian Unit Costs Compared—Six Case Studies

	Case A U.S. %	Case A Aust. %	Case B U.S. %	Case B Aust. %	Case C U.S. %	Case C Aust. %	Case D U.S. %	Case D Aust. %	Case E U.S. %	Case E Aust. %	Case F U.S. %	Case F Aust. %
Manufacturing labour cost[a]	31·5	28·9	57·6[c]	17·1	5·2	6·7	26	26	3·9	5·1	35	24
Direct materials cost	19·4	33·3	20·1	32·2	67·0	73·2	44	48	82·2	81·2	50	69
Depreciation	4·6	2·4	2·8	2·9	} 27·8	} 20·1	6	4	1·3	1·6	} 15	2
Other overheads	44·5	35·4	19·5	47·8			24	22	12·6	12·1		5
Total unit production cost	100·0	100·0	100·0	100·0	100·0	100·0	100·0	100·0	100·0	100·0	100·0	100·0
Australian unit cost as a percentage of American		80		95		100		105		112		125
Total output of product by Australian firm as a percentage of American output		7		10						10		5
Average remuneration received by Australian employees as a percentage of that received by American employees		b		27		b		66		45		62
Product involved	Metal tool		Electrical control device		Toilet article (1)		Item of apparel		Toilet article (2)		Heavy engineering product	

a The interpretation placed on the listed cost categories varied from company to company. With the exception of Case B, however, it is believed that the American and Australian figures are shown on a directly comparable basis in each case.

b Not known by the company concerned.

c Cost categories not comparable.

d Not available for separate disclosure.

TABLE VII-3 American and Australian Unit Costs Compared—Five More Case Studies

	Case G		Case H		Case I		Case J		Case K	
	U.S. %	Aust. %	U.S. %	Aust. %	U.S. %	Aust. %	U.S. %	Aust. %	U.S. %	Aust. %
Manufacturing labour cost[a]	19·2	19·9	17	10	4·8	11·4	4	10	14	6
Direct materials cost	46·1	37·9	49	69	76·9	53·3	75	46	45	78
Depreciation	} 34·7	} 42·2	8	6	} 18·3	} 35·3	3	16	} 41	} 16
Other overheads			26	15			18	28		
Total unit production cost	100·0	100·0	100·0	100·0	100·0	100·0	100·0	100·0	100·0	100·0
Australian unit cost as a percentage of American		128		130		134		150		183
Total output of product by Australian firm as a percentage of American output		8		b		1		4		1
Average remuneration received by Australian employees as a percentage of that received by American employees		40		36		e		50		c
Product involved	Building accessory (metal)		Motor vehicle		Food product		Industrial chemical		Item of electrical equipment	

a See Note a to Table VII-2.
b See Note d to Table VII-2.
c See Note b to Table VII-2.

167

foreseeable volume would the Australian company be able to justify the local production of all components of the product concerned.

The effects of low volume on unit costs may be seen most clearly in Cases G, I, and J in Table VII-3. In two of these cases, I and J, expenditure on raw materials by the Australian operation is not only relatively but also absolutely smaller per unit than is American expenditure, and in Case G Australian unit expenditure on materials is little higher than the American. In all three cases, however, labour and overhead costs in Australia are significantly higher than those in America because of the influence of scale.

A firm's small scale of operation will often impose an additional burden in the form of more expensive materials cost. Firms that are able to buy in bulk are frequently able to secure significantly cheaper materials both because of the economies available to the supplying firm and the greater bargaining power in the hands of the purchaser. Case H in Table VII-3 offers an illustration of this point. Though the relatively higher Australian expenditure on materials reflects in part the fact that the Australian firm tends to buy in more of its components in a finished form than does the American firm (itself a manifestation of the small size of the Australian operation), it also reflects a higher price which the Australian firm has to pay for Australian-made components because of the relatively small volume of its orders. The company felt a doubling of local volume would be required to reduce total unit cost to the American level. Case F in Table VII-2 offers another illustration of this, while an engineering company not included in either table commented that every steel item it purchases in Australia is more expensive than in America with the sole exception of raw steel.

Materials were more expensive in Australia than in the U.S. for other reasons than the small size of the supplier or the small size of the order given by the local subsidiary. More than one firm complained of the high cost of cardboard packaging materials in Australia, while others mentioned freight and, sometimes, tariff charges on materials not produced in Australia. These charges were mentioned, for example, by the company concerned with Case D in Table VII-2, though comparatively low Australian labour productivity (despite the use of substantially similar equipment by the plants in both countries) was an even more important factor in this company's somewhat higher Australian unit cost. (Most of the components used in the local assembly of the item concerned in Case K in Table VII-3 were also imported, but the very high cost of these components was principally due not to freight or tariff charges but to the fact that they were purchased from an affiliated company at prices above those ruling in a competitive market.)

Other factors received only occasional mention. One firm complained that packaging costs are higher in Australia partly because of the strict regulations imposed by the Australian Postmaster-General's Department on the wrapping of parcels for posting. Another firm lamented the multitudinous variety of municipal regulations which compel it to produce not one model of a particular electrical appliance but as many as fifty if it wishes to sell throughout Australia. A third felt that local government specifications (for a product mainly bought by public authorities) are too severe, and this necessitated the employment of thirty-five men on inspection duties alone, where the American firm felt five to be adequate. And in quite a different area of costs, another company commented that inventory charges are disproportionately great in Australia because of the small range of production of the local firm: to keep a reasonable range of the product concerned in stock, the Australian firm was forced in 1962 to maintain an inventory/sales ratio of almost 40 per cent, compared with a figure of 22 per cent for the British affiliate and only 3·2 per cent for the American parent.

Many of the difficulties experienced by American subsidiaries in Australia assume their most acute form in the chemical industry. In this industry, the cost of constructing a plant of given size in Australia may differ little from the cost in the U.S., the relatively low Australian wage level tending to offset the American advantage in specialized process equipment. But there are very considerable economies of scale in the construction of chemical plants, which mean that the large American plants have a major initial advantage over plants designed for the small Australian market.[4] It is not only capital costs per unit of capacity which are lower in large plants than in small: operating costs per unit of output also are much lower in large plants. This is principally because large plants involve lower charges for depreciation and maintenance (because of the low initial capital cost) and a staff little larger than that required by a small plant. When to these difficulties are added those of frequently more expensive raw materials, and widely dispersed markets, it is not hard to see why Australian unit costs in the chemical industry are so often above those in the U.S.[5]

No attempt was made during the present survey to compare unit costs in American-affiliated firms with those prevailing in Australian-

[4] At the time that Australian Synthetic Rubber Co. Ltd decided to produce synthetic rubber in Australia, it was calculated that to build a plant of 15,000 tons annual capacity would have cost £3·5 million: to construct a plant of double that capacity involved an additional cost of only £1·5 million (*T.B.R.* 1962j: 5).

[5] For good discussions of the cost disadvantages of the Australian chemical industry, see Hunter and Webb (1963: 323-6); and Zeidler (1961).

owned companies. Not only would this information have been extremely difficult if not impossible to obtain, in many cases there are no Australian-owned firms producing similar goods with which comparison could be made. Instead, the operating performance of American-affiliated firms is compared with that of other firms manufacturing in Australia by using a broader, if less satisfactory, measure, that of value of production per person employed.

Table VII-4 shows the value of production per person employed in the factories of ninety-nine American-affiliated firms compared with the same measure in Australian industry as a whole in 1961/2. In aggregate, the value of production per person employed in the American-affiliated firms is seen to have been about 36 per cent higher than that in Australian industry generally.[6] What is even more interesting is that in eight of the ten individual industries in which comparison is possible, the value productivity of the American-affiliated companies was higher than the level prevailing within that industry. In other words, the higher value productivity of labour in American-affiliated companies is not merely due to their concentration in industries in which the labour productivity of all companies is above the national average. Admittedly, the two industries in which American-affiliated companies appear to fall short of the average performance are major ones—motor vehicles and industrial chemicals. The explanation of the relatively low value productivity of labour in the industrial chemicals industry is not obvious, but there are sound reasons for believing that the figures shown in the table for the motor vehicle industry are almost meaningless because of the way in which some of the companies concerned complete their Factory Returns.[7] If this industry be ignored, the value productivity of the American-affiliated firms exceeded the relevant industry average in eight out of nine industries and the average value produc-

[6] A remarkably similar difference between the value of production per employee in a group of American-controlled enterprises in Canada and that in Canadian manufacturing industry as a whole was noted by Blyth and Carty (1956: 452).

[7] Companies engaged only in assembly work are instructed by the Commonwealth Bureau of Census and Statistics to exclude the value of components bought from other establishments from the figures they present for both cost of materials and value of output. The latter should include, however, 'the actual labour cost of assembling the parts, costs of fuel and power used, any additional expenses of assembly, and profit made on such work'. It is believed that at least one (and probably more) of the large motor vehicle manufacturers does not complete its Factory Returns in this way. This company shows its value of output on the basis of a fixed percentage mark-up on its costs of production (excluding the cost of purchased components), and this appears to give a figure for value of output which could not possibly accommodate the company's profit.

TABLE VII–4 Value of Production and Book Value of Capital Per Employee in Australian and American-affiliated Factories in 1961/2, by Industry[a]

Industry	Value of production per person employed £A	Value of land and buildings per person employed £A	Value of plant and machinery per person employed £A
Industrial chemicals	3,298 (3,618)	2,034 (2,186)	9,477 (5,269)
Pharmaceuticals and toilet preparations	6,354 (4,188)	1,478 (1,839)	924 (725)
Plant, equipment, and machinery	2,733 (1,843)	1,566 (955)	975 (596)
Electrical machinery, cables, and apparatus	1,814 (1,758)	815 (869)	601 (524)
Motor vehicle construction and assembly, and motor bodies	1,807 (1,857)	1,169 (1,158)	1,185 (859)
Motor accessories	3,014 (2,002)	1,187 (1,008)	2,185 (1,169)
Other metal products	2,635 (1,748)	2,079 (1,038)	3,533 (1,213)
Foundation garments	1,973 (1,344)	805 (504)	137 (134)
Food, drink, tobacco	3,216 (2,315)	1,139 (1,340)	1,076 (1,311)
Paper, stationery, printing, etc.	3,973 (2,214)	2,081 (1,154)	2,518 (1,244)
Other products	4,843	2,318	7,109
Total	2,597	1,403	2,179
Total manufacturing	(1,905)	(1,042)	(1,089)

[a] Figures not in parentheses refer to the factory operations of 99 American-affiliated companies; those in parentheses relate to the whole of the Australian industry concerned, including the American-affiliated companies. For further explanatory notes, see Appendix B.

171

tivity for the remaining American-affiliated firms in 1961/2 rises from
£2,597 to £3,177.

When these figures are further dissected the impression is at
first clouded. Somewhat less than two-thirds of the total number of
plants operated by these American-affiliated firms enjoyed labour
productivity above the average for their industry, and of the total
employment of the group of 56,430 more than half (or 30,518) were
employed in plants of which the productivity was below the industry
average. Certainly the great size of the motor vehicle plants exercises
a considerable influence on this result, but even if they are subtracted
from the total the number employed in plants operating at above
average labour productivity was little more than half. In fairness it
should be added, however, that this situation appears to be the
result primarily of the relatively poor labour productivity obtaining
in a small number of large and long-established companies and of
the initial difficulties encountered by a number of newly-established
firms. On a company basis, it seems significant that sixty-eight out of
ninety-four companies (leaving firms mainly engaged in the motor
vehicle industry out of account) conducted most of their operations
in plants operating above the industry average in terms of value
productivity. Moreover, the industries in which American-affiliated
companies operate are frequently those in which subsidiaries of other
foreign companies also operate, a fact which implies that the comparisons given are in some cases less between American-affiliated and
Australian-owned companies than between American-affiliated companies on the one hand and British- and European-affiliated companies on the other.

Value productivity figures are not easy to interpret. They reflect
values or prices and may not be closely related to physical quantities.
They are influenced by tariff levels. But the magnitude of the difference between figures for Australian industry and those for American-
affiliated companies makes it seem likely that even in physical terms
labour productivity was higher in American-affiliated firms in 1961/2
than in the remainder of Australian industry. No one explanation
is adequate to account for this. The fact that the factories of
American-affiliated companies are generally much larger than is
typical in Australia, as shown in Tables B-2 and B-3 in Appendix
B, must have had an influence on productivity. It seems reasonable
to assume that the modern techniques of management and production available to many American-affiliated companies would result
in their having a higher labour productivity even if their capital-
labour ratio were the same as for Australian-owned companies. And
American-affiliated firms do appear to employ significantly more
machinery per employee than does Australian industry as a whole.

Some indication of this is found in Table VII-4, where values of land and buildings on the one hand and plant and machinery on the other are shown on a 'per employee' basis. Though these figures represent book values only, and so probably overstate the use of machinery by American-affiliated companies relative to Australian industry as a whole, figures of rated horsepower of engines per wages employee, shown in Table B-9, point in the same direction.

A few comments should be made on the difference, if any, in the performance of wholly American companies and jointly-owned ones. In 1961/2 the plants of participating wholly American companies enjoyed a value of production per employee of £2,508, compared with a figure of £2,864 in jointly-owned companies. If motor vehicle plants are excluded from the wholly American group, however, the average performance of the remaining companies in that category is, at £3,419, well above that of the jointly-owned companies. But a further qualification is required: the much higher figure for value productivity in wholly American firms (excluding plants in the motor vehicle industry) is the result of the concentration of wholly American firms in industries, such as the pharmaceuticals and toilet preparations industry, where value of production per employee is particularly high. When comparison is made with the relevant industry productivity, it is found that, even ignoring the plants in the motor vehicle industry, more persons were employed in wholly American plants of which the productivity fell short of the industry average than were employed in wholly American plants which exceeded the industry figure. (The figures are respectively 9,732 and 8,626.) By contrast, only 5,962 persons were employed in jointly-owned plants of which the productivity fell short of the industry average, and 8,209 were employed in jointly-owned plants which exceeded the industry figure. The data contain numerous deficiencies; the industrial classification used is too broad; and the number of companies participating in the survey *within each industry* is too small to permit close comparisons between companies of different ownership patterns. For these reasons definite judgment must be withheld; nevertheless the figures are interesting.

When attention is turned to *growth* in the value of production per employee in American-affiliated firms, the picture is so obscure that it has been decided not even to present the data gathered.[8] Even if the information collected clearly indicated that value productivity in American-affiliated firms has been growing moie

---

[8] This paragraph and the one immediately following summarize the conclusions arising out of a large amount of rather conflicting statistical material which may be seen in substantially complete form in the thesis version of this study.

rapidly than that in Australian industry as a whole (or vice versa), meaningful conclusions could only be drawn on the assumption that the rate of price increase in the industries in which American-affiliated companies figure prominently has been the same as that for the economy as a whole. And there are valid reasons for believing that in some of the major areas of American investment in Australia, notably motor vehicles, industrial chemicals, and oil products, the rate of price increase has been substantially less than any general index of consumer or wholesale prices. All that it appears safe to conclude is that, over the decade 1952/3 to 1961/2, American-affiliated firms approximately maintained their superior position in terms of value of production per person employed in relation to the industries in which they operated.

Some difficulties were encountered even in comparing the growth in total size of American-affiliated companies with that of Australian industry generally. It was clear that over the period 1952/3 to 1961/2 most American-affiliated companies expanded both value of production and manufacturing employment more rapidly than did Australian industry as a whole, but it was equally clear that in some cases part of the explanation for this lay in a faster than average *industry* growth rate.

Because of the deficiencies in the manufacturing data, companies were also asked to indicate changes in their market shares over the eight-year period 1954/5 to 1961/2. Of the twenty-two companies that were able to provide figures for these years, fifteen felt their market share had increased between the two years, two that it had remained about the same, and only five that it had declined. These figures support the view that American-affiliated firms have for the most part grown more rapidly than other firms even within their own industries.

An American affiliation is not a guarantee of success. In chapter X a number of cases will be mentioned in which an American interest has been sold out or a subsidiary liquidated. Others are noted in Appendix A. It should be mentioned here that several companies were encountered which felt that there are disadvantages in their foreign affiliation. One firm, controlled in the first instance by a British company, felt that its competitive position is seriously impaired by the fact that it is unable to introduce a new model of its product until it has been thoroughly tested and marketed by the U.K. company. At the time of the survey the Australian subsidiary wanted to introduce a product recently developed in the U.S., but was prevented from doing this because it was not permitted to contact the ultimate American parent company directly and the British company felt no need to introduce the product in the U.K. Another firm, dependent on its U.S. parent for design work and on its U.K. sister subsidiary for components, felt that its wholly Australian competitor has an advantage because it does its own design work and can buy components on the open market. This gives the Australian company the great advantage of flexibility. Even in the ordering of components, the American-affiliated firm felt itself to be at a disadvantage—it is required to order twelve months in advance to meet the budgeting requirements of its associates. As a result of these factors, the American subsidiary had achieved a sales growth of less than 50 per cent over a recent six-year period, which contrasted unfavourably with the growth of 95 per cent which the Australian-owned company was believed to have achieved over the same period. The executive of a third company, referring to another American subsidiary which operates as a competitor, expressed confidence in the future of his own company, particularly stressing the disadvantage under which his competitor labours because of its lack of Australian research facilities suitable for solving the technical problems of customers. But on balance an American affiliation usually appears to confer an advantage over domestic competitors not enjoying such an affiliation, and it seems significant that the executive interviewed in the first of the companies quoted above described his company as 'the most profitable in Australia'. The executive who lamented the slow rate of growth of his company's sales in relation to the growth achieved by his Australian-owned competitor yet admitted that the ratio of profit to sales in his own company was significantly higher than the ratio in the Australian-owned company. It seems unlikely that an American affiliation is in many cases a *net* disadvantage to the company concerned.

It is a source of considerable regret to the writer that, although it provides a number of interesting impressions, this chapter does not permit definitive answers to be given to several important questions. First, no final judgment can be made on whether the productivity of American direct-investment enterprises in Australia in terms of *total inputs* is higher than that of other companies operating in Australia. Secondly, it is not possible to decide whether, again in terms of total inputs, wholly American companies are more efficient than jointly-owned firms. No firm answers could be given to these questions without a great deal more study than was devoted to them in this survey. But as indicated in the preceding paragraph it does seem fair to assume that access to American managerial and technical know-how usually confers advantages on the companies enjoying such access, and the evidence of the present chapter appears to support this assumption.

VIII

Some Effects on Australians

In what ways has American investment affected Australian incomes? Only a theoretical analysis of the kind attempted in chapter XI can provide a complete answer to this question, but for the moment some useful observations may be made from the empirical material available.

One of the most obvious effects is the impact American investment has had on labour incomes. Though it has been seen in chapter V that most American-affiliated firms pay wages no higher than they are compelled to by local regulation or competitive conditions, the increased demand for workers to staff the new and expanded factories which have been the result of American investment must have had an important influence on the general wage and salary level. In particular cases the advent of an American-owned company has created a demand for a new type of skilled labour, and the pioneering company finds itself having to train Australian labour for the purpose. The frequency with which American-affiliated firms send employees to the U.S. parent company for a period of training or familiarization has already been mentioned. The following example helps to emphasize the importance of training in Australia. When construction of the Altona petrochemical complex commenced late in 1959, the shortage of welders qualified in the particular skills needed for the project necessitated the introduction of a special training programme. Under it, 102,000 man-hours were spent in training the men and approximately two hundred men were qualified (Australian Chemical Industry Council 1964: II, 75). For the later operation of only one of the plants in the complex, that of the Altona Petrochemical Company Pty Ltd, fifty-six skilled operators were required: twenty-two of these had previously been unskilled, twenty-eight had been semi-skilled, and only six had been skilled. 'The weekly earnings of these men as qualified shift operators averaged, in one period of 12 months, £27 a week compared with the general average for the group of £18 to £19 a week before joining

176

the company. This increase of about 50% in weekly wages represents the addition of a further £25,000 a year to their purchasing power.' (Ibid.: I, 26-7.)

The inflow of capital from abroad has been an important factor in the smooth absorption of the large number of immigrants who have come to Australia from the United Kingdom and Continental Europe in the post-war period. About 50 per cent of the workforce of General Motors-Holden's was made up of migrant labour in the early sixties, and other companies were probably in a similar situation, if on a less spectacular scale.

Another obvious benefit accruing to Australia from the operation of American-affiliated companies is the contribution the latter make to tax revenue. Published figures do not permit a precise calculation of the tax paid by American-affiliated firms in this country but it would appear that income tax of about £35 million was levied on income accruing to shareholders in North America in 1963/4, and this figure does not include a further amount of approximately £5 million which was paid on dividends accruing to shareholders in the U.S. and Canada.[1] In addition, many of the royalties and service charges accruing to American parents are taxable at company tax rates in Australia. Admittedly American-affiliated firms sometimes adopt stratagems to avoid the payment of withholding tax, as was noted in chapter IV, and the extent to which Australian tax is avoided by the manipulation of intra-company pricing arrangements and the careful use of nomenclature to describe 'service charges' is dealt with in the next two chapters. Moreover, not all tax paid by American-affiliated companies is a *net* gain to Australia, both because the profits on which American-affiliated companies pay tax are won to some extent at the expense of the profits of other companies, and because American-affiliated firms receive *from* the Australian community many offsetting services. Nevertheless it seems likely that significant net benefit does accrue to Australia from this source.[2]

[1] It is not possible to derive precise figures for these amounts because of the absence of published Australian figures for the remittance of branch profits to North America. This lack prevents precise calculation of withholding tax, since none is levied on the remittance of branch profits, and this in turn prevents exact estimation of after-tax profit. The figure of £35 million is, however, likely to be a fairly close estimate on the assumption of an average company tax of 40 per cent. If anything, it understates the tax paid by subsidiaries of North American companies because many of the latter invest in Australia via third countries. (Figures used were derived from Commonwealth Bureau of Census and Statistics 1965b.)

[2] It should be noted that the point made in the text, and a number of the others made in this chapter, depend on the assumption that the total capital stock in the Australian economy has been increased above what it would have

(Continued on next page)

N

The dealers and distributors of many American-affiliated firms have benefited greatly by the growth of the latter. The importance of this group is most obvious in the motor vehicle and agricultural equipment industries—General Motors-Holden's alone estimated that in 1962 it had over 600 distributors and dealers, with employment of approximately 18,000 and total assets of close to £50 million —but it is very significant in other areas also. Frequently American-affiliated companies assume the responsibility of training their dealers, and while this clearly is of benefit to the American companies themselves, the benefit is mutual. One firm producing soft drink concentrate, for example, conducts training courses in the U.S. for overseas personnel (mainly from locally-owned bottling companies) twice annually, and eighteen Australians from companies engaged in the distribution of abrasives produced by another American subsidiary have been to the U.S. parent company over the years for periods of training. The writer was told by the managing director of a company in the food industry that it had been the absolute insistence of Kraft Holdings Ltd on the orderly and hygienic presentation of its products that had first introduced modern food marketing techniques to much of Australia's grocery trade. On the other hand some dealers handling the products of American-affiliated firms feel themselves to have been harshly treated: petrol retailers in particular have made bitter complaint at the unrestricted construction of new service stations on the part of the international oil companies, and it was reported in 1961 that of twenty-five service stations in Sydney selected for investigation by the New South Wales Prices Commissioner more than half were trading at a loss (*A.F.R.*, 27 April 1961).

The techniques of American subsidiaries tend to become disseminated throughout the economy in a number of ways. Executives with experience in American-owned companies often move to Australian-owned companies, though as so many of the larger companies in Australian industry are foreign-owned this effect may be of smaller benefit than is sometimes imagined. Nearly forty American-affiliated firms were members of local productivity groups in 1963, and through these contacts American techniques in at least some areas of management are shared. (Indeed, a former managing director of the Ford Motor Company of Australia was chairman of the Australian Productivity Council for some time, in addition to his membership of the Australian Export Council and the Technical Education Advisory Council.) The writer met one highly trained

---

been in the absence of a capital inflow by roughly the amount of the inflow itself. This may not be a valid assumption, but it appears to be at least as probable as any alternative assumption. See also chapter XI.

company secretary who quite often gives lectures on management techniques to groups of businessmen. In addition this man had recently spent considerable time trying to help the executives of one Australian company master 'some of the more elementary techniques'. He admitted, however, that his company does not encourage him to spend his time in this way. Several American-affiliated companies have organized plant tours for visitors—both General Motors-Holden's and H. J. Heinz claim that more than 14,000 visitors tour their plants each year—and the intangible effect these have, apart from their public relations value, must be considerable. Often the mere example of American-affiliated firms is sufficient to induce a change in the operating methods of Australian firms: one widely known Australian industrialist told the writer that when he first began manufacturing operations he had observed General Motors-Holden's closely. He commented that 'if you follow General Motors' methods you won't go far wrong'.

Of relatively small importance in total money value but of considerable significance to those immediately affected are the scholarships awarded by some American-affiliated firms. By far the best known of these are the twenty-five awards made annually to Australian students by General Motors-Holden's to permit them to further their studies at a post-graduate level. The same company annually makes an award to encourage Australian theatre. The large-scale financial aid given to universities and research institutions by companies in the U.S. is almost unknown in Australia, but there is no evidence that American subsidiaries are any more reluctant to contribute in this way than are Australian-owned companies. In certain fields, such as pharmaceutical research, there is evidence that some American-affiliated firms are active in their encouragement of local research in universities and teaching hospitals.

Australian companies which find themselves in competition with American-owned companies are among those most directly affected by American investment. In many cases Australian companies find themselves at a serious competitive disadvantage: the foreign companies not only have free access to the technical and managerial know-how of their parent companies, but are also usually able to draw heavily, at least initially, on the financial resources of their parents. Even where the parent company is not prepared to support the subsidiary financially, the reputation or guarantee of the former is of considerable benefit to the latter in raising finance locally. Subsidiaries may be able to purchase materials at lower cost than can Australian-owned companies, either because their parent companies buy in bulk from American suppliers or because their parents can afford to supply them at little more than marginal cost. Since the establishment of an Australian plant is a relatively minor under-taking for most American firms, the American subsidiary in Australia is often able to commence operations on a scale substantially above that possible for an Australian-financed company, thus giving it a major advantage in securing economies of scale. The international advertising of many American products may also be an important factor helping the American-owned company.

Certainly many Australian companies have complained at the competition they have experienced from American-owned sub-sidiaries. Frequent complaints have come, for example, from firms in the food and drink industry, where newly-arrived American firms have recently been running substantial losses in an effort to secure larger market shares. Typical of the comments made in recent years was that by the chairman of the Australian firm of Cottee's Ltd in 1964:

> Competition in the processed food industry springs, in no small measure, from companies of overseas origin. These companies, some already well established and some seeking to become well established, have the use of considerable capital resources which their principals invest often without requiring an immediate profit return. Although, as an Australian company, we have been able to meet this competition it has not been without some reduction in profit margins. (*Sydney Morning Herald*, 7 July 1964.)

From the other side of the competitive battle, the company secretary of a wholly American firm in a related industry stated:

> Ours is really a very profitable business but we have been making losses because of heavy advertising expenditure. The U.S. company has been making loans to us on inter-company account to cover these expenses and losses. . . . There is still a lot of shaking up to take place in the Australian industry. . . . Ultimately, the firms that will survive will be those with overseas financial backing which can support an Australian company making losses over a lengthy period.

Such behaviour appears to be in all respects tantamount to price discrimination between markets with the intention of reducing competition in a particular market, and in the U.S. might fall under the purview of restrictive trade practices authorities. Though the practice has obvious benefits to Australian advertising agencies and shareholders in Australian advertising media, there would seem to be much in favour of refusing to accept such expenditures as deductible for taxation purposes in any case (whether foreign com-panies are involved or not) where an intention to seriously reduce competition can be established.

Competition need not be as fierce as in the above example. It may be quite gradual. It is none the less real. One American firm in the agricultural equipment industry expressed the view that 'a large number—perhaps 250—of the 400 firms at present operating in this industry in Australia will go under'. Local coal-mining firms have in recent years made frequent complaint about the unbalanced production pattern of some of the major oil refining companies, a pattern which results in the production of an 'excessive' percentage of fuel oil. In evidence before the Tariff Board in early 1965, the chairman of the Joint Coal Board contended that the price of furnace oil had declined from about £16 per ton in 1958 to little more than £6 per ton in 1965. From newspaper reports, he appears to have argued that furnace oil is offered at such reduced prices only when it is directly competitive with coal. When sold for use in ships' bunkers, the price is substantially higher at more than £10 per ton (in 1963/4). He is reported to have claimed further that the Sydney retail price (presumably net of excise tax) of most premium grade motor spirit is higher than that in any West European country except West Germany. The obvious conclusion to be drawn is that the oil refining companies (almost all American or British in ownership) indulge in a form of price discrimination detrimental to the coal producers (*A.F.R.*, 1 Mar. 1965). Whether or not this is another case of 'unfair competition'—and because fuel oil and motor spirit are produced jointly any charge of price discrimination based on relative costs of production is very difficult to sustain—it is hardly surprising that companies engaged in coal production dislike the pressure on them.

The effects of the operation of American-affiliated companies on competitors are not always detrimental and often, because of the concentration of foreign ownership in particular industries, the greatest impact is felt by other foreign-owned companies. The comment of an executive of an Australian-owned company engaged in the production of household cleansers is interesting in this connection:

> In 1956, Ajax, produced by Colgate-Palmolive, hit the market. It cut our sales by 11 per cent and drove Old Dutch [produced by another American-affiliated company] out of business. But Ajax did the market a lot of good—intensive advertising developed many new uses for our type of cleansers, and we are almost back to our peak sales again, though Ajax is much more important in the Australian market than we are now.

And though the growth of General Motors-Holden's has undoubtedly been one of the factors impeding the progress of the only significant

Australian-owned firm engaged in the assembly of motor vehicles, nobody would deny that the great weight of competitive pressure generated by that company is borne not by Australian-owned companies but by Ford, Chrysler, British Motor Corporation, and Volkswagen, all of them having their entire ordinary capital held abroad (1965).

Sometimes the pressure of competition from American-owned firms induces Australian-owned firms to modernize their methods to their own long-term benefit. Not infrequently this is done by establishing a licensing arrangement with another foreign company. An executive in one long-established subsidiary explained that when his company first commenced Australian operations in the thirties, standard cost accounting and advanced techniques of cash forecasting were used at a time when they were almost unknown in Australia. 'We pioneered many new techniques and local competition was forced to follow us.' A spokesman for the oil industry also has contended that the significant increase in the efficiency of the local coal industry which has occurred over the past decade (an increase which has permitted a fall in coal prices of 17 per cent between 1953 and 1964 at a time of steadily rising wage rates) has not been unrelated to the competitive pressure of the oil refining industry, which first became established as an important force at the beginning of the fifties (*Australian*, 19 Aug. 1964).

Moreover, what is loss to Australian-owned companies competing with American subsidiaries is often gain to Australian consumers. The establishment of a foreign subsidiary may be the only practical way to destroy a local monopoly, and there have been some spectacular examples of this in recent years. Probably the best known of these was the invasion in the mid-fifties of the Australian cigarette market—previously dominated by the Anglo-Australian firm of British Tobacco Co. (Aust.) Ltd—by Rothmans of Pall Mall (Aust.) Ltd, another Anglo-Australian firm, and Philip Morris (Aust.) Ltd, an American-Australian firm. From holding almost the entire Australian cigarette market in 1955, British Tobacco's share of the market is believed to have slipped to below 50 per cent in 1965. Another example, this time involving a clash between a wholly British company and a wholly American firm, has occurred in recent years in the soap flake and detergent market. For many years, Unilever Australia (Holdings) Pty Ltd had held, through its various subsidiaries, almost the entire Australian market for such products. It was not until Colgate-Palmolive introduced Fab that any serious competitor challenged the British giant on the local scene. As J. A. Bushnell has observed, 'The actual or potential entry of overseas firms into oligopolist Australian markets through locally established factories is an important, but seldom mentioned, limitation on oligopolist profits and inefficiency.' (1961: 133.)

The Australian consumer may also benefit from the more rapid introduction of new products than if the Australian market were served only by importing from the United States. American direct-investment enterprises have manufactured many hundreds of products for the first time in Australia. One company indicated that it never introduces a new product to the Australian market until its stocks of the old line have been cleared, and in this case it is possible that the American investment actually delays the introduction of the new product. But most of the companies which commented on the time-lag between the introduction of a new product in the U.S. and its introduction in Australia felt that the delay involved is very short or determined by local market conditions. One executive commented that 'new products are available in Australia immediately they are developed in the U.S.', while another in the foundation garment industry remarked that one special type of brassiere was introduced to the Australian market only six weeks after its first sale in New York. An executive in one pharmaceutical company even felt that because of new U.S. laws controlling the sale of drugs, there have been cases in which products have been manufactured in Australia before they have been marketed in the U.S. Several companies supplying industrial components felt that their American affiliation always enabled them to be prepared well in advance of any new demand emanating from their customers.

The savings made by some of the customers of American subsidiaries through the reduction in inventories that their proximity makes possible have already been noted in chapter III. The example quoted where customer companies were able to save more than £100,000 annually in inventory charges is not an isolated case. One firm in the chemical industry explained how it had won orders in New Zealand because customer companies could reduce stocks from a full year's supply to those needed for three months. Another firm felt that its presence in Australia made it possible for customers to reduce inventories from those needed for six months' operations to those needed for four weeks.

The presence of an American manufacturing operation in Australia often means that the Australian customer is particularly well served in terms of technical training and after-sales attention. This appears to be especially true in the chemical industry. Most of the companies in the Altona petrochemical complex, for example, maintain laboratories for the solution of the technical problems of customers, and the older firms appear to offer similar service. One very small firm, with 1962 employment of less than twenty-five, maintains a technical service manager and two technicians who run demonstrations and tests in customers' plants explaining how to use their product and showing how money can be saved.

Help of a different kind has been provided by another American-affiliated firm in the chemical industry, C.S.R.C.-Dow Pty Ltd. In 1963 it was reported that the company

> recently sponsored representatives of 10 companies in New South Wales and Victoria at a course of work simplification methods. . . . The program presented covered the improvement of existing methods of plant lay-out, improvement in the planning of work, the use of manpower, and the effectiveness of all employees. (*A.F.R.*, 10 Sept. 1963.)

'Technical services selling' appears to characterize the marketing of many American-affiliated firms. Norton Australia Pty Ltd, then known as Behr-Manning (Aust.) Pty Ltd, indicated to the Tariff Board in 1959 that 'since 1952, qualified products engineers have been used to boost sales by demonstrating to industry the correct use of abrasives. They also assist in the design of machines and techniques which will enable the user to reduce his grinding or finishing costs. Workshop clinics have been established in four States where user problems can be discussed.' Summing up the evidence, the Tariff Board commented that

> various witnesses referred to the difference in the selling techniques of Behr-Manning, 3M [Minnesota Mining and Manufacturing Co. (Aust.) Pty Ltd] and Carborundum on the one hand and distributors of United Kingdom finished products on the other. It appears that these three companies have adopted 'American' selling techniques which provide considerable technical service direct to users. (*T.B.R.* 1959b: 4, 9.)

In another industry, the Lincoln Electric Company has frequently advertised that

> for over a generation we have been helping manufacturers get more welding productivity. Sometimes the results have been spectacular—cutting welding time by 90%, for example. Almost every time a new customer calls on us, there is some worthwhile improvement to be made, if only a 5% or 6% increase in productivity. The man from Lincoln *thinks* productivity . . . When he is in your shop he is working not for us but for you.

In a different sector of the electrical industry, I.B.M. has trained several hundred personnel from customer companies in data processing techniques, though of course this programme is probably not intimately dependent on the company's Australian manufacturing activities.

No simple answer can be given to the question of the effect which

American investment in Australia has had on the prices of the products supplied by the American affiliates. There have certainly been some dramatic cases in which the prices of goods produced by American-affiliated firms have risen very much less rapidly than the price level in Australia generally. Probably the best known of these examples relates to the price of the Holden car. The list price of the Holden standard sedan, excluding tax, rose in a series of steps from £675 in November 1948 to £945 in June 1952, a rise of 40 per cent. Over the same period the rise in the Australian retail price index was in excess of 50 per cent. During the next few years the price of this car declined until in October 1958 it reached £885, at which price it still remained in 1965. At this level it was only 31 per cent above that of 1948, despite considerable improvements in the car itself and a rise in the Australian retail price index of 106 per cent during the same period. Needless to say, the competitive pressure of this company has compelled other companies, including other American subsidiaries, to make parallel price reductions so that today cars are substantially cheaper, in relative terms, than they were at the beginning of the fifties.

Because of the considerable importance of this subject a number of other examples may be cited. In the electrical equipment industry American-affiliated firms have made some remarkable price reductions. In February 1963 Lincoln Electric illustrated the success of its profit sharing and job incentive scheme by the following statement:

> During the years 1939-1957 when the wholesale price index of goods manufactured rose by 200 per cent, the price of one of Lincoln's main sales items—welding electrode—rose by only 45 per cent. As another example, a particular type of farm welding machine sold in 1951 for £133. Today, the price of a newer type having 65 per cent more output is only £114.[3]

Thomas Electronics of Australia Pty Ltd, a wholly American subsidiary until early in 1962, was cited by the Australian Tariff Board in 1960 as the company which, while seeking high protection with other manufacturers in 1957, had indicated that it did not expect to need such protection by 1958. The Board's 1960 report on cathode ray tubes noted that between 1957 and 1960 this company had reduced the selling price of one of its major products by about one-third. In 1963 the Tariff Board also noted with approval that competition between members of the Australian portable electric tool industry was vigorous and that prices 'and consequently profit levels' were being reduced. The American-owned firm of Black and

[3] Originally a statement of this kind appeared in *Business Review*, January 1959. Figures amended to February 1963 were supplied directly by the company.

Decker (Australasia) is one of the two largest producers in that industry. The chairman of Australian Controls Ltd, a jointly-owned venture, announced at the company's annual general meeting in 1964 that 'for some years now we have been steadily reducing our selling prices across a wide range of our products. A continuation of this process is something which we should regard as probable and necessary.'

Australian prices of locally produced chemicals fell between 1953 and 1963 by 16 per cent, a fall greater than that in any of the major chemical manufacturing countries with the exception of Japan. Both Monsanto Chemicals (Australia) and Union Carbide Australia feel that this price fall was typical of their own experience (Australian Chemical Industry Council 1964: II, 72).

Similar reductions in price have occurred in the food industry. The H. J. Heinz Company supplied price data on four of its main product categories for the three years 1953, 1958, and 1963. The net-into-store prices of all four advanced between 1953 and 1958, but in three cases this increase was less than the increase in the Australian wholesale price index. The prices of all four groups declined significantly between 1958 and 1963, so that indexes of the 1963 price of each product (with base 1953 = 100) were respectively 87, 93, 94, and 107. These compare with a 6 per cent increase in the Australian wholesale price index over the whole period and an increase of 58 per cent in an index of wages provided by the company. Since 1963, the writer understands there have been still further price reductions, in part no doubt because of increasing competition from the entry of other foreign subsidiaries into the field. The imminent entry of the American-owned Nabisco Pty Ltd into the Australian biscuit market also appears to be having a beneficial impact on prices. It is reported that the dominant company in the industry 'has now dropped its policy of price maintenance on biscuits in N.S.W.' as part of its new marketing drive (*A.F.R.*, 3 July 1964).

In the foundation garment industry, one American-affiliated firm mentioned that the reorganization of production which followed the establishment of its American association had made it possible on one occasion to maintain prices despite a general price rise throughout the industry of about 10 per cent. Another American-affiliated company in the industry recently introduced a brassiere which it claims to be of high quality at a price less than half that at which most brassieres are sold.

A number of examples from an earlier period may also be given. The Wiltshire File Company contended before the Tariff Board in 1953 that between 1944 and 1950 the 'company's files were purchased by merchants at prices equal to or less than they could have been landed from the United Kingdom free of duty and primage. For the three years, 1946 to 1948 inclusive, the cost of Australian files was as much as 14 per cent less than the duty free landed cost of United Kingdom files.' (*T.B.R.* 1953: 4.) In 1955 the Tariff Board (1955b: 10) described as 'a highly creditable performance' the fact that International Harvester had refrained from increasing the price of its tractors since 1951 despite increased costs for labour and raw materials. Very much earlier, in 1914, the managing director of Kodak (Australasia) argued at a tariff hearing that the manufacture of photographic film by his company in Australia had reduced the price of such film to the world market price, which was apparently 'considerably lower' than the price prevailing before this (*Inter-State Commission of Australia. Tariff Investigation: Report*, p. 66).

It is not imagined, of course, that American-affiliated firms reduce their selling prices simply out of concern for Australian consumers. Often prices are reduced because of competition from imports or other local companies. In some industries prices are reduced in order to increase profits through the expansion in sales volume which the price reduction makes possible. One firm specifically stated that a price reduction from £125 to £99 on one of its major products more than doubled turnover and thus increased overall profitability. It is also obvious that prices in some industries would have fallen even without the influence of American investment. But it does seem reasonable to conclude that American investment has been an influence slowing the rate of price increase in some areas and that Australian purchasers of the products involved have thereby benefited.

Unfortunately, this benefit has not been by any means universal. There is, for example, substantial evidence that prices charged by pharmaceutical companies in Australia, including many American subsidiaries, are very much higher than necessary. The Federal Minister for Health, Senator Wade, gave a number of price comparisons in September 1963 which showed that the prices of drugs supplied to the National Health Scheme by companies in Australia are frequently more than 100 per cent higher than the prices of identical drugs when supplied to the British government's health scheme.[4] The result of this is that the average cost of a prescription to the Australian health scheme was stated in 1963 to be more than double the average cost of a prescription in England and Wales

[4] Senator Wade's examples included the following: prednisone, 30 x 5 mg. tablets, British price 8s. 2d., Australian price 18s. 6d.; cortisone, 40 x 25 mg. tablets, British price 31s. 11d., Australian price 50s.; erythromycin, 250 mg. tablets, British price 26s. 7d. per 25, Australian price 51s. 9d. per 16. (*A.F.R.*, 19 Sept. 1963.)

(*Commonwealth Parliamentary Debates*, vol. H. of R. 39 (n.s.), p. 643). In part, of course, these high prices may be the result of higher Australian unit costs. In part also, they are the result of substantially higher distribution margins in Australia. But these are not the only influences on price, as the following comment from a senior executive in one wholly American company indicates:

> Pricing policy varies but the most important influence is what price the government can be prevailed upon to pay to the chemist for the final product under the pharmaceutical benefits scheme. Some lines are in fairly strong competition, but in others there is no competition and in still others there is a gentleman's agreement on prices.

In recent years the federal government has been exerting considerable pressure on pharmaceutical companies to reduce their prices, pressure which has been accompanied by overt ministerial threats. The policy has met with a significant measure of success. A sample list of price reductions secured by the government tabled in the House of Representatives early in 1964 showed that price reductions in many drugs exceeded 25 per cent over a two-year period (*Commonwealth Parliamentary Debates*, vol. H. of R. 41 (n.s.), p. 1129), and there is some evidence that because of this pressure there are now a number of cases in which Australian drug prices to the pharmaceutical benefits scheme are on a par with British prices. As far as one can judge, however, government action has had little influence on the prices of proprietary lines sold directly to consumers, and these still appear high by international standards. An experiment conducted by the writer, admittedly with a sample much too small to permit of dogmatic conclusions, indicated that the Australian prices of proprietary medicines tend to be higher even than those in New Zealand—in the most extreme case, the price of 100 capsules of a brand of halibut liver oil capsules marketed in Australia by one of the large American branch operations was more than five times the New Zealand price.[5] Despite the inadequacy of the sample and insufficient information on the tariff and marketing arrangements involved in each country, it is hard to avoid the feeling that there might be some relevance to Australia in the conclusion reached by the Special Committee on Pharmaceutical Benefits set up by the New Zealand government:

[5] The content of the pills in each country was, however, not quite identical. In Australia the pills were labelled as containing not less than 5,000 I.U. of Vitamin A and 1,000 I.U. of Vitamin D. In New Zealand the pills contained 5,000 I.U. of Vitamin A but only 'not less than' 410 I.U. of Vitamin D. To the layman the difference does not appear sufficient to explain a fivefold price differential.

When drugs are manufactured in New Zealand, even if this merely amounts to processing and packaging, production costs tend to be high, and a monopolistic situation may be created. Purchasing with limited competition in this small market tends towards high prices. (N.Z. Dept. of Health 1963: 59.)[6]

It is not immediately clear how many American direct-investment enterprises indulge in restrictive trade practices in Australia. Certainly there are many that do. It is common knowledge that the two American-affiliated companies in the rubber industry are parties to the agreement fixing prices and discounts in the tyre replacement market: indeed, Forster (1964: 56) has noted that one of the reasons for Goodyear's profitable début in the Australian market in the late twenties was the issue of uniform tyre price lists by all the local tyre manufacturing companies in 1928. A witness before a Tariff Board hearing on rubber conveyor belting in 1961 provided documentary evidence of price collusion by the local manufacturers of this item, again including Goodyear's Australian subsidiary (*A.F.R.*, 25 May 1961). In the supply of petroleum products also, it is common to hear complaints from local government authorities of price collusion on the part of supplying companies, which certainly include several large American-affiliated companies. It was reported recently that in the case of oral contraceptives 'all the manufacturers make their product available at the same price to the chemists' (*A.F.R.*, 15 Oct. 1964), and American subsidiaries are undoubtedly implicated in that statement. Very many pharmaceuticals and cosmetics are in fact covered by retail price maintenance agreements, and while these schemes are sometimes initiated by pharmacists they are usually agreed to readily by manufacturers.[7] In both fields American subsidiaries and branches are prominently represented.

[6] Of course, if this view does have relevance to Australia it suggests measures to deal with restrictive trade practices and monopolistic abuses in the industry as a whole.

[7] The writer was fortunate in securing access to a copy of the retail price list issued by the Federated Pharmaceutical Service Guild of Australia (N.S.W. Branch) in 1963. This document not only specifies retail prices and profit margins but also indicates the 'credit rating' of each product. This is judged on whether the company concerned sells only through pharmaceutical chemists, whether it supports price maintenance, what profit margin it affords to retailers, etc. Products with a high rating, marked 'G' for 'gold', merit 'utmost support'. Those with a low rating, marked 'R' for 'red', should be accorded 'no display, no support, sell only on demand'. It is interesting that all the products of several wholly American companies, especially those producing mainly toilet preparations and toothpaste, were given a low rating, indicating among other things their unwillingness to participate in the price fixing agreements of the Guild. On the other hand, all the products of several American subsidiaries whose operations are more concerned with pharmaceuticals were given a high rating.

Many other examples could be adduced. Among firms encountered during the present survey was one which fixed its prices in accordance with an international price agreement on its product, an agreement which appears to cover all producing countries outside the Soviet bloc except Japan. The chief executive of another company commented that when he read the proposed federal legislation on restrictive trade practices 'I thought Sir Garfield had been reading our own marketing arrangements—we break all the laws'. An executive in a third company admitted that a public denial he had made some years ago of a market sharing arrangement of which his company had been accused was made 'for the benefit of our attorneys in the U.S. who are always worried about antitrust laws'. Still another American-affiliated firm complained that its Anglo-Australian competitor would not come to any agreement 'to stabilise prices'.[8]

Whatever comment one might wish to make about the society which tolerates such abuses of the competitive system, there appears little doubt that a significant fraction of American-affiliated firms in Australia do participate in restrictive trade practices.

There are a number of products manufactured by American-affiliated companies which are marketed at a common list price. Electrical consumer durables are the most popularly known, but there has been evidence in recent years that competition through the granting of grossly unrealistic 'trade-in allowances' has been very vigorous. Referring to the local manufacturers of electric shavers in 1962, moreover, the Tariff Board expressed the view that 'the evidence indicates that there is no pricing agreement between them' despite the identical prices which each quotes. Similarly, though the three American subsidiaries producing coated abrasives in Australia quote 'virtually the same prices' (prices which, incidentally, are considerably higher than those quoted by the British subsidiary in the industry), the Tariff Board 'does not conclude that there is collusion between the companies in the setting of prices but only that, as a matter of company policy, each would appear to follow the lead of the largest supplier of the three in setting its prices for a particular market'. (*T.B.R.* 1959b: 9.)

Several companies were encountered which refuse to have anything to do with industry agreements on price or marketing. The only one of these whose position with regard to price agreements is sufficiently widely known to permit its citation here is General

---

[8] In fact the Anglo-Australian competitor had its own restrictive trade practice. Having enjoyed a monopoly of the Australian market in its particular product until the arrival of the American-affiliated company, it embarked on an aggressive policy of price-cutting which compelled the new company, after a period of heavy losses, to sell out to the original monopolist.

Motors-Holden's, a company which refuses to 'co-operate' with other manufacturers in the marketing of either motor vehicles or domestic appliances. But there are a number of others. These firms, with only two exceptions, all mentioned a fear of American antitrust legislation as the explanation of their behaviour. None of them dared 'talk price' with any other manufacturer and at least one of them, in a dominant position in its industry, was afraid to offer discounts to Australian customers lest it be accused of trying to stifle competition. Writing of American subsidiaries in Canada, Kingman Brewster, jr, noted that 'if the U.S. parent can be said to have dictated or even acquiesced in the cartel activities of its foreign subsidiaries, an antitrust charge may be made against the parent even though the subsidiary in question is not itself subject to the power of a U.S. court' (1960: 10). It appears beyond doubt that, in the absence of effective Australian legislation against restrictive trade practices, this country has derived some benefit from the legislation of the United States.

It is also probable that some American subsidiaries which now participate in industry agreements do so only reluctantly. In recent years the experience of Parsons General Foods Pty Ltd has received considerable publicity in this connection. When the company attempted to launch its Maxwell House instant coffee on the Australian market without price maintenance, it is reported that Australian retailers exerted such pressure on the company that it was forced to follow the policy of other manufacturers and 'maintain price'. When tactics were changed and the company advertised one free jar of coffee for each one purchased, retailers again complained that their profit margins were being jeopardized (*A.F.R.*, 3 July 1964).

If most American-affiliated companies do indulge in restrictive trade practices, and this seems probable, they are only following the example set by the great majority of Australian-owned and other companies in Australia. Alex Hunter concluded in 1961 that 'however conservatively the position is stated, it is clear that Australia is well, even handsomely, endowed with trade associations and restrictive practices' (1961: 32). Two years later he published an estimate that between 40 and 50 per cent of all public expenditure on acquiring supplies in Australia was affected by level tendering (1963). No evidence has been produced to suggest that he exaggerated the prevalence of such practices.[9] Again it is obvious that what is

---

[9] In a recent survey of manufacturing industry conducted in Western Australia, John Hutton (1964) discovered that almost two-thirds of the major firms contacted worked within the framework of an orderly marketing scheme.

(*Continued on next page*)

required is not an attack on foreign subsidiaries but adequate measures to combat restrictive trade practices.

One of the most crucial questions that may be asked of American investment concerns the prices at which the products of American affiliates are marketed in relation to the prices of equivalent imported products. Firms participating in the present survey were asked to compare the ex-factory price of their main product line with the landed duty-paid price of the same product if it were imported from their parent company. In all, twenty-five firms provided such data, though the basis for comparison was not identical in all cases. Twenty-one companies felt the Australian ex-factory price to be lower than the landed duty-paid price if the same product were imported from their American parent, and four felt it to be higher.[10] Ten of the companies that felt the Australian price to be lower, moreover, felt it to be less than 75 per cent of the imported price, and of the four that felt Australian prices to be higher than those of imported products, one company was using as a basis for comparison the U.S. price which an Australian customer could secure if he placed his whole annual order with the U.S. parent at one time, something very unlikely to occur in practice.

At first sight, these figures might convey the impression that the operation of American subsidiaries in Australia helps Australian consumers to purchase goods at prices lower than they would have to pay if dependent on imports. The industrial distribution of companies which responded to this question, though including few industrial chemical companies, was fairly wide, further strengthening this impression. Two important qualifications must be taken into account, however. First, the assumed price of the American import included an element of Australian tariff. While the tariff clearly influences the price at which Australian *consumers* can buy, it probably has little influence on the price at which *Australia* can buy. A saving available to the Australian consumer by the purchase of a locally-produced article may be more than offset by a loss in taxation revenue. To shed further light on this matter, participating firms were also requested to compare their ex-factory price with the landed price of the same product if imported from their parent company without customs duty. Of the twenty-five firms mentioned, only thirteen felt their Australian price to be below the American import price in

---

The report of the Tasmanian Royal Commissioner on prices and restrictive trade practices, released in 1965, found that two-thirds of about seventy Tasmanian trade associations were involved in restrictive trade practices.

[10] It is possible for the Australian price to be higher than the import price in some cases where the local company has sole Australian distribution rights for its affiliates.

such circumstances, two felt it to be the same, and ten felt it to be higher. Moreover, had a greater number of chemical companies been included among those which answered this question, the proportion of those which felt their Australian price to be above that of the imported product would certainly have been considerably higher.

The second qualification which must be taken into account is that in at least some cases the American prices used for the purpose of comparison were not typical of those at which imports are available to Australia. In the case of some products, imports are now available more cheaply from Japan or West Germany. Moreover, the American prices used appear in most instances to have been full cost prices, and as such are probably significantly higher than the actual prices at which Australia can buy on the world market. The two companies which compared the Australian price of their motor vehicle with the price of a comparable product imported from the U.S. are both believed to have used the price of a fully-assembled vehicle, again perhaps overstating the benefit to Australia of local manufacture.

To sum up the available evidence on the price of goods produced by American direct-investment enterprises in Australia, it appears that, *if it is granted that local manufacture of the goods concerned is desirable for other reasons,* American investment has reduced the prices of many goods to Australian consumers. There are, however, some notable exceptions to this generalization. It also appears likely that many prices would be significantly lower than they are at present were it not for the participation of many American-affiliated companies in industry agreements to maintain price levels. But there still remains the most serious question of whether or not the manufacture of some items now made in Australia by American affiliates should have been encouraged at all. Clearly there are some products, particularly in the metal-working industries and probably also in the food industry, whose Australian prices are lower than those in most overseas countries. Equally clearly, however, there are some products (especially, perhaps, in the field of industrial chemicals) which from a purely economic point of view it would pay Australia not to produce, either now or in the foreseeable future; for if the cost—after allowing for all external economies—of certain locally-manufactured goods is higher than that at which imports are available against an increase in Australian export production, not only is Australian real income adversely affected but the Australian balance of payments is also harmed (as will be explained in chapter XI).[11]

[11] There may, of course, still be grounds for local manufacture from a defence point of view, though it is doubtful (because of dependence on imported raw materials) if such an argument could carry much weight in the case of some investment in the Australian chemical industry.

o

American investment (or more correctly, the oligopolistic situation it may create) may be blamed in some cases for fragmenting an already small market and thereby maintaining costs and prices at an unnecessarily high level,[12] but, fundamentally, blame for the production of 'uneconomic products' in Australia must fall on the Tariff Board and the government which lays down its terms of reference.

One important influence on the incomes of Australians not so far examined is the impact which American-affiliated companies have through their purchases of goods and services. In aggregate these purchases are very large. Table B-7, in Appendix B, shows that the expenditure of ninety-nine American-affiliated manufacturing companies in 1961/2 on certain materials, fuel, power, etc. was in excess of £200 million. While this amount includes considerable expenditure on imported parts and materials, it almost certainly understates the total expenditure on Australian-made products because most finished parts bought by the American-owned motor vehicle manufacturers are excluded from the figures. Not included at all, moreover, is expenditure on a multitude of services, perhaps the most important of which is advertising.[13] Of the ten largest daily-press advertisers (among industrial companies) in 1962, four were wholly American subsidiaries, one was a jointly Australian-American firm, and one was in the process of acquiring a large American minority interest (*A.F.R.*, 30 April 1963). Public authorities are also among the beneficiaries, to the extent that the price paid by American-affiliated firms for electricity, the use of roads, freight services, etc. exceeds the marginal cost of providing these utilities.[14]

In his survey of American investment in Britain, J. H. Dunning found that many companies supplying American direct-investment enterprises with parts and materials benefited considerably from the operation of their American-owned customers. Many companies felt that the strict adherence to technical tolerances demanded by American subsidiaries had compelled them to improve their manufacturing methods, and a majority of those he interviewed felt that they had received some specific benefit in the form of materials

[12] In this connection the Australian Tariff Board was critical of the two local manufacturers of styrene monomer, Australian Petrochemicals and C.S.R.C.-Dow, both companies with American affiliations (*T.B.R.* 1962h: 8). W. P. Hogan (1961) has made a similar criticism.

[13] The U.S. Department of Commerce (1960: 115) estimated the total expenditure of all U.S. direct investments in Australia on materials and services in 1957 (other than expenditure by trading organizations) at £347 million.

[14] It may be debated, of course, perhaps especially in the case of road use, whether the price paid by American-affiliated (and other) firms for the use of public utilities *does* exceed the marginal cost of providing them.

formulae, manufacturing methods, or machinery design (1958: esp. 224-5). A detailed study of supplying companies was not undertaken during the present survey, but some light is shed on this subject by questions asked a number of the American subsidiaries themselves. It appears beyond doubt that most American subsidiaries provide their suppliers with detailed specifications and blueprints, but on the other hand it seems that very few give additional help. Of twenty-two companies asked the question:

> Have you found it necessary, in order to improve the quality of components, to provide Australian producers with information on new techniques, materials, or formulae?

twelve replied in the negative. Typical of the comments made by executives of these companies was one that 'we give drawings to suppliers and sub-contractors but nothing else. We had some difficulty with tubing for a time so we imported it.' Only one of these companies noted that, though it had not provided any technical information to its suppliers directly, most of these had in fact made contact with the American parent company while on overseas trips.

Of the ten companies which answered the question in the affirmative (all, incidentally, wholly American in ownership), four had provided such assistance only on very rare occasions. One of these indicated that 'normally we don't try to do our supplier's business for him', but went on to admit that on one occasion detailed information had been passed on to a local British subsidiary to help the latter make a particular type of bronze. Against the American company's wishes, the supplier had made use of the formulae when supplying the company's competitors. The initial reaction of another firm, in the motor vehicle industry, was that no help had been provided to suppliers, but as an afterthought it was mentioned that one supplier had been assisted with technical information some years previously. When an executive of the supplying company was contacted, however, he expressed the view that the American information 'really only confirmed an opinion we had had before'.

Two more companies had provided considerable information to suppliers only in the years immediately after their establishment in Australia and felt that because of the improvement in the standards of their suppliers this was no longer significant. In one case, the technical liaison had been important:

> We laid down certain manufacturing tolerances and made our suppliers live up to them. We had our own inspection shop and our rigorous standards compelled our suppliers to install inspection shops too. Right from the start, we demanded quality and educated our suppliers to produce it.

But in only four cases of the twenty-two queried on this point did the writer gain the impression that the flow of technical information from American subsidiary to Australian supplier is of continuing importance. One of these firms is in the motor vehicle industry, but since a more detailed comment is made below on the relationship between American companies and their suppliers in this industry no further mention is made of this company here. The comments of the other three companies are worth quoting at length. An executive of a company producing electric shavers stated:

> Australian electrical steels and plastic components had to be made to dimensional tolerances which were difficult to achieve in the beginning, but with the provision of process by process details from the U.S., Australian production of these highly specialized components was upgraded to meet the necessary standards and specifications on the blueprints supplied from America. . . . At all times there has been a free flow of process information from the U.S. company to the Australian plant and sub-contractors. Some of this information has been invaluable in the manufacture of products entirely unconnected with the electric shaver industry.

In the food industry, an American subsidiary gives help on a similar scale:

> Contracts are issued to growers during the winter, and planting out of seedlings begins during August. Field officers of the company supervise the preparation of the ground, the amount of fertilizer to be used, the planting out of seedlings, the spraying of the crop with pesticides and fungicides for crop protection purposes, and advise on the general care of the crop.

Finally, the financial director of a company engaged in the production of toilet preparations commented:

> Our Australian raw material and packaging suppliers are not only being constantly alerted to new trends but are also given exacting quality control standards and advice on operations where applicable. . . . Fairly constant pressure has to be put on some suppliers to make them keep up to standard.

It is clear that some American subsidiaries go to considerable lengths to help their suppliers to meet required standards of quality and price, and it seems likely that the Australian companies involved benefit significantly from this. But if Dunning's impression of the help passed to supplying companies in Britain is correct, an explanation of why so few American subsidiaries in Australia behave in this way seems necessary. The most important part of the explanation is probably to be found in the relatively small scale of the Australian operations of many American companies. A number of companies in the metal-working industries, for example, are engaged primarily in the assembly of imported components, and probably a majority of the subsidiaries in the Australian pharmaceutical industry are engaged only in making pills or capsules from imported materials. It is no accident that all the four companies which were noted above as providing considerable information to supplying companies are large, and all but one of them have been established in Australia for more than thirty years. Another factor to be taken into account is that suppliers and sub-contractors in very many industries are already in contact with an overseas affiliate, either as subsidiaries or licensees, and so perhaps are not often in need of advice.

There is yet another reason why some Australian suppliers do not receive technical information from American subsidiaries: in many cases, they have already been galvanized into efficient operation by the influence of the largest American subsidiary of all, General Motors-Holden's. The Australian managing director of a large domestic appliance company, answering the question on help provided to suppliers, indicated the complete adequacy of Australian-made parts in the following terms:

> I think G.M.H. did the best possible job for Australia: nobody in Australia knew anything about mass production until G.M.H. came along. Australian manufacturers are now served by efficient sub-contractors and in the early years this was mainly G.M.H.'s contribution.

It was this remark, and many in a similar vein made by other executives, which prompted the writer to make a particular study of the impact of American subsidiaries in the motor vehicle industry on their Australian suppliers.

To the outside observer the most obvious benefit to the Australian manufacturers of automotive parts has been the very rapid growth of the motor vehicle industry, a phenomenon for which the American subsidiaries have themselves in large measure been responsible. From being concerned principally with the replacement market and the original market for only a few rather elementary components, the industry has graduated to the stage at which it can now produce the full range of parts needed for the modern motor vehicle. In 1962 General Motors-Holden's alone paid £84,172,000 to suppliers of goods and services, a figure which had grown from less than £10 million in 1948, the first year of Holden production. The company estimated in 1962 that 31,000 people employed by its several thousand Australian supplying companies were dependent for their livelihood on the success of its activities. Both Ford and

General Motors-Holden's boast an Australian content in their main passenger vehicles in excess of 95 per cent.

Not infrequently, the motor vehicle companies have paid a considerable premium above the price of equivalent imports to Australian suppliers to encourage local production. This appears to be less significant now than in earlier years, but is still paid in some cases. The policy has been of importance in building up local suppliers to the point where they can produce at a more economic volume. Not all the American subsidiaries have adopted the policy but it appears to have been particularly important for General Motors-Holden's, the company which first embarked on complete car manufacture in Australia.

The benefit derived by many suppliers has been very great. An executive in one of the American-affiliated companies participating in the present survey was quite neurotically fearful that the vehicle manufacturers would secure access to the profit figures of his company, while another company declined to provide its sales figures lest 'the motor companies want some of the gravy'. Another prosperous company, Australian-owned, commented that without the car companies 'we wouldn't be on the breadline, we would be below it'.

In an attempt to discover the attitude of the supplying companies towards the American-owned vehicle manufacturers, a total of seven such companies (six wholly Australian in ownership and one foreign subsidiary) were interviewed. The results of this short study may be biased, inasmuch as the seven were chosen from a list of major suppliers provided by one of the manufacturers and from press advertisements in a newspaper supplement on the motor vehicle industry. But this bias does not seem to have been unduly significant, and all the companies interviewed are believed to supply parts to all the major vehicle manufacturers.

Attention was concentrated on three main questions. First, do Australian suppliers generally have difficulty meeting the technical standards demanded by the American-owned vehicle manufacturers? By and large, they do not. All seven companies felt that the most consistent pressure on technical standards had come from only one of the American subsidiaries, and if anything some of the suppliers resented the sudden fluctuations in the standards demanded by some of the other subsidiaries. Almost all had felt at one stage that this pressure was unreasonable but there was a very general realization at the time of the survey that they had gained from it in the long run.

Do Australian suppliers have difficulty meeting the delivery dates and scheduling requirements of the American subsidiaries? Again it appears that they do not. All the firms interviewed appreciated the need for precise delivery dates and exact ordering, and again the only complaint voiced was that some of the American subsidiaries are very inept at forecasting their demands and very inconsiderate to their suppliers when orders have to be changed at short notice. One of the American firms was again singled out for its special ability in this field and also for the thoughtful manner in which it deals with suppliers when orders must be changed at short notice.[15]

But part of the explanation of the negative answers to the first two questions is found in the answers to the third question: have Australian suppliers received any assistance, either in the form of technical information or managerial techniques, from the American subsidiaries? In describing the answers received to this question, the writer finds himself in a particularly embarrassing position, for almost without exception,[16] all the seven companies visited contrasted the very considerable help they had received from one of the American subsidiaries with the usually complete absence of such help from the other American subsidiaries (indeed, all the other companies) in the industry. While it has been deliberate policy to avoid giving company names in such situations, not to do so here would be rather clumsy. Besides, every Australian familiar with the motor vehicle industry could name the company concerned in any case. Some justice may be done in naming the company, moreover, since more than any other it has incurred the resentment of Australians at the profitability of overseas investment in this country. Some explanation for its achievement may be found in the fact that it was the first company of any nationality to embark upon the complete manufacture of a motor vehicle in Australia. Its name, of course, is General Motors-Holden's.

G.M.H. has taken a lively interest in the manufacturing methods used by its suppliers since its inception in Australia. Forster (1964: 43) gives an interesting account of General Motors' very close tech-

[15] This company was particularly considerate during the recession in the motor vehicle industry in 1961-2. A number of suppliers were aware that the company could have stopped all buying for several months till its inventories were reduced to a level commensurate with its sales, but instead the company 'smoothed' the reduction in its orders over a period. One firm indicated that when it reached its overdraft limit during this difficult period it rang the American subsidiary and successfully requested it to pay certain bills before the due date. In the most remarkable case, when one foreign subsidiary which had expanded its inventory at the request of the American subsidiary found itself in liquidity difficulties in 1961-2, the American subsidiary negotiated a bank overdraft running into six figures on its behalf and agreed to increase the price of its purchases to cover the interest charges.

[16] The one exception was the foreign subsidiary interviewed, which felt it needed no technical advice because of its existing overseas connections.

nical liaison with Holden's Motor Body Builders Ltd in the twenties, though Hartnett (1964: 49, 62) has argued that the company really did not appreciate the problems of manufacturing in a small market at that stage. It was after World War II when planning for Holden production commenced in earnest that the company made its biggest impact on Australian suppliers. While the company itself provided considerable information on this aspect of its activities, the impression is more vivid as described by the suppliers.

One of these, a company which sells 95 per cent of its output to the motor vehicle industry, has experienced a six-fold growth in total profits over the past decade. Its growth in export sales has been even more dramatic, from less than £10,000 in 1949 to over £1 million in 1963. A senior executive felt that both achievements were in important measure due to assistance from G.M.H.:

> By forcing suppliers like ourselves to meet their specification requirements, they brought about something of a revolution in components manufacture. They encouraged association with other U.S. companies and also provided direct technical assistance. Because of this initial pressure, we have become better manufacturers and with competence in one field we have been led into other fields such as precision equipment.

This company also received benefit from G.M.H. through the fact that several of its senior executives originally learnt that company's methods in its employment.

Another company, engaged in die-casting, felt that technical information passed on from the American subsidiary had not been at all significant, but it did feel that it had learnt a great deal from G.M.H. in the field of management techniques. In particular G.M.H. had helped the company improve its inspection techniques by showing it all its own manuals on inspection.

In the case of three of the suppliers visited, help of both a technical and managerial kind from G.M.H. had been of such considerable assistance that some of the comments made are reproduced in some detail:

> (a) In 1954 we resented [G.M.H.'s] pushing—this was when we first went into die-casting for the car industry. They have marvellous forecasting and scheduling systems and we said, when they wanted us to schedule our work in the same way, you can't schedule jobbing work. But they insisted—and now we schedule all our work up to twelve months ahead. We now set out targets and can in retrospect check our performance—this is a very big thing. We can talk the same language as G.M.H. They simply told us we must have strict schedule observance—they didn't *tell* us how to do it, but they suggested we could do it their way. At our

request they showed us how to operate their time sheet system, how to finance our production and how to sell it. And they have done this for lots of companies. . . .

Everybody in the supplying industry says G.M.H. demands technical standards which are too high—we say it too. But we're not right—it's only an excuse. In insisting on quality, they have brought the quality up to their standards. They have revolutionized standards in many industries. We have very strict quality control—but it was put in at their suggestion. . . .

On many occasions we have sent people overseas with G.M.H. backing—I have gone myself. We go to Melbourne and ask for an introduction—without that contact you wouldn't get beyond the front door in America. As it is, we go over there, are met by the head man in the plant or division we want to see and he gives us a guide for the rest of the day. We sent one senior man to the U.S. every year between 1954 and 1960. . . . General Motors are very free with information. We are quite at liberty to take notes in all G.M. plants and they answer all our questions—on costs, rates of flow per hour—the lot, all without charge. . . . And with G.M. you can keep on writing back for years, getting further help.

(b) We always think G.M.H. standards are too high—but they always prove to be right. This country owes a helluva lot to G.M. In the early years we cursed them up hill and down dale: we damn nearly had to rebuild our factory to meet their quality demands. But they help us meet their standards—all G.M. factories are open to us and we visit them almost every year. They don't encourage us to take up licensing agreements with other foreign companies —it's not that they're opposed to it but just that in our line of business, General Motors owns the best factory in the world. And we have also had entries into many other factories through the good offices of G.M.H. . . . And G.M.H. doesn't make any charge for this help: they even lend us their technical staff to help us solve problems without any charge. . . .

G.M.H. taught me purchasing. After the war we didn't have any special purchasing department: purchasing was done by me, the company secretary. A G.M.H. man came up for three or four days, all without charge, and taught us how to operate a modern scheduling system, and we're still using basically the same system. At the moment we're thinking of installing a teleprinter, so last week I went across to the G.M.H. plant at Pagewood to see how they use theirs. And I'm going down to Melbourne next year to examine their e.d.p. system. . . . Is there another company in the world which has done so much for one national economy?

(c) Without a question of doubt, G.M.H. have contributed more than any other car company to this country—especially with their methods and quality control. Before I met G.M.H., I thought I knew all about producing the particular component in which we specialize, but I really didn't know the first thing about mass production methods and when they told me what prices they were prepared to pay I told them it couldn't be done. They not only showed me how I could meet their prices but also showed me how I could make a very good profit doing it. But you have to let G.M.H. boss you round, because they know what they're doing. They put quality control into this company. They helped us enormously: they told us the systems they use and they sent people up for weeks on end to help us with these systems, without any charge. This benefits everybody, including G.M.H.'s competitors of course. I have a great admiration for G.M. . . . . G.M.H. even suggest what plant we should get sometimes: just recently we ordered a machine which is much more expensive than other machines of its kind at G.M.H.'s suggestion. But it is so much better as a machine that we just couldn't afford not to have it. They put us on to all the new stuff coming out of the States in our field.

G.M.H. have also given us a new attitude to many things we had previously taken for granted. For example, when they gave us an order, they would ask us how we intended to transport the products to Victoria. We would name the trucking company we planned to use and they would reply that this company was very frequently behind schedule in its deliveries. This gave us a new interest in transport efficiency. . . .

This company was established in 1952 because of the expected growth of the car industry. Eleven years ago we employed six people—now we work two shifts with a total employment of over 400. . . . We have just begun exporting to the U.K. and expect this trade to grow rapidly because of the relative cheapness of the Australian article—which in turn is due basically to our better manufacturing techniques and management procedures.

The extent of the benefit derived from G.M.H. by Australian manufacturers of automotive parts seems difficult to exaggerate. The testimonies offered by the suppliers interviewed are the more remarkable in that, human nature being what it is, one might almost have expected some resentment against the company so many of them depend upon for their prosperity. The contribution which G.M.H. has made to the efficiency of Australian industry over the past twenty years must undoubtedly be rated among the greatest benefits which Australia has received American investment.

IX

Imports and Exports

One of the more controversial aspects of foreign investment in Australia is the alleged restriction on the freedom of foreign subsidiaries to buy and sell where they please. Australian firms sometimes feel that they are at an unfair competitive disadvantage in tendering for the supply of foreign subsidiaries because the latter are directed to purchase many of their materials from affiliated firms, while public displeasure has been voiced frequently at the international market-sharing arrangements which are believed to restrict the growth of Australia's exports. This chapter sets out the relevant data gathered during the present survey and attempts answers to some of the questions of immediate public concern. The chapter specifically does not deal with the impact of American investment on Australia's overall balance of payments position, discussion of this subject being deferred until chapter XI.

Seventy-seven companies provided information on their expenditure on imports in 1961/2. Though neither of the two very large American-owned oil refining companies is included in that total,[1] the number is believed to represent a reasonable cross-section of American investment in other sectors of Australian industry. Between them, these companies spent in excess of £92 million on imports in that year, and the figure does not include some expenditure on capital equipment bought from the local agents of overseas manufacturers, or some exporting by parent companies to non-affiliated companies in Australia.[2] Most of the total import

[1] One of the major American oil refining companies provided import figures but because of a company reorganization during the year their use proved impossible.

[2] A number of companies could provide only an estimate of imports, so that the accuracy of the figures shown both in the text and in succeeding tables is

(Continued on next page)

203

bill was expenditure on raw materials, components, and finished goods for resale without further processing, and together these were equivalent to nearly 19 per cent of the total sales of the companies concerned.

Table IX-1 shows this information by the industry of the importing company. As might be expected, the direct import content of the sales of companies in the food and drink industry was very low, while that in the electrical equipment industry (where a number of companies were still engaged primarily in the assembly of imported components) was considerably higher. Some of the other ratios shown may be deceptive. The high ratio shown for companies in 'Plant, equipment, machinery' is largely the result of substantial importations of finished goods by one company, while the ratio of 24·5 per cent shown in 'Other industries' is heavily influenced by expenditure on crude oil imports by one of the smaller American-affiliated oil companies.

If comparison is confined to imports of materials on the one hand and total sales on the other, none of the aggregate ratios appears high. Admittedly, a comparison of imports of materials with sales is not very satisfactory and for this reason an attempt was made to compare materials imports with total cost of production as shown on the Commonwealth Statistician's Factory Return. The difficulty with this comparison is that the Statistician requests the exclusion from the total cost of production of the cost of components which are merely assembled by the reporting factory. But if companies which are thought to exclude significant amounts of assembled components in this way be left out of account, there are still sixty-four companies which can be used for meaningful comparisons. Of the total, the ratio of imported materials to total manufacturing cost was less than 20 per cent in thirty cases, and less than 30 per cent in forty-one cases. In only eleven cases was the ratio greater than 50 per cent, and several of these companies, having but recently begun manufacture, were accumulating stocks of imported materials. Unfortunately, since information could not be obtained on indirect import content, no comparison can be made of the total import content of

----

somewhat spurious. Most of the large companies, however, provided figures accurate to the nearest £1,000. Though the questionnaire failed to specify the basis of valuation on which figures were required, it is thought that the figures presented approximate a c.i.f. valuation. By verbal questioning, it is known that most companies provided figures in this form, though some gave f.o.b. figures and others added Australian tariff to the c.i.f. valuation. In a number of cases, companies which included Australian tariff were able to provide an estimate of this component, and this permitted a rough estimate of the c.i.f. figure. As with other data, many companies did not provide figures for the year ended 30 June 1962, but instead used their own company year ending in 1962.

TABLE IX–1 Imports of 77 American-affiliated Companies in 1961/2, by Industry and Type of Import

| Industry | Imports of | | | Total imports^b £A('000) | Total sales in 1962 £A('000) | Imports of materials and finished goods as percentage of sales | No. companies covered |
	Materials £A('000)	Finished goods £A('000)	Capital equipment £A('000)				
Plant, equipment, machinery	2,741^a	5,200^a	107	8,048	27,669	28·7^a	16
Motor vehicles	40,039	6,380	6,888	53,306	262,491^c	17·7	4
Electrical equipment, instruments, etc.	5,004^a	3,478^a	125	8,607	38,317	22·1^a	14
Food and drink	211	7	190	408	26,500	0·8	6
Industrial chemicals and plastics	2,870	2,070	173	5,113	23,215	21·3	8
Pharmaceutical and toilet preparations	2,686	121	61	2,869	15,863	17·7	6
Other industries	10,485	1,830	1,399	13,714	50,232	24·5	23
Total^b	64,037^a	19,086^a	8,943	92,066	444,288^c	18·7^a	77

[a] Four companies failed to classify part of their imports by type. In each case the unclassified portion has been allocated to the class which is the most nearly appropriate. This results in a small error in the figures indicated.

[b] Detail may not add to totals because of rounding.

[c] To safeguard the secrecy of the sales figures of a very small participating company in the motor vehicles industry, this figure actually includes the sales of one company which provided no information on its imports. The overstatement is substantially less than £1 million, however.

NOTES: (1) Figures shown are believed to approximate a cost-insurance-freight valuation.
(2) There is some understatement of the total imports of these companies. See text for explanation.

205

the production of American-affiliated firms on the one hand with the import content of Australian manufacturing industry as a whole on the other. It might be expected, however, that since so many American ventures begin life in Australia as primarily assembly or packaging operations, the import content of the production of American-affiliated firms would be significantly higher than for Australian industry generally.

At first sight Table IX-2 appears to show that wholly American companies were significantly more dependent on imported products in 1961/2 than were jointly-owned firms. While 13 of 15 jointly-owned firms manufacturing in Australia before 1957 had a direct import content in their 1962 sales of less than 20 per cent, the comparable ratio among wholly American firms was only 11 out of 25. Of those which began manufacture in or after 1957, almost half the jointly-owned ones had ratios of less than 20 per cent, but only one-third of the wholly American ones could lay claim to a similar ratio. Ratios of imported materials to manufacturing cost confirm this impression, though with a smaller sample of companies.

These figures must be interpreted with considerable caution, however. Many jointly-owned companies were in fact manufacturing long before an American company acquired an interest in them and in this situation purchasing patterns were often laid down before the American investment. Of the companies shown in Table IX-2 as being less than 50 per cent American in ownership and as commencing manufacture 'in or after 1957', for example, three of the four which had a direct import content in sales of less than 20 per cent had been manufacturing in Australia long before the American interest was acquired. Often an Australian-American partnership begins life in answer to a need felt by a previously wholly Australian venture for technical information or capital. By contrast, the wholly American firm often has its genesis in the desire of an American company to circumvent Australian trade barriers by assembling components imported from the U.S. Because it was so rarely possible to compare companies of different ownership pattern *within the same industry*, it is impossible to be certain from the above evidence that wholly American companies import a greater proportion of their materials than do jointly-owned firms in the same situation.

During early interviews conducted as part of the present survey, participating companies were asked a series of questions on their use of Australian-made materials and components. As time went on, however, it became increasingly apparent that most of the questions were inadequate to elicit much useful information on this topic and several of them were not asked in later interviews. Too often, executives stated that 'we buy locally wherever possible', in deference, it is

TABLE IX-2   Materials and Finished Goods Imported by 77 American-affiliated Companies in 1961/2, by Percentage of American Ownership and Period in which Manufacture Began

Percentage U.S. ownership and period in which Australian manufacture began[a]	No. companies covered	Imports of materials and finished goods £A('000)	Total sales in 1962 £A('000)	Imports of materials and finished goods as percentage of sales	Ratio of imported materials and finished goods to sales (%)					
					0–9	10–19	20–29	30–39	40–49	50 and over
25–49%: Manufacture began—										
before 1957	7	8,268	31,697	26·1	2	3	..	1	1	..
in or after 1957	8	865	8,614	10·0	3	1	..	1	2	.
50–99%: Manufacture began—										
before 1957	8	2,297	22,073	10·4	5	3	..	..	..	..
in or after 1957	11	1,641	8,734	18·8	4	1	1	2	1	2
100%: Manufacture began—										
before 1957	25	65,300	357,064[b]	18·3	8	3	7	4	1	2
in or after 1957	18	4,752	16,106	29·5	2	4	..	6	3	3
Total	77	83,123	444,288[b]	18·7	24	15	8	14	8	8

[a] The year in which manufacture began is taken to be the year in which an American equity of at least 25 per cent was first acquired in the case of companies manufacturing previously as Australian-owned ventures.

[b] See Note [e] to Table IX-1.

thought, to current popular opinion.[3] Some companies undoubtedly import a very high proportion of their raw materials—in the extreme case, a company in the chemical industry 'calculated' its imports in 1961/2 by referring to its total expenditure on materials as recorded on its Factory Return. A number of companies in the pharmaceutical industry are in a similar situation. In other cases, particularly in the food industry, dependence on imported materials was found to be extremely low or negligible. Almost always, companies importing materials or components explained that the required volume of the imported product was insufficient to justify local manufacture or that it involved a raw material not found in Australia at all. One of the few executives who gave a different reason stated that his company (predominantly Australian-owned) imported steel occasionally because the local steel monopoly is so difficult to deal with.

The most useful information obtained on the use of Australian materials emerged from an examination of changes in the use of imported materials over a period. Companies were asked to provide data on their imports for 1954/5 and 1959/60, as well as for 1961/2, where relevant. Twenty-three companies provided information for all three years.[4] Unfortunately, half of these firms either did not provide information on their manufacturing activities over this whole period or exclude all assembled components from the figure they report for cost of production on their Factory Return. But of the eleven cases in which comparison between imported materials and total manufacturing cost was possible, eight showed an increase in 'Australian content' and only two a decrease. The impression is not so clear if the twenty-nine additional comparisons available for the more limited period 1959/60 to 1961/2 are examined. Here, seventeen showed an increase in 'Australian content' and eleven showed a decrease. Too much should not be read into these figures on their own, however: relating to individual years as they do, they are likely to have been significantly affected by changes in stocks of materials, particularly since between 1959/60 and 1961/2 there was not only a change in government policy on import controls but also a complete change in the cyclical position of the economy.

Probably of greater interest are the answers to a question asking

[3] John Lindeman and Donald Armstrong found the same difficulty in their study of American investment in Canada: 'Of course all company executives interviewed expressed a strong preference for Canadian-made goods and services; it would take an unusually frank man to express any other view. However, further investigation showed that there were degrees of preference.' (1960: 53.)

[4] These statistics were presented, in aggregate form, in the thesis version of this study. Because of the difficulty of attaching any precise meaning to them, however, they have been omitted here.

companies which had begun manufacture in Australia before 1957 to compare the Australian content of production in 1962 with that 'five years ago'. Of the seventeen companies which answered this question, four felt the question to be not very meaningful because their dependence on imports of materials had for long been negligible, six felt Australian content to be 'about the same', and seven felt it to be 'greater'. Fourteen companies which had begun manufacture in 1957 or subsequently were asked whether Australian content had increased since manufacture began: all but three of these felt that it had, and one of the three had used exclusively Australian materials since establishment. The other two felt Australian content had remained 'about the same'. All those companies which felt Australian content had increased expected this trend to continue, though one felt the growth in local content would be slow and another that it would never go beyond a certain point.

It would be misleading to create the impression that all American-affiliated companies are assiduously engaged in increasing the Australian content of their production. There have certainly been a few cases, particularly since the removal of import restrictions in 1960, in which American subsidiaries have decreased their Australian content in favour of a greater dependence on imported components bought from affiliates. But for the most part the trend seems to have been in the opposite direction. Sometimes this is because of cost factors associated with importing. One firm in the electrical equipment industry explained that, when the Australian operation was confined to the assembly of components imported from the U.S., inventory costs were very high because the American company only produces components for 240-volt apparatus twice yearly. This factor was resulting in a steady increase in Australian content. Another company had a deliberate policy of increasing local content because the products it supplies are subject to sharp and unpredictable fluctuations in demand and local suppliers are able to deliver components more rapidly than foreign. Sometimes an American-affiliated firm is able to increase its local content because of an improvement in the quality of domestically-made goods: a firm in the garment industry, for example, indicated that Australian content had increased from about 40 per cent in 1959 to about 60 per cent in 1963 because of increased technical contact between local suppliers and overseas firms. But probably the most important single factor leading to an increase in Australian content is Australian tariff policy. Several firms indicated that they had embarked on programmes to increase Australian content under agreements with the Customs Department to allow the importation of certain components free of duty provided the firm made determined efforts to increase the over-

P

all Australian content of its production. Several others indicated that Australian content had been increased after a sharp rise in the tariff on specific items.

Very few companies could be positively identified as following a policy of paying a price premium for Australian-made supplies as part of a policy to develop local industry, though as noted in chapter III it is the practice of companies in some industries to pay a rather higher price for local supplies in order to have the flexibility associated with local manufacture. It is thought that some companies in the motor vehicle industry pay such a price penalty, and L. J. Hartnett (1964: 77) has told how, when he assumed control of General Motors-Holden's in the thirties, he changed the policy of that company from one of purchasing components imported from affiliates unless the locally-supplied product was 10 per cent cheaper than the import to one of purchasing locally-supplied products unless the import was 10 per cent cheaper. The managing director of another wholly American company, in the chemical industry, stated that 'in years past, we were prepared to pay a premium of up to 10 per cent for Australian supplies—to help boost Australian industry and so on—but we have had to harden our attitude lately. We can't afford such a luxury since our customers buy in the cheapest market.' The American executive of one jointly-owned firm explained that he felt that foreign companies should behave as 'guests' with profit motive 'almost secondary'. This implies 'we shouldn't import too much on principle'. But such an attitude to imports seemed extremely rare.

This is hardly surprising. There is little evidence to suggest that many Australian-owned companies pay a premium for Australian-made supplies, except in so far as it is to their own immediate advantage to do so. Foreign subsidiaries have even less reason to purchase supplies locally. Clearly, the sale of a component by an American company to its subsidiary in Australia entails a profit to the parent company provided the sale price is above its marginal cost. Unless protected by import controls or substantial tariffs, local suppliers must therefore compete not with the average full cost price of the parent company but with its marginal cost price, a price very likely to be below even the marginal cost of the Australian producer. This is so whatever the price at which the transaction is actually registered in the company's books, unless, as is sometimes the case, the local affiliate retains the right to buy supplies wherever it pleases.

A number of American companies with subsidiaries in Australia are widely known to practise a policy of international specialization of production, and in this situation the Australian subsidiary is hardly likely to purchase a component from an Australian supplier even if it is somewhat cheaper than the imported product. The same forces may inhibit the manufacturing activities of the American subsidiary itself, and at least one company is known to have temporarily delayed the expansion of its local activities because of the construction of new plants by affiliates in the U.S. and the U.K. Such use of imported components may cause resentment on the part of some domestic companies. Most Australian companies have no difficulty in securing substantial tariff protection from the Tariff Board, however, and with a few notable exceptions the imports of materials on account of American affiliates in Australia genuinely seem to be of articles not produced in Australia or of product models required in quantities which would make domestic manufacture extremely uneconomic.

Most of the imports of American-owned companies are purchased from affiliated firms, though in some cases 'through' affiliated firms is a more correct description than 'from'. Table IX-3 shows that of the imports of the seventy-six companies which provided information on the source of their imports in 1961/2, more than 91 per cent came from U.S. parent companies or their subsidiaries. Wholly American firms, moreover, bought a greater proportion of their imports from affiliates than did jointly-owned firms. For them the percentage was 94·7 per cent, but for jointly-owned companies only 74·4 per cent. Indeed the figure for jointly-owned companies is artificially inflated by the crude oil imports of one company, and

TABLE IX–3 Source of the Imports of 76 American-affiliated Companies in 1961/2, by Percentage of American Ownership
£A('000)

Source of imports	Percentage U.S. ownership			Total[a]
	25–49	50–99	100	
Imports from U.S. parent companies and their foreign subsidiaries				
U.S. parent company	892	2,509	23,134	26,535
Foreign subsidiaries[b]	6,728[c]	735	19,296	26,759
Unclassified[d]	..	..	30,837	30,837
Total[a]	7,620[c]	3,244	73,268	84,132
Other imports from				
U.S.	317	811	978	2,106
Other countries	2,055	557	3,116	5,728
Total[a]	9,992	4,612	77,362	91,966

[a] Detail may not add to totals because of rounding.
[b] Mostly British and Canadian.
[c] A substantial fraction of this amount is the crude oil imports of one company.
[d] Mostly American, British and Canadian.
NOTE: For the number of companies involved in each category of ownership, see Table IX–4.

TABLE IX–4   Ratio of Imports from U.S. Parent Company and its Foreign
Subsidiaries to Total Imports in 76 American-affiliated Companies in 1961/2,
by Percentage of American Ownership

Ratio of imports from U.S. parent company and its foreign subsidiaries to total imports (%)	Percentage U.S. ownership			No. companies covered
	25–49	50–99	100	
0–9	3	4	1	8
10–19	2	1	1	4
20–29	1	1	1	3
30–39	..	..	..	..
40–49	1	2	..	3
50–59	1	..	1	2
60–69	1	..	4	5
70–79	..	2	1	3
80–89	2	1	1	4
90–99	1	2	12	15
100	3	6	20	29
Total	15	19	42	76

without that company the figure would have been much lower. The
difference between jointly-owned and wholly American companies is
even more clearly seen in Table IX-4: while only 19 of 34 jointly-
owned companies purchased 50 per cent or more of their imports
from affiliated companies, the number of wholly American companies
buying such a ratio from affiliated companies was 39 out of 42. The
evidence lends considerable support to the view that the import of
direct investment capital has a significant influence on the source of
a country's commodity imports.

Because figures in Table IX-3 include imports of capital equipment, no direct comparison is possible with figures published by the
U.S. Department of Commerce for the exports of U.S. companies to
their foreign manufacturing affiliates. Figures published by that
Department (1964: no. 12, p. 24) show that products (other than
capital equipment) bought from U.S. parent companies by foreign
manufacturing affiliates were equal to about 9 per cent of total
affiliate sales in 1962. If two-thirds of the 'unclassified' imports in the
table were purchased from U.S. parent companies (an arbitrary but
not unreasonable assumption in view of the companies concerned),
it seems likely that the ratio applicable to U.S. affiliates in Australia
is closely similar to the average figure, even allowing for the possible
error involved in the inclusion of figures for capital equipment
imports.

It is probably true that imports of capital equipment are more
often bought on the open market than are imports of materials.
Indeed, as noted earlier, many imports of capital equipment are
thought to be excluded from the import figures presented in this

chapter, since companies often purchase imported equipment from local firms and so fail to classify such expenditure as on imports. Only nine participating companies are known to have purchased second-hand capital equipment from affiliated companies, and not all of these made their purchases in 1961/2. (This probably understates the true situation, however.) In most cases the amount of equipment involved was not large, and in all cases but two, executives of the subsidiaries concerned either did not comment on its price or specifically stated that such equipment had been bought at 'very reasonable' or 'give-away' prices.[5] Both the firms which felt they had been overcharged for equipment were relatively small, jointly-owned, companies, but the comment of the secretary of one of them serves to illustrate the danger sometimes attached to buying second-hand equipment in this way:

> Our first two casting machines were reconditioned equipment discarded by the U.S. company—it was certainly not of the latest design nor was it bought at a bargain price. Now, when we are spending £100,000 on a new machine, we have to buy another of this older design because if we bought a new machine parts would not be interchangeable with our two existing machines.

The general problem of the pricing of imports bought from affiliated companies has aroused a good deal of attention in Australia of recent years, mainly because of a widespread belief that foreign subsidiaries in the oil industry are paying their affiliates more than the open market price for both crude oil and the transport facilities needed to bring it to Australia. Because of the large volume of imports purchased from affiliated firms (and the figures shown include almost none of the very considerable expenditure on crude oil imports by the American-affiliated oil refining companies operating here in 1962), this subject is obviously of great importance. At the same time, it is a subject of daunting complexity, because in so many cases a 'world market price' does not exist. The discussion is only meaningful if the prices actually paid by foreign subsidiaries can be compared with some notional price which *would* be payable by the same companies if they were independent units. The difficulties in such an approach are obviously immense, though some useful observations may perhaps be made nevertheless.

If oil companies are left aside for the moment, there appear to be three main factors which might lead American companies to 'overcharge' their Australian subsidiaries, bearing in mind the complete absence of restrictions on the remittance of dividends and service

[5] In one case, a company purchased a piece of second-hand equipment from its parent for £45. When a second machine of the same type was required, it had to be bought new—and cost £1,700.

charges from Australia. The first is considerations of public relations. By charging a high price for commodities sold to the subsidiary, the profits of the latter may be reduced and its 'image', in a country highly sensitive to the profitability of foreign subsidiaries, improved. It is hard to believe that much overcharging has taken place on this count, however, at least until 1962, because the profits of most foreign-owned companies have been secure from public scrutiny. This factor may be of more importance in the future. Secondly, the American company has an obvious incentive to charge the maximum price feasible if the subsidiary is jointly-owned. Some tendency to charge jointly-owned companies more for imports than would be charged to wholly owned companies probably does operate,[6] but there appears little doubt that most American companies temper the desire to maximize their own profits in the short term by the desire to preserve harmonious relationships with local management and shareholders.

The third factor, taxation, emerges as by far the most important to be considered. If the rate of Australian company tax were higher than in the country of residence of the affiliate exporting to the Australian subsidiary, or if company tax payable by the Australian subsidiary plus Australian withholding tax levied on dividends were higher than the tax payable if profits were made in the exporting country, there would appear to be every incentive to overcharge the Australian subsidiary. There is little danger of this happening at present, however, whether the exporting country is the U.S., the U.K., or Canada, for in all these countries, the rate of company tax is somewhat higher than the Australian. Only if the rate of dividend remittance were very high would there seem some incentive to 'load' prices to Australian subsidiaries. Indeed, under most circumstances, there is a positive tax incentive to reduce below the open market level the price of exports from affiliates in these countries to Australian subsidiaries. Only where it is possible to 'export' to Australia from a tax-haven country would there appear to be a strong incentive to overcharge the Australian subsidiary to avoid Australian tax liability.

[6] The only conclusive item of empirical support for this *a priori* reasoning was found in the case of a company in which the American equity was little more than 25 per cent. Shortly before the survey was conducted, this company lost its right to distribute certain of the parent company's products in Australia, the parent company setting up a separate distributing company instead. The joint venture was not disturbed by this, however, since it was itself to have a 25 per cent equity in the new distributing company. Because the new distributing company was to buy at substantially lower prices from the American parent than had the original joint venture, the latter felt its profits would not suffer at all.

What is the situation in practice? Leaving out of account the wholly American oil companies, seventy-one companies were asked the following question:

On what basis are you charged for imports purchased from your American associate or one of its affiliates?

One company gave an answer which is believed to be false and another six gave answers which are impossible to classify. The chief executive of one of these companies frankly admitted that the parent company is continually 'playing' with the inter-affiliate pricing structure in order to generate funds where they are most needed for expansion, while the secretary of another very large firm stated that affiliated companies 'leave less profit here than we would like'. But in none of these cases was there sufficient evidence to form a clear impression of the situation.

In nine of the remaining sixty-four companies, two of them jointly-owned, there was clear evidence that the Australian subsidiary is charged a 'high'[7] price for materials purchased from affiliated companies. One of the two jointly-owned companies believed its U.S. parent took a profit of between 100 and 300 per cent on the total cost of items sold to the Australian company. In the case of one item which the American parent bought from another U.S. company in bulk, it charged the Australian company £6. 6s. 8d. per item; the Australian company was eventually able to switch its purchases to the local subsidiary of the American supplying company and buy these items, including a 40 per cent tariff, at £3. 4s. 10d.[8] Not surprisingly, the management of this company felt the U.S. company had recouped all the cash it had invested in the Australian company, through royalties and profits from the sale of components, within two years of the original investment. A company in the pharmaceutical industry felt that it would be meaningless to compare Australian and American unit production cost because the great bulk of Australian unit cost is accounted for by purchases of materials from the international division of the parent company, based in a tax-haven country. The international division 'makes a very handsome profit' on the sale of these materials—calculated by the manager of the company for one purchase at twice the profit made on the sale of

[7] In this context, 'high' is used to include prices that are designed to leave relatively large profits in the exporting company even if, as in a few cases, there is some doubt that the local company would be able to purchase materials more cheaply elsewhere because of patent restrictions.

[8] The company was inhibited from dealing with the U.S. supplying company directly because under its agreement with the Customs Department to increase Australian content, duty-free admission of imports applied only to goods bought from its own parent company.

the final product in Australia. In the most remarkable case of all, an executive was encountered who believed that profits made by the American parent company on sales to the wholly-owned Australian subsidiary were sufficient to cover the annual dividend on the American company's entire capital. It was contended, in fact, that one unexpected result of the Australian Federal Treasurer's stringent fiscal measures in 1960 was the drastic reduction of the parent company's dividend when sales to the Australian operation fell off sharply!

It should be obvious, of course, that before their establishment in Australia *no* part of the profit from the sale of the products of these companies incurred Australian taxation. As long as the Australian profits of the companies concerned are not artificially inflated by Australian tariffs, therefore (and in remarkably few, if any, of the nine cases uncovered were prices dependent on Australian tariffs), there may still be a net gain to Australia from the taxation of the profits of these companies. The gain is undoubtedly less than it might be, however, were the Taxation Commissioner able to police import prices more closely.[9]

The motives for this 'overcharging' appeared to vary. Only three of the nine companies are known to have used a tax-haven country, and only two of the total were jointly-owned companies. Only one was required to publish its accounts before the Uniform Companies Act of 1961, and this was one of the companies using a tax-haven country. In one of the remaining cases, the motive may have been to boost parent company profit while being able to claim to American shareholders that almost all foreign profits were being reinvested abroad. Twice, 'overcharging' seemed to be the result of a desire on the part of a non-American affiliate to increase its profit, in one case because of natural inter-affiliate rivalry and in the other because of the inefficiency of the exporting affiliate. In the latter case, an executive of the Australian company commented:

> We have to pay more for components than if we purchased them competitively. This sort of thing happens in a family group like ours, especially if somebody is trying to cover up an inefficient operation or trying to avoid a loss.

In the ninth case the policy appeared to be quite without rational basis and may be only a by-product of a policy primarily designed for countries which prevent the remittance of dividends or service charges.

---

[9] An offsetting advantage to Australia may operate in some cases. Where companies are free to buy locally at will, and jointly-owned companies and some wholly American ones are often free in this way, they may divert expenditure to locally produced materials.

Such overcharging occurred in only a minority of the companies studied. To avoid betraying the classification of a few very large companies, it is not possible to disclose the volume of imports purchased from affiliated companies by Australian firms in various categories of 'import price'. But it can be stated that the imports bought from affiliated firms by subsidiaries in Australia which were bought at 'fair' or 'very fair' prices exceeded those purchased at 'high' prices more than three times over.

The classification of other company responses to the question on import pricing was inevitably arbitrary. As far as could be gauged, however, twenty-nine companies (of the sixty-four referred to above) paid 'fair' prices for imports from affiliated firms, interpreting 'fair' as being roughly equivalent to the open market price. Seventeen of these companies were jointly-owned. This adherence to the open market price was often necessary because jointly-owned firms retained the right to buy where they pleased, but wholly-owned subsidiaries of companies which encourage their affiliates to maximize their profit almost independently of each other frequently followed the same practice. The secretary of one jointly-owned company commented that the American parent company is 'not slugging us'. He stated that his company had 'obtained quotes from all over the world and while we could get some materials slightly more cheaply from Japan, U.S. delivery dates are absolutely reliable'. The chief executive of a wholly American company explained that 'we buy some supplies from our parent and some from a competitor—both quote the same price'. The financial director of yet another wholly American company stated that 'we are charged competitive prices—and we had a chance to check on this when setting up a new plant in Malaysia recently. The U.S. company might take 5 to 7 per cent, but nothing appreciable.'

Another twenty companies (six jointly-owned) felt the prices they pay for imports from affiliated companies are 'very fair', or slightly below the open market price. American-affiliated companies in Australia often benefit from the volume discounts obtained on the bulk purchases of their parent companies and this was one of the most common reasons for a company to contend that prices of imports from its American parent were somewhat less than those payable if the goods were bought on the open market. Several wholly American firms felt the prices paid were 'very competitive' or 'cost plus 10 per cent' because 'we don't have to buy from our associates'. One jointly-owned company purchases components 'at some nominal mark-up', and buys finished products at a 5 per cent preference over other manufacturers buying at comparable volume: as far as was known in the local company, wholly-owned subsidiaries of the

American company pay for imports on the same basis. The secretary of another jointly-owned company, which uses its American associate as a buying agent, stated:

> We get a very good deal out of them really. They only handle the stuff for us, and charge us a handling charge of 5 per cent. For this, they do all our ordering, pay all our bills, and freight the stuff on a 90-day draft.

Nine companies (only one of them jointly-owned) indicated that for imports from affiliates they pay considerably below the world price for similar goods. In at least one of these cases, the Customs Department refuses to accept the invoice valuation as the true valuation for duty purposes. A comment made by the chief executive of a small wholly American company was typical: 'We buy finished products at 70 per cent of the "best" retail price [i.e. that based on the largest volume order] regardless of how small our order is.' Another firm indicated that all fully-assembled products are bought at the 'subsidiary discount price'—40 per cent below retail price— and components are bought at the same price as that paid by the U.S. assembly line. Surprisingly, only two of the nine appeared to be adopting this policy deliberately to secure the advantage of lower Australian company tax rates—and one executive was sure that such a policy had never occurred to his parent company. Often, the prices paid by the Australian subsidiary, though lower than world market levels, are no different from those paid by subsidiaries in countries where the tax situation is very different.

In summary, therefore, and still leaving oil companies to one side, it appears that in 1962 relatively few American-affiliated companies felt they were being overcharged for imports purchased from affiliated companies—a fact which, because of the great difficulty of the Taxation Commissioner's establishing a 'fair price' for such imports, is particularly fortunate. If anything, local subsidiaries on balance secure imports at prices better than those available to independent companies. It is further likely that following the passage of the U.S. Revenue Act of 1962 (which was intended, among other things, to prevent the abuse of 'tax-havens') the situation for Australia will improve still more.

When attention is turned to foreign oil companies in Australia (and the comments apply to British-owned companies as well as to American), the situation is quite different. Local subsidiaries buy their supplies of crude petroleum from affiliated companies in oil-producing countries, mainly the Middle East, Brunei, and Indonesia. At first sight, since Australian company tax is in most cases substantially lower than the combined imposts of governments in the oil-producing countries, there would appear to be every incentive to make most profits in Australia by charging Australian subsidiaries low prices for crude oil. But two other points have to be taken into consideration. First, international oil companies are usually able to claim substantial credits against tax liabilities in their base country by utilizing depletion allowances permitted on profits attributable to the production of *crude* oil. Secondly, it appears that the governments of most oil-producing countries demand a fixed percentage of an agreed 'posted price', and that if the price of oil falls below this posted price, the oil-producing companies themselves bear the *full* brunt of the price reduction. In contrast, if Australian subsidiaries are charged the full posted price, it is Australian taxation revenue which suffers part of the loss if oil could in fact be purchased more cheaply elsewhere.

There is some evidence to suggest that for some years after independent refining companies became able to purchase supplies of oil at prices significantly below posted prices in the second half of the fifties, the Australian subsidiaries of overseas oil companies did pay the full posted price. The Australian Tariff Board referred to this subject in its report on the industry in 1959, and also complained that local subsidiaries were being overcharged for freighting crude oil to Australia. In its 1961 report, the Board was satisfied on the latter point and noted that local refineries were in some cases either already receiving or about to receive significant discounts on their purchases of oil. The 1965 report noted still further reductions, both in freight charges and in prices paid for crude. But the Australian Taxation Commissioner has clearly not yet been satisfied that oil companies purchase crude from the cheapest possible source, and at the time of writing most of the foreign oil companies had recently announced tax provisions very considerably greater than consideration of their after-tax profit would indicate to be necessary. E. L. Wheelwright (1963: 149) has suggested that the prices paid by local oil companies for crude oil and freight facilities result in an overpayment of something like £20 million annually (at current levels of oil imports—little more than £120 million annually), though of course even if his estimate is correct, the loss to Australia in a situation where almost all oil refineries are owned abroad is not that total sum, as he argues, but only the tax on that sum. (This conclusion depends on the assumption, which seems reasonable at least in the case of motor spirit, that the prices of petroleum end-products are established in Australia independently of the price of crude.)

There seems little doubt that, for a period of perhaps several years, Australian tax revenue was substantially less than it might have been had the Taxation Commissioner adopted a more rigorous policy towards foreign oil companies in Australia; but there is also little doubt that at present the Taxation Commissioner is looking at this situation very critically, even, it is said, to the extent of examining the 'true' tax liability of foreign-owned oil companies in past years. Some assurance for the future lies in the increasing publicity being given to the prices paid by independent oil refiners in other countries, though, as noted earlier, the difficulty of establishing a 'fair' price for tax purposes would be hard to exaggerate.

Compared with their imports, the exports of American-affiliated firms in Australia in 1961/2 were small.[10] Probably because the federal government's tax incentives to increase exports of manufactured goods encourage companies to keep detailed records of their export activities, ninety-eight companies were able to supply information on their exports for at least 1961/2. Two of these companies (only one of which had significant exports) did not supply sales data as a basis for comparison, one was an oil company whose most important single activity in the 'export field' was the supply of fuel for ships and aircraft calling at Australia, and two were engaged principally in the processing of Australian raw materials (mainly copper and meat) for export in an early stage of manufacture. These five companies had combined exports in 1961/2 of more than £24 million. For the balance of the chapter, however, attention is concentrated on the remaining ninety-three companies in an attempt to measure the performance of American-affiliated firms in the 'export of manufactured goods' as usually understood.

In total, these ninety-three companies had exports of £10·4 million in 1961/2, compared with sales of £456·8 million.[11] Twenty-six companies sold no products outside Australia at all in 1961/2 (and only one of these had ever exported before) but in all of the main industry groups there were some companies exporting, and in most

[10] Seventy-six companies provided figures for both imports and exports in 1961/2. Their total imports for that year were £91·4 million, compared with exports of £9·5 million. As with import figures, companies often provided export data for their own company financial year. Export figures have a higher degree of accuracy than import figures, however, because most companies keep detailed records of exports for taxation purposes.

[11] For a reason which is not entirely clear, the ratio of exports to sales indicated here, 2·3 per cent, is substantially lower than the figure of 5·3 per cent revealed by the census conducted by the U.S. Department of Commerce (1960: 110) for American direct investments in Australian manufacturing in 1957. The explanation may lie in the inclusion in the Department's figures of the export activities of at least one of the five companies referred to in the text as being excluded from the figures shown here.

TABLE IX-5 Ratio of Exports to Sales in 93 American-affiliated Companies in 1961/2, by Industry

Industry	Ratio of exports to sales (%)						No. companies covered
	Nil	0·01– 0·99	1·00– 2·99	3·00– 4·99	5·00– 9·99	10·00 and over	
Plant, equipment, machinery	9	5	3	1	..	1	19
Motor vehicles	1	2	1	1	..	..	5
Motor accessories	3	2	..	..	..	..	5
Metal manufactures, n.e.i.	1	..	1	..	..	3	5
Electrical equipment, instruments, etc.	1	6	4	2	2	..	15
Food and drink	3	1	2	..	..	1	7
Industrial chemicals and plastics	2	4	..	1	2	2	11
Pharmaceutical and toilet preparations	..	3	2	2	1	1	9
Other industries	6	7	2	..	2	..	17
Total	26	30	15	7	7	8	93

those exporting constituted the majority. It is clear from Table IX-5, however, that for most companies foreign sales constituted a very small part of total sales in 1962. Only eight companies sold 10 per cent or more of their sales volume overseas in that year and the exports of only one of these exceeded 20 per cent of total sales. This contrasts sharply with the high proportion of total sales exported by many American affiliates in the United Kingdom and Germany (Dunning 1958: 291-8; Philipps 1960: 38-9).

What are the reasons for this apparently 'poor performance'? In particular, is the fact of American affiliation itself responsible for this situation, as is often alleged? Quite obviously there is no simple answer. The first point which should be made is that Australian manufacturing industry as a whole has, in the past, not been noted for its 'export consciousness'. Shielded from the worst rigours of import competition and made complacent by domestic inflation throughout the fifties, local manufacturers have had few motives to venture forth into foreign markets.[12] There is no reason to suppose that Australian-owned manufacturing companies exported a larger proportion of their output in 1961/2 than did the ninety-three companies under consideration, and it is interesting to observe that the exports of the group were a distinctly higher proportion of total manufactured exports in 1961/2 (10·2 per cent) than was the ratio of their manufacturing production to total Australian manufacturing production in the same year (6·5 per cent), though understatement of the value of production of American subsidiaries in the motor vehicle industry may result in some exaggeration of this difference. No comparison has been made in the present survey of the export performance of American-affiliated firms with that of Australian-owned companies in the same industries, and indeed such a comparison would be impossible in many industries because of the small number or absence of Australian-owned companies in them. In a study made by A. E. Safarian in Canada, however, the data suggested 'that any problems which inhibit Canadian exports are generally common to both [Canadian- and foreign-owned] firms, and that in the typical case ownership as such is not a significant deterrent to the exports of nonresident-owned firms' (1964: 456).

[12] This has been noted by many observers. The American National Industrial Conference Board has quoted the example of an American company that would not consider licensing a company in Japan 'where there is a very strong export drive' but which 'felt that a licensing agreement in Australia did not expose it to much risk of licensee competition in other export markets because there is a sizable Australian domestic market, and prevailing business ethics there are such that the licensee would almost certainly confine his sales efforts to the territory for which he was licensed' (Enid Baird Lovell 1958: 43).

It is perhaps only to be expected that a number of American-affiliated firms would export only a small proportion of their total output: as seen in chapter III, very many American companies invest in Australia primarily in order to surmount trade barriers. The very existence of a tariff suggests that Australian operations are not competitive on the world market. Ten of the companies which were not exporting at all in 1962 gave as explanation for this that they did not consider exporting would be profitable. Among companies which were exporting, high Australian cost was the most frequently mentioned reason for relatively small export volume. As an executive of a company supplying a specialized form of machinery explained, 'the U.K. affiliate can always under-cut our prices by about 20 per cent and I suspect that even then we have a lower mark-up than they do.' This company's only exports are spare parts sent to New Zealand occasionally for the sake of speedy delivery.

Related to high cost of production is the small size of many American-affiliated firms in Australia. Though a close correlation between export performance and company size would not be expected, not least because of differences in the importance of economies of scale in different industries, Table IX-6 does seem to indicate some tendency for export performance to improve with an increase in the size of the firm concerned. All companies with exports equal to at least 10 per cent of total sales were relatively small, however.

How important are restrictions imposed by American companies on the export freedom of their Australian affiliates?[13] Companies participating in the present survey were asked to indicate to which of twelve suggested areas (broadly embracing the whole world) they were permitted to export by their 'export franchise'. The answers received are extremely difficult to summarize and almost equally difficult to assess. Of the ninety-three companies under study, the answers of fourteen could not be incorporated in Tables IX-7 and IX-8, dealing with export franchise restrictions. Two of the fourteen had been established in Australia so recently that no decision on export franchise had been made at the time of the survey, and another company which may have been in the same position did not answer the question. Two more companies were engaged in the manufacture of products the nature of which made exporting, even in the distant future, very unlikely. In another case, a predominantly Australian-owned company was excluded from the tables because of

[13] For a discussion of the motives of American companies in imposing restrictions on the export franchise of their foreign affiliates, see Irving Brecher and S. S. Reisman (1957: 143-4).

TABLE IX-6 Ratio of Exports to Sales in 93 American-affiliated Companies in 1961/2, by Sales

Total sales in 1962 £A	Ratio of exports to sales (%)						No. companies covered
	Nil	0·01–0·99	1·00–2·99	3·00–4·99	5·00–9·99	10·00 and over	
500,000 and under	13	8	3	4	..	3	31
Over 500,000 and not above 1,000,000	6	2	..	1	2	2	13
Over 1,000,000 and not above 3,000,000	5	11	4	1	..	3	24
Over 3,000,000 and not above 5,000,000	2	3	1	..	2	..	8
Over 5,000,000 and not above 7,500,000	..	2	2	..	..	..	4
Over 7,500,000 and not above 10,000,000	..	1	4	..	2	..	7
Over 10,000,000	..	3	1	1	1	..	6
Total	26	30	15	7	7	8	93

the great variety of the export restrictions imposed upon it by its numerous overseas affiliates. Most of the balance were excluded because of uncertainty concerning the true nature of the restriction. Typical of this group was the pharmaceutical company which indicated that it could export to Australian Territories, New Zealand, and the islands of the Pacific—but the company secretary insisted that there was no 'specific limitation' on exports other than the high cost of Australian production. In several cases of this kind it was not clear whether exports had been restricted at the initiative of the parent company or whether the decision had been taken locally.

Even with these fourteen companies eliminated, the problem of interpretation is difficult. In some cases, markets allocated to the Australian affiliate by the American company merely recognize the inability of the Australian company to compete on markets also served by the more industrialized countries of the world. One company, exporting mainly to New Zealand and the islands of the South Pacific, explained that 'if we could export to other markets our parent company probably wouldn't have any objection'. The firm's main difficulty was high freight charges on a very bulky product. Another company, in the chemical industry, indicated that it was free to export to New Zealand only, but since there were no customers for its product in the South Pacific or in Australian Territories it was no disadvantage not to possess the right to export to these markets. It had investigated the possibility of exporting to Indonesia, but high freight charges and Indonesian currency difficulties had inhibited any trade. In other parts of Asia, Japanese competition made exporting impossible.

Frequently, even companies with a wide franchise were unable to make significant exports. Eight of the nineteen companies which indicated that they were free to export to all of the twelve areas enumerated, for example, had exports which amounted to less than 1 per cent of their sales revenue in 1962. There were other factors at work besides cost of production and freight. The former manager of a subsidiary in the cosmetics industry explained that not only were Australian costs higher than British or American, but also Australian colours were usually not in demand in Asian countries. Several companies complained of import quotas against their products in the New Zealand market, while others were having such difficulty meeting local market demand that the possibility of exporting had not yet arisen.

Yet other companies were free to export some products to any market of their choosing but others to only a limited number of countries. This situation usually prevailed when the Australian company was the only member of its family to produce a particular

Q

article, perhaps an article produced by a previously Australian-owned company before the acquisition of an American interest.[14] At least one company had been chosen to supply all non-American affiliates with one particular part of a larger item of equipment. The Australian company in turn assembled parts supplied by affiliates in many other countries. In such situations the question of 'export franchise' was rather irrelevant. In all the above cases, however, all the markets which companies were permitted to export to—even if permission extended to only a part of the company's product range —have been considered as part of that company's franchise.

In a surprising number of cases, companies answered the question on export franchise restrictions in vivid awareness of the U.S. anti-trust laws forbidding a wide range of market sharing arrangements.[15] Executives of six companies even referred to these laws by name. Several of the companies which were aware of the influence of American legislation on their exporting freedom seemed genuinely to be allowed a great deal of freedom, though usually even these companies were directed to sell through affiliated companies in countries where the U.S. parent had other subsidiaries. But in a number of cases export freedom was actually strictly circumscribed. Two companies stated that 'technically' or 'officially' they are permitted to export anywhere but 'in practice we don't sell outside Australasia'. One company stated that despite the freedom extended by its licensing agreement with its parent company it is not allowed to export *anywhere*; even the New Zealand market was recently acquired by the British affiliate. In all cases of this kind, the response included in Tables IX-7 and IX-8 is not that provided by the company on its questionnaire but the probably more accurate response conveyed to the writer verbally during the course of survey interviews.[16]

It is obvious, therefore, that the data presented on export franchises must be treated with caution.

Table IX-7 shows the number of mentions accorded each of the twelve areas by the seventy-nine companies included in the tabula-

[14] Of the eight companies which had been completely Australian-owned and which provided export figures for at least one year before and after the acquisition of an American interest, the exports of seven were higher (and in several cases much higher) after the American investment than before it.

[15] For discussion of U.S. antitrust laws and international market sharing arrangements, see Enid Baird Lovell (1958: 38-44); and Kingman Brewster, jr (1960: 9-22).

[16] Widespread evasion of the intention of American antitrust legislation in this field must make one sceptical of the practical effect of often-suggested Australian legislation to 'abolish' such export restrictions.

tion.[17] It is clear that almost all of these companies were free to export at least to Australian Territories overseas (mainly Papua-New Guinea), and that a large majority of companies were also free to export to New Zealand and the islands of the Pacific (usually

TABLE IX–7   Export Franchise Restrictions—Number of Times Each of 12 Markets Was Indicated as Being Open to 79 American-affiliated Companies in 1963, by Percentage of American Ownership

Markets open to Australian company		Percentage U.S. ownership			Total
		25–49	50–99	100	
Australian Territories:	A	3	10	19	32
	B	9	10	21	40
New Zealand:	A	1	8	14	23
	B	9	12	23	44
Pacific Islands[a]:	A	1	5	10	16
	B	9	10	25	44
South-East Asia[b]:	A	..	4	3	7
	B	9	10	30	49
Other Asia[c]:	A	..	1	1	2
	B	6	11	18	35
Middle East		5	6	14	25
Africa		6	8	15	29
Continental Europe		5	6	13	24
United States		5	5	9	19
Canada		5	5	10	20
South America		6	8	14	28
United Kingdom		5	8	13	26
Number of companies covered		14	21	44	79

A: Companies which enjoy this market as an 'exclusive territory'. See text for explanation. There may be some degree of understatement in a few cases because of uncertainty as to whether some companies had exclusive or non-exclusive rights. When in doubt, companies were included in 'B'.

B: Companies which do not enjoy this market as an 'exclusive territory'. All markets beyond 'Other Asia' were non-exclusive for the companies in this table.

a Usually interpreted to include islands in the South Pacific only.
b Usually interpreted to include the area bounded by Burma, Indonesia, and the Philippines.
c All of Asia not included in 'South-East Asia'. See Note b.

NOTE: In the thesis version of this study, companies which began manufacture before 1957 and those which began manufacture subsequently were classified separately in this and the immediately succeeding table. There seemed to be a slight tendency for the older firms to have greater freedom than the more recently established.

[17] The number of companies in each ownership class of the table is shown in Table IX-8. By way of explanation it should be added that when an Australian company enjoys an 'exclusive market' in, say, New Zealand, this merely means that other affiliates regard New Zealand as the sales territory of the Australian company. It does not, in all cases, mean that no other affiliate exports to New Zealand but just that when it does so it must pay the Australian company a commission on all sales in the area. The commission involved can range as high as 9 or 10 per cent and is often at least 5 per cent. On the other hand, of course, when the Australian company exports into the 'exclusive market' of another affiliate, it must pay the latter a commission.

TABLE IX–8 Export Franchise Restrictions—A Classification of 79 American-affiliated Companies by the Degree of Marketing Freedom Allowed in 1963, by Percentage of American Ownership

Marketing freedom	Percentage U.S. ownership			Total
	25–49	50–99	100	
Companies which could sell in				
Australia only	2	..	2	4
Australia and Australian Territories only	..	1	2	3
Australia, Australian Territories, and N.Z. only	2	2	2	6
Oceania only[a]	..	3	3	6
Oceania and S.E. Asia only	2	..	9	11
Limited parts of Oceania and/or Asia only	2	3	6	11
Oceania, S.E. Asia, and other Asia only	..	3	3	6
Oceania, S.E. Asia, and between one and six other markets[b]	1	4	8	13
Any market	5	5	9	19
Number of companies covered	14	21	44	79

[a] 'Oceania' is used for the sake of brevity to describe Australia, New Zealand, Australian Territories, and the islands of the South Pacific.

[b] The 'markets' referred to are those enumerated in Table IX–7.

NOTE: This table should be read in conjunction with Table IX–7 and the comments on both tables in the text.

interpreted to mean 'South Pacific'). On the other hand, only nineteen companies indicated that they could export to the U.S. and these are the companies listed in Table IX-8 as being free from all geographical restraint on exports.

Only four companies are shown in Table IX-8 as being forbidden to sell outside Australia at all, though the exports of a further three companies were confined to Australian Territories. It is interesting that only eight of the twenty-six companies not exporting in 1962 gave parental restriction as the main reason for this 'failure'.

The number of companies permitted to export beyond Australasia into South-East Asia is surprisingly large—fifty-six of the total. This contrasts favourably with the position found by the Department of Trade survey analysed by H. W. Arndt and D. R. Sherk in 1959, though the difference between the two surveys is certainly exaggerated by the inclusion of Australian companies working under licence to American companies in the Department's survey.[18] Of the 102 companies with American affiliations examined by Arndt and Sherk,

[18] As Arndt and Sherk (1959: 239) note, it is reasonable to expect subsidiaries to have wider export franchises than companies operating under licensing agreements.

the franchise of 79 (by coincidence) could be classified by area. Only 38 of these were free to sell in 'Australia, New Zealand, South Pacific Islands and Asia'. It is understood that a survey conducted by the Department in 1961-2—embracing a somewhat wider sample of American-affiliated companies than this study and distinguishing between those companies operating as subsidiaries and those operating only as licensees of foreign companies—indicated an even lower percentage of companies free to export into South-East Asia than did the 1959 study. The reason for this discrepancy between the Department's later study and the present one is not clear, though a difference in classification, a difference in size of sample, or a difference in period covered (at a time when, as suggested below, there is evidence that export franchise restrictions were under close scrutiny by many companies) could all offer part of the explanation. Because of the frankness of many qualifying comments, the writer does not believe that the responses actually tendered by participating companies in the present survey are subject to doubt as to their reliability.

Some of the most open comments came from companies which contended that they are free to export to any of the areas suggested. The exports of the majority were restricted in some way despite the absence of any overt restriction on markets. In some cases, as mentioned earlier, this restriction took the form of a limitation of the range of products which could be exported; in others, the necessity to sell all exports through affiliated firms. One jointly-owned company was permitted to sell products bearing its parent's brandname in the Australasian area only, but could export identical products under another brand to any country of its choosing. One wholly American company could export to any country in the world provided it did not reduce its export price below 80 per cent of its Australian retail price. A third company could sell in any market provided it quoted an unvarying f.o.b. price at Melbourne for all exports and sold through affiliates wherever applicable. The company was quite free to price its exports on a marginal cost basis, provided the same price was charged in all foreign markets. The only exception to the 'flat price' rule was in a situation where the Australian company was at a disadvantage because of foreign tariff preference in favour of the American article. Yet another company—whose parent insists that it compete on international markets for fear of U.S. antitrust legislation—always refers export orders to its U.S. parent, though this is 'for advice rather than approval'. The Australian company is prevented from competing with other affiliates on price because of a world-wide agreement entered into by its parent and other international companies to maintain price, and its parent will not tolerate any competition by 'unfair' means. What this latter stipulation entails was vividly illustrated when the local company, after testing an improved form of packaging on the New Zealand market and deciding to use it in all future export sales, received a vigorous complaint from its parent against such a move.

The median ratio of exports to sales of the nineteen companies which claimed no territorial limitation to exports was, at $1 \cdot 1$ per cent, not very much higher than the median for the group of ninety-three companies as a whole ($0 \cdot 5$ per cent), though what part factors unrelated to parent company direction played in this situation is difficult to judge.

The necessity to sell exports through affiliated companies is not, as is sometimes imagined, by any means always a disadvantage. It may, in fact, be of considerable assistance to the exports of the Australian company. Provided the c.i.f. price which the Australian company can quote is competitive with that of other affiliates, the use of the distribution facilities of an affiliated company can provide the local firm with ready-made sales outlets. This appears to have been an important consideration in the growth in exports of American-owned companies in the motor vehicle, agricultural equipment, and earth-moving equipment industries, all fields where distribution facilities and after-sales service are of vital importance.

Some companies appear to be allowed complete freedom in where and how they sell their products. Though the number of these seems to be small, they include some of the most substantial American subsidiaries in Australia. Executives of several companies made comments indicating that no member of their group has an exclusive market and that 'as soon as we get our costs down a bit more we'll be taking the New Zealand market off the British affiliate like a shot'. A 'usually reliable authority' has informed the writer that at least one wholly American company is even exporting to the People's Republic of China, though whether this reflects a large measure of marketing autonomy enjoyed by the local company or a deliberate attempt on the part of an American company to evade U.S. legislation forbidding trade with that country is not known.

Because franchise limitations may so often merely reflect competitive conditions, it is difficult to form any clear impression from the above evidence. While it is obvious that because of high Australian cost structures relatively few American subsidiaries would have been major exporters in 1962 even in the absence of parental restrictions, it is also abundantly clear that in the absence of such restrictions there are a number of companies which could have exported a very much larger fraction of their total output than they did. One jointly-owned company, the only overseas affiliate of an American company in the metal industry, was convinced that it could export economically to the West Coast of the United States, but because its parent feared that manufacturers in California might turn their attention to its own market in the Eastern States in such a situation, such sales were forbidden. Another jointly-owned company had, at the time of the survey, only just had its right to sell in the New Zealand market recognized by the British affiliate, and other affiliates 'preferred' it not to export into South-East Asia. The executive interviewed explained that he felt embarrassed by this situation and felt rather sorry for the Australian Trade Commissioners who often referred Asian customers to the company for supplies. 'We have to think up some excuse to put their inquiries off politely—that we haven't got the capacity at the moment, that we can't meet their delivery dates, etc.' The writer was told by a senior official of one of Australia's recent 'trade ships' that one of the largest American subsidiaries here had planned to participate in this trade display in the Asian area but had been compelled to withdraw its exhibit at the last minute because of pressure from its parent.

Some companies, moreover, would be in a better position to reduce their unit costs, and so justify their 'right' to a larger market, if they could only *get* a larger market. An executive of one large firm whose exports are currently confined to New Zealand, the islands of the South Pacific, and small parts of South-East Asia commented that his company would be given more markets if its costs were lower—'but we can't get our costs down without the increased volume we could get from exporting!' The executive anticipated that in the relatively near future the Australian company would be given an export order to fill because of lack of capacity in some other affiliate—'and once we get a leg in they'll never get it out again'.

It is argued in chapter XI that the effect on the Australian balance of payments of restrictions on the export franchise of American-affiliated companies is considerably less than is frequently implied in popular discussion of the subject. It nevertheless appears beyond doubt that some export franchise restrictions do have a detrimental impact on Australia's balance of payments, and in addition they must act to stifle the initiative of subsidiaries.

It is interesting to compare the position of jointly-owned firms with that of wholly American ones in the export field. The evidence is ambiguous, both in those tables showing export franchise restrictions and in Table IX-9, which shows ratios of exports to sales in companies of different ownership patterns. Within each ownership group the export performance of those companies which had been operating in Australia with an American affiliation for more than five or six years in 1962 was better than that of direct investments more recently established. If attention is confined to those companies

TABLE IX–9 Ratio of Exports to Sales in 93 American-affiliated Companies in 1961/2, by Percentage of American Ownership and Period in which Manufacture Began

Percentage U.S. ownership and period in which Australian manufacture began[a]	Ratio of exports to sales (%)						No. companies covered
	Nil	0·01–0·99	1·00–2·99	3·00–4·99	5·00–9·99	10·00 and over	
25–49%: Manufacture began—							
before 1957	1	4	..	..	1	1	7
in or after 1957	3	4	..	..	1	1	9
50–99%: Manufacture began—							
before 1957	1	2	4	2	1	1	11
in or after 1957	7	3	2	..	..	2	14
100%: Manufacture began—							
before 1957	4	8	7	4	3	2	28
in or after 1957	10	9	2	1	1	1	24
Total	26	30	15	7	7	8	93

a See Note a to Table IX–2.

which began manufacture in Australia before 1957, those with an Australian equity of up to 50 per cent seemed to do rather better than the wholly American companies, while both groups did better than those in which the American equity was less than 50 per cent. But there simply are not sufficient cases in which wholly American companies can be compared with jointly-owned ones of roughly similar size in the same industry to make a definite judgment from such evidence possible. Moreover, it is not the fact of sharing ownership with *Australians* which might be expected to exercise an influence on a company's freedom to export but the fact of sharing ownership with *any* other shareholder. And several of the companies classified as wholly American have two or even three major American shareholders.

A priori, one would expect companies which are jointly-owned to be allowed less export freedom than those which are wholly owned by one American company, and what little evidence there is seems to support this view.[19] One wholly American company was allocated the whole of the Asian and Pacific area as its export territory, despite the fact that its parent has an affiliate in Japan. The reason for this, it was explained, is that the American interest in the Japanese firm is less than 20 per cent. On the other hand, an executive of an Anglo-American firm explained that, since there was no formal restriction inhibiting the Australian company's exports, it had recently 'just started to export'. The company was severely reprimanded for its action because both shareholders had wholly-owned subsidiaries which could supply the Asian area. Another jointly-owned company, this time one in which Australian shareholders have a substantial minority interest, was free to export products peculiar to the Australian company to any market of its choosing, but could not sell products associated with the parent company's brandname outside Australia. The parent company, it was stated, naturally serves foreign markets for these products from the U.S. 'or from some other 100 per cent owned company established in the area'. In one of the most remarkable cases, a company which had been owned in partnership with a number of other shareholders changed its position in the export field when it became wholly American in ownership. Before this, exports seem to have been confined mainly to New Zealand, but when the American parent acquired complete ownership it closed its similar plant in the United Kingdom, doubled the capacity of the Australian plant and, at the time of the survey, expected the Australian plant to export a large fraction of its output to the United Kingdom, Canada, and Japan.

---

[19] Interestingly, W. P. Hogan (1965) reached an exactly parallel conclusion in his study of British-affiliated companies in Australian industry.

By extension, one would expect even jointly-owned companies to have wider export franchises than wholly Australian licensees, but the only concrete evidence for this view encountered by the writer was the comment of a licensee who was preparing to make a large share issue to the American licenser:

> Under our licensing agreement we can't export outside Australia but there is a sort of gentleman's agreement that if we can get our volume up and our costs down we will be given more territory. And we will probably get more territory when they take up their equity.

It is understood that the 1961-2 survey of the Department of Trade on this subject revealed that, within each nationality of overseas affiliate, a significantly higher fraction of licensees than of financial affiliates was confined to Australia in their sales.

To digress briefly, there has been controversy ever since Arndt and Sherk published their analysis of the Department of Trade's study in 1959 on whether British affiliates are more restricted in their export freedom than are American affiliates. The figures published by Arndt and Sherk showed American affiliates to have a much greater freedom in the Asian area than had British affiliates, and the difference was understated, according to the authors, because of the higher proportion of licensees in the American figures than in the British. The authors suggested that the reasons for this difference probably lay both in the greater frequency with which British parent companies might be expected to have established direct connections in the Asian area, and in the post-war dollar shortage which might be expected to have led American companies to channel Asian orders to their soft-currency Australian subsidiaries. If it is true that British affiliates in Australia are more often jointly-owned than are American, this may provide another part of the answer. Obviously the present study does not permit of comment on this matter. It is understood, however, that the 1961-2 survey of the Department of Trade, while showing a markedly greater freedom for both American licensees and American subsidiaries to sell in the New Zealand and South Pacific area than for British, showed only a small difference in the freedom of affiliates of the two countries to export outside the Australasian area as a whole. This could be explained by a difference in ownership policy between British and American companies, if such a difference exists, but may also be explained by the probably greater number of British investments in New Zealand than of American.

In practice, most American-affiliated companies, whether wholly American or jointly-owned, depended heavily on markets in New

Zealand, Australian Territories, and the South Pacific—regardless of the export freedom they enjoyed. This is clearly brought out in Tables IX-10 and IX-11. A significant fraction of total exports also went to Asia but, despite the substantial volume of unclassified exports, it is safe to conclude that the share of exports going to the Middle East, Europe, United Kingdom, and the Americas in 1961/2 was very small.

Regrettably perhaps, no attempt was made to discover what fraction of total exports was channelled through affiliated companies overseas. Certainly there was little exporting to American parents by the companies under study, though the unclassified exports of at least two jointly-owned companies are known to have been primarily to the parent company. (In one of these two cases, indeed, the American interest in the Australian company had been acquired in large measure with a view to its supplying the American company with a particular product not required by the latter in a volume large

TABLE IX–10   Destination of the Exports of 93 American-affiliated
Companies in 1961/2, by Percentage of American Ownership
£A('000)

| | Percentage U.S. ownership | | | |
	25–49	50–99	100	Total[d]
Exports classified by destination				
Australian Territories	55	1	580	637
New Zealand	222	228	4,441	4,891
Pacific Islands[a]	5	..	535	541
South-East Asia[b]	51	339	743	1,133
Other Asia[c]	140	93	1,141	1,373
Middle East	..	..	20	20
Africa	14	68	521	603
Continental Europe	[e]	4	72	76
United States	..	..	66	66
Canada	..	..	..	..
South America	..	3	76	79
United Kingdom	..	6	49	55
Unclassified exports	81	659	193	934
Total exports[d]	569	1,401	8,436	10,405
Total sales	41,082	45,075	370,624	456,781

[a] Usually interpreted to include islands in the South Pacific only.
[b] Usually interpreted to include the area bounded by Burma, Indonesia, and the Philippines.
[c] All of Asia not included in 'South-East Asia'. See Note [b].
[d] Detail may not add to totals because of rounding.
[e] Less than £500.

NOTE: In the thesis version of this study, companies which began manufacture before 1957 and those which began manufacture subsequently were classified separately in this and the immediately succeeding table. There was some tendency for the older firms to export outside the Australasian area more often than did the more recently established.

TABLE IX–11   Number of Companies Engaged in the Export Trade Depicted
in Table IX–10

| | Percentage U.S. ownership | | | |
	25–49	50–99	100	Total
Number of companies indicating exports going to				
Australian Territories	4	1	9	14
New Zealand	7	11	30	48
Pacific Islands[a]	3	..	11	14
South-East Asia[b]	4	7	15	26
Other Asia[c]	3	2	8	13
Middle East	..	..	1	1
Africa	2	2	4	8
Continental Europe	1	1	4	6
United States	..	..	2	2
Canada	..	..	..	..
South America	..	1	4	5
United Kingdom	..	1	2	3
Companies which left some exports unclassified	4	4	5	13
Number of companies exporting	12	17	38	67
Number of companies covered	16	25	52	93

[a] See Note [a] to Table IX–10.
[b] See Note [b] to Table IX–10.
[c] See Note [c] to Table IX–10.

enough to give it a cost advantage.) There were a number of other companies engaged in the export to the U.S. of products not produced by the parent company, but these firms were mainly associated with the extraction or processing of raw materials of one kind or another and have not, even in those few cases when they provided relevant figures, been included in the present tabulation. It is known that at least one of these companies still sells part of its output to its parent at a price which is lower than it might wish, and one of the others was compelled to sell all its output to its parent at considerably less than world market prices until government intervention ended the practice towards the end of the forties. One manufacturing company is known to export at marginal cost to a tax-haven company in Hong Kong, from where the products are sent on to Japan at a substantially higher price. But because of recent American tax legislation and the fact that so many of the exports of the companies under consideration are sent to New Zealand and closely surrounding markets, it seems unlikely that such tax evasion is significant.

The speed at which the exports of the companies under study are growing is remarkable. The twenty-seven companies that provided export data for the three years 1954/5, 1959/60 and 1961/2 experienced a growth in total exports of from £2·8 million in the first of these years to £7·4 million in the last. Not all of the twenty-seven companies provided production data for the same three years, so that changes in the ratio of exports to manufacturing output are known in only nineteen cases. Two of these companies exported nothing in either 1954/5 or 1961/2, but of the other seventeen, ten registered an increase in their ratio of exports to 'selling value of output' while only seven registered a fall. More impressive was the change that occurred between 1959/60 and 1961/2: of the fifty-five comparisons available, eleven companies exported nothing in either year, thirty-one registered an increase in their ratio of exports to selling value of output, and only thirteen experienced a fall.

It is not surprising then that the exports of American-affiliated companies appear to be rising much more rapidly than their imports: the exports of the twenty-one companies which provided data for both imports and exports for 1954/5, 1959/60 and 1961/2 rose by 167 per cent between 1954/5 and 1961/2, compared with a growth of only 30 per cent in their imports. The exports of the thirty companies which provided data for both imports and exports for only 1959/60 and 1961/2 fell by 13 per cent between the two years —but their imports fell by 26 per cent.

The number of companies which have recently started exporting is substantial. Of the twenty-seven companies which provided data for 1954/5, 1959/60, and 1961/2, only sixteen were exporting in 1954/5—but twenty-five were exporting in 1961/2. Of the thirty-eight which provided data for 1959/60 and 1961/2 only, eighteen were exporting in the earlier year as against twenty-seven in the later. All but four of the twenty-six American-affiliated companies known to be not exporting in 1961/2 expected to be exporting in the future, and in a number of cases exporting was imminent.

Very many of the companies which were exporting in 1961/2 were anticipating substantial increases in their export sales. One company with exports of less than £4,000 in 1961/2 expected exports to be 'at least £50,000' in 1963/4. Another firm, established only five or six years in 1962, sold exports worth only £2,000 in that year but exports worth over £20,000 in 1962/3. While most of these exports went to New Zealand, the company had recently given the travelling representative of the American company in Asia an Australian price list to carry with him, and the Australian company anticipated sending its own representative into Asia in the near future. Yet another company (one not participating in the present survey) achieved a 320 per cent increase in exports between 1961/2 and 1962/3, to the point where exports were about 10 per cent of total sales. Another small company, with no exports in 1961/2, expected to begin exporting to overseas affiliates on a large scale in 1965. Most of its affiliates sub-contracted the manufacture of the products made by the Australian company and most contracts were due to expire in 1965. In a different industry, a company with exports of £97,000 in 1961/2 made overseas sales of £250,000 in 1962/3. Clearly it would be over-stating the case to imply that these examples are typical of all the companies studied, but the list of similar instances could certainly be extended considerably.

The great expansion of exports achieved by many American-affiliated companies has been well-publicized. General Motors-Holden's alone claimed that its exports in 1965 would earn Australia at least £10 million in foreign exchange, compared with a figure of only £3·7 million in 1962 (*A.F.R.*, 26 May 1965). The company has even developed a left-hand drive model of the Holden, especially for export markets, and Holdens are now assembled in no less than four overseas countries. Chrysler, too, despite very small exports in 1962 and the first part of 1963, announced early in 1965 that more than 10 per cent of its vehicles were exported in 1964 (*A.F.R.*, 15 Jan. 1965). In the electrical equipment industry, S.T.C. was stated to have increased the percentage of its production exported almost six-fold between 1961/2 and 1963/4 (*Australian*, 19 March 1965), while a company in the engineering industry with exports of less than £10,000 in 1959/60 claimed that it had export orders of £600,000 in 1962/3, £200,000 of the total being on account of Japanese customers. During 1964-5, at least two American subsidiaries secured export contracts worth substantially in excess of £1 million, and one of these was termed by the Minister of Trade and Industry 'the biggest single sale an Australian manufacturer has made overseas' (*Sydney Morning Herald*, 30 Jan. 1964). Many similar cases could be cited and it is hardly surprising that American subsidiaries have figured prominently in recent years among those receiving awards for export achievement from the Associated Chambers of Manufactures of Australia.

The reasons for this sudden expansion are not hard to find. In part, it reflects a growing awareness throughout Australian industry of the importance of manufactured exports in Australia's future growth, and the profitability of exporting even if this has to be done on a marginal cost basis. In part, it is a direct result of the government's tax incentives for exports, which, of course, are partly responsible for the growth in export 'consciousness'. Of 102 companies which answered questions on export promotion and the use of government tax incentives and facilities, 60 companies were engaged in some form of promotion. In the case of 21 of these companies this 'promotion' seemed to be largely market research, but other companies pursued a more active programme. Eight companies specifically mentioned having a sales branch in at least one overseas country (usually New Zealand, though in three cases Singapore or Hong Kong) while several of the 9 companies with manufacturing subsidiaries in other countries (almost exclusively New Zealand) sold considerable quantities through these outlets. Only 8 companies used official overseas trade missions as a means of export promotion. Seventy-three of the total of 102 companies used at least one of the government's export incentives or facilities: 62 used payroll-tax rebates, 60 'market development allowances', and 10 the Export Payments Insurance Corporation. (Surprisingly, only two companies made specific mention of help received from Australian Trade Commissioners, though since this was not one of the suggested 'government facilities' listed on the survey questionnaire the number of responses may be in no way representative.) How important these incentives are is not generally known but one company described the taxation rebates and allowances as 'the one thing that really makes exporting pay'.

There are other factors encouraging the exports of American-affiliated companies. At least one company has experienced a major breakthrough in exports because its 'Australian content' has reached the level needed to qualify it for British preferential tariff treatment in the New Zealand market. Another company was able to displace its British affiliate in Asian markets as its unit cost fell with the growth of local sales. A third firm was allocated the Asian market because it is so much better placed than the American company to give prompt after-sales service. One major company has expanded its exports sharply after a large increase in its local research expenditure: in solving a problem associated with the Australian market, it found it had developed a product with considerable sales potential in the Asian area.

Many export franchise restrictions have undoubtedly been relaxed in recent years also. Sometimes this relaxation has been associated with a prior reduction in Australian unit cost, but sometimes with other pressures. One non-American subsidiary in the motor vehicle industry, for example, is understood to have received a much wider export franchise in recent years to enable it to expand its volume sufficiently to meet the Australian government's directives on increasing Australian content of vehicles, and this factor may well have been at work in the case of some American firms too. One large American company has sharply increased its exports in recent years because it fears that the government may soon legislate to limit the imports a company may purchase to the value of its exports. The fruit of government pressure on export franchises may be seen from the fact that, apart from the two companies which indicated that no decision had yet been made on their export franchise, no fewer than twenty of the companies interviewed in 1963 stated that they were negotiating to have their export restrictions removed or reduced.

In conclusion, there seems little doubt that a great many American-affiliated companies are rapidly assuming a major role in the expansion of Australian manufactured exports. The most hopeful sign for the future is that local management often seems keen to expand Australian exports whatever the actual ownership of the company concerned. This 'internal' pressure is reinforced to an important extent by the threat of American antitrust action and measures taken by the Australian government to make exporting more profitable.

X

How Profitable is American Investment in Australia?

The income earned by foreign-owned companies in Australia probably generates more widespread concern than any other single aspect
of foreign investment. In its most popular form, this concern is
frankly mercantilist in its preoccupation with 'money flowing out of
the country', while added to this fear is indignation at the 'rapacious
profits' which foreign companies are believed to earn in Australia.
At a more sophisticated level, concern is usually expressed in terms
of the effect which Australia's growing liability on account of international investment income has, or will have, on the country's
balance of payments.

What are the facts? Certainly, the total level of profits and interest
accruing to foreign investors has grown rapidly in the post-war
period. From only £26 million in 1947/8, company income payable
overseas expanded more than fivefold in the years to 1963/4 and, as
Table X-1 shows, the growth in income due to shareholders in North
America has been even more rapid than the average. The ratio of
company income payable overseas to Australia's total external
receipts is also substantially higher at present than it was in the late
forties, though it is interesting to note that the rapid rise in this
ratio which took place in the fifties and which gave so much concern
to commentators at that time (e.g. Arndt 1957: 251) appears to have
been at least temporarily halted. Further discussion of the significance of changes in this ratio is deferred until chapter XI (where an
attempt is made to assess the overall impact of foreign investment on
the Australian balance of payments), and attention is confined for
the moment to the *profitability* of American investment.

Australian statistics make it impossible to make a precise calculation of the return on foreign investment in Australia. The best available official estimates, recently published by the Commonwealth
Treasury (and reproduced in Table X-2), suggest that the average
return on foreign investment in companies has probably fluctuated

TABLE X-1   Annual Investment Income Payable Overseas by Companies, Compared with Australia's External Earnings

Year ended 30 June	Investment income payable to				Total external earnings £A(m.)	Ratio of investment income to earnings (%)
	U.S.A. & Canada	U.K. £A(m.)	Other countries	Total		
1948	4·4	18·8	2·5	25·7	468	5·5
1949	4·6	15·5	2·6	22·7	591	3·8
1950	6·6	25·4	2·8	34·8	679	5·1
1951	11·2	31·0	2·4	44·6	1,073	4·2
1952	14·7	28·3	3·2	46·2	771	6·0
1953	15·4	29·7	2·5	47·6	954	5·0
1954	30·5	35·2	4·1	69·8	927	7·5
1955	28·3	39·6	4·5	72·4	885	8·2
1956	32·0	48·1	5·5	85·6	904	9·5
1957	32·9	49·6	7·0	89·5	1,135	7·9
1958	38·0	48·9	7·8	94·7	975	9·7
1959	48·0	56·0	10·7	114·7	977	11·7
1960	51·8	61·9	8·8	122·5	1,117	11·0
1961	49·7	54·7	12·4	116·8	1,135	10·3
1962	37·1	50·8	9·6	97·5	1,292	7·5
1963	44·9	70·2	11·5	126·6	1,303	9·7
1964	49·1	74·9	11·9	135·9	1,661	8·2

SOURCE: Commonwealth Bureau of Census and Statistics 1965a and b.

TABLE X–2   Estimated 'Earning Rates' on North American,
United Kingdom, and Total Overseas Investment in Companies in Australia[a]

Year ended 30 June	Investment income payable as percentage of total overseas investment in companies in Australia from		
	U.S.A. & Canada (%)	U.K. (%)	All overseas countries (%)
1948	7·3	7·7	8·0
1949	6·9	5·6	6·3
1950	9·4	8·2	8·7
1951	13·9	8·5	9·5
1952	14·5	7·0	8·6
1953	11·7	6·6	7·6
1954	22·8	7·4	10·7
1955	18·7	7·6	10·1
1956	16·8	8·4	10·4
1957	14·8	7·7	9·5
1958	15·2	6·9	9·1
1959	17·3	7·3	10·0
1960	16·0	7·4	9·6
1961	12·8	5·8	8·0
1962	7·8	4·8	5·7
1963	8·2	6·3	6·8
1964	7·7	6·1	6·6

[a] Annual estimates of the value of overseas investment in companies in Australia were reached by adding estimates of annual capital inflow to an assumed value of private overseas investment at 30 June 1947. In each case the investment income payable has been compared with the value of investment at the *beginning* of the year in question. Because figures showing the domicile of the overseas investor do not provide a classification of direct and portfolio investment, the above 'earning rates' refer to both types of investment combined. The approximate nature of the estimates is obvious even from figures shown for 1947/8, where 'earning rates' for both North American and British investment are shown as being below the average for all countries, despite the heavy preponderance of investment from those two areas.

SOURCE: Commonwealth Treasury 1965a.

between about 6 and 11 per cent over the period under consideration. This is clearly not a high return and in several recent years has been lower than the return on shareholders' funds in Australian public companies.[1] But the table does reveal that the return on American investment has been considerably greater than the average, or—and this is almost another way of saying the same thing—considerably greater than the return on British investment in Australia.

Various explanations have been offered for the relatively high profits earned by American investment in Australia in the fifties,

[1] The Treasury (1965a: 19) noted that figures published by the Reserve Bank of Australia for a large group of Australian public companies (excluding finance companies, those engaged in mining or primary industry, and overseas companies) reveal a net return on shareholders' funds for the years 1959 to 1963 of 9·7, 9·3, 6·8, 6·8, and 7·4 per cent respectively.

and the apparent decline in these profits since the beginning of the sixties. Treasury itself offered three possible answers. First, it was suggested that discrimination against dollar imports into Australia up to 1959 enhanced the scarcity value of American-designed products and so increased the profitability of producing these locally. Secondly, it was claimed that America's technological superiority over Australia and other countries was greater during the fifties than it has since become, 'so that North American firms operating in Australia at that time possessed initial advantages over their competitors' (1965a: 20). Thirdly, American investors may have adopted a more discriminating approach to investment in Australia in the years when this was a relatively new field for their interest than did British investors. Some have offered yet another explanation of the greater profitability of American investment: British firms, the theory runs, only invest overseas when tariff barriers in their export markets compel them to do so, while American firms retain the initiative by actively seeking out profitable investment opportunities.

None of these explanations is entirely satisfactory. The last in particular, which suggests a different motivation for investment by British and American firms, is quite unacceptable. As shown in chapter III, trade barriers have been of great importance in the decisions of American investors to manufacture in Australia. It is also a little difficult to accept that import restrictions on dollar goods were a major factor in the profitability of American firms, since American-designed goods would have been available to a large extent from American subsidiaries in the United Kingdom. On the other hand, it does seem likely that import restrictions in general played an important part in enhancing the profitability of American firms, as probably also of many Australian-owned firms. It is possible that America's technological superiority over Australia has declined since the fifties, but it seems at least as likely that the competitive advantage enjoyed by old-established American firms in Australia has been whittled away, not by a relative advance in *Australian* technology, but by the establishment of more *American* ventures (and the expansion of some of the older ones) in Australia.

Perhaps after all this is not unrelated to Treasury's third reason for the decline in the profitability of American investment, that American investors are accepting a lower rate of return as their familiarity with the Australian market increases. Certainly part of the recent fall in aggregate profitability revealed in Treasury estimates reflects not a decline in the profitability of long-established companies but the positive *unprofitability* of a number of very large investments made since 1960. One has only to think of American investments in the Altona petrochemical complex, in aluminium, in the food industry, and in new marketing networks for the distribution of motor spirit—and to recall the dimension of the losses incurred by these companies in the early sixties—to recognize that any generalizations from aggregate figures on profitability must be treated with caution.

There may be a further reason why American investment in Australia has appeared to be more profitable than British, a reason which bears no relation to the inherent profitability of the respective investments. If American-affiliated companies tend to be wholly-owned subsidiaries more often than do their British counterparts, there may be a tendency for a larger part of the 'profits' of British affiliates to accrue to their parent companies in the form of technical service fees, or profits on the sale of goods exported to the affiliate in Australia, than is the case with American affiliates. But the evidence necessary for generalization in this area is entirely lacking and any comment must be mere speculation. Lack of data also prevents conclusions being drawn from the probably different industry distribution of American and British investments in Australia.

Calculations presented in Table X-3, based on data published by the U.S. Department of Commerce, show that it has been in the manufacturing sector that American-owned companies have secured the highest return on their investment, though the rate of return on the much smaller American investment in 'Mining and smelting' has not been significantly lower. Moreover, the relatively low profitability of American investment in 'Other' industries was primarily the result of the low return on American investment in the Australian oil industry, and this in turn was probably, at least in part, the result of the crude oil pricing practices referred to in chapter IX. There appears to have been a downward trend in the profitability of American investment in Australian manufacturing over the period, but these data suggest that, after making due allowance for the 1961-2 recession, there has been no sharp reduction in the profitability of American-affiliated companies in manufacturing since the end of the fifties. Certainly their profitability in 1962 can only be described as very satisfactory, though because the figures are based on book values of investment there is undoubtedly some overstatement of the 'true' rate of profit.

The present survey also sought information on profits. As mentioned in chapter IV, some difficulty was experienced in securing consistent figures in this field. Even if satisfactory profit figures were available, there would still remain the problem of what to measure them against. A comparison of profit with the par value of the paid-up capital of the firms concerned—the measure of profitability so beloved of Australian financial journalists—is obviously quite in-

TABLE X–3   Estimated 'Earning Rates' on American Direct Investments in
Australia, by Sector[a]

Calendar year	Investment income payable as percentage of U.S. direct investment in			
	Manufacturing (%)	Mining and smelting[b] (%)	Other[c] (%)	Total (%)
1951	28·6	18·2	7·6	17·9
1952	18·9	25·0	6·0	13·3
1953	26·5	14·3	9·1	18·2
1954	28·5	40·0	7·3	20·1
1955	25·4	15·0	7·1	17·2
1956	17·5	20·0	7·5	13·0
1957	20·9	17·2	7·7	14·9
1958	21·5	9·1	8·7	15·4
1959	20·0	27·3	9·2	15·6
1960	18·8	29·6	5·7	13·5
1961	12·4	24·2	2·9	9·0
1962	18·6	13·9	3·1	11·7
Unweighted arithmetic average	21·5	21·2	6·8	15·0

a In accordance with the method used by the Commonwealth Treasury in deriving the estimates in Table X–2, the investment income payable in each case has been compared with the value of U.S. direct investment in the industry at the *beginning* of the year in question. American data on overseas investment on which these estimates are based are derived from actual book values of investment, however, and in this respect are unlike those used by Treasury.

b Because the absolute dimension of income accruing to U.S. investors in this industry is small, 'rounding' in the raw data may account for part of the violent fluctuation in earning rates revealed in the figures.

c Includes 'Petroleum', which is in fact substantially the largest category of investment within the total. Published figures do not make it possible to calculate the return on U.S. direct investment in this industry, but it is possible to arrive at close estimates for at least the years 1958 and 1959. In these years, the rates of return on U.S. investment in this industry were 7·4 and 8·2 per cent respectively. It is likely that the sharp falling off in the return on 'Other' investment after 1960 was due almost exclusively to a fall in the rate of return on petroleum investment.

SOURCE: 1951–9, derived from U.S. Department of Commerce 1963b.
1960–2, derived from information supplied directly by the U.S. Department of Commerce.

admissible, since the paid-up value of the share capital of most American-affiliated companies grossly understates the value of the American investment. It does not even represent the value of the 'original investment', as noted in chapter IV, though even if it did it would still have no value as a measure of profitability. More valid would be a comparison of profit with shareholders' funds, but even this significantly understates the book value of the parent company's investment in many cases by ignoring the frequently important advances made to the subsidiary on inter-company account. The best measure of profitability would appear to be a comparison of profit accruing to the U.S. shareholder with the combined total of shareholders' funds due to him and credit extended by him on inter-company account. This is by no means a perfect measure, since the book value of the shareholders' funds of long-established companies considerably understates the real worth of the assets they represent. However, it appears to be the best measure available, and provided the imprecise nature of the data being presented is borne in mind, some interesting observations may be made.

Table X-4 presents ratios of profit to this estimate of total American investment, by percentage of American ownership. Seventy-nine companies are covered in the table, and of these sixty-two were operating at a profit in 1962. The total income accruing to U.S. shareholders from the whole group was £32 million, after allowing for aggregate losses of about £2 million. The table reveals a distinct tendency for companies established before 1957 to be profitable more often than those established subsequently, which is scarcely surprising. Average profit rates also appear to reveal a tendency for wholly American companies to be more profitable than jointly-owned ones, at least if attention be confined to those established before 1957. But the appearance is deceptive. The median profitability of the seventeen jointly-owned firms established prior to 1957 was 10·4 per cent—as compared with 10·8 per cent for the median profitability of the twenty-seven wholly American firms established before 1957. If the considerable profitability of one very large company, General Motors-Holden's, is excluded from the average for all wholly American companies established before 1957, the average for that group falls from 14·5 per cent to only 10·1 per cent—a level much nearer the averages of 8·4 and 9·3 per cent obtaining for the two categories of jointly-owned companies.

The explanation of differences in the profitability of companies of different ownership pattern is probably to be found in large measure in the fact that ownership patterns often coincide with industry patterns. All participating companies in the pharmaceutical industry, for example, were wholly American in 1962, and all but the smallest of the participating companies in the motor vehicle industry were also wholly American. As Table X-5 shows, these two industries were among the most profitable for American investment in Australia in 1962. Because of this concentration of companies of one ownership pattern within particular industries, it is not possible to assess the relative profitability of companies of different ownership patterns under approximately similar circumstances.

The overall profitability of the whole group of companies, 11·4 per cent, is not nearly as high as the rate of 18·6 per cent shown in Table X-3 for the profitability of all American investment in Australian manufacturing in 1962, though it is substantially higher than

TABLE X–4 Ratio of Net Profit to Total American Investment in 79 American-affiliated Companies in 1961/2,
by Percentage of American Ownership and Period in which Manufacture Began

Percentage U.S. ownership and period in which Australian manufacture began[a]	Companies incurring a loss	Ratio of U.S. share in net profit to total American investment (%)							No. companies covered	Average ratio, profitable companies (%)	Average ratio, all companies[b] (%)
		0–4.9	5.0–9.9	10.0–14.9	15.0–19.9	20.0–24.9	25.0–29.9	30.0 and over			
25–49%: Manufacture began—											
before 1957	..	2	2	3	..	..	..	..	7	8·4	8·4
in or after 1957	1	..	3	1	..	..	..	..	5	10·9	0·5
50–99%: Manufacture began—											
before 1957	1	2	1	4	1	1	..	..	10	9·3	9·3
in or after 1957	7	..	1	2	2	..	..	..	12	14·4	—1·8
100%: Manufacture began—											
before 1957	3	3	7	6	2	2	3	1	27	14·7	14·5
in or after 1957	5	4	4	1	..	..	2	2	18	9·5	—0·1
Total	17	11	18	17	5	3	5	3	79	13·4	11·4

[a] The year in which manufacture began is taken to be the year in which an American equity of at least 25 per cent was first acquired in the case of companies manufacturing previously as Australian-owned ventures.

[b] A loss is denoted by a minus sign.

NOTE: The U.S. share in after-tax profit has been compared with the American share of shareholders' funds plus credit extended by the American company at the end of the year to which profits refer. As elsewhere, not all companies gave figures for the year ended 30 June 1962, and the aggregate figures have a bias towards calendar 1962.

TABLE X–5 Ratio of Net Profit to Total American Investment in 79 American-affiliated Companies in 1961/2, by Industry

Industry	Companies incurring a loss	Ratio of U.S. share in net profit to total American investment (%)							No. companies covered	Average ratio, profitable companies (%)	Average ratio, all companies[a] (%)
		0– 4·9	5·0– 9·9	10·0– 14·9	15·0– 19·9	20·0– 24·9	25·0– 29·9	30·0 and over			
Plant, equipment, machinery	2	2	5	5	1	..	..	..	15	7·5	7·2
Motor vehicles	1	..	2	1	..	1	..	..	5	16·1	16·1
Metal manufactures, n.e.i.	2	..	2	2	..	..	..	..	6	8·5	5·8
Electrical equipment, instruments, etc.	1	4	2	5	..	..	1	..	13	11·4	11·4
Food and drink	1	2	..	..	..	1	1	..	5	10·9	10·1
Industrial chemicals and plastics	6	1	1	1	..	..	1	..	10	7·5	–2·3
Pharmaceutical and toilet preparations	1	..	2	..	2	..	2	2	9	19·0	17·8
Other industries	3	2	4	3	2	1	..	1	16	9·8	8·7
Total	17	11	18	17	5	3	5	3	79	13·4	11·4

[a] A loss is denoted by a minus sign.

the Treasury estimate of 7·8 per cent shown in Table X-2 for the return on *all* North American investment in Australia in 1961/2. The figures are not directly comparable, however. They cover different aggregates, refer to different time periods (at a time when the Australian economy was just emerging from a recession), and are based on different methods. Companies in the present survey were asked to provide profit figures for the year ended 30 June 1962 or their nearest accounting period, and a number of the largest firms in fact provided figures for the calendar year 1962. In this respect, the figures presented here are more nearly similar to those collected by the U.S. Department of Commerce, which are collected on a calendar year basis. But the profit rate for 1962 in Table X-3 was calculated by comparing the earnings generated in 1962 with the value of investment at the beginning of 1962, whereas the figures based on data collected in the present survey compare profit in 1961/2 with investment at the end of that year (for lack of other data). This difference in method certainly accounts for at least part of the difference in the two profit estimates: had the profit recorded by the U.S. Department of Commerce as accruing to U.S. share-holders in 1962 been compared with the value of U.S. investment at the *end* of 1962, the profit rate would have been 16·2 per cent instead of 18·6 per cent. The source of the remaining difference is not known with certainty: there were some extremely profitable companies which declined to participate in this survey and it is possible, in view of current Australian sentiment on this matter, that on average non-participating companies were more profitable in 1962 than were participating companies. This, together with the fact that many companies in the present survey provided data for the year ended 30 June 1962, may explain the remaining discrepancy, but it is impossible to be sure. It seems reasonable to assume that data published by the U.S. Department of Commerce are the most reliable available, if only because all American companies with investments abroad are obliged to supply information on their activities to that Department.

Whichever rate is accepted, it is clear that American direct investment in Australian manufacturing was considerably more profitable on average in 1962 than was Australian enterprise: a large group of Australian-owned manufacturing companies surveyed by the Reserve Bank of Australia earned only 6·9 per cent on shareholders' funds in that year.[2] Yet if attention is confined to data collected in the present survey, it appears that the proportion of American-affiliated

[2] In 1963 the earning rate was only a little higher, at 7·4 per cent (Reserve Bank of Australia 1965).

companies earning a profit of more than 6·9 per cent in 1962 was not startlingly large. Of the total of 79 companies, only 43 earned more than 6·9 per cent on the value of their American investment, though admittedly 31 of the 44 which commenced operations before 1957 did so.

It is also interesting that if General Motors-Holden's is omitted from the table altogether, the rate of return on investment in profitable companies falls from 13·4 to 10·0 per cent, and in all companies from 11·4 to 7·7 per cent. There can be little doubt that the high profitability of General Motors-Holden's, and the considerable size of the company even in relation to total American investment in Australian manufacturing, has been an important factor contributing to the high profitability of that investment throughout the fifties. In several years during that decade, the profits of General Motors-Holden's alone exceeded 40 per cent of total U.S. earnings on direct investments in Australian manufacturing. In several years, the company's net trading profit (after depreciation and tax) exceeded 30 per cent of the parent company's total investment in Australia at the end of the year in question.

Indeed, if the distribution of rates of profit shown in Table X-4 is typical, it would appear that perhaps the most striking feature of the earning rates of American-affiliated companies is the great range they cover. General Motors-Holden's is undoubtedly a very profitable company, but it is by no means the most profitable American subsidiary in Australia. Twelve of the seventy-nine companies in Table X-4 had a higher rate of return on total investment in 1962 than did G.M.H., and in one case after-tax profit exceeded 100 per cent of the total American investment. (This high profitability was, incidentally, not associated with substantial borrowings from Australian sources.) At the other extreme, one company established in the early fifties incurred a loss in 1962 which exceeded in value the parent company's total remaining investment in the firm at the end of the year. A total of seventeen firms made a loss, and four of these had been operating for more than five or six years in 1962. Certainly, in two of the seventeen cases, the loss incurred was entirely the result of very heavy advertising expenditure, manufacturing operations having been very profitable, but in the other cases the loss primarily reflected unprofitable manufacturing operations. Between these two extremes lay the great bulk of the firms covered, mainly earning from 5 to 15 per cent on total investment.

Of course it is well known that the profitability of some American-affiliated companies is not adequately reflected in their after-tax profit figures. The profits of the local enterprise may be considerably affected by the price paid for materials bought from the parent company, though as noted in chapter IX it seems likely that, if oil companies are excepted,[3] the profits of American-affiliated companies in Australia are inflated as often as they are deflated by this factor. At least one manufacturing subsidiary sells its output to the local sales branch of its American parent at a price which one company executive felt was designed to leave an important part of the profit in the branch—and again it is difficult to assess what meaning is to be attached to the profit figure of the manufacturing operation.

An attempt was made, however, to examine the importance of interest payments, royalties, technical assistance fees, engineering fees, and so on as means by which American parent companies receive a reward on their Australian investment.[4] Of the seventy-nine companies included in Tables X-4 and X-5, seven either declined to provide information on such payments or felt that their description on the questionnaire, as 'service charges', did not cover the kind of payment made by their company. Admittedly, the problem of defining such payments is not easy. As mentioned in chapter VI, some companies regard payment of technical assistance fees as just another method of transferring profits, while others contend that their payments are only sufficient to cover the actual cost to the American parent of passing on information to the Australian company. Several of the latter in particular declined to provide details of such payments because they did not regard them as 'service charges'. But if the higher return on direct investment than on fixed interest borrowing is to be explained in terms of the former's contribution of technical and managerial expertise, it seems reasonable to examine *total* payments for such know-how, and not just disclosed profits.

Of the seventy-two companies which did provide full information on profits, interest payments, and royalties and technical assistance fees paid to their U.S. shareholder,[5] nine declared no dividend and paid neither interest nor fee in 1962 (Table X-6). On the other

[3] The profits of neither of the two major American oil subsidiaries operating in Australia in 1962 are included in the figures given in this chapter. One of the two did provide profit figures but these have not been included because of the difficulty of interpreting such figures for an operation which includes very substantial marketing activities.

[4] The Commonwealth Statistician includes interest payments in his published figures for investment income payable. The U.S. Department of Commerce does not include interest in figures on 'earnings' but does include it in figures on 'income'. Neither includes royalties or other fees in their published figures for earnings, though the U.S. Department of Commerce does publish such figures separately for a small number of major areas of U.S. investment.

[5] Royalties and technical assistance fees paid to non-affiliated bodies by a small number of companies have been ignored.

TABLE X-6 Number of Companies Paying Dividends, Interest, or Fees to Their Parent Companies Among 72 American-affiliated Companies in 1961/2, by Percentage of American Ownership and Period in which Manufacture Began[a]

Percentage U.S. ownership and period in which Australian manufacture began[b]	Companies making no payment to their parent company	Companies making payment to their parent companies of							No. companies covered
		Dividend only[a]	Interest only	Fee only[a]	Dividend & interest	Dividend & fee	Interest & fee	Dividend, interest, & fee	
25–49%: Manufacture began—									
before 1957	..	1	..	1	1	3	..	1	7
in or after 1957	1	1	1	1	..	..	..	1	5
50–99%: Manufacture began—									
before 1957	..	1	..	..	..	8	1	..	10
in or after 1957	2	..	1	3	..	3	..	1	10
100%: Manufacture began—									
before 1957	3	1	..	5	..	6	4	5	24
in or after 1957	3	..	2	6	..	5	..	..	16
Total	9	4	4	16	1	25	5	8	72

[a] The term 'fee' is used to include any kind of technical assistance fee, contribution towards home office expenses, engineering fee, or royalty. The term 'dividend' is used to include the remittance of branch profits.

[b] See Note[a] to Table X-4.

hand, eight companies declared a dividend and made payment of both interest and at least one service charge in that year. By percentage of American ownership, no clear pattern emerges, except that a higher proportion of jointly-owned than of wholly American companies paid dividends in that year. Remarkably similar proportions of both types of affiliate paid fees of one kind or another, and, of the total, fifty-four (or 75 per cent) paid some kind of fee. Nor did a significant pattern emerge from a reclassification of the data in Table X-6 by industry, though it was interesting that eight of the nine companies in the industrial chemicals industry were paying a fee of some dimension, even though only three of the nine were operating at a profit in that year.

When the combined total of interest payments and fees which accrue to the U.S. shareholder (net of Australian taxation) is compared with the profits which accrue to him, it is still not easy to see any clear pattern, either by the percentage of American ownership or by the industry in which the Australian company operates. Table X-7 presents ratios of interest payments and fees on the one hand to profit accruing on the other for the fifty-seven companies in Table X-6 which were operating at a profit in 1962. But interpretation of the data is difficult, not least because the recession of 1961-2 caused a more abrupt contraction in the profits of some American subsidiaries in Australia than it did in the interest and fees they were required to remit abroad. One result of this is seen in the table where five companies, four of them wholly American, remitted more in interest and fees in 1962 than accrued to their parent companies in after-tax profit—but only one of the companies earned a profit of more than 3 per cent on its investment in that year. Similar influences affected other companies to a greater or less extent, and because of the doubtful meaning of these ratios no classification by industry is shown. Only two points may be made with safety. The first is that, in the case of thirty-four of the fifty-seven companies covered in the table, interest and fees accruing to parent companies amounted to less than one-third of the profit accruing to them. Secondly, a few companies appeared to be using such payments in an attempt to disguise an extremely profitable operation in Australia. One wholly American firm, for example, made a pre-tax profit of 32 per cent on sales in 1962, and paid royalties and management fees totalling a further 13 per cent. A second wholly American company made a pre-tax profit equal to 28 per cent on total sales, and paid a management fee of a further 9 per cent. (A jointly-owned company with pre-tax profits of 20 per cent on sales remitted 'engineering fees' of 8 per cent to its American parent, but the motive for this was probably less associated with public relations than with the

TABLE X–7 Ratio of Interest and Fees Payable to Parent Companies, after Australian Taxation, to U.S. Share in Net Profit in 57 American-affiliated Companies in 1961/2, by Percentage of American Ownership and Period in which Manufacture Began[a]

Percentage U.S. ownership and period in which Australian manufacture began[b]	Ratio of interest and fees payable to U.S. share in net profit (%)							Average ratio (%)	No. companies covered
	Nil	1–19	20–39	40–59	60–79	80–99	100 and over		
25–49%: Manufacture began—									
before 1957	1	3	2	..	..	..	1	31·4	7
in or after 1957	2	..	..	1	1	..	..	41·0	4
50–99%: Manufacture began—									
before 1957	1	4	2	2	..	..	..	6·8	9
in or after 1957	..	1	1	..	1	1	..	76·7	4
100%: Manufacture began—									
before 1957	2	8	4	2	2	..	3	28·0	21
in or after 1957	2	2	3	1	1	2	1	41·9	12
Total	8	18	12	6	5	3	5	25·3	57

[a] The 57 companies referred to in this table are all the companies operating at a profit in 1961/2 among the 72 companies covered in Table X–6. See Note [a] to Table X–6 for definition of 'fees'.

[b] See Note [a] to Table X–4.

desire of the American parent to receive a reward for the technical know-how made available to the Australian subsidiary.)

The most interesting feature of the aggregate figures on interest payments and fees supplied by the seventy-two companies under study is their total size, especially in relation to the total of dividends or profits remitted by the same companies. This is clearly brought out in Table X-8. Total remittances of interest and fees, after Australian tax, at £4·4 million, were only fractionally below total remittances of dividends and profits, after withholding tax, by the same group of companies. In the case of wholly American companies, remittances of interest and fees actually exceeded dividends and profits remitted. The same was true in several individual industries.[6] But it is not possible for such ratios of fees to dividends to hold true for foreign investment in Australia generally: while interest payments are already included in the Commonwealth Statistician's figures for investment income payable, and royalties are not out of proportion to the total paid by Australia, the ratio of technical assistance and other fees to dividends remitted (almost 70 per cent) indicates a level of fees, if it were applicable to all foreign investment, substantially larger than any relevant balance of payments debit.

The amount of Australian tax paid on interest payments, royalties, and fees of all kinds is also of special interest. When the survey questionnaires were sent to companies, the writer was not fully aware of the tax issues involved in this area, and it was only after discussions with a number of companies that some of the important points began to clarify. For this reason no mention was made of taxation in that part of the questionnaire dealing with service charges. Most companies were asked about this matter orally, but Australian tax payments by some companies (or their parents) had to be estimated from knowledge of the tax usually applied to particular kinds of remittances. The error involved does not appear to be large enough to invalidate the general impression conveyed by the tables.

Broadly, cash dividends due to foreign residents from companies incorporated in Australia are subject to Australian withholding tax, equal to not more than 15 per cent in the case of shareholders resident in countries with which Australia has a double-tax agreement (including the U.S. and the United Kingdom).[7] Remittances of branch profits are not subject to any such tax, however. Since it is the foreign shareholder who is liable to the withholding tax, he is able to claim a tax credit for this in the U.S.

---

[6] Those seeking a classification of the data in Table X-8 by industry should consult the thesis version of this study.

[7] Stock dividends, not being subject to American tax, are subject to a heavier Australian withholding tax.

TABLE X-8 Dividends, Interest, and Fees Payable to the Parent Companies of 72 American-affiliated Companies in 1961/2, by Percentage of American Ownership and Period in which Manufacture Began[a]

£A('000)

Percentage U.S. ownership and period in which Australian manufacture began[b]	U.S. share in net profit[c]	Dividends, interest, and fees accruing to the U.S.							Dividends, interest, and fees remitted to the U.S.[d]			
		Dividends gross[e]	Interest		Royalties		Other fees		Dividends		Total interest, royalties, and fees	
			gross	net[f]	gross	net[f]	gross	net[f]	gross	net[f]	gross	net[f]
25–49%: Manufacture began—												
before 1957	624	354	41	25	140	110	61	61	216	184	191	147
in or after 1957	5	4	6	4	4	3	13	13	3	3	23	19
50–99%: Manufacture began—												
before 1957	3,287	2,126	1	g	43	39	201	192	1,731	1,470	246	232
in or after 1957	(238)	63	26	15	32	29	173	171	44	38	211	203
100%: Manufacture began—												
before 1957	10,827	3,349	397	394	969	646	2,079	2,078	2,899	2,555	3,410	3,084
in or after 1957	(127)	328	5	3	82	73	756	611	328	279	843	687
Total[h]	14,377	6,224	477	441	1,269	900	3,283	3,126	5,222	4,528	4,924	4,372

a See Note a to Table X-6.

b See Note c to Table X-4.

c Parentheses denote a loss. Note that the losses of unprofitable companies have been offset against the after-tax profits of profitable ones.

d The difference between sums accruing and those remitted is, of course, the amount held in Australia, often on inter-company account with the affiliated company.

e No column shows dividends accruing to the U.S. net of Australian withholding tax because dividends held in Australia can sometimes avoid withholding tax by being paid to a holding company registered in Australia.

f Net of Australian taxation. See text for explanation.

g Less than £500.

h Detail may not add to totals because of rounding.

257

In the case of interest payments to overseas lenders, however, it is the *Australian* company which is liable to company tax, and this means that the American recipient of interest payments from an Australian source is not able to claim a tax credit for the amount of the Australian tax.[8] It is often better, indeed, for the parent of a wholly-owned subsidiary not to charge interest on advances to the Australian subsidiary at all, and to receive all return on its investment in the form of dividends. There are circumstances, however, in which the Australian company can avoid the payment of tax on interest paid to a foreign resident: this is the case if the local subsidiary can prove it is obliged to pay the full amount of the interest, without any deduction on account of taxation, to the overseas resident, perhaps because the loan to the Australian subsidiary was negotiated under the laws of another country. It is interesting that, so far as is known, only eleven of the eighteen companies in Table X-8 paying interest abroad were being taxed on these amounts, and all those not paying tax were wholly American in ownership. Because by far the greater part of total interest payments by the eighteen firms was on account of wholly American companies, the average rate of Australian tax on interest accruing to U.S. parent companies was very low.

Royalties are taxed in Australia in the hands of the recipient company, and, as in the case of dividends, that company can claim a tax credit in the U.S. for tax paid in Australia. In some cases, companies claim that a royalty (or part thereof) is payment for legitimate business expenses incurred in Australia, so that the average rate of tax shown in the tables falls short of company tax rates in 1961/2. Indeed, of twenty parent companies receiving royalties from Australia in that year, only seventeen are thought to have paid tax on them at all.

When attention is turned to other technical assistance fees, contributions to home office expenses or to parent company expenditure on research and development, the tax position is much more complex. Such payments are usually exempt from Australian tax on the grounds that they represent expenditure on the purchase of technical or other information, and not income from real property in Australia as in the case of royalties. But if the Taxation Commissioner can establish that such payments are in reality in lieu of royalties or in some other way attempts to avoid Australian taxation (and some executives frankly admitted that this is their primary function), they may be subject, at least in part, to Australian com-

[8] For information on the Australian tax position with regard to interest and royalties paid to overseas residents, see Sections 125, 255, and 256 of the Income Tax and Social Services Contribution Assessment Act 1936-1962.

pany tax. Certainly some parent companies are subject to Australian tax on such payments, but it seems that by and large they are tax exempt. Several companies mentioned that the tax position with regard to these payments had recently undergone change (in the direction of an increased Australian tax liability) and this may reflect an increased effort on the part of the Taxation Commissioner to levy these amounts. It appears that, unless the payments can escape American taxation by means of a tax-haven country, such increased Australian tax has no detrimental effect on the return received by American companies on their investment in Australia, though the return to the American economy as a whole is clearly reduced.

But of course interest payments, royalties, and fees, though a debit on Australia's balance of payments, cannot simply be added to after-tax profit accruing to American shareholders to gain an idea of the 'true' profitability of their investment; for even if not subject to Australian tax, such payments *are* subject to American tax, unless channelled to a tax-haven country. Moreover, although the *marginal* cost of extending technical information or licensing a trademark to an Australian company may be very low or negligible in many cases, in others the fee charged to the Australian company is specifically designed to cover only the marginal cost involved. Thus it is impossible to get an absolutely accurate idea of the 'true' profitability of American direct investments in Australia. The estimates shown in Tables X-9 and X-10 are, therefore, only approximations. They refer to the seventy-two companies shown in Table X-8 and were calculated by assuming the 'true net profit' of the Australian operation (so far as the American shareholder is concerned) to be the U.S. share of the actual net profit, plus 50 per cent of interest payments net of Australian tax (where applicable), plus 50 per cent of royalties and other fees gross of Australian tax.[9] It is further assumed, as a very rough approximation, that there is no marginal cost to the American company of transmitting information to the Australian company, or licensing it to produce an American product. As before, the value of American investment is taken to be the American share in shareholders' funds, plus advances by the American company on intercompany account.

[9] To the extent that part of the actual net profit is earned by branch operations in Australia (and so is subject to an additional American tax), and another part is paid out in dividends (and so incurs Australian withholding tax), this procedure overstates the 'return' to the American shareholder. On the other hand, to the extent that interest, royalties, and other fees can avoid the payment of American tax (assumed for these purposes to be 50 per cent), there is some understatement of the 'return' on the Australian investment.

TABLE X-9 Ratio of Net Profit, Interest, and Fees to Total American Investment in 72 American-affiliated Companies in 1961/2, by Percentage of American Ownership and Period in which Manufacture Began[a]

Percentage U.S. ownership and period in which Australian manufacture began[b]	Com-panies incurring a loss[c]	Ratio of U.S. share in net profit, interest, and fees to total American investment (%)[a]							No. com-panies covered	Average ratio, profitable companies[d] (%)	Average ratio, all companies[d][e] (%)
		0– 4.9	5.0– 9.9	10.0– 14.9	15.0– 19.9	20.0– 24.9	25.0– 29.9	30.0 and over			
25–49%: Manufacture began—											
before 1957	..	1	3	2	1	..	..	..	7	9.9 (8.4)	9.9 (8.4)
in or after 1957	1	..	2	1	1	..	..	..	5	13.4 (10.9)	1.5 (0.5)
50–99%: Manufacture began—											
before 1957	..	3	1	2	3	1	..	..	10	9.6 (9.3)	9.6 (9.3)
in or after 1957	6	..	1	1	..	1	1	..	10	22.3 (16.0)	–3.2 (–5.9)
100%: Manufacture began—											
before 1957	3	2	7	5	2	..	2	3	24	11.7 (10.2)	11.4 (9.9)
in or after 1957	4	3	4	1	..	..	1	3	16	12.7 (10.1)	1.2 (–0.5)
Total	14	9	18	12	7	2	4	6	72	11.3 (10.0)	9.2 (7.9)

[a] These ratios compare the U.S. share in net profit, plus 50 per cent of interest payments net of Australian tax, plus 50 per cent of royalties and fees gross of Australian tax on the one hand, with total American investment on the other. See text for explanation.

[b] See Note a to Table X–4.

[c] The term 'loss' is used here to indicate a negative return on investment, after taking into account receipts of interest, royalties, and other fees.

[d] Figures in parentheses show the ratio of the U.S. share in net profit to total American investment, and are parallel to figures shown in Table X–4. They permit an assessment of the importance of receipts of interest, royalties, and other fees after all taxes.

[e] A loss is denoted by a minus sign.

TABLE X-10   Ratio of Net Profit, Interest, and Fees to Total American Investment in 72 American-affiliated Companies in 1961/2, by Industry[a]

Industry	Companies incurring a loss[b]	Ratio of U.S. share in net profit, interest, and fees to total American investment (%)[a]							No. companies covered	Average ratio, profitable companies[c] (%)	Average ratio, all companies[c][d] (%)
		0–4.9	5.0–9.9	10.0–14.9	15.0–19.9	20.0–24.9	25.0–29.9	30.0 and over			
Plant, equipment, machinery	2	1	5	4	1	..	1	..	14	9·8 (7·7)	9·4 (7·4)
Motor vehicles	1	..	2	1	..	..	..	..	4	10·6 (9·4)	10·5 (9·3)
Metal manufactures, n.e.i.	1	..	1	3	..	..	..	..	5	8·6 (8·5)	8·0 (7·9)
Electrical equipment, instruments, etc.	..	5	2	3	2	..	..	1	13	14·4 (11·4)	14·4 (11·4)
Food and drink	1	2	..	..	..	..	1	1	5	12·4 (10·9)	11·6 (10·1)
Industrial chemicals and plastics	6	1	1	..	..	..	..	1	9	9·4 (7·4)	—1·0 (—2·5)
Pharmaceutical and toilet preparations	1	..	2	..	1	..	2	2	8	22·6 (20·1)	20·7 (18·3)
Other industries	2	..	5	1	3	2	..	1	14	10·6 (9·9)	9·6 (8·8)
Total	14	9	18	12	7	2	4	6	72	11·3 (10·0)	9·2 (7·9)

a See Note a to Table X–9.
b See Note b to Table X–9.
c See Note d to Table X–9.
d See Note e to Table X–9.

Though the inclusion of interest and fees in the calculus makes an appreciable difference to the recorded profitability of particular industries and companies of particular ownership, it is clear from both tables that the overall difference made by the inclusion of such payments is relatively small. For all the seventy-two companies covered, the difference is only that between 7·9 and 9·2 per cent, or about 16 per cent, and this, as noted above, is based on the assumption that there is no marginal cost to the American company of transmitting technical information to the Australian affiliate.

The time taken by American-affiliated companies in Australia to reach profitable operation varies enormously from company to company. As shown in both Table X-4 and Table X-9, companies established before 1957 were, in each category of ownership, more profitable than those established subsequently. (That this was not true in general when attention is confined to the average earning rates for profitable companies is due partly to the establishment of a small number of particularly profitable companies in recent years and also to the fact that, as explained in notes to the tables, some companies which are taken to have begun manufacture 'in or after 1957' actually began operations before 1957.) In part the period of time taken to reach a 'reasonable' level of profitability depends on the industry in question: pharmaceutical companies which confine their Australian operations to forming fully-imported ingredients into capsules, for example, frequently can merely appropriate a part of the parent company's profit, and so may be in a position to make substantial profits from the moment local operations begin. On the other hand, chemical companies which must expand local demand for their product before economic production is possible must often operate on (or below) the margin of profitability for a number of years. The marketing policy adopted is also relevant: some companies with very profitable manufacturing operations incur losses only because of heavy advertising expenditure designed to expand their market share or even, as in one case encountered, to sell products imported from the parent company.

Many companies in the present survey provided information on taxable income for years before 1961/2—a considerable number provided such information for every year between 1950/1 and 1961/2. In the absence of balance sheet (or other) data for most years prior to 1961/2, and because of the great difficulty involved in adding profit data over a period of years for companies which began manufacture at widely different times, these data have not been put to any detailed use. A profit series could in any case only have been an incomplete version of statistics published by the Commonwealth Statistician. The figures gathered do serve to illustrate the divergent experiences of American-affiliated companies in Australia, however: at the one extreme was a company which made a pre-tax profit of little more than £20,000 in 1950/1 but of substantially more than £1 million in 1961/2; at the other was the company which incurred losses in every year for eight years after its establishment in Australia. They also show that, though the profitability of many of the companies which provided data for 1962 was affected by the recession in the Australian economy in that year, the absolute profit of almost two-thirds of those which provided data for both 1961 and 1962 was higher in the latter year than in the former, and in many cases absolute profit was higher in 1962 than in any previous year in the company's history.

Have the results of American-affiliated companies in Australia lived up to the expectations of their parent companies? Twenty-four firms which began local operations before 1957 were questioned on this point, and all but one felt that Australian results had been fully up to expectations. Ten of these felt that results had exceeded expectations. An attempt was made to compare the profitability of subsidiaries in Australia with that of their parent companies in the U.S. by seeking information on relative profit margins on sales in the two countries. Some individually interesting examples were obtained in this way but it proved impossible to gauge relative profitability on investment, even when subsidiary and parent operated in a substantially similar manner. The difficulty is exemplified by the comments of two chemical companies on the question: one felt that profit margin on sales is higher in Australia than in the U.S., but that this does not result in a higher rate of profit on investment in Australia because the small size of Australian operations leads to disproportionately heavy investment per unit of output. The other company felt that profit margin on sales is lower in Australia than in the U.S., but that because of the cheapness of capital equipment in Australia the rate of profit on investment is higher in Australia.

As an alternative method of comparing the profitability of American-affiliated companies in Australia with that of their parent companies, the ratios shown in Table X-9 for companies which began operation here before 1957 were compared with figures published in *Fortune* (July 1963) for return on the shareholders' funds of parent companies. Such a comparison can only give rise to very approximate results, since some U.S. companies consolidate their overseas subsidiaries with their own figures.[10] In all, thirty-three

[10] Indeed, in some cases American companies include the value of their investment in foreign subsidiaries in their books but do not include earnings on this investment except to the extent of actual receipt of dividends. This clearly results in understatement of the profitability of the American companies.

comparisons were possible. In eighteen of these the profitability of the Australian company exceeded that of the U.S. parent, and in fifteen it fell short of the American figure. Though profit ratios of the Australian companies covered a much greater range than did those of their American parents, the median of both sets of ratios was identical, $10·7$ per cent. It is possible that the Australian ratios were affected significantly by the recession of 1961-2, and of course even if the average return on investment in Australia was below that in the U.S. it is not possible to conclude that the Australian investment is below expectations, or was not warranted, since the comparison must be between the return on a company's marginal investment in the U.S. and the return on its investment in Australia. But the impression is not without interest.

Twenty-seven companies which began operations in 1957 or subsequently were also asked how their results to date compared with expectations. Three felt that it was still too early to judge, seven that expectations had been exceeded, and ten that they had been met. Seven were disappointed. There were various reasons for this disappointment, though probably the most frequently mentioned factor was the 1961-2 recession, which caught some companies in their establishment period. The removal of import quotas early in 1960 also damaged the prospects of several companies, especially in the petrochemical industry. A surprising number of companies—at least five—explicitly criticized the market survey which Americans from the parent company had made before establishment here. One described the pre-establishment market survey as 'far too optimistic', and another criticized the 'complete misconception on the part of the American company of the saleability' of its products. The chief executive of a third company stated that he had recently been talking to the managing director of the largest firm in their industry 'and we agreed that both our firms could fold up completely and the industry would hardly notice the difference'. An executive from this company's American parent had described Australia as a 'goddam market', and neither man felt there had been an adequate market survey conducted before the original investment. Much criticism has been levelled against some members of the Altona petrochemical complex for misjudging the growth in the Australian market for their products: an American in a related industry expressed the view that one part of the complex had been set up 'almost intuitively', with a justification for the investment decision being worked out after the decision had been taken. Over-estimation of the Australian market certainly appears to be a mistake to which some Americans are particularly prone, and though it is the American shareholders who often have to pay the heaviest penalty for this, there may also be a cost to Australia if such error leads to premature investment, consequent pressure for increased tariff protection, and misallocation of complementary Australian resources.

Many American companies have withdrawn from operations in Australia. It was noted in chapter II that twenty-six American-affiliated companies which had either severed their American connections or been liquidated before 1962 were encountered during the course of the survey. There must undoubtedly have been others which escaped notice. Some of the better known ones are mentioned in Appendix A but there were others, such as Westclox (Aust.) Pty Ltd, makers of spring alarm clocks; Reichhold Chemical Inc. (Aust.) Pty Ltd, chemical manufacturers; the Bon Ami Co. of Australia Pty Ltd, manufacturers of household cleansers; and Murfett Publishers Pty Ltd, engaged in the printing of greeting cards. Among the smaller firms were the A. C. Horn Co. of Australia Pty Ltd (building materials),[11] Harris Calorific (Aust.) Pty Ltd (gas welding equipment), Australian Packers Corporation Pty Ltd (food processing), Muralo Co. (Aust.) Pty Ltd (water paints), Wah Chang (Aust.) Pty Ltd (mainly chemical manufacture), Greenwich Pty Ltd (lead pencils), Australian Plexon Pty Ltd (plastic coating of fibre), Carpco Australasia Pty Ltd (mining equipment for the rutile industry), and Yorkaire Pty Ltd (air-conditioning equipment).

Not all the American companies which sold interests in Australia before 1962 did so because of the poor performance of the Australian company. No reason for the sale of the American interest is known in seven of the twenty-six cases examined. In four cases it is known that the primary motive for selling the Australian interest was the urgent need of the parent company for funds in the U.S., a need which bore little relationship to the profitability of the Australian company.[12] In another case, an American company sold a minority interest at a very good price to the majority shareholder simply because of the latter's desire for complete ownership. General Electric sold out of an Australian partnership in 1955 primarily because of American antitrust considerations. The 40 per cent interest of another American company was sold to permit the owner of the American holding company to consolidate his estate. In still another

[11] A. C. Horn Co. of Australia Pty Ltd appears to have been established in 1959 as a joint venture between an American company and New Zealand interests. The American interest was sold in 1961 and the company became wholly New Zealand-owned. It was acquired by other American interests in 1964 when the wholly American holding company, W. R. Grace Australia Pty Ltd, purchased all the shares in the company.

[12] In one case, for example, the American parent was compelled to sell its only two overseas subsidiaries because a senior executive of the parent company embezzled substantial funds in the U.S.

case an American holding company sold its interests in a particular industry in the U.S. and so had to dispose of parallel interests in Australia. But in eight cases repeated losses or very low profits were the primary reason for sale, and in three other cases a deterioration in growth prospects caused the sale. In some of these cases, companies were unable to meet import competition. One company was unable to secure sufficient import licences; the principal market of another collapsed unexpectedly. The reasons for sale were, in short, almost infinitely varied.

The American-affiliated companies operating in Australia in 1962 were not without their difficulties. Of thirty-six questioned on the adequacy of their protection against imports, fourteen firms (six of them in the chemical industry) felt increased tariff protection would be very desirable. Several companies complained of the small size of the Australian market and two objected to the methods used by government departments in letting contracts, but with only one exception—a company which felt its American parent was worried by the political unrest to the north of Australia—none of the complaints made by American-affiliated companies were peculiar to American companies. The great majority of American affiliates interviewed felt their future prospects in Australia to be good or, in many cases, excellent.

In conclusion, it appears that even were reliable statistics on the profitability of American-affiliated companies in Australia available, sweeping generalizations would be out of place. It is clear that American direct investment in Australian manufacturing has, on average, been considerably more profitable than Australian or British investment in that sector, but for most companies the rate of return has certainly not been as high as is frequently implied in popular discussion.

XI

Conclusions

Many of the most important questions concerning foreign investment have not yet been answered. This is because, as so often in economics, they cannot be finally answered from empirical observation alone. Chapter VIII looked in an *ad hoc* way at some of the more readily discernible effects of U.S. investment on the incomes of Australians, but no explicit answer has yet been attempted to the question: what is the overall effect of foreign investment on Australian incomes? Chapter IX examined the imports and exports, and chapter X the profitability, of American-affiliated firms, but again no explicit answer has been given to the question: what is the total effect of foreign investment on Australia's balance of payments? Though a highly theoretical analysis of these questions would be out of place in a study of this kind, some discussion of foreign investment in its broader aspects is essential.[1]

In looking at the effects of foreign investment on domestic incomes, it is important to recognize at the outset that foreign investment would be of no benefit to Australia if it operated in an 'enclave', unconnected with the economy in any way. The mere operation of foreign-owned capacity within the geographical borders of the country would not of itself confer economic benefit. While it is impossible to imagine a foreign investment of this type occurring in Australia[2]—an investment which employed no Australian labour, purchased no Australian goods and services, paid no Australian taxation, and sold all its produce abroad—a recognition of this hypo-

[1] No reader familiar with the literature on international capital movements will fail to detect the debt this chapter owes to the work of many earlier writers, perhaps most especially G. D. A. MacDougall (1960), and T. Balogh and P. P. Streeten (1960).

[2] Foreign investments which approximate to this type have occurred in some underdeveloped countries, however; see Singer (1950).

267

thetical limiting case serves to direct attention to ways in which foreign investment actually *does* confer benefit. It is only through the 'links' which the foreign investment has with the domestic economy that it can assist that economy.

The potential variety of these links can be clearly seen if we imagine that a foreign corporation establishes a new factory in, say, the car industry of the capital-importing country. (Assume that this industry is completely protected from import competition by a tariff.) Even if the technology of the new foreign firm is identical with that of the previously-operating firms and there is no taxation on its profits, the borrowing country is affected in a number of ways. Perhaps the most immediately obvious effect arises from the increased demand for labour, not only to staff the new car factory but also to expand output in all those industries affected by the expansion of the car industry. This increased demand for labour generates higher wages and/or higher levels of employment. Alternatively, where the capital-importing country has a vigorous immigration policy, the foreign investment may permit the absorption of this labour inflow without a fall in domestic wages.

By making the car industry more competitive, the foreign investment is also likely to result in relatively lower car prices and in the production of better cars. This confers immediate benefit on all new car buyers.

The effect of the foreign investment on the profits of previously-operating companies depends on a number of conflicting forces. All companies are likely to find they have to pay higher wages as the car industry's increased demand for labour gradually makes itself felt throughout the economy, while companies producing cars and other directly competitive forms of transport experience further pressure as a result of the reduction in car prices. If these were the only influences exerted on the profits of other companies by the foreign investment, the overall gain to domestic real incomes would, under present assumptions, vary directly with the extent of the foreign ownership of previously-operating companies. This is so because the reduction in company profits almost exactly measures the gain to domestic labour and domestic consumers: only to the extent that the redistribution of income implicit in the new investment results in a reduction in the income accruing to previously-operating *foreign-owned* companies does the income of *domestic* residents benefit.

This last is no mere academic point, as consideration of foreign investment in the Australian car industry indicates: additional foreign investment in that industry results in a substantial redistribution of income from other foreign firms in the industry to Australian residents. But apart altogether from this gain there is another, for the effect of a new foreign investment on profits is by no means entirely negative. Some companies may become *more* profitable as a result of the foreign investment, despite their need to pay higher wages. These are the companies producing goods and services used by the car industry or goods used jointly with cars, such as petrol. The profits of these companies benefit because the increased demand for their products permits them to reduce unit costs by utilizing capacity more fully and securing economies of scale generally.

If the capital-importing country levies a tax on company profits—and of course Australia and most other countries do—there is a further very important gain to domestic incomes, through the tax raised by levying the profits earned by foreign-owned companies. Though there is no need to elaborate this point, it is regarded by many writers as one of the most important benefits to the recipient economy from foreign investment.

The capital-importing country may benefit in yet another way if the foreign investment results in some improvement in the country's terms of trade. We have assumed that the foreign investment takes place in a sector already protected from imports by a tariff, so that investment does not, in this case, lead to any direct reduction in the demand for imports. Even had the industry not been protected from imports, the reduction in the capital-importing country's demand for imports as a result of the foreign investment would not be likely in practice to result in any appreciable reduction in import prices.[3] But in both these cases the export prices of the capital-importing country would benefit from the relative decrease in the supply of its exports which would, in principle, follow the movement of labour into the car industry, though it must be admitted that even this beneficial effect on the terms of trade may not be large in reality.[4]

[3] No special consideration is given here to the other effects of foreign investment on domestic incomes when the industry receiving foreign capital is not protected from imports. It is clear, however, that such investment would lead to a smaller reduction in the prices charged to domestic consumers (because until all imports are displaced the import price will govern the sale price of competitive domestically-manufactured products), but on the other hand to smaller loss to domestic companies in competition with the new investment (because a reduction in imports absorbs at least part of the impact of the increased local production).

[4] If foreign investment occurs in the export sector, however, its adverse effect on the barter terms of trade of the host economy may be relatively large. There is nothing logically inconsistent about this apparently perverse result: it is quite possible in theory, and often occurs in practice, that the host economy is a relatively large part of world supply for the goods it exports but a relatively small part of world demand for the goods it imports. There is, however, some

(Continued on next page)

Up to this point three important assumptions have been made. One of these was that the foreign corporation establishes a new factory in the car industry of the capital-importing country. Capital inflow may, of course, take the form not of the setting up of new companies but of the take-over of existing ones: this is a form of foreign investment with which Australians have in fact become very familiar. But no fundamental change in the analysis is needed. Some of the foreign capital spent on buying out the domestic shareholders may leak into consumption expenditure, but the bulk of it seems likely to lead either fairly directly to other real investment (in the case, say, of a corporate shareholder with interests in several industries) or indirectly to the same end through the financial system (in the case of private shareholders). The final result is that capacity is increased not in the car industry but in other industries, and it is from these that many of the effects of 'foreign investment'—higher wages, lower prices, etc.—emanate.

The second assumption made was that the foreign-owned car company uses the same technology as that used by domestic companies. In practice this is unlikely. If the foreign company employs a technology which permits it to produce a given output of cars at a lower cost in total factor inputs than can previously-operating companies, several changes must be made in the original analysis. The profits of competing companies are likely to suffer more severely and, if the more advanced technology permits a reduction in the use of labour per unit produced, the rise in labour incomes may be smaller than under the previous assumption. But this relative loss (which will, as noted, be borne in part by other foreign-owned companies if these are present) is offset by a greater reduction in the price of cars and/or by a rise in the revenue raised by taxing the profits of the foreign-owned company. Companies supplying materials for the car industry and those supplying products used jointly with cars are both likely to benefit as the increased reduction in price of cars (and so the increased use of cars) further stimulates demand for their output. Of far greater importance than these influences, however, may be the effect of the new technology on the methods used by domestic companies. The extent to which other companies benefit

---

automatic limit imposed on the adverse effects that might result from an excess of foreign investment in the export sector: any decline in export prices as a result of foreign investment in the export sector would itself bring about a reduction in the flow of foreign investment into that sector, thus limiting the deterioration in the terms of trade. (The danger is one of reaction lags.) Moreover, if a deterioration in the terms of trade were due to such an export bias in production by foreign capital, 'it is possible that the factoral and the income terms of trade might still improve even though the commodity terms worsen' (Meier 1963: 99).

from the improved technology of the foreign firm depends in part, of course, on just how much more advanced the new technology is than that already in use. A number of other factors are also relevant, however, such as the attitude of the company employing the new technology to the dissemination of its techniques, the proportion of the company's materials which are purchased from domestic sources (this is likely to influence the amount of technical information passed to supplying companies), and the extent to which the new technology is peculiar to the production of a particular type of output. From this last point it would appear that other companies gain the greatest benefit from the introduction of improved management skills by the foreign-owned car firm and the least benefit from an improvement in a manufacturing process peculiar to the production of cars. Indeed, this is true not only because of the greater applicability of management skills beyond the car industry but also because of the greater difficulty in maintaining secrecy around management skills because of personnel movement between firms, etc. But whatever the type of technology introduced, it seems likely that in the situation described the capital-importing country benefits by more than in the 'constant technology' case considered initially.

It is possible, of course, especially if foreign-owned companies uncritically imitate the technology of their parents, that the techniques introduced by the foreign firm will be less suitable than the ones already in use in the capital-importing country. It may be, for example, that capital-intensive production methods are introduced into the capital-importing country and that these are inappropriate both to its relative factor endowment and to its absolute size. In this case the gain to the capital-importing country may be *less* than under the 'constant technology' assumption, especially because of the likelihood that the foreign-owned company will operate much less profitably than it would if its technology were more appropriate, and domestic taxation revenue will suffer (relatively to the original situation examined) as a result. But even in this situation there is no actual loss to the capital-importing country, as compared with the situation without capital inflow.

The third assumption made (implicitly) was that the level of tariff protection is a datum. It is obvious that a protective tariff involves the payment of a subsidy by the economy as a whole to the producers in the industry protected. The most usual justification of this in economic theory is that the growth and development of the pro- tected industry will eventually compensate the society, through external economies of one kind or another, for its present sacrifice— and compensate it more highly than if it gave a special subsidy to some other industry (the 'infant industry' argument). If a tariff *can* be justified on these grounds, there is a gain to the economy no matter what the ownership of the companies which invest in the protected industry, for by definition the protected industry eventually repays society as a whole for its initial subsidy. On the other hand, if a tariff can *not* be justified on these grounds, there is economic loss to the society as a whole and the loss is the greater if the subsidy is initially paid not to local shareholders but to foreign shareholders.

There are several features of the Australian tariff system which are particularly unfortunate in this regard. The most important is the basis on which tariff protection is given. Though it is not by any means easy to isolate the principles applied by the Australian Tariff Board, it appears that an industry can usually be fairly confident of winning protection for itself if it is operating at the time it makes an appeal, can prove its *technical* efficiency, and is at a cost disadvantage *vis-à-vis* overseas producers. It should be clear that there is no necessary relationship between these criteria and the infant industry approach outlined above. Another undesirable feature of the Australian system is the considerable number of goods which, though allowed into the country free of duty under 'by-law' in the absence or inadequacy of domestic production, are nominally dutiable at protective rates of duty. Many of these products are in the 'not elsewhere included' classifications, catch-all categories designed to include a wide assortment of otherwise undefined goods. It is hard to avoid the impression that some of the products in these categories are granted nominal protection without any careful analysis of the desirability of such protection. Though the tariff may remain a dead letter for years, it remains ready to protect the first company to commence the local production of the goods in question.

Because it is well known then that any company commencing manufacture in Australia can be fairly sure either of winning tariff protection or of being able to make use of an already-existing tariff, there is a constant fear on the part of those serving the Australian market by imports that some company will commence local production and effectively exclude imports forthwith. This fear is heightened if the Australian market is small in relation to the optimum plant size, and the chances of becoming the *second* firm to commence local manufacture are correspondingly reduced. This is a highly unstable situation which, in theory, might provoke a move towards local manufacture either by an Australian firm or by a foreign manufacturer serving the Australian market by exporting. But in practice it is the foreign manufacturer who is most likely to make the move: by definition, he has the know-how needed to make the product; he is also more likely to be in a position to sustain the temporary losses which may have to be borne before adequate tariff protection can be won. If local production should not be subsidized on economic grounds, such a move involves economic loss to society as a whole. This loss is enhanced if the tariff protection obtained is tailored in such a way that it protects the foreign company from paying the penalty it should incur for adopting production methods unsuited to the Australian market or for building plant capacity in excess of market demand.

It should be stressed that these comments are a criticism of *Australian tariff policy*, not of foreign investment *per se*. The foreign companies are merely responding rationally to an environment of Australia's making. But in any assessment of the gains and losses accruing to the capital-importing country, the subsidies paid to foreign-owned companies must be subtracted from the benefits which the operation of the latter confers. It is probable that applying such arithmetic to some of the highly protected foreign investments in Australia (one thinks in particular of petrochemicals among American investments and textiles among British) would produce a negative answer.

Of course *all* the subsidies paid by the capital-importing country must be included in the calculation. In the Australian context it would be unfair to single out tariffs. State government competition to attract industry often results in the payment of a substantial subsidy to foreign-affiliated firms (for example through agreements to enter into preferential purchasing arrangements), while if public services used by foreign-owned companies are provided at less than cost this is another subsidy which must be taken into account.

But even after allowing for all these offsetting costs, it seems likely that in most circumstances foreign investment results in a rise in domestic real incomes. It may do this through a redistribution of income away from other foreign-owned companies in the economy, through the provision of external economies to other producers through its purchases in the market place, through its effect on increasing taxation revenue, through the spread of its more advanced technology to domestic producers, or through its effect on the terms of trade of the capital-importing country. To some extent these are the benefits of *any* increase in capital stock, whether financed domestically or from abroad. In other words, Australia (or any other capital-importing country) could secure many of these benefits for itself in the future if it were prepared to save more now—the benefit of foreign investment can thus be measured by the savings the economy does *not* have to make to reach a given standard of living in the future. It should be recognized, however, that the savings

T

which would have to be made if foreign investment were to be foresworn would *exceed* the apparent capital inflow in the event of continued dependence on foreign capital. As discussed in chapter III, it is not usually the greater volume of funds available to the foreign company which prompts it to invest abroad but its advantage over the companies in other countries in terms of know-how, reputation, or familiarity with international markets. While the *transfer* of these advantages to another country may involve a very low marginal cost for a company already possessing them in its home country, the *acquisition* of such advantages may involve a very substantial cost to the 'capital-importing country' which decides to curb foreign investment. This cost could well impose such severe restraints on present standards of living that other policy goals—such as the immigration programme in Australia—would become unattainable.

It is in the context of these general theoretical considerations that the full significance of many of the observations made in the empirical chapters can be seen. This is true in particular of the discussion of the impact of American investment on domestic prices, on the after-sales service and technical advice available to consumers, on labour incomes, and on the spread of more efficient techniques to Australian-owned companies. The analysis also suggests that several aspects of the debate on foreign investment in this country are substantially irrelevant. One of these aspects is the question of whether foreign-affiliated firms should be encouraged to sell part of their equity to Australians. To the extent that Australian share participation would be an alternative to increased investment of *foreign* funds, it should be obvious that such participation would positively reduce the benefit to Australia. Even where Australian equity participation did not replace foreign investment, it could hinder the flow of technical know-how and harm Australian tax revenue by encouraging the foreign affiliate to pay its parent for such information (see also chapter IV).[5] The profits earned by foreign subsidiaries are also seen to be relevant only to the extent that the incomes of Australians are adversely affected as compared with their level *in the absence of foreign investment*. Indeed, provided no harm is done directly to the incomes of Australians, the higher the profits of foreign-owned companies the better—because of the substantial equity in these profits enjoyed by the Australian Taxation Commissioner.

At the same time, it is plain that Australia can *increase* the net

---

[5] It is possible that in some underdeveloped countries there could be economic gain to the host country in urging foreign companies to share their equity with local investors. This might be the case if joint ventures with foreign firms are one of the very few ways of training domestic 'entrepreneurs'.

benefit it receives from foreign investment, and ways in which this might be done have been suggested by inference at various points. One such might be enactment of legislation similar to that in force in the U.S. to deal with restrictive trade practices and monopolies, for if a foreign company (or a domestic company, for that matter) is able to secure a monopolistic position in a previously competitive industry and raise prices to the 'import-parity' level there may well be a net loss to the capital-importing country from its operation. Another way might be a more rigorous approach by the Taxation Commissioner to tax avoidance, both through the pricing of imports and exports and through the payment of arbitrary 'service charges' and 'engineering fees'. And if the employment of non-Australians in foreign subsidiaries ever reached the stage where the failure to employ Australians involved a greater cost than would be incurred if the non-Australians were *not* employed (and this situation has clearly not been reached in most American-affiliated companies in Australia) the tax concessions now enjoyed by such foreign personnel could be withdrawn. Imperfections in the Australian capital market may make it possible for the subsidiaries of internationally-known corporations to assume control over large blocks of fixed interest funds from the Australian market when domestically-owned companies are short of funds, and this situation also may require positive policy measures. Probably more important than any of these measures in the Australian environment is a careful examination of the costs of present tariff policy, especially as it bears on foreign investment. There can also be little justification for the continued subsidization of foreign-affiliated companies implicit in state government competition for industry: it was seen in chapter III that state government inducements to foreign companies are almost never significant in increasing the total flow of foreign investment to Australia, and are probably only significant in a minority of cases in the location of a foreign-sponsored investment.

The fundamental problem is to ensure that foreign investment—indeed, *all* investment—occurs in sectors where its value to the economy as a whole (or social productivity) is at an optimum. This is never easy. To begin with there is the familiar divergence between social and private marginal productivity. The foreign investor is not primarily interested in the extent to which his investment increases the returns to other factors in the host economy, nor does he often take into account the possibility of his investment altering the terms of trade of the capital-importing country. This suggests the need for some kind of government interference in the market mechanism. But there are two important difficulties in the way of this, at least one of which seems insurmountable.

The first and perhaps more intractable is this: even if private marginal productivity could be made to reflect social marginal productivity there is good reason to doubt that foreign capital would react in the socially desirable manner. For foreign capital of the direct investment variety tends to move from a particular sector in the capital-exporting country to the *corresponding* sector in the capital-importing, induced by a profitable investment opportunity *in that sector*.[6] The fact that there might appear to be a higher profit to be made in some other sector of the capital-importing country, or for that matter in some other sector of the capital-exporting country, tends to be quite irrelevant to the investment decision. This tendency for foreign capital to be 'sector-specific' implies that for an American, say, soft-drink company, the choice is between investing in the Australian soft-drink industry or not investing in Australia at all. The fact that Australian authorities might prefer it to invest in oil exploration or chemicals production is likely to be entirely irrelevant to its decision. Australia can reduce the extent to which its *own* resources are 'misallocated' by denying the soft-drink subsidiary access to the Australian capital market, but it would appear difficult if not impossible to re-allocate the foreign investment itself.

The second problem is that it is not easy to decide what the socially optimal allocation of investment is. Even investment in soft-drink production (used here because the industry is so often held up as an example of the kind of foreign investment Australia does *not* want) may reduce prices below their level in the absence of foreign investment, increase wages, and benefit tax revenue. Moreover, if the foreign investment is through the acquisition of a domestic company, domestic capital is released for use in other sectors. (Indeed, far from discouraging foreign take-overs in industries where capacity is already in over-abundance, there appears to be much to be said for *encouraging* them, inasmuch as they free domestic resources for investment in sectors where social marginal productivity may be higher. This may be one way to combat the 'sector-specific' problem.) It may be simpler to decide where investment is *not* required (for example in industries likely to be heavily dependent on tariff protection for an indefinite period) than to encourage

[6] Various writers (e.g. Penrose 1956, Behrman 1962c: 151, Guth 1963: 34) have commented on this. The explanation for this behaviour, of course, lies in the fact noted in chapter III that manufacturing companies usually invest abroad not primarily to exploit a profitable opportunity for the investment of capital as such but to exploit some advantage of know-how or reputation peculiar to a *particular* industry which trade barriers prevent their exploiting in the normal way.

it to sectors where it *is* required. But while it may not be easy to implement a policy of the type suggested in practice, the nature of the problem is clear.[7]

Until now, the discussion has skirted explicit mention of the impact of foreign investment on the balance of payments of the recipient country. This is a complex subject, and one around which a whole literature has grown up. For the purpose of this study two questions are relevant, the first being 'What effect does foreign investment have on the balance of payments during the period in which it is actually being received?' and the second 'What effect does the *operation* of the new productive capacity have on the balance of payments after the transitional reactions associated with the receipt of the foreign investment have worked themselves out?' In practice, of course, these effects are impossible to distinguish, but analytically it is desirable to treat them separately.

The reaction of most Australians to the two questions would be that, while the receipt of foreign capital might help the balance of payments in the short run by providing funds for necessary imports, there is a real danger that the profits from the operation of foreign-affiliated firms will eventually pose a serious problem for the balance of payments. This long-term problem is exacerbated, moreover, by the restrictions on export freedom under which, it is widely believed, most foreign-affiliated firms labour. It is the purpose of the following discussion to suggest that this approach is misleading.

For convenience we shall begin with the second question: what effect does the *operation* of the new productive capacity have on the

[7] No mention has been made in the text of the 'infant firm' argument for protecting locally-owned companies against competition from the subsidiaries of foreign companies. This argument, claimed to be parallel to the 'infant industry' argument in tariff theory by its supporters, suggests that given time and special assistance domestically-owned companies could grow to play the role which will otherwise be played by foreign-owned companies. But in fact the 'infant firm' argument and the 'infant industry' argument are not parallel. The 'infant industry' argument justifies tariff protection for an industry on the grounds that the industry will eventually be able to reward society for initial support more richly than if support were given to some other industry. It is by no means immediately apparent that the future economic advantages to society of having its main industries locally controlled—in a situation where the society retains sovereign rights to control monopolies, levy taxation, impose tariffs, and legislate in other ways having a direct bearing on industry—could justify the substantial current sacrifices needed to achieve such a goal. If society is in a mood to make sacrifices, it might do very much better to channel resources into sectors where foreign investment could not be expected to go. (See also the comments later in this chapter on the question of foreign control of the economy.)

balance of payments? It has been argued by various writers (e.g. Polak 1943, Arndt 1957) that the crucial factor in gauging the effect of foreign investment on the balance of payments is whether it is sufficiently biased in favour of export-generating or import-replacing industries. But there is no *necessary* presumption that investment in import-replacement or export-creation will improve the balance of payments, nor that investment concentrated on the production of home-trade goods and services will worsen the balance of payments.[8] This can best be illustrated by taking the limiting case. Imagine, if possible, that a foreign company establishes a fully automated, fully integrated, operation (i.e. using neither domestic factors nor domestic materials) for the production of 'bricks' in the capital-importing country. ('Bricks' are used as representative of home-trade products.) Assume also that there is no taxation and that the investment of the foreign company results in some reduction in the price of 'bricks'.[9] In this situation all expenditure on the 'bricks' produced by the foreign subsidiary accrues overseas and so is a debit on the balance of payments. But if total expenditure by domestic residents remains unchanged—and there is little reason in the present example why it should not—the expenditure which has been diverted to the products of the foreign subsidiary must, at least in part, be instead of expenditure on imports and exportables. The decline in expenditure on imports and exportables produces some direct benefit to the balance of payments, which partly offsets the debit arising from the operation of the foreign subsidiary. Some of the expenditure now devoted to the purchase of 'bricks' produced by the foreign subsidiary would, presumably, have been diverted from the purchase of other home-trade goods and services. Such diversion produces no *direct* benefit to the balance of payments, to be sure, but it does free resources for production in sectors which do have a direct impact on the balance of payments.

The movement of these factors may pose problems. On the assumption that domestic factors were being employed up to the margin of profitability in the international-trade sectors *before* the foreign

---

[8] See, for example, Nurkse (1953: 136-8, 1961: 259-63); Meier (1963: 110-11); Kahn (1951). Kindleberger applies this reasoning specifically to Australia in the 1963 edition of his *International Economics* (p. 417).

[9] It is implicitly assumed that the fall in price of 'bricks' results in an increase in total expenditure on 'bricks'—or, in the terminology of economics, that the price elasticity of demand for 'bricks' exceeds unity. This may not be a valid assumption but it seems hard to imagine foreign investment in fact taking place in many industries producing goods of which the price elasticity of demand falls short of unity. An alternative assumption—that the product manufactured by the foreign firm is new to the capital-importing country—would have produced a result similar to that in the text.

investment, the absorption of factors displaced from the home-trade sector in sectors producing internationally traded goods requires not only factor mobility but also some improvement in the competitive position of the international-trade sectors. If exchange rates must be accepted as sacrosanct, some reduction in the price of the factors affected is required. This reduction may not need to be great: indeed, it may not need to be an absolute reduction at all, if world prices are rising. But if some absolute adjustment *is* required and if factor incomes (especially wages) are inflexible downwards, the maintenance of employment levels in this situation is likely to be inconsistent with balance of payments equilibrium. In the case of foreign investment in the international-trade sectors, fewer adjustments—both to the allocation of domestic factors and to their prices —are required if pre-foreign-investment levels of domestic factor employment are to be maintained in consistency with balance of payments equilibrium. To this extent there is an advantage in foreign investment being in international- as compared with home-trade sectors. (The overwhelming majority of American direct investment in Australia has, of course, been in international-trade sectors.)

Though not useful in assessing the processes of adjustment required in any particular situation, there is a fundamental sense in which the effect of foreign investment on the balance of payments can be measured by the basic equation of national income analysis:

$$X - M = Y - E,$$

where x is exports of all goods and services, m is imports of all goods and services (including profits accruing abroad), y is income accruing to domestic factors, and e is national expenditure. Any decrease in income y, with total expenditure (or demand) e being unchanged, necessarily produces an increased deficit in the balance of payments, as one would expect. An obvious corollary of this equation is that, given total expenditure, the investment which produces the maximum increase in domestic incomes also produces the maximum benefit for the balance of payments.

This is frequently forgotten in popular discussion of the balance of payments. The way to reduce the balance of payments deficit, it is often suggested, is to produce locally more of the goods hitherto imported, even if this results in a higher domestic price for these goods. But clearly, if the price increase results in a net fall in domestic real incomes, the balance of payments deficit is *increased*, not diminished—unless total demand can be reduced commensurately with the fall in real income. Another form of the popular fallacy is that the contribution which a company makes to the country's balance of payments can be measured by a comparison of its imports and exports: it is said, for example, that the contribution of a foreign-owned mining company may be measured by a comparison of the profits which accrue abroad from its operations on the one hand and the value of its exports on the other. But were it not for the company's contribution to domestic incomes through the payment of wages, taxes, and royalties, the *entire* value of its exports would accrue as profits to the foreign shareholder. Moreover, if the capital employed in the mining venture could make a greater contribution to domestic real incomes in, say, the construction of roads, its employment in mining is sub-optimal from a balance of payments viewpoint.

It was seen in the earlier discussion that foreign investment usually does benefit domestic real income, though this benefit may vary considerably from case to case. If total demand were unchanged by the operation of the foreign investment, the balance of payments of the host economy would clearly improve.

But it is probable that total demand also will be higher in the post-capital-inflow period than in the pre-inflow period. To begin with, any increase in incomes is likely to produce some increase in consumption expenditure, though this is usually less than the increase in incomes. Secondly, to the extent that the marginal propensity to consume out of wages is higher than that out of profits, and to the extent that the operation of the new foreign-owned capacity produces a *relative* increase in labour's income, there is another reason to expect an increase in consumption expenditure as a result of the foreign investment. There may be a still further increase in consumption because of a 'demonstration effect'—the influence foreign investment has on consumption through its introduction to local consumers of new products and consumption standards.[10] Finally, levels of consumption may be raised as a result of an increase in factor incomes during the actual construction of the foreign-owned capacity (as will be discussed more fully later).

It is not possible to be precise about the effect of the capital inflow on domestically-financed investment expenditure. It may be fair to say that in the medium to long term the divergence of the

[10] In the Australian context, it is difficult to believe that American investment has had a significant effect on consumption through this particular effect, since almost all the products manufactured here by American companies were well known in Australia prior to the American investment, either through other domestic production, through imports, or through international advertising. To the extent that the local subsidiary of a foreign company is more anxious to expand its sales in Australia than a parent company is to expand its exports to Australia, the demonstration effect may nevertheless have some impact on consumption even in this country.

level of investment from its level before the capital inflow will be a function of the divergence of consumption from its level in the period before the inflow. Since there is ample reason to expect consumption expenditure to be higher after the foreign investment than before, it appears likely that investment expenditure also will tend to be higher after the inflow.

When all relevant factors are taken into account, therefore, it is difficult to predict whether the operation of any unit of foreign-owned capacity will (in the absence of policy measures designed to restrict expenditure) increase domestic incomes by more or less than it will increase domestic expenditures. The result will depend on the particular circumstances of each case. The outcome is of paramount importance, however, because if demand is expanded by more than incomes the balance of payments must be adversely affected; and this is only another way of saying that the capacity of the host economy to finance its own capital formation is reduced. In the long term this even affects domestic incomes, unless there is to be indefinite reliance on foreign investment.

It is important to repeat, then, that the foreign investment which makes the greatest contribution to domestic real incomes (after allowing for possible costs of relative factor movement if too much investment occurs in home-trade sectors) and stimulates domestic demand the least also makes the greatest contribution to the balance of payments. This emphasizes the significance of measures suggested earlier whereby the benefit that Australia derives from foreign investment can be enhanced. It suggests that responsibility for the preservation of long-term balance of payments equilibrium rests primarily on domestic Australian authorities. It suggests further that this responsibility can best be discharged not by compelling foreign-affiliated companies to invite Australians to share their equity but by containing the growth of aggregate demand within the growth in Australian income—bearing in mind that foreign investment is likely to increase *both*.

All this appears very obvious yet it is a point of view that is frequently overlooked. Even ignoring crudely fallacious arguments which seek to assess the effect of foreign investment on the balance of payments by comparing 'new capital inflow' with 'profit remittance', there is a considerable amount of misunderstanding on this subject. Attention has already been directed to the essentially incomplete views expressed by Polak, Arndt, and others concerning the allocation of foreign investment between international-trade industries on the one hand and home-trade industries on the other. Preoccupation with the ratio of profit remittance to a country's external earnings is also misleading if a rise in that ratio is too simply taken to indicate that foreign investment is causing a strain on the balance of payments.[11]

The effect of export franchise restrictions on the balance of payments is not easy to measure. Suggestions that a reduction in such restrictions would produce a large increase in exports and an equivalent benefit to the balance of payments are, of course, quite untenable: even if the increase in exports were forthcoming, this would not of itself produce an improvement in the balance of payments of equivalent magnitude.[12] This is because if foreign companies divert sales from the home market to overseas markets, and if total domestic demand is given, the overseas sales of the foreign companies must bring about either a reduction in the exports of Australian companies or an increase in Australia's imports. The argument that export franchise restrictions damage Australia's balance of payments must rest on the assumption that an increase in the exports of foreign-owned companies would increase the incomes of Australians by more than an equivalent increase in the exports of Australian-owned companies. This *may* be a valid assumption: the exports of Australian-owned companies may, for example, face a less elastic foreign demand curve than the exports of foreign-owned companies (though there seems no special reason why this should be true, at least as between foreign and domestic companies in the manufacturing sector), or the economies of scale available to foreign-owned companies which expand their output by exporting may be greater than those available to domestic companies which expand their output by exporting. But the gains are of this 'marginal' kind, not the absolute gains so often referred to in public debate.[13]

When attention is turned to the other question of relevance to the balance of payments—what effect does foreign investment have on the balance of payments during the period in which it is actually being received?—the position is again rather different from that usually implied. The most popular view in Australia is that it has only been the receipt of large amounts of private foreign capital which has permitted the country to import significantly more than it has exported over the years since 1945. In a sense, of course, this

[11] The writer himself probably placed undue emphasis on this investment service ratio in his *New Zealand's Debt Servicing Capacity*.

[12] It has been noted in chapter IX that many export franchise restrictions merely reflect the fact that Australian products are not competitive internationally. The opinion has even been expressed to the writer that the abolition of all market sharing arrangements would actually *reduce* Australia's exports because companies which now enjoy a limited overseas market on an exclusive basis would then face competition from affiliates in these markets.

[13] See also Perkins (1960), especially p. 82.

is correct, but it ignores the fact that *it is the capital inflow itself which has very largely generated the high level of imports.*

Economists debated for many years how a flow of money from one country to another could lead to a flow of goods and services of similar magnitude (i.e. a deficit of similar magnitude in the current account of the balance of payments). Obviously, without such a flow of real resources the flow of money could mean little. Early writers believed the real transfer would be brought about by relative price adjustments which would make the capital-exporting country a more attractive market in which to buy and the capital-importing country a less attractive market. Later, attention was focused on income changes in the two countries but there was pessimism that income changes alone would suffice to transfer the capital in full (Metzler 1942). It was only when economists took into account the possible reactions of the banking system of the country receiving the foreign investment (Polak 1943) and made full allowance for the fact that foreign *direct* investment usually involves not merely the transfer of purchasing power but the net creation of productive capacity (e.g. Kindleberger 1958b: 400-1; Arndt 1957: 253-4) that it was recognized that international capital movements may cause the balance of payments of recipient countries to *over*-compensate for the receipt of foreign resources. In other words, it was recognized for the first time that foreign investment may generate a balance of payments deficit on current account larger than the foreign investment itself.

This 'perverse' result may occur because of the far-reaching effect foreign direct investment often has on the level of domestic activity. The process of constructing the new capacity itself generates additional spending throughout the economy—some of which is directed towards imports—through familiar multiplier effects. Were this the only effect operating, it can be shown that under most circumstances the deficit in the current account of the balance of payments would fall short of the foreign investment (Metzler 1942). But any increase in manufacturing capacity provides some stimulus to investment in other areas of the economy, the extent of this stimulus varying with the amount of excess capacity already in existence and with the importance, in terms of linkages, of the initial investment. It would not be surprising to find that, in an economy already operating at near full capacity, the establishment of, say, a car industry by a foreign company would provide a very substantial stimulus to domestically financed investment.[14] In this situation it is probable

[14] The effect on the balance of payments is similar if the increased 'domestically financed investment' represents not investment in industries complementary to that in which the foreign investment occurs but the absorption of domestic

(Continued on next page)

that monetary and fiscal authorities will find themselves having to restrain domestic demand for the sake of containing the current account deficit in the balance of payments within limits set by receipts of foreign capital.

More serious than this aspect of the problem is the fact that the receipt of foreign investment results in the economy becoming 'geared' to a deficit in the current account of the balance of payments. This means first that factor incomes are raised to a level at which, with a given level of employment, the balance of payments is in deficit. It means also that there is a relative re-allocation of resources away from the international-trade sectors towards the home-trade sector.[15] Neither of these changes would pose any problem if foreign investment could be relied upon to flow into the economy indefinitely on a stable basis. But it is clear from Table I-1 that foreign investment cannot be relied upon in this way. Indeed, the unpredictability of the flow of foreign investment must probably be rated its most serious cost, for any sudden fall in the rate of capital inflow requires readjustment of factor prices (if employment levels are to be maintained in consistency with a reduction in the balance of payments deficit on current account) and re-allocation of resources (from home-trade sectors to international-trade sectors). The greater the degree of instability in the capital inflow the greater the social cost involved in adjusting to it.

It should nevertheless be observed that this instability of capital inflow and the problems it generates are not very different from the effects of the instability of export receipts. In combating this latter instability, the importance of maintaining substantial foreign exchange reserves is recognized and vigorous attempts are made to diversify the composition of exports and the markets to which they are sent. Few would suggest that the gains which arise from international specialization and trade should be abjured simply because

---

resources for use by the foreign company. The greater the extent to which foreign companies rely on domestic funds for their investment, covering only the direct foreign exchange content of the investment with funds from abroad, the greater is the pressure on domestic resources and so the likelihood of the foreign investment creating a balance of payments problem. This suggests that pressure on foreign-owned companies to accept local equity participation could accentuate problems of this kind.

15 This re-allocation takes place partly because foreign direct investment is almost certain to create a relatively large increase in demand for goods which by their nature cannot be imported—principally factory buildings—and partly because the increase in domestic costs which occurs as a result of the expansion fostered by foreign investment tends to shift the relative profitability of investment away from international-trade sectors to those more remote from international competition (Hall 1963: 194).

of the unpredictability of export receipts, and the same conclusion seems to be the most logical in the case of foreign investment. The instability problem can be reduced to some extent by the maintenance of adequate foreign exchange reserves (though this itself entails some cost). There may also be some scope to diversify the sources of foreign investment in Australia—the growth in importance of American investment is itself a significant diversification from traditional reliance on the British capital market—while, when private foreign investment slackens temporarily, government borrowing abroad may be able to supply some of the foreign resources needed to avoid the structural adjustments which would otherwise be necessary.[16]

Several questions of relevance have still to be discussed. For example, given the total level of foreign investment in Australia, would the country be better off if government were to give less encouragement to private direct investment and 'replace' some of the private capital inflow with government fixed-interest borrowing abroad? It has just been suggested that the two forms of 'borrowing' are, in some senses, alternatives: both permit a continued deficit in the current account of the balance of payments and so obviate structural adjustments in the economy which might otherwise be necessary. In most senses, of course, the two forms are not alternatives, either from the point of view of the capital-exporting country or from that of the capital-importing country. From the stand-point of the capital-exporting country, the two forms of investment take place in response to different forces and tap different supplies of capital: it is by no means obvious that Australia could replace private direct investment by government borrowing on any substantial scale. From the stand-point of the capital-importing country, fixed interest borrowing brings none of the know-how usually associated with private direct investment and has the disadvantage that it imposes on the borrowing country a fixed charge for debt service which must be paid

[16] The writer has been accused of being hopelessly unrealistic in suggesting that government overseas borrowing could be used to offset fluctuations in private direct investment in this way, and difficulties encountered by the Australian government in borrowing abroad in 1965 (at a time when it was widely feared that British and American government measures would result in a sharp fall in private capital inflow) have been adduced as proof. Perhaps so, but it seems likely that some increased government overseas borrowing could have been done if the rate of interest offered had been raised. Admittedly the rate of interest offered might have had to be very high, but it might still have been a smaller cost to pay than the social costs which might have been involved had the economy faced the need to adjust to a temporary fall in the rate of capital inflow.

independently of the productivity of the investment which it finances and of the state of the economy in general. But fundamentally the question posed is irrelevant. As long as private direct investment benefits Australia, it should be encouraged. Similarly, if government can invest funds locally to yield a return above the rate of interest in international capital markets, it should borrow abroad to do so. The only economic caution which must be made is that the total level of capital inflow should be as stable as possible over time. This suggests a need for moderation.

One economic argument in favour of foreign investment not so far mentioned is the converse of Keynes's oft-quoted argument *against* capital export by the United Kingdom: the capital-importing country may derive considerable advantage if a foreign subsidiary goes bankrupt leaving a legacy of real assets behind it.[17] Another point worthy of mention is that in times of war or international crisis the formal ownership of productive capacity in a capital-importing country is likely to be of small importance.

On the other hand, a number of economic disadvantages can be added to those already mentioned. One such is the possibility that foreign investment, partly because it so often reflects the oligopolistic structure of the industries whence it springs, may encourage the undue proliferation of production units in a small market, a situation which could prevent the reaping of economies of scale but which might not necessarily lead to greater competition in markets as heavily rationalized as are many in Australia.[18] Another drawback of foreign investment is the fact that foreign-affiliated companies have access to supplies of credit not under the control of domestic monetary authorities. This complicates the already difficult task of economic management and suggests the need to place increasing reliance on fiscal measures to control the economy's progress.

Should 'economic control' also be listed as one of the 'costs' of foreign investment? For three reasons it seems hard to answer this question in the affirmative. First, it is clear from chapter V that the local subsidiaries of American companies are in many cases allowed a considerable measure of autonomy in most areas of management decision-making. Secondly, it is hard to see how even the strict control exercised in some fields by most parent companies could

[17] Keynes (1924: 586). The passage to which reference is made in the text has been quoted, for example, by Kemp (1962a: 61) and Murphy (1960: 12). The argument assumes, of course, that capital markets are imperfect. In a perfect capital market, the liquidating company could sell its assets to the host country for their full economic value.

[18] It must be admitted, however, that *one* of the forces leading to such proliferation of small production units in Australia—state government competition for industry—is, in principle, within Australia's powers to change.

work to Australia's disadvantage. Investment decisions, those subject to the greatest degree of American control, are under normal circumstances likely to be governed primarily by local market conditions and prospects, and as such may differ little from the decisions taken by a 'self-financed' company of Australian ownership.[19] If a foreign subsidiary adopts a policy of high profit remittance at the insistence of its parent company, this cannot (again under normal circumstances) be rated a 'disadvantage' to Australia except to the extent that all capital inflow (including profit reinvestment) may be to Australia's advantage. In any case, it has been seen in chapter IV that American control over the dividend policies of local subsidiaries frequently means the adoption of a very conservative policy. Thirdly, and perhaps most important of all, ultimate control rests to an important extent with Australia. In times of severe economic crisis, the government could restrict or even prohibit profit remittance and capital repatriation. It could control import prices and make it uncomfortable for those companies not exporting. Even in normal times, the government wields very important powers (especially over investment decisions) through its control of tariff and fiscal policies. In an important sense, a foreign company investing in Australia submits itself to potential *Australian* control.

But can policy towards foreign investment be decided on economic grounds alone? Obviously not, and there are many Australians who feel that economic factors are much less important in coming to a policy on foreign investment than are political, social, and moral factors. Negatively, some fear the political influence which large foreign companies may exert; others fear that Australia's continuing dependence on foreign investment may dictate the country's foreign policy. Still others fear the 'Americanization' of the Australian way of life; a few suspect that on moral grounds Australia should be a capital exporter. Positively, there is a large body of opinion—with representatives on both the right and left of the political divide—which would welcome foreign investment from Britain and the U.S. even if it entailed some economic cost, because of the 'guarantee' such investment provides for the nation's future defence.

Some of these arguments must be allowed weight. Because of the economic and social costs of adjusting the balance of payments to a sharp fall in capital inflow, there may be some reluctance to adopt otherwise agreed-upon policies which could 'frighten' foreign investors. And American investment in this country may well hasten the

---

[19] This view depends on the assumption that Australia and the market of the capital-exporting country are either actually or potentially two distinct markets. The assumption appears the only one possible in the Australian situation but may not be valid for a political dependency *vis-à-vis* the metropolitan power.

'Americanization' of the 'Australian way of life'. But the former problem is only an aspect of the wider problem of the instability of foreign capital inflow and in an extremity could be met in part by a prohibition on profit remittance, while in a situation where American magazines and films appear prominently on bookstall and television screen American *investment* can only in part be blamed for the 'Americanization'. The 'political influence' of large foreign companies is impossible for the layman to assess but there is little reason to suspect that a large American-owned company in, say, the chemical industry would behave very differently in this respect from a large Australian-owned company in the same industry. It is hard to imagine an 'American front' being adopted by the American subsidiaries here in any situation not involving discriminatory legislation against them. The moral argument that Australia, a wealthy country in a capital-hungry world, should be a net capital exporter is one with which the writer personally has much sympathy. But this end cannot be achieved by preventing foreign companies investing in Australia because foreign companies do not, in most circumstances, regard investment in Australia and investment in, say, an Asian country as genuine alternatives. To make Australia a net capital exporter, or a less voracious capital importer, requires an increase in Australian investment abroad, not a reduction in foreign investment in Australia.

Whatever view is adopted towards these non-economic factors—and this survey is clearly not competent to pronounce final judgment on them—it is of first importance to have the economic costs and benefits in clear perspective. There *are* economic costs of foreign investment, the most important of which is almost certainly the instability of its flow. But these costs appear small when set beside the gains. It is certain that from an economic point of view United States direct investment has made a major contribution to Australia's industrial development in the past. Given sensible policies on the part of Australian authorities, there seems little doubt that it will continue to be of value in the future.

Appendix A

Survey of American-affiliated Companies Known to be Manufacturing in Australia at 30 June 1962

Aggregate statistics alone provide a rather barren picture. Though it has been deliberate policy to mention company names only on rare occasions to avoid disclosing information supplied on a confidential basis, there appears to be considerable advantage in providing some background to figures of the kind presented in chapter II by attempting to place individual American-affiliated companies in their industrial setting. This appendix is directed to that end.[1]

Automotive and Related Industries

By far the largest American investment in Australian manufacturing is in the motor industry, and of the companies in this industry General Motors-Holden's Pty Ltd stands out as the giant. In 1926 General Motors (Australia) Pty Ltd established its first assembly plant in Melbourne, and plants in all other mainland states quickly followed. At this stage the company confined its operations to assembly, importing chassis and engines and buying bodies from an Australian company, Holden's Motor Body Builders Ltd. Despite this, more than 2,000 Australians were employed by the company by 1929 (Forster 1964:47). Two years later, General Motors absorbed Holden's and General Motors-Holden's Ltd was born. This move was essentially defensive in character, designed to assure the American subsidiary of its supply of bodies in a situation where the prosperity of the Australian firm was seriously threatened by the depression. The new company itself was soon in some difficulty, with a substantial accumulated

---

[1] Readers should be aware that, for the most part, company names used in this appendix were those in use in 1962. It should also be noted that almost all points made are based on published material, though for the sake of economy most reference footnotes have been omitted. Research workers desiring to follow up the references may consult the original doctoral thesis (held at the Menzies Library of the Australian National University) on which this book is based. The writer wishes to acknowledge in particular the very considerable amount of information drawn from the *Australian Financial Review* and from Tariff Board Reports.

U

loss by the end of 1932, and consideration was given in New York
to winding up the whole operation (Hartnett 1964: 50).[2] However,
after a change in management and an extensive reorganization of
the company in 1934, G.M.H. (as the company became known
throughout Australia) never looked back. A major new plant was constructed at Fishermen's Bend, near Melbourne, in 1936 and in 1937
the company made a profit of a million pounds for the first time. By
the end of the thirties, the total employment of G.M.H. was 11,000.

During World War II, G.M.H. was heavily preoccupied with production of the weapons of war. Indeed, even before 1939, the firm
had been associated with a small number of other large companies
in the production of military aircraft. As the war drew to a close,
increasing attention was given by the company to the possibility of
complete car manufacture in Australia, to replace the partial manufacture undertaken up to that time. The federal government had
been keen to encourage such complete manufacture for some years,
as had been shown in 1939-40 with the passage of the Motor Vehicle
Engine Bounty Act and the Motor Vehicle Agreement Act which
together gave Australian Consolidated Industries Ltd substantial
financial encouragement to manufacture motor vehicle engines and
chassis. No manufacture was actually undertaken by A.C.I. and the
Acts were repealed in 1945. In 1944 the government sent a letter of
invitation to all interested parties to submit proposals for car manufacture. The letter contained the implied threat that if 'satisfactory
proposals are not received as a result of the invitation to interested
parties, the Government should set up a Corporation to manufacture
a complete car'. It was this challenge that G.M.H. took up.

G.M.H. was not the only company to accept the government's
challenge. Indeed, three other American companies also accepted it
—Chrysler Australia Ltd, the Ford Motor Company of Australia
Pty Ltd, and the International Harvester Company of Australia Pty
Ltd. But while the last three planned to increase the Australian
content of their vehicles over a period, the plans of G.M.H. called for
the almost complete manufacture of a car in one step. It can fairly
be said that in successfully bringing these plans to fruition, G.M.H.
did more than any other single company towards building the Australian motor vehicle industry. In so doing, the company played a
vital role—perhaps the most important individual role—in the
development of Australian industry in the fifteen years after 1945.

The company requested no additional tariff protection and no
bounty. While its staff were kept employed in the manufacture of
household goods, work on the design and tooling for the new car

[2] The debit balance at the end of 1932 is reported to have been £464,139,
though the company showed a profit of £134,160 in 1933.

proceeded apace both in America and in Australia. The result: little more than four years after the government extended its invitation to the car companies to submit their proposals, the first Holden, as the new car was named, made its public appearance. The date was 29 November 1948. Initially, only ten Holdens were produced daily and by the end of 1948 a total of only 163 had been produced. But expansion was continuous. Daily output had reached 100 by 1951. Early in 1956 total production of the Holden reached 250,000. By 1962, when the millionth Holden was produced, the company had spent almost £75 million on the expansion of its facilities since World War II; it owned or leased 3,179 acres of land and occupied plants which covered more than 7 million square feet of floor space; it was planning further expansion which would raise Holden production to 730 each working day (or 175,000 a year) and total production, including the assembly of other General Motors products, to 200,000 vehicles annually. With a total employment of 21,607 at the end of 1962, the company was easily the second largest industrial employer in Australia.

Though substantially the largest, the General Motors subsidiary was not the first American-controlled motor vehicle company established in this country. That honour belongs to the Ford Motor Company of Australia Pty Ltd. In October 1924 it was announced that Ford planned to establish five assembly plants and one body-building plant in Australia at an estimated cost of £1,400,000. On 31 March 1925, the *Geelong Advertiser* carried front-page headlines announcing the acquisition of more than 100 acres of land by Ford in the town. Geelong was to be Ford's Australian headquarters and the *Advertiser* referred to the announcement as 'perhaps the most important statement that has ever been issued in connection with industrial undertakings at Geelong'. The paper went on enthusiastically:

> A link with America is indeed a great achievement, because at the present time it is amazingly prosperous and has become the recognized barometer of the world's finance. . . . So serious has the accumulation of wealth in America become that financial economists are busy speculating as to the right remedies to be applied to relieve the nation of the consequence of its embarrassment of riches. On the other hand it is one of the problems of Australia to secure capital to develop its resources.

Production of Ford's famous Model T began almost at once in a number of temporary quarters including Dalgety's old wool store at Geelong. By the end of 1926 plants were operating in all mainland states. In 1928 the company switched to the Model A, and in 1935 to the V-8. With the latter model Australia saw its first example of all-steel body building. After the war, as noted above, Ford Australia was one of the four companies to accept the government's invitation to embark on complete motor vehicle manufacture, though, unlike G.M.H., the company planned to do this in stages. From a peak employment in 1925 of only 776, the company grew to have an employment of 4,600 in 1950, and of 8,000 in 1963.

The smallest of the American companies engaged in the manufacture of passenger cars in Australia is Chrysler Australia Ltd. In the twenties there were two large Australian-owned motor body builders operating in South Australia: Holden's Motor Body Builders Ltd and T. J. Richards & Sons Ltd. The former was absorbed by General Motors (Australia) Pty Ltd and the latter eventually became Chrysler Australia Ltd. The first step in the transformation occurred in 1922 when the South Australian distributors of Dodge cars gave T. J. Richards a contract to build car bodies. In 1936 Chrysler Dodge Distributors (Aust.) Pty Ltd was set up and a controlling interest in T. J. Richards was acquired in 1939. The company became Chrysler Dodge De Soto Distributors Ltd in 1947 and Chrysler Australia Ltd in 1951 when the Chrysler Corporation of the U.S. first took up an equity interest in the firm (85 per cent). Though the firm maintained production capacity in military aircraft for a number of years after the outbreak of hostilities in Korea, its primary activity remained the production of motor cars and trucks. Like Ford, Chrysler embarked on a plan to increase gradually the local content of its vehicles during the fifties.

All the three companies dealt with so far—G.M.H., Ford, and Chrysler—sell trucks as well as passenger cars. But all these companies confine their operations for the most part to modifying imported engines to suit local conditions or to producing parts of the upper-structure of the bodywork. The International Harvester Company of Australia Pty Ltd, however, incorporates a very substantial Australian content in the trucks it produces. Established in Australia in 1912, International Harvester commenced production of trucks as an adjunct to its tractor operations in 1949. In so doing, it became the second company in Australia to engage in the complete manufacture of motor vehicle engines. By 1962 the company held almost one-quarter of the whole Australian truck market.

If the impression conveyed is that the Australian motor vehicle industry was entirely the creation of American companies, the case has been overstated. Significant body-building operations were being conducted here before American subsidiaries arrived in the field. But these activities were inherently unstable, being dependent on decisions made by foreign companies catering for markets many times the size of the Australian. Gradually two of the largest of these

Australian firms became dependent on the orders of two American companies, while most of the others were squeezed out of the industry. British companies made no attempt to establish assembly plants in Australia before the war and a Tariff Board report of 1937 stated that at that time G.M.H. supplied 39 per cent of the vehicle market, Ford Australia about 22 per cent, and Chrysler Dodge Distributors (Aust.) about 15 per cent, with a further 14 per cent of the market being held by chassis of American origin assembled by other importers. After 1945 British companies increased their share of the market temporarily because of the dollar shortage. But the currency restrictions on dollar imports which helped the British in the short term cost them dearly in the long term. Through lack of necessity or lack of foresight, they still failed to establish production facilities in Australia and soon lost their advantage to their American rivals, who had been compelled by the difficulty of procuring supplies from dollar sources to embark on complete car manufacture in Australia. Maxcy has observed that 'it was not until the mid-fifties that shipments of built-up vehicles from England [to Australia] ceased to be significant.' (1963: 505.) When the Tariff Board discussed the motor vehicle industry in 1957, the only companies it considered to be properly 'manufacturing' in Australia were the four American ones discussed above.

Though they did not create the industry unaided, American companies must receive the lion's share of the credit. Their dominant position in the local industry in the early sixties is clearly illustrated in Table A-1.

But not all the American-affiliated firms in the vehicle industry have been as successful as the ones described. Willys Motors (Aust.) Pty Ltd, a joint venture between Willys Motors Inc. of the U.S. and a number of Australian firms, mainly vehicle distributors, has been one of those to fare poorly. Established on a sub-contracting basis in 1957, it began its own manufacturing in Brisbane in 1961. By the end of June 1962, accumulated losses totalled more than £500,000 and the company's market share was at a low ebb. Products of the firm are confined mainly to the jeep type of vehicle. Not very different has been the experience of a company on the periphery of the industry, Fruehauf Trailers (Aust.) Pty Ltd. This firm was formed in 1957 also, and it too is a joint venture. By 30 June 1962, the production of trailers had earned the firm only an accumulated loss of more than £238,000. In the case of C.C.C. Carriers Pty Ltd, established in 1959 for the production of specialized heavy-duty trucks and mobile crane carriers, progress was so discouraging that the firm was sold to Australian interests in 1963. The total employment of these three companies in 1962 was less than 200.

TABLE A–1   Percentage Share of American-affiliated Companies in New Vehicle Registrations, 1960 to 1963

Company	Cars and station wagons				Panel vans, utilities, hearses, ambulances				Trucks and omnibuses			
	'60	'61	'62	'63	'60	'61	'62	'63	'60	'61	'62	'63
G.M.H.	44·8	49·7	44·0	45·7	53·8	56·3	49·1	51·9	30·0	33·9	34·0	31·8
Ford	15·6	17·9	19·5	16·9	14·5	17·4	21·8	19·2	15·4	12·3	11·0	11·9
Chrysler	4·5	2·8	5·7	6·8	2·3	2·0	1·5	1·4	6·3	6·0	6·7	8·2
I.H.	..	..	..	..	1·9	2·0	3·7	3·5	22·0	22·0	21·0	19·2
Willys	..	..	..	..	1·3	1·3	0·5	0·4	1·0	0·9	0·6	0·6
Totalª	65·0	70·4	69·2	69·5	73·8	79·1	76·7	76·4	74·7	75·2	73·3	71·6
Total registrations ('000)	245	188	267	307	45	34	39	44	20	15	17	22

ª Detail may not add to totals because of rounding.

NOTE: American vehicles imported by companies other than those listed above are not included in the table.

SOURCE: Commonwealth Bureau of Census and Statistics 1960–3.

The influence of the developing motor vehicle industry has been felt throughout the economy. Not unnaturally, American companies have been among those attracted into the supply of parts for the growing industry. The Goodyear Tyre & Rubber Company (Aust.) Ltd was one of the first of these. A company to distribute Goodyear products was formed in Australia as early as 1915, and in 1927, one year after Goodyear became the largest rubber manufacturer in the world, the company set up its first Australian manufacturing facilities at Granville, in New South Wales. By the end of 1929, the company's plant covered eight acres and its production was playing a significant role in making Australia almost completely independent of tyre imports. In the middle of 1930 plant was installed for the manufacture of a range of industrial rubber products, including various kinds of belting and industrial hose. By 1952, when the company celebrated its silver jubilee of manufacture in Australia, the company's plant covered $17\frac{1}{2}$ acres and annual production had expanded more than ten times above that of the first year of production. Ten years later sales exceeded £20 million, and it was estimated that the company, with 26-27 per cent of the Australian tyre market, was the largest tyre manufacturer in the country.

B. F. Goodrich Australia Pty Ltd, another company engaged in tyre manufacture, is a joint venture in which the B. F. Goodrich Company of the U.S. holds 56 per cent of the equity and Ampol Petroleum Ltd most of the balance. Though production did not commence till 1960, the company was estimated to have secured 11-12 per cent of the tyre market by 1963. Goodrich is not the last of the American tyre companies to establish operations in Australia: since this survey was conducted, U.S. Rubber has purchased a substantial minority interest in S.A. Rubber Holdings Ltd of Adelaide and the company plans to embark on tyre manufacture. At the time of writing, there were rumours that still another of the American giants was contemplating investment in the industry.

Among the very earliest American-affiliated firms supplying parts or materials to the emerging car industry were three firms either no longer in existence or no longer connected with their American partner in 1962. One of these was the United States Light and Heat Corporation (Aust.) Ltd, one of the three chief Australian producers of storage batteries during the twenties. The company claimed in 1927 to have capacity for the production of 120,000 car batteries per annum, but it appears that operations ceased during the depression of the thirties. In 1928, Du Pont de Nemours and Imperial Chemical Industries of London jointly acquired a 40 per cent interest in British Australian Lead Manufacturers as part of an agreement under which the latter obtained Du Pont's duco rights, and a plant was erected in the same year to produce the newly-discovered paint. One year later, Nobel Chemical Finishes (Australasia) Ltd was formed as a joint venture between I.C.I. (51 per cent) and Du Pont (49 per cent) to produce leather-cloth and rubber-cloth, principally for use in car upholstery. Renamed Leathercloth Pty Ltd in 1930, it was acquired by I.C.I.A.N.Z. in 1935.[3]

Most of the American companies now producing components for the motor vehicle industry in Australia began operations after World War II. By far the largest of these is Borg-Warner (Aust.) Ltd. This company was formed in 1956 by the take-over of an Australian firm, Coote & Jorgensen Ltd, and now is the only independent producer of automotive axle transmissions and gears in Australia. Indeed, apart from G.M.H., the firm is the only producer of such items in Australia. While the other American-affiliated firms in the industry are much smaller than Borg-Warner in terms of employment, several of them occupy positions at least as important in the market for their own particular products. For example, Bendix-Tecnico (Automotive) Pty Ltd, in which the Bendix Corporation of the U.S. holds an indirect interest of about 42 per cent, has been the only manufacturer of carburettors in Australia since its establishment in 1958, and its share of the carburettor market was estimated at well over 80 per cent in 1964. Schrader-Scovill Co. Pty Ltd also is the only company manufacturing tyre valves in Australia and is believed to hold a substantial share of the total market. On the other hand, the Champion Spark Plug Company (Aust.) Pty Ltd, though holding a substantial fraction of the total market for spark plugs in Australia, is one of a number of manufacturers, all with overseas affiliations. Similarly, Trico Pty Ltd, engaged in the production of windscreen-wiper arms and blades and windscreen washers, and Steerings Pty Ltd, producing automotive steering gears, share their respective industries with several other firms.

So far, attention has been paid mainly to those companies which are almost entirely geared to the motor vehicle industry. There are a number of others which, though catering to industry generally, lean on the vehicle industry for a significant part of their orders. Some of these are long established companies like the Carr Fastener Company of Australia Ltd, which was set up as early as 1928 and is currently producing a wide range of fasteners for the aircraft, automotive, radio, television, and clothing industries. And not only fasteners: among the products supplied to the motor vehicle industry by this firm are such diverse items as frames for headlights, window regulators, seat adjusters, and gaskets for spark plugs. Since 1954, Bundy

---

[3] Information supplied by Imperial Chemical Industries of Australia and New Zealand Ltd, letter dated 21 Jan. 1965.

Tubing Co. (Aust.) Pty Ltd, in which the majority shareholding is held by a predominantly British-owned firm, Tubemakers of Australia Pty Ltd, has manufactured the specialized small diameter tubing sold under the name of Bundyweld, and the automotive industry is a vital market. Australian Timken Pty Ltd, the only company to produce tapered roller bearings in Australia since it began production in 1958, sells the principal part of its output to the vehicle industry. Even Engelhard Industries Pty Ltd, a company with substantial interests in the refining of precious metals, supplies microid starter and generator bushes to the industry, while the Sheffield Corporation of Australia Pty Ltd, though not strictly a supplier of components, is heavily dependent for its existence on the motor industry's demand for gauges and tooling in general.

From the electrical equipment industry too come a wide range of parts. It is not surprising to find that Willard Australia Pty Ltd is closely associated with the motor industry, since it produces automotive storage batteries. But many others also play an important role: Aircraft-Marine Products (Aust.) Pty Ltd, for example, supplies solderless terminals for electrical wiring, and Ducon Industries Ltd, in which P. R. Mallory & Co. Inc. had a minority interest until Ducon was taken over by Plessey Co. Ltd of the U.K. in 1963, supplies ignition condensers.

Electrical Products

American investment in the motor vehicle and related industries is clearly varied as well as substantial. But it is of course only one of the areas, though the best known, in which American capital in Australia is engaged. Reference has just been made to American firms in the electrical equipment industry. Undoubtedly the largest American firm in terms of employment in this industry is Standard Telephones & Cables Pty Ltd. This company began the production of telephone equipment on a small scale in the mid-twenties and in 1928 had an average employment of only 66. Even this modest achievement was at least partially dependent on the assistance of the Postmaster-General's Department. But the company survived and prospered, and thirty years later was one of two companies supplying that Department with more than 80 per cent of its automatic switching equipment requirements. After 1945, S.T.C. also ventured into the home appliance market with the acquisition in 1946 of all the assets of Silovac Electrical Products Pty Ltd. Radio and television receivers were produced in the fifties too, but, like so many others, the company withdrew from this market in the recession of 1961-2. Part of the firm's influence is wielded through Austral Standard Cables Pty Ltd, a company in which S.T.C. holds a 40 per cent interest and the British-controlled company, Metal Manufacturers Ltd, the balance. The company was initially established in 1948 as a 50/50 joint venture to acquire the existing telephone-cable manufacturing plant of Metal Manufacturers at Port Kembla and the new plant being established at that time at Maribyrnong in Victoria. Since its inception the company has effectively dominated the whole Australian market for underground cable, and its annual capacity of 750,000 pair-miles of cable in the early sixties represented a capacity almost eight times that of Metal Manufacturers in 1945.

Automatic Electric Telephones Pty Ltd appears to have been another company established in the Australian telecommunication industry at an early date but its parent sold the company to Clyde Industries Ltd in 1958.[4] It was never large.

One of the very largest American-affiliated firms in the electrical equipment industry is no longer in existence—or rather has been resurrected in a very different form from that in which it died. This is Australian General Electric Pty Ltd. The company began operations in Australia in 1898 as a selling organization only but moved into manufacture during the twenties. 'By 1929 the range of regular production included the following: traction motors, traction controllers and certain parts of control equipment, squirrel cage motors and star delta starters, Hotpoint electric irons and toasters, air break switches and certain street lighting fittings.' (Forster 1964: 119.) British capital was introduced into the company in 1930 and the firm remained an Anglo-American venture till American antitrust action compelled the U.S. parent company to liquidate its holding in 1955. Under the name of A.E.I. Ltd, the local company remains a force in the electrical goods industry, though after a period of Anglo-Australian ownership the company is now wholly British-owned. Not until 1961 did the American company re-enter the Australian market. When it did so, manufacturing operations were initially a comparatively small part of its interest, though the company did establish a minority holding in James N. Kirby Manufacturing Pty Ltd and set up Australian General Electric (Appliances) Pty Ltd to produce small home appliances in Victoria.

More American companies are operating in the home appliance section of the electrical products industry than in any other. Almost certainly the best known of these is Sunbeam Corporation Ltd, which has been manufacturing in Australia since 1934. The company now produces a wide range of appliances including toasters, frypans, beaters and mixers, irons, electric kettles, shavers, electric clocks,

---

[4] The parent company of Automatic Electric Telephones Pty Ltd, the Automatic Electric Company of Chicago, sold its very small interest in Telephone & Electrical Industries Pty Ltd in the same year.

hair-dryers, electric lawn-mowers and electric hedge trimmers. In several products, such as domestic electric clocks, the firm is the chief local manufacturer. It was among the earliest, if not the first, to manufacture electric shavers in Australia in 1952 and was closely followed in that industry by another American company, Remington-Rand (Aust.) Pty Ltd. The latter increased its sales of shavers by 1,000 per cent in the decade after its establishment here, and in 1962 was thought to head the electric shaver market, just one place ahead of Sunbeam. In third place came a Dutch company and in fourth another American, Ronson Pty Ltd, but though both these companies conducted some manufacture of shavers in Australia in the late fifties, both ceased production after import controls on shavers were lifted in 1960, leaving the manufacturing side of the industry to Sunbeam and Remington.

In the field of larger appliances, the name of Hoover has become almost synonymous with vacuum cleaners: production of these began from substantially imported parts in 1954 and the company is now by far the largest Australian manufacturer/assembler of these products. It is also a major producer of washing machines and steam irons. The only American-affiliated company engaged in the production of radio and television receivers at the time of writing was James N. Kirby Manufacturing.[5] Marketing its products under the General Electric brandname since 1961, the company caused a considerable stir in the industry in 1964 by introducing the portable television receiver to Australia. The company's success in producing other appliances, such as refrigerators and washing machines, has also been such as to encourage General Electric to increase its minority holding of 1961 to a controlling interest in the company in 1964. G.M.H., in addition to its production of cars, is an important producer of home appliances marketed under its Frigidaire brand, while the names of Singer and Black & Decker, in the fields of sewing machines and portable electric tools respectively, are as well known in Australia as they are throughout the world.

Other American firms are scattered widely through the electrical products industry. In one section of the industry is IBM Australia Pty Ltd. This company was incorporated in Australia in 1932 but did not begin manufacturing here till 1949. In that year the firm began the local assembly of 'time systems', a company expression used to denote everything from electronic master clocks to attend-

[5] Admiral of Australia Pty Ltd, a joint Australian-American venture, produced television receivers from 1955 to 1961 (when the American interest was sold), however, and Thomas Electronics of Australia Pty Ltd, a company producing cathode ray picture tubes for television receivers, was wholly American-owned from its inception in 1956 until early in 1962.

ance recorders. In 1957 IBM Australia began the assembly of electric typewriters and in the following year the first Australian assembly of complex data processing equipment. In another section of the industry, the Lincoln Electric Company (Aust.) Pty Ltd markets a wide range of welding equipment and electrodes. Two small companies, Arrow Switches (Aust.) Pty Ltd and Heinemann Electric (Aust.) Pty Ltd, produce electric switching gear of various kinds. Every television-receiver manufacturer in Australia drew supplies of capacitors from Ducon Industries Ltd in 1962, and the company was also a major supplier of other kinds of capacitors, potentiometers, and electrical porcelain. Bendix-Tecnico Pty Ltd supplies aircraft electrical equipment, Cannon Electric (Aust.) Pty Ltd highly technical electrical connectors, and Westrex Australia Pty Ltd communications equipment. British companies dominated the early years of the Australian gramophone record industry, but today three well-known companies have American affiliations: the Australian Record Co. Ltd, associated with Columbia Records Inc.; Festival Records Pty Ltd, jointly owned by the Ampar Record Corporation Inc. and a large Sydney newspaper chain; and the long established RCA of Australia Pty Ltd.

Five companies with American affiliations produce between them a wide range of controls—from thermostatic controls for domestic appliances to flowmeters for the control of giant oil refineries. Australian Controls Ltd, in which Ranco Inc. holds a minority interest, is substantially the largest of those engaged in the production of domestic thermostats, and supplies these for incorporation in refrigerators, air-conditioning units, stoves, washing machines, etc. Texas Instruments Australia Ltd, too, is in the broad field of thermostats for domestic appliances but the company tends to concentrate on providing for the needs of 'table-top' appliances. Moreover, an important part of the company's activities is in the non-ferrous metal rolling industry. Robertshaw Controls (Aust.) Pty Ltd, on the other hand, is more directly in competition with Australian Controls, but the company again has an alternative interest, in the manufacture of LP-gas equipment. Engaged in the production of process control equipment in Australia are Taylor Instrument Companies of Australia Pty Ltd and Fischer & Porter Pty Ltd.

Other Metal Industries

The number of American companies in other parts of the Australian metal-working industry is so great as to defy adequate description in short compass. In the extraction and refining of non-ferrous metals, Mount Isa Mines Ltd is by far the largest American interest. For some years the company has been mainly concerned in the production of copper, though it was founded to mine lead, zinc, and silver. Its importance to Australia is apparent from the fact that during the industrial dispute at Mount Isa in 1964-5 it was estimated that Australian copper production fell by 75 per cent. It is not only the existence of the Mount Isa township of 14,000 people which is completely dependent on the activities of the company: it has even been claimed that much of the economic viability of Queensland itself is tied to its fortunes. Apart from the ore smelters operated by the parent company at the pithead, one subsidiary operates the largest copper refinery in Australia at Townsville, while another mines coal in the far north of the state.

Only two companies at present produce aluminium from bauxite in Australia and both are affiliated with American firms. Comalco Industries Pty Ltd, in which the Kaiser Aluminium & Chemical Corporation of the U.S. and the substantially British-owned Conzinc Riotinto Australia Ltd share equally, is one of these. It is the holding company for three main operating companies, Commonwealth Aluminium Corporation Pty Ltd, Comalco Products Pty Ltd, and Comalco Aluminium (Bell Bay) Ltd, in which the Tasmanian government has held a minority interest since the facilities of this company were sold to Comalco by the Tasmanian and federal governments in 1961. The Comalco group draws bauxite from its own leases at Weipa, in Queensland, refines its own alumina and smelts its own aluminium at Bell Bay in Tasmania,[6] and fabricates a significant part of this aluminium in New South Wales. The other company in the industry is Alcoa of Australia Pty Ltd which, though not in production at the time this survey was conducted in 1962, began production in 1963 and is now a major producer. This company is 51 per cent American, with three Australian mining companies holding the balance of the equity. The firm draws its bauxite from deposits in the Darling Ranges, Western Australia, refines it to alumina in a 210,000-ton refinery at nearby Kwinana, and conducts its smelting and fabricating operations at Geelong, Victoria.[7] These two companies, the scope of whose operations span every Australian state but one, together had an estimated capacity of 92,000 tons of primary aluminium at the end of 1963, more than enough to meet the estimated Australian demand for the metal in 1968.

[6] Since alumina capacity is inadequate, however, the company is currently importing alumina while its affiliates, in association with Alcan of Canada and Pechiney of France, construct a vast 600,000-ton refinery at Gladstone in Queensland.

[7] During 1965 Alcoa announced plans to increase alumina capacity at Kwinana to 410,000 tons.

Engaged in the refining of metals of quite a different kind and on a much smaller scale is Breckett Pty Ltd. This highly profitable firm specializes in the recovery of steel from slag dumps and operates under contract to the Broken Hill Proprietary Company Ltd. It is jointly owned by the Harsco Corporation of the U.S. and the locally-owned Brambles Industries Ltd.

In the agricultural equipment industry, American firms again play a significant role. The Australian tractor market is dominated by foreign-owned companies: the largest appears to be the Canadian company, Massey-Ferguson Holdings (Aust.) Ltd, but the next two in order of size are both American-owned: International Harvester and Ford. International Harvester, however, is the only one of the three engaged in tractor manufacture proper, as distinct from the assembly of imported parts, and it has been the largest company in this field ever since it began tractor production in 1948. The firm also produces a wide range of agricultural implements. On a much smaller scale, J. I. Case (Aust.) Pty Ltd, New Holland (Australasia) Pty Ltd, Oliver Australasia Pty Ltd, Ralph McKay Ltd (in which Borg-Warner has a minority interest), Buckner (Australasia) Pty Ltd, and Greenacres Farming Equipment Pty Ltd all produce a variety of agricultural machinery and implements, ranging from the irrigation sprinklers produced by Buckner to the discs made by Ralph McKay.

Le Tourneau-Westinghouse Pty Ltd has been a leader in the earth-moving equipment industry since its establishment at Rydalmere, New South Wales, in 1941. In that year the firm began the manufacture of drawn scrapers and by 1945 had widened its field of production to include tractor-scrapers. In 1963 it was reported to be producing twenty-two types of earth-moving and construction machinery. Caterpillar of Australia Pty Ltd arrived a little later. This company was incorporated in 1955 and now produces a variety of crawler tractors, front-end loaders, rippers, bulldozers, and graders. Like Le Tourneau, however, the company imports substantial sections of the units it sells, such as the engine and the transmission. In 1958 International Harvester, too, entered the earth-moving equipment industry, after the company had acquired the assets of Fowler Engineering Pty Ltd; while making up the complement of American companies significantly engaged in this industry in 1962 were Clark Equipment Australia Pty Ltd and Allis-Chalmers Australia Pty Ltd. All three companies, however, had important interests outside the earth-moving equipment industry. Though the primary concern of Allis-Chalmers, for example, was the production of motor graders for highway construction, the firm had diversified to such an extent that in 1964 it claimed to have produced the kiln for Australia's largest single cement-making unit.

Not surprisingly, the two companies supplying tenpin bowling equipment in 1962 were both associated with American firms. One, American Machine & Foundry Co. (Aust.) Pty Ltd, was formed in 1959 by the take-over of the Australian firm, Sterling Industries Pty Ltd. This company was already engaged in the production of bakery machinery and it was on this foundation that the tenpin bowling activities were built. The company is now a 50/50 joint venture with the predominantly Australian-owned British Tobacco Company (Aust.) Ltd. It continues to produce bakery machinery—and indeed has even ventured forth into such novel fields as the production of a bowling machine for use by cricketers—but since 1962 production of tenpin bowling equipment has virtually ceased. The second firm in the industry, originally named Brunswick of Australia Pty Ltd but renamed in turn Brunswick Bowling Equipment Pty Ltd and now Blacklock Industries Pty Ltd, is affiliated with the other great name in the American tenpin bowling industry, Brunswick Corporation. This company has only a small minority interest in Blacklock, though Hoyts Theatres Ltd, the Australian subsidiary of another American company, also holds an interest. Like A.M.F. (Aust.), Blacklock Industries has moved out of the production of tenpin bowling machinery since 1962.

In the field of sheet-metal working, Armco (Aust.) Pty Ltd specializes in the production of pre-fabricated steel buildings and steel culverts for drainage purposes. It has grown little, however, since its establishment before World War II. Much more spectacular has been the growth of Rheem Australia Industries Pty Ltd, which was also established in the thirties. The company is probably best known for its widely sold domestic water-heating appliances, but its main activity is undoubtedly the production of drums (and the reconditioning of old ones) for the petroleum industry. The company has long made steel containers of all sizes, from giant 150-cubic foot ore containers to small fuel tanks for outboard motors, but the early sixties saw a diversification into other forms of packaging, notably plastic squeeze tubes and bubble packs. By 1963 the company's total employment substantially exceeded 2,000. In sharp contrast was the brief experience of a company engaged in a more basic stage of manufacture, the production of pipes from cast iron scrap: Metters-Clow Pty Ltd. This company's plant did not commence manufacture till the very end of 1961 and, despite the considerable fanfare associated with its official opening by the Premier of Victoria in February 1962, had been sold to its only competitor by 1964.

Both the American-affiliated companies producing hand tools in Australia dominate the market for their particular product. Wiltshire File Co. Pty Ltd began production of a wide range of engineers' and saw files in early 1940 as a joint venture primarily owned by two Australian companies, the Broken Hill Proprietary Company Ltd and McPherson's Pty Ltd. The company claimed that its plant was capable of supplying files in 160 to 170 types, sizes and cuts, representing 90 to 95 per cent of the total Australian file market, and that its factory was capable of dealing with at least 800 dozen files daily. It was not until shortly after the Tariff Board made it clear that the company could expect to supply the great bulk of Australian file requirements that the Nicholson File Company of the United States, which had previously been supplying a substantial portion of the Australian market by exporting from Canada, took up a large minority interest in the Australian firm. Nicholson is the largest file manufacturer in the world and is no doubt at least partially responsible for Wiltshire's claim to have the most mechanized file works for its size in the world. It is not only the Australian file market that Wiltshire dominates: in 1950 the company branched out into the manufacture of forged cutlery and later further widened its activities to include knives made from stainless steel strip. By 1962 the company, operating through Wiltshire Cutlery Co. Pty Ltd, was still the only local manufacturer of forged stainless steel table, dessert, and steak knives.

H. K. Porter Australia Pty Ltd began operations in 1914 under the name of Henry Disston & Sons Inc. (Australasia) Ltd. At this time it was the subsidiary of Henry Disston & Sons Inc. of the U.S. and was engaged in the production of circular saw blades, veneer knives and planer knives. In 1958, following the acquisition of its parent company by H. K. Porter Co. Inc. of Pittsburgh in 1955, the company was sold to an Australian firm, Commonwealth Engineering Co. Ltd. But, in what is surely the only case in Australian industrial history of a foreign company buying *back* a subsidiary it has earlier sold, all the shares in Henry Disston & Sons Pty Ltd were repurchased by H. K. Porter Co. Inc. at the beginning of 1962 and the company renamed shortly afterwards. It is now Australia's principal manufacturer of hand saws.

More than a dozen companies which are either wholly or substantially American in ownership produce what can loosely be termed 'machinery'. Otis Elevator Pty Ltd was one of the first of these to be established: it began the manufacture of its lifts and escalators in the twenties. Ingersoll-Rand (Aust.) Pty Ltd was another early arrival, this time in the field of compressed air equipment, and before World War II it had been joined by another American company, Consolidated Pneumatic Tool Co. (Aust.) Pty Ltd. Though neither company manufactures domestically its entire output, the two companies are among the largest in the Australian industry. Gilbert

& Barker Manufacturing Co. (Aust.) Pty Ltd began the production of petrol pumps for service stations in 1930 and is now substantially the larger of the two Australian producers of these. It is also an important manufacturer of such items as industrial lubricating equipment, airport refuelling equipment, paint reticulation systems, and domestic and industrial oil-burning heaters. Since 1945 many more American companies have entered into the production of plant and machinery in Australia. F.M.C. (Aust.) Ltd was born in 1948 when the American F.M.C. Corporation acquired a two-thirds interest in the old established Australian firm, Austral Otis Engineering Co. Ltd.[8] The company currently produces a wide range of food processing machinery, together with packaging equipment, orchard sprayers, irrigation systems, and even hydraulic brake presses. Following the acquisition of D. W. Bingham & Co. Pty Ltd, food and milk machinery engineers, in 1961, the company was judged to be by far the largest in its field in Australia. Wallace & Tiernan Pty Ltd began the production of chlorinators in 1957 and is one of only two companies engaged in the local manufacture of these items. The company also produces a variety of other engineering products, particularly specialized chemical pumps. In quite a different field, Joy Manufacturing Co. Pty Ltd is the major manufacturer of mining equipment in Australia, while Cummins Diesel Australia is one of the few manufacturers of large diesel engines. Even mechanized cattle feeding equipment is made in Australia by an American firm, Keith Engineering (Aust.) Pty Ltd. In 1962 the manufacturing activities of Addressograph-Multigraph of Australia Pty Ltd were confined to the rebuilding and repair of the office machines it sold, but the assembly of several of the company's products was already being planned and this commenced in 1963.

American-affiliated companies hold a position of particular importance in the production of forklift trucks. Of the four largest names in the industry in the early sixties, three were closely connected with an American firm. One, Towmotor, was produced at that time under licence from the Towmotor Corporation of Cleveland by Freighters Ltd, an Australian firm, and distributed through Towmotor (Aust.) Pty Ltd.[9] A second, Hyster, was originally produced under licence by another Australian company, Sonnerdale Ltd, and distributed by an Australian-American venture, Hyster-Sonnerdale Ltd, but after incurring heavy losses Sonnerdale sold out its interest, and manufacture has been undertaken since 1962 by Hyster Australia Pty Ltd, a wholly-American company. The third well known name is

[8] F.M.C. was originally known as Food Machinery (Aust.) Ltd.

[9] In 1965, however, Towmotor (Aust.) Pty Ltd announced the intention to embark on its own manufacture.

V

Clark, produced by Clark Equipment Australia Pty Ltd, a joint venture between the American Clark Equipment Company and the Australian-owned Tutt Bryant group.

Comparatively few of the American companies in the metal-working industries, apart from those engaged in the production of electrical goods, produce goods for direct sale to the consumer. There are some which do, however. Outboard Marine Australia Pty Ltd, for example, sells chain saws and outboard motors, and the familiarity of the Johnson and Evinrude brandnames among boating enthusiasts testifies to the company's success. Even better known are the products of Gillette (Aust.) Pty Ltd; by 1962, the company had been manufacturing its famous razor blades in Australia for five years, though the razors themselves were still imported. In other fields Ronson Pty Ltd produces cigarette lighters and lighter accessories, Aladdin Industries Pty Ltd kerosene lamps and stoves, and Hobart Manufacturing Co. Pty Ltd a variety of equipment for food preparation and dishwashing.

Sporting Arms Ltd, in which Omark Industries Inc. had a minority interest in 1962, produces 'consumer goods' in the form of sporting firearms, but since the acquisition of the American interest in the company in 1958, the firm has also moved into the production of fastening equipment for the construction industry. The only other company engaged in the production of powder-actuated fastening equipment in Australia, Ramset Fastener (Aust.) Pty Ltd, publicly claims to be 'the largest manufacturer in the field'. It too is partly owned by an American company, the Olin Mathieson Chemical Corporation.

Still the supply of American-affiliated companies in the Australian metal-working industries is not exhausted. Fenner Dodge (Aust.) Pty Ltd is engaged in the production of power transmission equipment, particularly the manufacture of taper lock pulleys. Unbrako (Aust.) Pty Ltd, a company jointly owned by the Standard Pressed Steel Company of the U.S. and McPherson's Ltd of Australia, produces specialized screws. Vickers-Detroit Hydraulics Pty Ltd manufactures a wide range of hydraulic controls for use in the production of earth-moving equipment, forklift trucks, and machinery of many different kinds, while the Lindberg Engineering Company (Aust.) Pty Ltd produces industrial furnaces for use by the automotive and other engineering industries. One of the main companies engaged in the production of iron and steel chain in Australia is Pitt Waddell Bennett Chains Pty Ltd, which, since March 1962, has been owned to the extent of 43 per cent by the Columbus McKinnon Corporation of the U.S. In a not too dissimilar field, the P. & M. Company (Aust.) Pty Ltd has been engaged in the production of specialized metal forgings for rail anchors and scaffold fittings since the twenties.

Another early arrival was the British United Shoe Machinery Company of Australia Pty Ltd which, despite its name, is associated indirectly with what must surely be the world's largest manufacturer of shoemaking machinery, the United Shoe Machinery Corporation of Boston. B.U.S.M. not only supplies the bulk of the shoemaking machinery used in Australia but has also branched out into other fields such as the production of nails, tacks, and pins. An associate company, Tucker Industries Pty Ltd, was one of the four companies producing eyelets in Australia in 1962 and, like B.U.S.M. itself, the company also produces a range of metal pressings. Another of the four companies in the eyelet industry in 1962 was Carr Fastener, a company mentioned earlier in connection with the motor vehicle components industry. This company appears to be the only Australian manufacturer of snap fasteners, principally for use in the clothing industry. The company began this activity in 1928 and now claims to offer 'a complete range of brass snap fasteners, not matched by any other single organization in the world'. (*T.B.R.* 1962e: 4.) Also engaged in the production of light metal pressings in 1962 was American Flange & Manufacturing Co. Inc., a firm specializing in the manufacture of drum closures.

In 1959, P. & H. Power Cranes and Shovels Pty Ltd was established as a joint venture between the American Harnischfeger Corporation and the locally-owned firm, Industrial Engineering Ltd. The company still produces truck cranes and excavators, as its name adequately explains, but early in 1963 it was announced that the Australian shareholder had been bought out. Others also have changed their ownership patterns recently. Richardson Scale Co. (Aust.) Pty Ltd exchanged its majority American shareholder for a majority Canadian one when the latter took over the former in 1963, while since the middle of 1962 the indirect American interest in the Walter Kidde Company (Aust.) Pty Ltd, a subsidiary of Wormald Brothers Industries Ltd engaged in the production of fire extinguishers, has been exchanged for an interest in Wormald Brothers itself.

Reference has already been made to the production of refrigerators by James N. Kirby Manufacturing and G.M.H. G. H. Stuart Pty Ltd, in which the Hill Corporation of the U.S. holds a minority interest, is engaged in the same industry but caters only for the commercial refrigeration market.

Food and Drink

American investment in the Australian food and drink industry probably ranks second only to that in the motor vehicle industry in its capacity to generate controversy over the whole question of foreign investment in this country. In 1963 the Deputy Prime

Minister and Leader of the Country Party, the Rt Hon. J. McEwen, tabled in Federal Parliament a list of thirty-four Australian food companies which had been acquired by foreign concerns during the preceding few years (*Commonwealth Parliamentary Debates*, vol. H. of R. 40 (n.s.), p. 1823), and it is this aspect—the take-over of established Australian companies in an industry where, it is felt, the technology of the invaders is little better than that of the local companies—which has aroused the greatest popular feeling. The extent of American involvement in this take-over movement is considerable and has been carefully noted. On one occasion, a financial editor commented that 'it would take an expert dietician now to show us how to keep body and soul together without helping to send dividends abroad, and especially to the United States.' (*Sydney Morning Herald*, 28 Sept. 1963.)

One of the areas most under the domination of American-controlled companies is the breakfast cereal market. In the 'ready-to-eat' section of that market, the name of Kellogg (Aust.) Pty Ltd has been well known since the firm began manufacturing at its plant in Sydney in 1926. Following the pattern established by its American parent, Kelloggs almost certainly holds by far the largest single share of this market. American interests in this industry were further widened when the National Biscuit Company of the U.S. purchased Purina Grain Foods Pty Ltd in 1960 and formed Nabisco Pty Ltd. Under such names as Vita Brits and Weeties, this company too can claim a large share of the industry. While the company plans an assault on the Australian biscuit market—as none who witnessed the firm's vain struggle for ownership of Swallow & Ariell Ltd in 1964 is soon likely to forget—its main activity in 1965 was in the prepared breakfast cereal market. At the time of writing, the last American firm to enter this market was Ralston Purina, which acquired the Australian firm Robert Harper & Co. Ltd late in 1962.

In the same year that the National Biscuit Company was making its entry into the Australian prepared cereal market, the Quaker Oats Company entered the rolled oats market with the take-over of Creamoata Ltd. With its acquisition, Quaker Oats has become one of the largest suppliers in this field. American influence in the industry was further increased when Corn Products acquired Clifford Love & Co. Ltd, makers of Uncle Toby's Oats, in 1965.

Parsons General Foods Pty Ltd, a company created by the acquisition of the locally-owned Parsons Foods Pty Ltd by General Foods Corporation in 1961, also produces breakfast cereals, but this appears to be becoming a less significant part of the firm's operations following the introduction of a number of General Foods' products to its range. The most important of these is undoubtedly Maxwell House coffee, with which the company claimed to have secured almost 20 per cent of the Australian instant coffee market by 1964.

In the Australian soup market, the most recent American arrival at the time of writing was Campbell's Soups (Aust.) Pty Ltd. This company acquired the food division of Kia Ora Industries Ltd late in 1959 and has since built a large plant at Shepparton, Victoria. In addition to the product lines it acquired by the purchase of part of Kia Ora Industries—Kia Ora soups and cordials—the firm has made some inroads under its own brandnames, Campbells and V-8. But the company is substantially smaller than the first American company in the Australian soup industry, H. J. Heinz Co. Pty Ltd. This firm was established in Australia as early as 1935 and currently dominates the market for canned soup with an estimated share of 40 per cent in 1963. Its share of the total canned and packaged soup market has been estimated at 27 per cent.

H. J. Heinz is also dominant in another section of the food industry: that of baby foods. The company pioneered the manufacture of strained baby foods in Australia and estimated its market share in 1964 at about 80 per cent, with the balance shared between an Australian company selling under the American brandname, Gerber, and a Swiss-owned company, the Nestlé Co. (Aust.) Ltd.

An American company which has an important place in the Australian processed cheese market is Kraft Holdings Ltd. This firm was born in 1926 as Kraft-Walker Cheese Company, a joint venture between an American firm and F. Walker, an Australian who had been producing an unpasteurized cheese previously. In 1950 the name of the firm was changed to its present title and the company made its first public share issue. The company prospered and by July 1954 the 20s. shares, which had been issued at par, had reached 36s. 3d. (Bushnell 1961: 214). However, the Australian shareholding was bought out in 1959 by exchanging the 32 per cent Australian holding in the local company for shares in the American parent company, National Dairy Products Corporation. By the beginning of the sixties, Kraft Holdings was a large producer of both processed and natural cheeses,[10] of sandwich spreads such as Vegemite, of canned and frozen vegetables, and of mayonnaise and salad dressings. In September 1961 the company acquired the fish canning business of Green's Products Ltd, the largest canners of tuna fish and salmon in Australia, and three months later purchased the capital of Dewcrisp Products Ltd, a company engaged in the freezing and canning of peas and in the dehydration of a number of other vegetables. Even before the company's entry into the markets

[10] The company's *Annual Report, 1958* claimed: 'Kraft sales of cheese of all varieties now exceed 50% of the total cheese consumed in Australia.'

for peanut butter and jam in 1962, Kraft was thus a major force in the Australian food industry.

Two other American companies have interests in the Australian dairy products industry, the main one being the Carnation Company Pty Ltd, a firm well known since the early fifties for its production of condensed milk. The other is Swift Australian Co. (Pty) Ltd, a company with small interests in cheese manufacture.

By far the most important activity of Swift Australian, however, concerns the meat industry, where Swift has long been one of the three largest meat exporting companies in Australia. Indeed, Swift Australian began the processing of meat for export before World War I, and that has been its major interest ever since. The take-over of the domestically orientated Mayfair Hams Ltd late in 1963 may herald a change in this emphasis. The only other American investment in the Australian meat industry appears to be Wilson Meats Pty Ltd, a company incorporated in 1935 under the title of Brisbane Wholesale Meat Pty Ltd. The company is currently engaged in the processing of meat for export, but the firm is very much smaller than Swift Australian.

On the fringe of the meat industry are four American companies engaged in the production of sausage casings. Little is known about these firms because of the secretive and closely-knit nature of the industry but all except one of them seem to have begun operations prior to World War II. Their names are British-American Bye-Products Pty Ltd, the Oppenheimer Casing Company of Australia Pty Ltd, Pacific By-Products Pty Ltd, and Sayer & Co. (N.S.W.) Pty Ltd. All appear small.

There has been very little American investment in the Australian confectionery industry. What there has been, however, began early. Lifesavers (Australasia) Ltd seems to have begun in Australia in 1922, but in 1926 MacRobertson Pty Ltd bought out the American interest in the company for £36,000.[11] The Wrigley Company Pty Ltd was incorporated in New South Wales as early as 1919 and seems to have begun manufacturing operations in the twenties. The company currently enjoys a dominant position in the chewing-gum market.

Three American-affiliated companies were engaged in the production of food mixes at the time this survey was conducted in 1962. One was Downyflake Food Corporation Pty Ltd, an American-Australian enterprise whose main interest is the supply of food mixes for the armed services. The company began operations in 1948. Swift Australian has had an interest in the production of pastry and scone mixes for some years, but its operations in this field are

---

[11] MacRobertson (Aust.) Ltd sold this interest for £1,044,000 at the beginning of 1964.

relatively small. The third company is White Wings Pty Ltd, a firm in which the Pillsbury Company of the U.S. purchased a 50 per cent interest from its former sole owners, Gillespie Bros. Holdings Ltd, in 1961. White Wings is a significant supplier of self-raising flour, especially in New South Wales, and was estimated in 1962 to hold more than half the Australian cake-mix market. The firm also produces pudding mixes.

Both the American cola giants, Coca-Cola and Pepsi-Cola, are represented in Australia and both have remarkably similar types of investment. Both produce part of the concentrate from which their drink is made in wholly-owned plants; both have most of their bottling carried out by Australian-owned licensees; and both own one bottling plant. The Coca-Cola Export Corporation supervises the larger of the two operations: Coca-Cola products, including those sold under the Fanta name, were reported to hold 25 per cent of the Sydney soft drink market in 1963, compared with a share of 11 per cent by Pepsi-Cola products. Coca-Cola began its operations in Australia in the late thirties by establishing a number of bottling plants, but all these had been sold by the company by the end of 1950. The company turned its attention to the production of concentrate, in line with world-wide policy to encourage local shareholders to own the bottling plants. In 1954, however, the company repurchased the Sydney bottling plant and this is still a majority-owned firm, Coca-Cola Bottlers (Sydney) Pty Ltd. In 1962 it was the only one of twenty-nine Coca-Cola bottling plants throughout Australia with an American shareholding. Pepsi-Cola Co. of Australia Pty Ltd began local production only in the early fifties and it also devotes attention primarily to product promotion and the supply of concentrate, while encouraging local investors to own bottling facilities. In 1962, only one Pepsi bottling plant was owned by Americans, that of the Pepsi-Cola Metropolitan Bottling Company Inc. in Sydney, and it was stated company policy that this plant would be sold, at least in major part, to Australian investors as soon as it was properly established. The plant was built following the take-over of the former Sydney bottler of Pepsi products, Consolidated Beverage Co. Ltd, by Tarax Drinks Holdings Ltd in 1961.

Chemicals and Related Products, except Pharmaceuticals and Cosmetics

In few Australian industries has foreign capital played a more prominent role than in the chemical industry.[12] Though the industry

---

[12] The Australian Chemical Industry Council (1964: I, 10) has estimated the weighted average foreign ownership of the Australian chemical industry at 61 per cent.

is dominated by the subsidiary of a British company, Imperial Chemical Industries of Australia and New Zealand Ltd, American capital has been of vital significance.

The first American company to be established in the Australian chemical industry, and indeed probably the first to be established in any industry, was the National Ammonia Company of Australia, to which reference has been made in chapter II.[13] Of the companies still in existence in 1962, the two with claims to have been the first in operation in Australia are Australian Cream Tartar Pty Ltd and Stauffer Chemical Co. (Aust.) Pty Ltd. Both companies stem from the formation in 1926 of the Australian Cream Tartar Company Pty Ltd to undertake the manufacture of cream of tartar and tartaric acid. At that time the company was only about one-quarter owned in the U.S., by the Stauffer Company, while Kemball Bishop & Co. Ltd of London and T. J. Edmonds Ltd of New Zealand also held about 25 per cent each. The balance of the shares were held in Australia. The company began manufacturing early in 1928 and widened its field of production to include citric acid in 1935. Over the years various minor changes in ownership occurred, and by the fifties Stauffer held 34 per cent of the ordinary shares in the company, Kemball Bishop 27 per cent, and T. J. Edmonds about 22 per cent. When in 1959 Charles Pfizer Inc. of New York acquired Kemball Bishop, the total American interest, both direct and indirect, increased to 61 per cent. This move was followed by a substantial reorganization in 1961 in which the assets of the Australian Cream Tartar Company Pty Ltd which were engaged in the production of cream of tartar, tartaric acid, and citric acid were sold to the Pfizer Corporation. Pfizer sold its interest in the Australian Cream Tartar Company Pty Ltd to Stauffer and formed another company, Australian Cream Tartar Pty Ltd, to acquire the assets bought from the original company. This new company remains the only Australian producer of tartrates. Stauffer, which now held 61 per cent of the shares in the original company, renamed it Stauffer Chemical Co. (Aust.) Pty Ltd. This company is now the holding company for four operating subsidiaries, most of which were formed before the change in company structure: Chrome Chemicals (Aust.) Pty Ltd, Wesco Paints Pty Ltd, Hunter River Chemicals Pty Ltd, and Pacific Chemical Industries Pty Ltd. The first was formed in 1940 while

[13] Control of both the National Ammonia Company of Australia and an affiliate, the Victoria Ammonia Company Pty Ltd, established in 1912, passed in 1928 from Du Pont (which had acquired a majority interest in them by taking over their parent company in the U.S.) to Imperial Chemical Industries of Australia and New Zealand Ltd. (Information supplied by I.C.I.A.N.Z. Ltd, letter dated 21 Jan. 1965.)

the last commenced production only in 1962. Products manufactured include carbon bisulphide, paints, chrome chemicals, and fluorocarbons.

Three other major American chemical companies began operations before World War II. One of these, the smallest of the three, is Dewey & Almy Pty Ltd.[14] The company commenced local operations in the middle of the thirties and now produces a variety of products including sealing compounds, soldering crystals, construction chemicals, and plastic packaging materials. In 1961 its American parent formed another subsidiary, this time in partnership with an Australian firm, W.J. Manufacturing Co. Ltd. The new firm, Waratah Chemicals Pty Ltd, manufactures phenolic resins.

Another of those with pre-war origins is Monsanto Chemicals (Aust.) Ltd, which began life as a 50/50 partnership with Nicholas Pty Ltd of Melbourne in 1929. The company was initially known as the Southern Cross Chemical Company but its name was changed shortly after formation. As the company grew the Australian shareholding gradually diminished, and before 1962 the last Australian-owned ordinary share had been sold. By that time, Monsanto had become one of the four largest chemical producers in Australia and supplied a very large range of both chemicals and plastic raw materials. Part of the company's recent growth has taken the form of the take-over of two Australian firms in 1958, D.H.A. (Chemicals) Pty Ltd and Beetle-Elliott Pty Ltd, both subsidiaries of Drug Houses of Australia Ltd. Beetle-Elliott had in turn been acquired only two years previously by D.H.A. and was at that time an important manufacturer of plastic moulding powders. Another part of Monsanto's growth has taken the form of the establishment of joint ventures with other companies: in 1960 Australian Fluorine Chemicals Pty Ltd was set up in association with Consolidated Zinc Pty Ltd (now Conzinc Riotinto Australia Ltd) to manufacture fluorocarbons, and the company was still one of only two in that industry in 1964.[15] Also in 1960, Monsanto entered a partnership with Petrochemical Holdings Ltd in the formation of Australian Petrochemicals Pty Ltd, a company producing styrene monomer for use by Monsanto itself in the production of polystyrene.

Union Carbide has been represented in Australia since 1934, when Eveready (Aust.) Pty Ltd was acquired from its British owners. For more than twenty years after that, Eveready specialized in the

[14] Dewey & Almy Pty Ltd has recently changed its name to W. R. Grace Australia Pty Ltd. Since 1962, moreover, it has established a majority holding in a number of new ventures.

[15] The only other manufacturer was Pacific Chemical Industries Pty Ltd, the Stauffer subsidiary mentioned earlier.

production of dry batteries and zinc strip but in 1957 the company began an era of expansion by merging with the Australian chemical company, Timbrol Ltd.[16] The company, renamed Union Carbide Australia Ltd, remains the only Australian producer of dry cells, and in addition manufactures a considerable number of basic industrial chemicals including xanthates, bisphenol A, and chlorine products. Early in 1962 the company further widened the scope of its operations by bringing on stream Australia's second low-density polyethylene plant, at Altona, Victoria.

The Altona petrochemical complex, as the group of petrochemical plants at Altona is widely known, is almost entirely the fruit of American initiative.[17] When the first unit came into operation in August 1961, Australia saw its first large-scale petrochemical capacity. The whole group of plants is built around that of the Altona Petrochemical Company Pty Ltd, a company initially owned by the Vacuum Oil Company Pty Ltd and now, since the division of that company's assets in 1962, owned equally by Mobil Oil Australia Pty Ltd and Esso Standard Eastern Inc., a wholly-owned subsidiary of Standard Oil Co. (N.J.). By steam cracking a heavy petroleum fraction, A.P.C. produces two chemicals, ethylene and butadiene, which form the basis for the rest of the complex. Ethylene is piped in part to the polyethylene plant of Union Carbide already mentioned, and in part to the Altona plant of C.S.R.C.-Dow Pty Ltd. This company, a 50/50 partnership between the American Dow Chemical Company and the Anglo-Australian firm, C.S.R. Chemicals Pty Ltd, uses ethylene to produce both ethylene dichloride and styrene monomer. Part of the latter is converted to polystyrene by C.S.R.C.-Dow's plant at Rhodes, New South Wales, making the company one of only two producers of that material in Australia. (The other, of course, is the Australian Petrochemicals-Monsanto group to which reference has already been made.) Ethylene dichloride is used in the production of vinyl chloride monomer and P.V.C. resin by a fourth member of the complex, B. F. Goodrich-C.S.R. Chemicals Pty Ltd, a company in which the American share interest is 60 per cent. As in the case of polyethylene and polystyrene, there is only one other producer of P.V.C. in Australia. The other basic chemical produced by A.P.C., butadiene, is piped to Australian

---

[16] Shareholders of Timbrol retained a 40 per cent interest in the new company.

[17] It should be stressed that the following description of the Altona complex refers to its structure in the period 1962-3. At the time of writing the construction of several other plants in the area was rumoured or planned, the most significant being a high-density polyethylene plant to be constructed by a large German firm, and a poly-butadiene rubber plant to be built by Australian Synthetic Rubber Co. Ltd.

Synthetic Rubber Co. Ltd, which produces styrene butadiene rubber (SBR synthetic rubber) with the help of styrene monomer drawn from C.S.R.C.-Dow. At the time of writing this company was still the only manufacturer of synthetic rubber in Australia, though this situation appeared certain to change with the imminent establishment of Phillips Imperial Chemicals Ltd—a company jointly owned by I.C.I.A.N.Z. and Phillips Petroleum Company of the U.S.—to produce poly-butadiene rubber. The ownership of Australian Synthetic Rubber is shared between three American or American-owned companies: Esso Standard Oil (Aust.) Ltd, Goodyear Tyre & Rubber Co. (Aust.) Ltd, and Mobil Petroleum Co. Inc.

Unconnected directly with the Altona complex itself but on a site nearby is Australian Carbon Black Pty Ltd. This firm began production of carbon black in 1959, and in 1965 was still the only firm in the Australian industry.

While compared with the massive capital inflow represented by recent American investment in the Australian petrochemical industry they were very small, there were at least four other American-affiliated chemical companies in existence in 1962 which had been set up in Australia since World War II. The first of these was a manufacturer of metallic paint driers and fungicides, Nuodex (Aust.) Pty Ltd, a company set up as a joint Australian-American venture in 1949. The second was Diversey (Australasia) Pty Ltd, set up in 1953 for the production of industrial bactericides and detergents. The third and fourth, Primal Chemical Pty Ltd and Hercules Powder Co. (Aust.) Pty Ltd, engaged in the production of acrylic emulsions and rosin-based products respectively, both began production early in 1962. At that time the former was a wholly-owned subsidiary of Rohm & Haas Company of Philadelphia while the latter was a joint venture between the American Hercules Powder Co. Inc. and the then predominantly Australian-owned Australian Chemical Holdings Ltd.

On the fringe of the chemical industry proper, in what the Commonwealth Statistician terms the 'Inks, Polishes, etc.' industry, at least six American firms are active. Four of these produce adhesives. Perhaps the first on the Australian scene was Bostik Australia Pty Ltd, a member of the British United Shoe Machinery group which was incorporated in Australia under the name of Boston Blacking Co. of Australia Pty Ltd in 1915. The company later changed its name to B.B. Chemical Co. of Australia Pty Ltd and again to its present title in 1962. The firm produces industrial adhesives and sealing compounds for a variety of industry. Another old-established company in this industry is Pabco Products Pty Ltd. Though this company was established in Australia during the thirties to serve the bituminous-roofing market, it has long been a major supplier of adhesives to the floor-covering industry. The company is also well known for its anti-corrosive paints. In 1949 Casco Adhesives Pty Ltd was established for the production of adhesives and glues from casein. Later the firm changed its name to Swift & Borden Chemical Co. Pty Ltd and widened its range of products. In 1962 the company was still an Australian-American venture but one year later the Australian interest was sold and the company's name was again changed, to Borden Chemical Co. Pty Ltd. Sidney Cooke (Printing Inks) Pty Ltd, in which an American firm has a minority holding, is also engaged in the supply of adhesives, though printing inks and industrial coatings make up a significant part of the firm's production.

Ferro Corporation (Aust.) Pty Ltd first began operations in Australia in association with Armco International Corporation, but shortly afterwards the company set up its own facilities in Sydney.[18] Since this beginning late in the thirties, the company has diversified from its principal product, porcelain enamels, into the production of enamelling equipment and other related lines, and has even entered the P.V.C. compounding industry. In quite a different field is S. C. Johnson & Son Pty Ltd. This company, which began production in Australia in 1929, is now widely known for its domestic and industrial polishes.

Cyanamid Australia Pty Ltd, established in Australia under the name of Titan Pty Ltd when an Australian firm of that name was acquired in 1951, is engaged in the production of tennis gut and surgical sutures from beef intestines. Despite the scope of Cyanamid's operations in the U.S., this activity was the only one belonging to the company which was actually manufacturing in Australia in mid-1962. Later that year, however, the fermentation of broad spectrum antibiotics, particularly tetracycline drugs, was started by another subsidiary, Cyanamid-D.H.A. Pty Ltd.

Pharmaceuticals, Toilet Preparations, Cosmetics

American-owned companies play a particularly vital role in the Australian pharmaceutical industry. Like investment in other sectors, however, this is not a new development. The largest American firm in the industry, and one of the two largest firms in the industry as a whole, is Parke, Davis & Co. This firm began operations in Australia as early as 1902 and set up manufacturing facilities at Rosebery in 1918. In 1954 operations were moved to new premises at

[18] Initially the company operated under the name Ferro-Enamels (Aust.) Pty Ltd.

Caringbah and the company now produces a very wide range of pharmaceuticals and veterinary preparations. In 1960 it was stated that the company was then producing about 350 different products, including the important antibiotic, chloramphenicol. Sterling Pharmaceuticals Pty Ltd is another large American company which had its origins in Australia before World War I, in the establishment of Frederick Stearns & Co. in 1910. When the American parent of Frederick Stearns was bought out by Sterling Drug Inc. in 1944, the local operation also changed hands. Sterling Drug had had another interest in Australia for a number of years, through a 50 per cent equity with a German firm in Bayer Pharma Pty Ltd. This firm was set up in 1935 for the compression of aspirin tablets from ingredients imported from Germany, but on the outbreak of war the German shareholding was acquired by the Controller of Enemy Property from where it eventually passed, in 1958, to Sterling Drug. Since that time, the manufacture of Bayer products in Australia has been conducted by Sterling Pharmaceuticals.[19] The whole group, through its three main operating divisions, Nyal Company, Winthrop Laboratories, and Glenbrook Laboratories, produces a very considerable number of pharmaceuticals, both ethical and proprietary.

Abbott Australian Holdings Pty Ltd, too, commenced operations many years ago. The firm was established under the name of Abbott Laboratories Pty Ltd in 1936, and through its operating subsidiaries now produces not only pharmaceutical products but also veterinary preparations and a range of basic chemicals used in the manufacture of pharmaceutical products. This last, the production of the basic chemicals used in drug production, was still rather rare in the Australian industry in 1962. Most American-owned plants, like those of other nationalities, imported the great bulk of their drug requirements. But there were cases other than that of Abbott where companies did engage in basic chemical manufacture for the pharmaceutical industry. Monsanto Chemicals, for example, had been manufacturing the chemical used in aspirin manufacture for very many years and by 1962 was also producing a range of sulpha drugs. Another example was Merck Sharp & Dohme (Aust.) Pty Ltd which since 1956 had produced the corticosteroid hormones in Australia. This company, which began Australian operations in 1953, is understood to be engaged also in the manufacture of thiabendazole, a chemical used in the treatment of parasites in farm animals. The firm specializes in the supply of ethical pharmaceuticals and veterinary products. (Reference has already been made

[19] The company apparently went to considerable pains to hide this fact, as the case of Bayer Pharma Pty Ltd *versus* Henry H. York & Co. Pty Ltd startlingly shows. For one view of the case, see *Nation*, 2 May 1964.

to the production of tetracycline drugs by Cyanamid-D.H.A. Pty Ltd, but this commenced after 30 June 1962.)

Five more American companies are engaged primarily in the supply of ethical pharmaceuticals. These are Smith Kline & French Laboratories (Aust.) Ltd, Eli Lilly (Aust.) Pty Ltd, Upjohn Pty Ltd, Wyeth Pharmaceuticals Pty Ltd, and Andrews Laboratories Pty Ltd. Wyeth and Andrews, however, are intimately connected with companies whose main interest lies outside the ethical field.

Some companies blend operations in both ethical and proprietary fields. Parke, Davis, Sterling, and Abbott have already been noted in this regard. The Pfizer Corporation began its pharmaceutical manufacturing operations in Australia in 1960 with primary emphasis on antibiotics, particularly the '-mycin' group, but has since entered the volatile market for popular slimming agents. Charles McDonald-Mead Johnson Pty Ltd, a company formed by the acquisition of the Australian firm Charles McDonald Pty Ltd in 1960, is mainly involved in the production of ethicals, but entered the market for slimming agents at the time of the American take-over. Though this début was not a lasting success, the company continues to supply a number of other proprietary lines, including diet supplements. Much longer has been the experience of Warner-Lambert Pty Ltd, one of the very first American companies established in Australia after the turn of the century. Warner-Lambert is now the holding company for three operating subsidiaries, one of which produces ethical pharmaceuticals, one proprietary products, and one the well-known range of Richard Hudnut beauty preparations. International Home Products (Aust.) Pty Ltd, which operated for many years under the name of Whitehall Pharmacal Company, produces a range of proprietaries, but its associated company, Wyeth Pharmaceuticals, is in the field of ethicals. Vick Products (Pty) Ltd, long known for its proprietary products, is also engaged in the supply of ethicals and veterinary products. The firm is now renamed Richardson-Merrell Pty Ltd. E. C. De Witt & Co. (Aust.) Pty Ltd, on the other hand, appears to concentrate principally on the manufacture of proprietary medicines, while Watkins Products Inc. produces toilet preparations and grocers' sundries in addition to proprietaries.

Johnson & Johnson Pty Ltd is one of the most remarkable firms in the industry, though many of its products can only with difficulty be termed 'pharmaceuticals'. The company was formed in Australia in 1932 and has been a household word almost ever since. It is the only Australian manufacturer of plaster dressings and holds a dominant position also in the local market for baby powder. Under its various brandnames, the firm is an important supplier of such diverse products as bandages, sanitary napkins, surgical sutures, contraceptives, and tooth brushes. At the beginning of the sixties the company purchased a majority shareholding in the locally-owned Andrews Laboratories, mentioned above, and thereby made a significant entry into the market for ethical pharmaceuticals.

The Australian toothpaste market is entirely the province of foreign-owned companies, and the dominant firms are American. Several of the pharmaceutical companies already mentioned produce their own brands—International Home Products, Sterling Pharmaceuticals, and Parke, Davis, for example, produce Kolynos, Nyal and Euthymol respectively—but the main American brands are Ipana and Colgate. The former is produced by Bristol-Myers Co. Pty Ltd, a company which set up manufacturing operations in Australia at the beginning of the twenties. Though the company has diversified into the manufacture of deodorants, shaving cream, and other toilet articles, the company was estimated to hold about 25 per cent of the whole Australian toothpaste market in 1962. At that time, this was a share exceeded only by Colgate, which, however, was estimated to hold roughly half the market. Colgate-Palmolive Pty Ltd began Australian manufacture at about the same time as Bristol-Myers and is also a large supplier of toilet requisites. Its Palmolive toilet soap has long been fully as well known as its Colgate toothpaste. The company also manufactures Ajax cleanser, introduced to the Australian market in 1956, and Fab detergent, introduced in 1960 to challenge the near-monopoly position held in the washing-powder market up to that time by the British group, Unilever. In 1964 Colgate-Palmolive claimed that 98 per cent of Australian homes used at least one of the company's products regularly.[20]

On a very much smaller scale, Cuticura Pty Ltd has been engaged in the production of toilet soap, ointment, and talcum powder, while Purex Australia Pty Ltd, an associate company, produces household cleansers. Purex was established in Australia many years ago under the name of Old Dutch Pty Ltd.

In the Australian cosmetics market, almost all the names which spring speedily to mind are American: Revlon, Helena Rubinstein, Max Factor, Elizabeth Arden, Richard Hudnut, Toni, Coty, Cutex, Mum, Pond's, Dorothy Gray, Odo-ro-no—all are the products of American-owned firms currently operating in Australia, and the list of brands could doubtless be extended. One of the odd quirks about the American domination of the industry is that one of its two widely-accepted leaders, Helena Rubinstein Pty Ltd, had its origin

[20] In 1963 Colgate claimed to hold 50 per cent of the Australian market for toilet soap, 50 per cent of the toothpaste market, 60 per cent of the scouring cleanser market, and 45 per cent of the household detergent market (*A.F.R.*, 2 July 1963).

not in the establishment of a local subsidiary by a large American corporation but in the genesis of the Helena Rubinstein organization itself: Miss Rubinstein established her first business in Melbourne and Helena Rubinstein Pty Ltd was formed soon afterwards in 1909. Though the company is now wholly owned in the United States, affiliated companies in the Rubinstein organization seem to bear a sisterly relationship towards each other rather than one of the parent-child variety.

In all other cases, however, the relationship is of the traditional kind. A recent survey of the industry placed Max Factor & Co. in a position of leadership with Helena Rubinstein, followed closely by Revlon (Aust.) Pty Ltd and Elizabeth Arden Pty Ltd. All four companies produce a wide variety of cosmetics. Chesebrough-Pond's International Ltd and Coty (England) Ltd are also important producers. The former established manufacturing facilities in Australia in 1953 and further widened the scope of its operations by the take-over of the local branch of the Northam Warren Corporation in 1959-60, at the same time that its parent was absorbing the Northam Warren Corporation itself in the U.S. Coty (England) Ltd, as its name betrays, has a British company as its immediate parent.

In the field of hair preparations, the name of Richard Hudnut has already been mentioned in connection with Warner-Lambert. The company produces other cosmetics also but is probably best known for these. Gillette (Aust.) Pty Ltd is prominent in the market for hair cosmetics, too, because of its production of goods sold under the Toni name. Waval Thermal of Australia Pty Ltd specializes in the supply of professional hair waving materials.

At the time of writing, it appeared that two more American names had entered the local industry since 30 June 1962: Helene Curtis (Aust.) Pty Ltd and Avon Products Pty Ltd. Both companies appeared to have begun manufacture since mid-1962 while a third, Dorothy Gray Pty Ltd, seemed to be in the distribution phase.

A company little known to the public but one which produces a substantial part of the lipstick made in Australia is Kolmar (Aust.) Pty Ltd. The company's output is understood to be sold under several of the leading brandnames.

Oil Products

Even those familiar with the Australian oil industry in mid-1962 may be surprised to learn that this section describes the activities of no fewer than five American-affiliated companies. Three of them are very large firms engaged in the refining end of the industry, with names well known to all, while two of them are very small.

One of the large companies is Mobil Oil Australia Pty Ltd, with its subsidiaries Petroleum Refineries (Aust.) Pty Ltd and Emoleum (Aust.) Ltd. This group operated under the name of Vacuum Oil Co. Pty Ltd for many years and, through the Standard-Vacuum Oil Company of the U.S., was jointly owned by Standard Oil Co. (New Jersey) and Socony Mobil Oil Co. As mentioned previously, the assets of Standard-Vacuum were divided between its two shareholders in March 1962, and Mobil Oil Australia is now owned wholly by Socony Mobil Oil, through Mobil Petroleum Co., Inc.[21] The origins of the group in Australia go back before the turn of the century, but at that time distribution of kerosene and other oil products was the main concern. The blending of lubrication oil and grease began at an early stage but it was not until after World War II that the company established oil refining facilities. Its first oil refinery came on stream at Altona in 1949, and this was greatly expanded during the fifties. In 1960 the company purchased the small Australian firm, Emoleum, a company manufacturing bituminous emulsions, but much more important was the heavy investment at that time in the Altona petrochemical complex and the new oil refinery near Halletts Cove, South Australia. When the latter came on stream in March 1963, the Mobil group controlled more than 24 per cent of total Australian crude oil refining capacity. The company also has extensive investment in marketing facilities and in oil exploration.

The second and third of the three large companies are affiliated. One of them, Australian Oil Refining Pty Ltd, is a wholly-owned subsidiary of the California Texas Oil Corporation of the U.S., a company representing the interests of both Standard Oil of California and Texaco, Inc. In 1962 this firm owned the largest single refinery in Australia, a plant with capacity equal to almost 26 per cent of the Australian total. Its output is marketed through the wholly-American affiliate, Caltex Oil (Aust.) Pty Ltd, and the predominantly Australian-owned firms, H. C. Sleigh Ltd and Ampol Petroleum Ltd, in both of which Caltex has a small financial interest. The other major American-affiliated firm in the industry is Bitumen & Oil Refineries (Aust.) Ltd, or Boral Ltd as it is now known. The Caltex group held a 40 per cent interest in this company at its inception in 1946 but this had declined to only 26 per cent by mid-1962. Since that time the American interest has fallen even further. Though the company has wide and ever-growing

---

[21] Some of Vacuum Oil's original assets, however, are now controlled by Standard Oil Company (N.J.): reference has been made to its interest in the Altona petrochemical complex, and in addition the firm has a 26 per cent interest in Petroleum Refineries (Aust.) Pty Ltd.

W

interests outside the oil industry—in coal mining and quarrying, for example—its primary activity still remains the refining of crude oil. Compared with those of other producers, both its refineries (one at Matraville, New South Wales, and one at Hamilton, Queensland) are small.

In the shadows of the giant corporations grow two very small firms dealing in oil products. Both began manufacturing operations in 1961. One, Lubrizol Australia, produces oil additives while the other, Wynn's Friction Proofing (Aust.) Pty Ltd, manufactures lubricants.

Since 1962, two more American-affiliated firms have made investments in oil refining—Australian Lubricating Oil Refinery Pty Ltd and Amoco Australia Pty Ltd. The former, as its name implies, is engaged in the production of lubricating oil, and when it came on stream in March 1964 it was declared to be the largest plant of its type in the southern hemisphere. H. C. Sleigh Ltd and Ampol Petroleum Ltd each hold 25 per cent of the equity while the Caltex group holds the remaining 50 per cent. Amoco Australia is a wholly-owned subsidiary of Standard Oil of Indiana. Its Brisbane refinery came on stream late in 1965.

Miscellaneous Products

American capital has made its impact felt in a multitude of other industries. The paper products industry is one of these. St Regis-Williams Pty Ltd, in which the St Regis Paper Company of the U.S. has a 50 per cent interest, holds a substantial share of the markets for multi-wall paper bags and Sisalkraft building materials through its two operating subsidiaries Bates (Australasia) Pty Ltd and Australian Sisalkraft Pty Ltd. The latter company began operations in 1932 and the former was started even earlier. Kimberly-Clark of Australia Pty Ltd also began operations in the thirties and its paper tissue products, Kleenex, Dawn, and Kotex are now widely known. Also engaged in the production of tissue products is Bowater-Scott Australia Pty Ltd, a joint venture between the giant British group, Bowater Paper Corporation Ltd, and Scott Paper Company of the U.S. This firm appeared on the Australian scene in the late fifties but already two of its brandnames, Scotties and Sorbent, are well known. The company is engaged in the production of tissue paper as well as in its conversion. Lily Cups Ltd, which began Australian operations by acquiring the paper cup division of its former licensee, Johnell Ltd (or Kia Ora Industries Ltd, as it had been known), in 1961, caters for the specialized market for disposable cups. One company whose products are little seen by the general public is Textile Cones and Tubes Pty Ltd. This firm stems from an old-established Australian family enterprise, Morris & Walker Pty Ltd, which in 1947 joined with another Australian firm and two foreign companies to form the present company. In 1962 the company was one-third owned by Sonoco Products Company of the U.S., and in addition to supplying a wide range of industrial containers made from paper was the only Australian manufacturer of paper cones for the textile industry. Australian Inhibitor Paper Pty Ltd, which produces anti-corrosive paper on a small scale, is another jointly-owned company.

One section of the paper products industry, the market for paper dress patterns, is effectively dominated by three American companies: Butterick Publishing Co. Pty Ltd (which also owns the Vogue trademark), McCall Publishing Co. (Australasia) Pty Ltd, and Simplicity Patterns Pty Ltd. All three firms have been operating in Australia for more than twenty years, though it appears that none produces in Australia the actual tissue paper from which the patterns are cut.

The Australian abrasives market is very largely the province of American-affiliated companies. Australian Abrasives Pty Ltd is by far the largest producer of bonded abrasives and has been ever since commencing production in 1940. Though there are small Australian and British shareholdings in the company, it is predominantly owned by two American firms, the Norton Company and the Carborundum Company. Both these American companies also have subsidiaries operating in the Australian market for surface-coated abrasives. Norton Australia Pty Ltd, or Behr-Manning (Aust.) Pty Ltd as it was known till 1963, set up a plant immediately after World War II for the production of pressure sensitive tape (sold under the Bear brand) and the conversion of imported rolls of abrasives to finished products. In 1952 the company extended its manufacturing activities to include the production of abrasive rolls from imported grains, and until 1961 remained the only company producing these in Australia. Carborundum Australia Pty Ltd commenced the conversion of imported rolls to finished products in 1956 and the production of abrasive rolls themselves in 1962. A third American company in the surface-coated abrasives industry began conversion operations before Carborundum, in 1953, but did not commence production of rolls till 1963. This was Minnesota Mining & Manufacturing (Aust.) Pty Ltd, a company, like Norton, also engaged in the manufacture of pressure sensitive tapes. In 1962 there was only one other major company in the Australian industry, and that was British-owned.

Four American-affiliated companies produce foundation garments in Australia. The largest firm in the industry is Australian-owned, though several of its main products are made under licence to American firms. In the second largest firm, however, one estimated to hold between 20 and 25 per cent of the total market, there is a substantial American minority holding. This is Dowd Associates Pty Ltd, which markets the Hickory brand. Formfit of Australia Ltd, until recently known as Merica Foundations Ltd, is also regarded as one of the chief producers and since 1959 a majority of the company's shares have been held by an American firm. The most recent arrival at the time of writing was the Lovable Brassiere Company (Aust.) Pty Ltd, another Australian-American joint venture, which was claiming from 12½ to 15 per cent of the brassiere market within three years of its commencement of manufacture in Australia in 1961. The fourth American firm in the industry, H. W. Gossard Co. (Aust.) Pty Ltd, was incorporated in Australia as early as 1931. It is the only wholly American firm of the four, but it is very small.

At least three other American firms have made investments in the Australian clothing industry but of these only one remained in 1962. The survivor was Jantzen (Aust.) Ltd, a firm initially formed in 1928 to specialize in the production of sports wear and swim suits. Both the other firms were engaged in the manufacture of lingerie. One, Julius Kayser (Aust.) Pty Ltd, was formed in 1929 by Julius Kayser & Co. of the U.S. and three local firms, Australian Knitting Mills Ltd, Yarra Falls Ltd, and Marks & Saulwick Pty Ltd. It became wholly American in ownership during the thirties but was sold in 1953 to a British company which itself had been formed by Julius Kayser & Co. The company now operates under the name of Kayser Pty Ltd. The other American firm in the industry, Holeproof Hosiery Co. (Aust.) Pty Ltd, was established at about the same time. It, too, was a jointly-owned company, this time with the Australian firm of Staley & Staley Ltd, but the American interest was sold a few years later.

American interest in the Australian textile industry has been very small. The Aberfoyle Manufacturing Company (Aust.) Pty Ltd was established as a wholly-American subsidiary in the thirties to mercerize cotton yarn, but before the end of June 1962 the company had been acquired by an Australian firm, Qualitaire Mills Pty Ltd. Much shorter was the life of Textured Yarns (Aust.) Pty Ltd. This firm, in which there was in any case only a minority American holding, operated for only a few years in the mid-fifties and was never large. Burlington Inc. of the U.S. held an interest which fell substantially short of 25 per cent in Burlington Mills (Aust.) Ltd when that company began operations immediately after World War

II, but even this small investment was repatriated early in the fifties.[22] The only American direct investment in the Australian textile industry at 30 June 1962 appears to have been a minority holding in Artflex Fabrics Australia Pty Ltd, a small company producing knitted elastic fabrics for the foundation garment industry.

Another industry in which American interest has been negligible is the plastic products industry. Only three small companies had substantial American shareholdings in 1962: Dentsply (Aust.) Pty Ltd, a firm producing artificial teeth; Amalgamated Plastics (Holdings) Pty Ltd, producing plastic products for household use; and U.K. Optical Bausch & Lomb Pty Ltd, producing frames for both sunglasses and spectacles. In no case was the American interest more than fifteen years old in 1962.

In the production of Australian furnishings, too, American companies have played a small part. Simmons Bedding Company began operations here in 1958 with the acquisition of John Lawler & Sons Pty Ltd, and is now a growing force in the mattress market. The only other American firm in the furnishing industry appears to be Hunter Douglas Ltd. This company dominates the venetian blind market and has in recent years diversified into the production of aluminium awnings, acoustic ceilings, building materials, and insect screens. The firm was established in Australia in 1954 and merged with an Australian firm, Mello-Lite Ltd, in 1961. Even before the merger, Hunter Douglas was reported to be Australia's largest single consumer of aluminium.

Dominating another industry is Kodak (Australasia) Pty Ltd. This company was formed in 1908 to merge the interests of an Australian firm, Baker & Rouse, with those of the Eastman Kodak Company. Baker & Rouse had been manufacturing sensitized materials in Australia since 1886, and by 1906 claimed to supply a substantial portion of the Australian demand for bromide and other sensitized papers at the same prices as similar papers were sold in Britain. The Australian partners were even engaged in the production of dry plates, though they supplied only a small part of the total market. With the imposition of a higher tariff on films in 1907, Baker visited the Eastman Kodak Company, for whom he had been the Australian agent for some years, and in the following year the two groups merged their interests, with the American firm holding a bare majority of the equity in the new company. The production of sensitized film was begun almost at once and within a few years the company claimed to supply 80 per cent of the Australian market for films. Ever since that time Kodak has dominated the Australian

[22] Information supplied by Bradford Cotton Mills Ltd, letter dated 18 Nov. 1964.

photographic market, though in recent years the company has been under increasingly severe pressure from imported products. In 1957 the company diversified into the production of box cameras and by 1962 was still one of only two producers so engaged in Australia. Now, however, the Australian shareholding is only nominal.

In the glass industry, Corning Glass Works commenced the local assembly of glass envelopes for the cathode ray tubes in television receivers in March 1959. The Tariff Board estimated that in 1960 Corning supplied about 50 per cent of the Australian market for these television bulbs, with the great majority of the remainder being imports. By the time of the Board's 1964 Report, Corning was one of two producers but was much the larger of the two. Indirectly affiliated with Corning is Australian Fibre Glass Pty Ltd. This firm was initially formed by Australian Consolidated Industries Ltd under the name of Glass Fibres (Aust.) Pty Ltd but since 1959, when the name was changed to its present form, 40 per cent of the equity has been held by the Owens-Corning Fibre Glass Corporation of the U.S. The company is the only Australian producer of fibre glass wool and the continuous filaments from which fibre glass textiles are produced.

In the market for writing instruments, the products of Parker-Eversharp (Aust.) Pty Ltd, Scripto Pens of Australia Pty Ltd, and W. A. Sheaffer Pen Co. (Aust.) Pty Ltd are well known. As far as manufacturing is concerned, Parker and Scripto are mainly engaged in the assembly of ball pens, while Sheaffer appears to concentrate more on pens and propelling pencils. All three companies began Australian operations during the fifties.

There was only one American firm with an investment in the Australian footwear industry in 1962. This was the International Shoe Company, which acquired a 60 per cent interest in Perry Shoes Pty Ltd in 1960. Since 1962 International Shoe has acquired interests in two more Australian firms, but its interest in Perry Shoes has been sold to the Australian shareholder, Bedggood & Co. Pty Ltd, which closed down the plant in 1963. A much more significant American investment in this industry occurred at the very beginning of the thirties when the Selby Shoe Company of the U.S. established Selby Shoes (Aust.) Pty Ltd in conjunction with the Sydney retailer, David Jones Ltd. This company prospered and flourished but the American equity, which was never more than 40 per cent, was sold to David Jones in 1959. In the related field of orthopaedic appliances, Scholl Manufacturing Co. Pty Ltd has been active since soon after World War II. The company is indirectly 51 per cent American, with an Australian firm, Associated Leathers Ltd, holding the balance of the shares.

The activities of the three companies which remain to be described cover widely different industries. A. G. Spalding & Bros. (Australasia) Pty Ltd, which began Australian manufacture in the twenties, produces a wide range of sporting goods, and Pearls Pty Ltd, an Australian-American company established in 1956, produces cultured pearls. Philip Morris (Aust.) Ltd, the last of the three, commenced cigarette production in 1955 and by 1965 claimed to have won almost 10 per cent of the fiercely competitive cigarette market.

Appendix B

Manufacturing Operations of Participating Companies

Part II of the first questionnaire used in the survey of American investment sought information parallel to that supplied by all manufacturing establishments to the Commonwealth Bureau of Census and Statistics. Considerable detail was requested for the financial year 1961/2, while information on the main aggregates of employment, wages, cost of materials, value of output, value of land and buildings, and value of plant and machinery was sought for as many of the previous years as possible. Relatively few companies were able to provide data for a useful number of years before 1961/2, but 100 were prepared to provide substantially complete data for 1961/2 itself. Indeed, willingness to complete Questionnaire I was taken as evidence of willingness to participate in the survey as a whole, as mentioned in chapter I. Of these 100 replies, one has not been included in the following tables because the company concerned began manufacture in Australia only in the very last weeks of 1961/2.

Information supplied by participating companies relating to their operations before 1961/2 is discussed in part in the body of the text. Some reference is also made there to the 1961/2 data, and the following tables present most of the material on which the discussion in the text is based. It is most important that they be read in conjunction with the numerous explanatory notes which follow them.

Except in Table B-2, figures not in parentheses refer to the manufacturing establishments of the ninety-nine participating companies included in the tables. Figures in parentheses refer to total manufacturing operations in the industry mentioned, and are drawn from tables published by the Commonwealth Bureau of Census and Statistics.

TABLE B-1 American-affiliated Companies, by Industry and Number of Factories Operating at 30 June 1962

Industry	One factory	Companies with Two factories	Companies with Three factories	More than three factories	Total factories[a]
Industrial chemicals	8	1	1	1	17
Pharmaceuticals and toilet preparations	9	1	..	..	11
Plant, equipment, and machinery	17	1	2	..	25
Electrical machinery, cables, and apparatus	9	5	..	..	19
Motor vehicle construction and assembly, and motor bodies	2	..	1	2	19
Motor accessories	5	..	..	..	5
Other metal products	7	1	1	1	25
Foundation garments	2	..	..	1	10
Food, drink, tobacco	5	..	..	3	28
Paper, stationery, printing, etc.	4	..	..	1	9
Other products	4	2	1	1	22
Total	72	11	6	10	190

[a] Note that in this table *companies* are classified, according to their main activity, by industry. This implies that not all *factories* actually operate in the industries shown.

329

TABLE B-2 Size of Australian and American-affiliated Factories, by Employment

Size of factories by employment	American-affiliated factories			All factories operating in Australian industry		
	Number	Employment	Percentage of total employment[a]	Number	Employment	Percentage of total employment
1–10	8	58	0·1	42,293	158,279	14·2
11–20	13	199	0·4	6,969	101,898	9·2
21–50	32	1,026	2·2	5,174	162,948	14·6
51–100	31	2,254	4·7	1,886	131,501	11·8
101–200	26	3,600	7·6	992	139,447	12·5
201–300	13	3,195	6·7	320	78,110	7·0
301–400	6	2,146	4·5	130	44,825	4·0
401–500	6	2,665	5·6	86	38,347	3·4
501–750	9	5,722	12·0	118	72,437	6·5
751–1000	2	1,513	3·2	46	39,779	3·6
Over 1000	10	25,176	52·9	66	144,844	13·0
Total	156	47,554	100·0	58,080	1,112,415	100·0

a Ten companies, which between them owned 34 factories employing 9,044 persons, gave 'consolidated' data for their several plants, thus making their classification by size impossible. Percentages shown leave the employment of these factories out of consideration.

TABLE B–3 Size of Australian and American-affiliated Factories, by Employment and Industry

Industry	1 to 50 persons F	1 to 50 persons P	51 to 100 persons F	51 to 100 persons P	More than 100 persons F	More than 100 persons P	Not classifiable F	Not classifiable P	Total F	Total P	Size of average factory (persons)
Industrial chemicals	2 (249)	21 (2,847)	4 (19)	284 (1,301)	4 (27)	606 (8,100)	7	2,216	17 (295)	3,127 (12,248)	184 (42)
Pharmaceuticals and toilet preparations	.. (165)	.. (2,048)	6 (28)	419 (2,020)	3 (18)	1,362 (3,846)	2	964	11 (211)	2,745 (7,914)	250 (38)
Plant, equipment, and machinery	9 (2,420)	255 (26,447)	2 (148)	168 (10,268)	12 (176)	3,518 (41,155)	3	229	26 (2,744)	4,170 (77,870)	160 (28)
Electrical machinery, cables, and apparatus	4 (1,158)	119 (11,532)	3 (73)	210 (5,169)	7 (118)	3,223 (36,469)	2	2,855	16 (1,349)	6,407 (53,170)	400 (39)
Motor vehicle construction and assembly, and motor bodies	1 (2,143)	30 (12,385)	1 (23)	51 (1,549)	14 (34)	23,820 (32,043)	..	..	16 (2,200)	23,901 (45,977)	1,494 (21)
Motor accessories	2 (252)	39 (2,318)	1 (16)	69 (1,169)	2 (32)	927 (8,803)	..	..	5 (300)	1,035 (12,290)	207 (41)
Other metal products	5 (16,831)	114 (105,881)	4 (399)	345 (27,934)	14 (370)	5,799 (175,923)	4	448	27 (17,600)	6,706 (309,738)	248 (18)
Foundation garments	3 (47)	114 (625)	5 (7)	320 (495)	2 (12)	506 (2,867)	..	..	10 (66)	940 (3,987)	94 (60)
Food, drink, tobacco	9 (6,773)	162 (50,044)	2 (232)	147 (16,318)	7 (246)	2,459 (63,754)	10	512	28 (7,251)	3,280 (130,116)	117 (18)
Paper, stationery, printing, etc.	4 (2,463)	108 (28,049)	1 (158)	89 (10,965)	3 (118)	515 (35,007)	4	250	12 (2,739)	962 (74,021)	80 (27)
Other products	14	321	2	152	4	1,282	2	1,570	22	3,325	151
Total	53	1,283	31	2,254	72	44,017	34	9,044	190	56,598	298
Total manufacturing	(54,436)	(423,125)	(1,886)	(131,501)	(1,758)	(557,789)			(58,080)	(1,112,415)	(19)

F = Factories; P = Persons.

TABLE B–4   Employment in Australian and American-affiliated Factories, by Industry and State[a]

Industry	N.S.W.	Vic.	Qld	S.A.	W.A.	Tas.	Not classifiable[b]	Total[a]
Industrial chemicals	265 (6,847)	553 (3,703)	c (414)	c (858)	c	c	2,216	3,034 (12,091)
Pharmaceuticals and toilet preparations	2,745 (4,214)	c (3,066)	c	c (473)	c	..	..	2,745 (7,910)
Plant, equipment, and machinery	1,901 (30,386)	2,267 (27,023)	c (5,950)	c (10,154)	c (3,432)	c (519)	..	4,168 (77,464)
Electrical machinery, cables, and apparatus	5,459 (32,432)	c (14,844)	c (2,235)	c (2,063)	c (1,061)	(283)	..	6,407 (52,918)
Motor vehicle construction and assembly, and motor bodies	2,416 (10,976)	11,767 (18,991)	c (2,193)	9,049	c (2,201)	c	..	23,901 (45,746)
Motor accessories	c (4,841)	c (5,678)	c (337)	c (1,095)	c	c	..	1,035 (12,273)
Other metal products	1,546 (143,025)	2,720 (84,800)	1,314 (26,502)	224 c	74 c	762 c	..	6,640 (308,574)
Foundation garments	c c	c (1,985)	c	..	..	..	..	940 (3,981)
Food, drink, tobacco	317 (40,202)	933 (38,999)	1,489 (25,895)	c (11,362)	22 (7,132)	(5,000)	512	3,273 (128,590)
Paper, stationery, printing, etc.	315 (31,006)	397 (24,940)	c (6,031)	c (4,698)	c (2,906)	(4,258)	250	962 (73,839)
Other products	860	2,341		25		..	..	3,325
Total	17,075	22,589	3,417	9,359	250	762	2,978	56,430
Total manufacturing	(455,442)	(372,745)	(99,657)	(97,204)	(49,812)	(29,691)	..	(1,104,551)

[a] Employment figures in Tables B–2 and B–3 are based on average employment over the period of operation of each plant, whereas figures in this and succeeding tables have been converted to annual equivalents.

[b] Four companies, each owning plants in more than one state, gave 'consolidated' data for their several plants, thus making their classification by location impossible.

[c] Not available for separate disclosure. Figures included in total.

TABLE B-5 Employment in Australian and American-affiliated Factories, by Industry, Category of Employee, and Sex[a]

Industry	Average number of persons employed								
	Managerial and clerical staff		Chemists, draftsmen, etc.		Wages staff		Total[b]		
	Male	Female	Male	Female	Male	Female	Male	Female	Persons
Industrial chemicals	348 (1,489)	205 (875)	349 (958)	4 (70)	1,858 (8,125)	270 (531)	2,555 (10,610)	479 (1,481)	3,034 (12,091)
Pharmaceuticals and toilet preparations	308 (725)	405 (776)	108 (392)	51 (133)	1,014 (2,395)	859 (3,443)	1,430 (3,548)	1,315 (4,362)	2,745 (7,910)
Plant, equipment, and machinery	701 (8,552)	395 (4,465)	204 (2,525)	15 (119)	2,717 (57,158)	136 (3,508)	3,622 (69,263)	546 (8,201)	4,168 (77,464)
Electrical machinery, cables, and apparatus	729 (5,434)	427 (3,430)	143 (1,500)	32 (113)	3,318 (33,092)	1,758 (8,807)	4,190 (40,522)	2,217 (12,396)	6,407 (52,918)
Motor vehicle construction and assembly, and motor bodies	2,595 (4,528)	690 (1,687)	790 (936)	15 (19)	19,309 (35,799)	502 (731)	22,694 (43,197)	1,207 (2,549)	23,901 (45,746)
Motor accessories	111 (1,461)	51 (874)	24 (388)	1 (48)	701 (6,980)	147 (2,373)	836 (8,961)	199 (3,312)	1,035 (12,273)
Other metal products	792 (23,861)	246 (12,648)	160 (5,788)	11 (365)	5,102 (237,805)	329 (15,949)	6,054 (278,679)	586 (29,895)	6,640 (308,574)
Foundation garments	52 (132)	92 (264)	5 (6)	6 (6)	95 (284)	690 (3,265)	152 (431)	788 (3,550)	940 (3,981)
Food, drink, tobacco	270 (10,228)	164 (7,174)	35 (1,584)	9 (493)	2,009 (76,493)	786 (26,709)	2,314 (92,782)	959 (35,808)	3,273 (128,590)
Paper, stationery, printing, etc.	101 (6,775)	69 (4,950)	16 (489)	4 (92)	526 (46,042)	246 (13,927)	643 (54,608)	319 (19,231)	962 (73,839)
Other products	297	192	224	28	2,128	456	2,649	319	3,325
Total	6,304	2,936	2,058	176	38,777	6,179	47,139	9,291	56,430
Total manufacturing	(86,594)	(53,837)	(18,055)	(1,998)	(702,991)	(201,362)	(841,507)	(263,044)	(1,104,551)

[a] See Note [a] to Table B-4.
[b] Figures for total employment shown in parentheses include small numbers of working proprietors not separately shown in the table. It has been assumed that no American-affiliated companies employed persons falling into that category.

333

TABLE B-6 Wages and Salaries Paid by Australian and American-affiliaᵛed Factories, by Industry, Category of Employee, and Sex
£A('000)

Industry	Managerial and clerical staff, chemists, draftsmen, etc.		Wages staff		Total[a]		Persons[b]
	Male	Female	Male	Female	Male	Female	
Industrial chemicals	1,372 (4,339)	179 (735)	2,698 (10,445)	233 (316)	4,070 (14,784)	412 (1,051)	4,481 (15,835)
Pharmaceuticals and toilet preparations	735 (2,333)	386 (831)	1,180 (2,568)	579 (2,132)	1,915 (4,901)	965 (2,963)	2,880 (7,864)
Plant, equipment, and machinery	1,483 (17,690)	318 (3,354)	3,229 (63,487)	94 (2,262)	4,712 (81,178)	411 (5,616)	5,123 (86,794)
Electrical machinery, cables, and apparatus	1,604 (10,837)	346 (2,682)	3,809 (37,506)	1,280 (5,994)	5,413 (48,343)	1,626 (8,676)	7,039 (57,020)
Motor vehicle construction and assembly, and motor bodies	5,936 (9,107)	621 (1,316)	23,927 (41,086)	378 (545)	29,863 (50,194)	998 (1,861)	30,861 (52,055)
Motor accessories	268 (2,922)	43 (693)	914 (8,057)	96 (1,608)	1,182 (10,979)	139 (2,301)	1,321 (13,280)
Other metal products	1,584 (46,106)	208 (9,105)	5,937 (261,449)	234 (10,944)	7,521 (307,555)	443 (20,049)	7,964 (327,604)
Foundation garments	95 (267)	77 (216)	98 (292)	400 (1,897)	193 (559)	478 (2,113)	671 (2,672)
Food, drink, tobacco	480 (18,327)	130 (5,481)	2,215 (84,912)	474 (17,954)	2,695 (103,239)	604 (23,436)	3,299 (126,674)
Paper, stationery, printing, etc.	309 (12,267)	54 (3,839)	594 (57,022)	169 (8,891)	903 (69,288)	223 (12,730)	1,126 (82,018)
Other products	1,009	167	2,586	300	3,595	468	4,062
Total[a]	14,874 (167,984)	2,530 (41,360)	47,187 (781,479)	4,236 (131,150)	62,061 (949,463)	6,765 (172,510)	68,827 (1,121,973)
Total manufacturing							

a Detail may not add to totals because of rounding.
b Excludes amounts drawn by working proprietors.

TABLE B–7 Various Costs, Value of Output, and Value of Production of Australian and American-affiliated Factories, by Industry

Industry	Value of output £A('000)	Power, fuel and light £A('000)	Lubricants and water £A('000)	Tools replaced and repairs £A('000)	Cost of Containers, packaging material, etc. £A('000)	All other materials used £A('000)	Total materials, fuel, etc. used[b] £A('000)	Value of production[a] £A('000)	Ratio of production to output (%)
Industrial chemicals	25,228 (96,711)	1,940 (5,347)	135 (415)	790 (2,542)	406 (2,890)	11,950 (41,769)	15,221 (52,962)	10,008 (43,749)	39·7 (45·2)
Pharmaceuticals and toilet preparations	28,088 (59,512)	158 (739)	19 (58)	180 (552)	3,098 (7,327)	7,193 (17,707)	10,647 (26,383)	17,441 (33,129)	62·1 (55·7)
Plant, equipment, and machinery	26,495 (294,964)	279 (3,274)	33 (485)	400 (4,551)	136 (1,232)	14,258 (142,681)	15,105 (152,222)	11,390 (142,742)	43·0 (48·4)
Electrical machinery, cables, and apparatus	27,874 (208,589)	345 (2,581)	34 (255)	431 (3,087)	449 (2,273)	14,993 (107,377)	16,253 (115,572)	11,621 (93,017)	41·7 (44·6)
Motor vehicle construction and assembly, and motor bodies	90,231 (188,044)	1,836 (2,739)	266 (378)	3,024 (4,387)	320 (340)	41,605 (95,248)	47,051 (103,092)	43,180 (84,952)	47·9 (45·2)
Motor accessories	5,246 (45,407)	112 (826)	28 (133)	181 (1,172)	45 (505)	1,760 (18,201)	2,126 (20,837)	3,120 (24,570)	59·5 (54·1)
Other metal products	58,693 (1,243,752)	2,480 (51,870)	105 (2,477)	1,540 (29,072)	146 (5,051)	36,926 (615,814)	41,198 (704,283)	17,495 (539,469)	29·8 (43·4)
Foundation garments	3,092 (11,181)	14 (44)	1 (5)	37 (89)	92 (243)	1,094 (5,448)	1,237 (5,829)	1,855 (5,352)	60·0 (47·9)
Food, drink, tobacco	25,205 (999,468)	321 (17,539)	25 (1,691)	296 (15,061)	3,224 (86,031)	10,812 (581,415)	14,678 (701,738)	10,527 (297,730)	41·8 (29·8)
Paper, stationery, printing, etc.	8,461 (322,383)	122 (6,140)	13 (526)	99 (4,738)	323 (2,805)	4,082 (144,703)	4,639 (158,911)	3,822 (163,472)	45·2 (50·7)
Other products	48,324	2,031	101	1,371	1,333	27,385	32,221	16,102	33·3
Total[b]	346,938	9,638	762	8,348	9,571	172,057	200,376	146,562	42·2
Total manufacturing	(5,087,231)	(137,337)	(9,670)	(98,213)	(140,810)	(2,596,896)	(2,982,926)	(2,104,305)	(41·4)

a Value added in process of manufacture, i.e. value of output less cost of materials, fuel, etc. used.
b Detail may not add to totals because of rounding.

TABLE B-8 Value of Land, Buildings, Plant, and Machinery Employed by Australian and American-affiliated Factories, by Industry
£A('000)

Industry	Land and buildings			Plant and machinery		
	Additions and replacements during 1961/2	Depreciation allowed during 1961/2	Value at 30 June 1962[a]	Additions and replacements during 1961/2	Depreciation allowed during 1961/2	Value at 30 June 1962[a]
Industrial chemicals	1,469 (4,930)	78 (479)	6,171 (26,427)	9,947 (32,261)	2,458 (6,366)	28,754 (63,707)
Pharmaceuticals and toilet preparations	340 (667)	104 (165)	4,056 (14,544)	411 (991)	311 (707)	2,537 (5,732)
Plant, equipment, and machinery	414 (5,673)	142 (542)	6,527 (74,008)	599 (8,327)	746 (5,280)	4,062 (46,177)
Electrical machinery, cables, and apparatus	319 (2,510)	111 (512)	5,220 (46,008)	1,014 (5,378)	601 (3,757)	3,849 (27,727)
Motor vehicle construction and assembly, and motor bodies	2,283 (3,202)	737 (936)	27,947 (52,990)	8,633 (9,356)	4,792 (6,606)	28,326 (39,313)
Motor accessories	2 (766)	[b] (30)	1,228 (12,369)	128 (2,173)	215 (1,586)	2,261 (14,348)
Other metal products	2,367 (22,984)	218 (4,518)	13,804 (320,403)	7,094 (78,146)	1,556 (33,840)	23,457 (374,165)
Foundation garments	52 (66)	1 (5)	757 (2,005)	10 (158)	21 (71)	129 (534)
Food, drink, tobacco	56 (9,717)	44 (2,105)	3,727 (172,357)	371 (28,227)	290 (16,501)	3,522 (168,620)
Paper, stationery, printing, etc.	391 (3,736)	[b] (544)	2,001 (85,219)	582 (13,993)	173 (9,514)	2,422 (91,862)
Other products	3,371	137	7,707	3,737	2,605	23,636
Total[c]	11,065	1,672	79,145	32,526	13,768	122,957
Total manufacturing	(74,731)	(12,629)	(1,150,930)	(248,791)	(123,6405)	(1,20,327)

[a] Depreciated or book value, including estimated value of rented premises, plant and machinery.
[b] Less than £500.
[c] Detail may not add to totals because of rounding.

336

TABLE B-9   Rated Horsepower of Engines Employed to Drive Machinery in Australian and American-affiliated Factories, by Industry

Industry	Rated h.p. of engines and motors Ordinarily in use	Rated h.p. of engines and motors In reserve or idle (excluding obsolete engines)	Rated h.p. of engines and motors ordinarily in use, per wages employee	Rated h.p. of all engines and motors (excluding obsolete engines) per wages employee
Industrial chemicals	51,332 (159,222)	8,181 (30,819)	24·12 (18·39)	27·97 (21·95)
Pharmaceuticals and toilet preparations	6,228 (20,322)	378 (3,588)	3·33 (3·48)	3·53 (4·10)
Plant, equipment, and machinery	15,510 (296,100)	693 (24,238)	5·44 (4·88)	5·68 (5·28)
Electrical machinery, cables, and apparatus	9,170 (128,326)	779 (9,556)	1·81 (3·06)	1·96 (3·29)
Motor vehicle construction and assembly, and motor bodies	103,833 (152,105)	4,457 (6,495)	5·24 (4·16)	5·47 (4·34)
Motor accessories	6,848 (48,947)	527 (5,194)	8·08 (5·23)	8·70 (5·79)
Other metal products	54,149 (1,786,090)	2,576 (183,385)	9·97 (7·04)	10·44 (7·76)
Foundation garments	516 (2,023)	37 (530)	0·66 (0·57)	0·70 (0·72)
Food, drink, tobacco	58,795 (931,017)	2,421 (149,262)	21·04 (9·02)	21·90 (10·47)
Paper, stationery, printing, etc.	3,591 (418,360)	667 (68,911)	4·65 (6·98)	5·52 (8·13)
Other products	41,072	4,905	15·89	17·79
Total	351,044	25,621	7·81	8·38
Total manufacturing	(6,000,529)	(811,527)	(6·64)	(7·53)

NOTES ON THE TABLES

1. *Scope of the Statistics and Period Covered*

(a) Of the 208 'eligible' companies approached in this survey of American investment, 100 supplied answers to Part II of Questionnaire I. As stated earlier, details of one company's operations are not included in the preceding tables. Moreover, two companies supplied details for their main plants only and for this reason the figures in the tables slightly understate the operations of even these ninety-nine firms. The understatement on this score, however, is negligible.

(b) From data presented in chapter I, it appears that the tables cover about three-quarters of the manufacturing activities of all companies operating in Australia in which there was an American shareholding of at least 25 per cent at 30 June 1962.

(c) The activities of the ninety-nine American-affiliated companies are compared with total manufacturing operations in Australia in the year ended 30 June 1962. Figures for these latter are derived from *Secondary Industries: Part I. Factory and Building Operations, 1961-62*, published by the Commonwealth Bureau of Census and Statistics, Canberra. Naturally, the figures shown for total Australian manufacturing operations include the activities of the American-affiliated firms.

(d) As with the figures supplied to the Commonwealth Bureau of Census and Statistics, a small number of companies supplied information relating to some other accounting period than that ending 30 June. In addition, one firm declined to provide data for the 1961/2 year because of an industrial dispute in that year, and provided figures for 1960/1 instead. The error involved, however, is small.

2. *Comparability of Data with that Provided on a Company Basis*

Most of the data presented elsewhere were gathered on a company basis. Information in the above tables, however, relates to manufacturing establishments or factories. This renders direct comparison of the two sets of figures impossible, the main difficulties being as follows:

(a) The industrial classification used in the above tables differs from that used to classify companies in the body of the text (see also Note 3). Moreover, in appendix tables each plant belongs to only one industry, whereas in company tables each company is classified according to its main activity.

(b) Many participating companies are engaged in some activity other than manufacture. The tables in this appendix refer only to their manufacturing activities and, in contrast to the company data, exclude employees engaged only in selling and distribution from employment figures and sales of goods to which no value has been added by the factory in question from the figures for value of output.

(c) Employment figures in this appendix are based on average employment over a period of time, while most of those elsewhere were given as at one point of time (see also Note 6).

(d) Since figures in the above tables refer to individual factories, companies operating plants at more than one stage of manufacture can have the value of the output of each plant added into the figures shown. Clearly, if the output of a plant at an early stage of manufacture is sold to a plant of the same company at a later stage, the sales of the company as a whole may fall short of the total value of the output of the plants taken together. This appears to be the situation with the operations of at least two of the companies included in the tables.

(e) In accordance with the instructions of the Commonwealth Bureau of Census and Statistics, figures shown for the cost of materials used and for the value of output produced generally exclude the value of components which are merely assembled by the factory in question. This factor is of major importance in such industries as the assembly of motor vehicles.

(f) Unlike figures given for company assets, figures shown in the above tables for the value of land, buildings, plant, and machinery used in manufacture include an estimate of the value of rented premises and plant and machinery.

(g) A few companies included relatively small operations in New Zealand in their aggregate figures. These operations are naturally not included in the appendix tables.

(h) As mentioned in Note 1, all the activities of one participating company and a part of the activity of two others are not included in the tables in this appendix.

3. *Industrial Classification*

The industrial classification used in these tables is thought to coincide as nearly as possible with that used for factory statistics by the Commonwealth Bureau of Census and Statistics. For many purposes this is not the most useful classification and, since the figures here presented cannot in any case be compared with company data, a somewhat different classification has been used in the body of the text. For purposes of comparison, however, the Bureau's classification has been followed as closely as possible for the factory statistics gathered.

(a) It was intended that 'Industrial chemicals', 'Pharmaceuticals and toilet preparations', 'Plant, equipment, and machinery', 'Electrical machinery, cables, and apparatus', 'Motor vehicle construction and assembly, and motor bodies', 'Motor accessories', and 'Foundation garments' be coincidental with Bureau classifications of similar or identical title. The classification 'Other metal products' represents the balance of the Bureau's 'Industrial Metals, Machines, Conveyances' classification, after the four sub-industries listed above it in the tables have been taken out. American firms are widely spread through the sub-industries covered by 'Other metal products' and are active in such Bureau classifications as 'Extracting and Refining of other Metals; Alloys', 'Cutlery and Small Hand Tools', 'Agricultural Machines and Implements', 'Non-ferrous Metals—Rolling and Extrusion', 'Sheet Metal Working, Pressing and Stamping', 'Pipes, Tubes and Fittings, Ferrous', 'Sewing machines', 'Wireless and Amplifying Apparatus' and 'Other Engineering'. In all cases, so few participating companies were active in each sub-industry that separate disclosure of the extent of American activities there was impossible. A similar difficulty applied to the 'Food, drink, tobacco' and 'Paper, stationery, printing, etc.' industries. The classification 'Other products' includes two companies in the Bureau's classification 'Glass (other than Bottles)', three companies in 'Oils, Mineral', and one in each of 'Treatment of Non-Metalliferous Mine and Quarry Products: Other', 'Plastic Moulding and Products', and 'Photographic Material (including Developing and Printing)'.

(b) In some cases it was extremely difficult to decide to which of several industries a factory should be allocated. Multi-product factories supplying only one answer to the questionnaire, and the very old classification still in use by the Commonwealth Bureau, made this allocation subject to a wide margin of error. In particular, attention should be drawn to the possibility that two large companies classified here under 'Pharmaceuticals and toilet preparations' are not so classified by the Bureau.

(c) It should be noted that some of the Bureau's classifications include activities other than those immediately apparent. For example, 'Plant, Equipment and Machinery, including Machine Tools' appears to include the manufacture of domestic refrigerators, and 'Motor Bodies' the manufacture of trailers and caravans. The manufacture of sewing machines is not included under the classification 'Electrical Machinery, Cables and Apparatus', and appears here under 'Other metal products'.

(d) To facilitate comparison of the American-affiliated factories with total Australian manufacturing, the operations of plants engaged in the 'Heat, Light and Power' industry have been excluded.

4. *Definition of Factory*

The Commonwealth Bureau of Census and Statistics defines a 'factory' as 'an establishment in which four or more persons are employed or where power (other than manual) is used in any manufacturing process'. Where two or more industries are conducted in the same establishment, however, and where separate returns are received for each industry, it appears that the one establishment is entered in the statistics as two or more 'factories'. The same policy has been adopted in the above tables in the three cases in which companies provided more than one reply to the questionnaire for operations conducted at the one establishment.

5. *Size Classification*

The class intervals used in Tables B-2 and B-3 were dictated by the need for comparability with those used by the Commonwealth Bureau. This explains the inadequacy of the classification in Table B-3: the Bureau provides no size classification of the kind used in Table B-2 by sub-industry.

6. *Employment*

(a) As with figures published by the Bureau, employment figures are shown on two bases. The first, used in Tables B-2 and B-3, is an 'aggregate of the average number of persons employed in each factory during its period of operation (whether the whole or only part of the year)'. The second, used in all other tables showing employment in this appendix, 'is calculated by reducing the average number working in the factories (irrespective of period of operation) to the equivalent number working for a full year'.

(b) Only persons employed in the manufacturing activities of a factory are counted as factory employees. Those engaged in selling and distribution are excluded.

(c) With reference to Table B-5, no American-affiliated factories were asked to supply details on the number of 'working proprietors' employed. It was assumed that American firms would have no employees in this category.

7. *Wages and Salaries*

All figures shown in Table B-6 exclude amounts drawn by working proprietors.

8. *Cost of Materials, Value of Output, Value of Production*

(a) The costs enumerated in Table B-7 are by no means all the costs incurred in the manufacturing process, and the figures cannot, therefore, be used to calculate profit or loss. Furthermore, as noted earlier, the value of materials used generally does not include the value of articles or materials which are merely repaired or assembled in the factory.

(b) The Commonwealth Bureau defines the value of factory output as
> the value of the goods manufactured or their value after passing through the particular process of manufacture and includes the amount received for repair work, work done on commission and receipts for other factory work. The basis of valuation of the output is the selling value of the goods at the factory, exclusive of all delivery costs and charges and excise duties, but inclusive of bounty and subsidy payments to the manufacturer of the finished article.

(c) The apparent simplicity of this definition of output is deceptive. In at least six different ways companies misinterpreted the definition or gave figures which for some reason mean very little:

(i) The most serious misinterpretation arose from an apparent ambiguity in the instructions supplied to all factories by the Commonwealth Bureau of Census and Statistics for the completion of their Factory Returns. On the Factory Return itself, factories are asked to give the 'Selling Value at Works (exclusive of all delivery costs or charges) . . .' but on the sheet of instructions which accompanies the Factory Return a note explains that what is required is the *'selling value at factory . . . after deducting all costs of selling and distribution'*. At least one company included in the present survey therefore regularly provides the Bureau with a figure for the value of its output which is net of its very substantial advertising bill. A more correct figure was obtained from the company concerned for use in this survey but no alteration was made to the Bureau's figures shown both to avoid disclosing the extent of the alteration and to avoid a 'double correction' if the Bureau has already made an alteration in its own editing process. The change makes a significant difference to the figures shown for one of the smaller industries.

(ii) Two companies provided output figures which in fact represented little more than factory cost. Again alteration was made to the survey figures, but not to the Bureau figures, after consultation with the companies concerned.

(iii) One small newly-established factory supplied a sales figure instead of a figure for value of output, and this too was altered after consultation with the company concerned.

(iv) At least one of the major American motor vehicle manufacturers appears to be misinterpreting the Bureau's instructions on the method of excluding assembled components from cost of materials and value of output. Not enough was known about this to make alteration possible and it should be noted that this misinterpretation may be causing some understatement of the value of output, and so of the value of production, of the motor vehicle industry.

(v) No alteration was made in the figure supplied by one company which sells its entire output to an affiliated sales company at little more than nominal mark-up.

(vi) One large factory in the 'Other products' industry included the value of materials processed by it in its figures for cost of materials and value of output for six months of the 1961/2 year but, following a company reorganization, excluded the value of such materials for the other six months. No allowance has been made for this in the figures shown.

(d) No correction has been made to any of the figures shown in Table B-7 for the fact that a number of factories commenced manufacture only after the beginning of the 1961/2 year. Production per employee figures shown elsewhere are not affected by this because of the correction made to employment figures, but direct comparison of the value of the output of American-affiliated companies with that of all manufacturing establishments is made more difficult. The error is only significant, however, where a considerable number of American-affiliated plants commenced operations during the year, as in the 'Industrial chemicals' classification.

(e) The Bureau of Census and Statistics defines the value of production as 'the value added to raw materials by the process of manufacture. It is calculated by deducting from the value of factory output the value (at the factory) of the materials used, containers and packaging, power, fuel, and light used, tools replaced, and materials used in repairs to plant (but not depreciation charges).'

(f) The exclusion of assembled components from the value of materials and the value of output tends to distort upwards the ratio of production to output for plants primarily engaged in assembly.

9. *Value of Land, Buildings, Plant, and Machinery*

As mentioned in Note 2, figures shown in Table B-8 for the value of land, buildings, plant, and machinery include an estimate of the value of rented premises and plant and machinery. The method used in arriving at these estimates was the same as that used by the Commonwealth Bureau.

10. *Horsepower of Engines Employed*

(a) Figures in parentheses include the horsepower of engines run on electricity generated in the factories concerned. Though this may give rise to some regrettable overstatement of the power available for use in the manufacturing process, it was made necessary by the failure to distinguish between such engines and those not so powered in the American investment questionnaire. In most industries the possible overstatement is small.

(b) For the calculation of 'horsepower per wages employee' figures, 'whole year' employment figures had to be used because the Bureau does not publish 'period of operation' figures by industry and kind of employee

Appendix C

Some Corporate 'Portfolio' Investments in Australian Companies

As explained in chapter I, the primary purpose of this survey was to examine American *direct* investment in Australian manufacturing industry. Inevitably, however, a number of companies were encountered in which the American equity fell short of 25 per cent. Though lack of time prevented their being visited, most of them completed a brief questionnaire on their American association. This appendix sets out the information gained.

In all, thirty-three such firms were encountered. It is unnecessary to list them all but the names of some of the more important ones illustrate their industrial diversity: Amalgamated Wireless Valve Co. Pty Ltd, Automotive Components Ltd, John Beith Holdings Ltd, the members of the Bradford Insulation group, Bradford Kendall Ltd, Commonwealth Engineering Co. Ltd, Consolidated Milk Industries Ltd, Freighters Ltd, Frigrite Ltd, Gibson Kelite Chemicals Ltd, Hanimex Corporation Ltd, Ernest Hiller Holdings Ltd, Pacific Oxygen Ltd (acquired since 1962 by Commonwealth Industrial Gases Ltd), and Unique Sash Balance Pty Ltd.

The twenty-eight firms which provided employment figures for 1962 had total employment of 17,296 in that year and the employment of the whole group was probably about 19,000. The smallest had employment of only 8 and the largest of 3,016. The twenty-three companies which provided sales figures for 1961/2 had total sales of a little more than £63 million. No accurate estimate can be made of the sales of the whole group, but since those which provided sales figures had employment of 14,452, it may be surmised that the sales of the whole group were in the region of £80-85 million.

The American shareholdings varied between 0·1 per cent and 24·0 per cent of ordinary capital. Only four holdings exceeded 20 per cent, however, and nineteen fell short of 10 per cent. The mean holding was 9·4 per cent and the median only 7·1 per cent. Of the total ordinary shares issued by the whole group of companies, almost 22 million shares in all, American companies held little more than 6·3 per cent. Nine of the companies had preference shares outstanding, but in only one case did the American company hold any—and this holding was quite negligible.

All companies were asked to state when and how the American shareholding had been taken up. Unfortunately, only seventeen companies gave a date for the American acquisition, possibly because the wording of the question made it easy to overlook this aspect. Of these seventeen holdings, one dated back to 1935, one to 1941, and one to 1953. All the balance had been taken up in 1955 or subsequently, and in fact seven holdings did not go back before 1960. The apparently rapid acceleration of such investments confirms the impression given by the data presented in chapter II.

342

Thirty companies indicated how the American shareholding had been acquired. The majority, nineteen, stated that shares had been issued to an American company in exchange for technical information, patents, and/or marketing rights. Three more explained that while some shares had been issued for cash, others had been issued in exchange for technical information and patents. In only eight cases had the shares been issued entirely for cash (sometimes in lieu of royalties due to the American company) or the supply of plant and machinery. (Sometimes, of course, even the share issues for cash were made at prices below ruling market levels in return for access to American know-how or patents.) Almost always the issue of shares by the Australian company was made as part of a licensing agreement with the American company.

The influence which American shareholders exercised on local management is not known. Even had a detailed survey of this aspect been made, it would have involved a study of the influence of licensers rather than of that of shareholders.[1] Certainly only a minority of the directors of the companies studied were American: the twenty-nine companies which provided information on the nationality of their directors had a total of 160 directors, of whom only six were Americans (two of them on the same Board). On the other hand, the influence which quite small equity holdings, in conjunction with a licensing agreement, can have is clearly illustrated by the failure of the proposed merger between John Beith Holdings Ltd and Jordan Chemicals Ltd in 1961-2. Somewhat more than 20 per cent of John Beith's ordinary shares were held in the U.S. in 1962 and the company also had significant, though smaller, corporate shareholders in the U.K. Jordan Chemicals had agreements with at least two American companies in that year, but the American shareholding seems to have been quite small. Despite this it was reported that the merger was 'postponed because of conflicting interests of the overseas principals of the two companies.' (*Jobson's Investment Digest: Year Book 1964*, p. 313.)

The American influence on the management *techniques* of the companies studied was not great. Only two of the thirty companies which answered this question felt that their overall management techniques had benefited strongly from the influence of their American affiliate, and only fourteen felt they had benefited 'moderately'. The balance felt that U.S. influence in this area had been negligible. (It is interesting to compare this evidence with that presented for direct-investment enterprises in chapter V: it was noted there that the greater the level of American equity, the more significant to the local operation did American managerial know-how become.)

On the other hand, technical information received from the U.S. was of much greater importance. Six companies stated that such information was 'vital' and another four that it was vital in the production of licensed products. Seventeen felt it was of 'moderate' importance, an answer which may well have meant 'vital in the production of a relatively small part of our turnover'. Only three companies felt that technical information from the American affiliate was of only marginal importance, and two of these qualified this by saying that they expected such information to be of greater importance in years to come.

Perhaps surprisingly, twenty-one of the thirty companies which answered this questionnaire paid a royalty or technical assistance fee based on sales of licensed products to their American associate. In other words, the share issue

---

[1] Some licensers hold very considerable authority over their licensees under certain circumstances. The writer was told of one case where the American licenser, who held none of the ordinary shares in the Australian company, was able to dismiss the entire senior management of the licensee when the latter got into financial difficulties.

made to the American company was often in addition to a service charge of the more conventional kind, though presumably the latter was lower than it would otherwise have been because of the share issue. Two of the twenty-one companies paying a royalty or fee based on sales also paid a fixed sum annually. Nothing is known about the general level of royalty: only two companies provided information on the rate of royalty paid, and one of these paid 1 per cent and the other 5 per cent.

Of the nine companies not making any special payment in 1962, one expected to start making such payments at a later date.

At least one of the companies not making any special payment for technical information or marketing rights had a licensing agreement which provided for the reciprocal exchange of all technical information without charge. This is perhaps the most desirable of all relationships if the Australian venture undertakes enough research or product development to make the arrangement of mutual benefit.

Because a significant number of direct-investment enterprises differentiated in conversation between where they were 'theoretically' allowed to export and where they might 'actually' export, the written answers received on the subject of export franchise restrictions from the companies currently under discussion must be treated with considerable caution. Moreover, these companies were not asked to indicate the actual extent of their export activities, and for this reason it is possible that a number of companies which indicated that they were not restricted in their export freedom might in fact have been engaged in the production of commodities the export of which was economically out of the question. As it was, two of the twenty-nine companies which answered this question stated that exporting was 'not relevant', though one added that restrictions might exist if exporting were feasible. With these serious reservations in mind, it may be noted that eleven companies indicated that they were not restricted in any way in their freedom to export. Sixteen stated that the export of licensed products was restricted to certain specified areas, and twelve of these indicated the areas concerned. Eight of the twelve could not sell outside Australasia (and one of these indeed was confined to Australia and its overseas territories) and two of the balance were not permitted to export beyond parts of Asia and Africa. The evidence is clearly not reliable enough to call into serious question the view expressed in chapter IX that licensees are likely to be more restricted in their export freedom than are subsidiaries, but the need for further study of this aspect is obvious.

Appendix D

Participating Companies and Those Supporting the Survey Financially

The following list of companies includes both those taken to be 'participating' in the present survey and those which responded to an appeal by Professor Sir John Crawford, Director of the Research School of Pacific Studies in the Australian National University, for finance to conduct the project. In fairness it should be added that a number of companies not included in the list did provide information for the survey. They have not been listed either because they did not feel able to answer at least the first main questionnaire used in the survey or because they were not manufacturing at 30 June 1962. (See also chapter I for further discussion of what constitutes a 'participating company'.) It should also be made clear that not all the companies listed were approached for financial support.

Companies have been listed according to their names at the time of the survey.

Addressograph-Multigraph of Australia Pty Ltd
Aircraft-Marine Products (Aust.) Pty Ltd
Altona Petrochemical Co. Pty Ltd
American Machine and Foundry Co. (Aust.) Pty Ltd
Armco (Aust.) Pty Ltd
Austral Standard Cables Pty Ltd
Australian Abrasives Pty Ltd
*Australian Carbon Black Pty Ltd
Australian Controls Ltd
Australian Cream Tartar Pty Ltd
Australian Fibre Glass Pty Ltd
Australian Petrochemicals Pty Ltd
Australian Synthetic Rubber Co. Ltd
Bendix-Tecnico Pty Ltd
Bendix-Tecnico (Automotive) Pty Ltd
Black and Decker (Australasia) Pty Ltd
Blacklock Industries Pty Ltd
Boral Ltd
*Borg-Warner (Aust.) Ltd
Bowater-Scott Australia Pty Ltd
Bristol-Myers Co. Pty Ltd

*Bundy Tubing Co. (Aust.) Pty Ltd
C.S.R.C.-Dow Pty Ltd
Cannon Electric (Aust.) Pty Ltd
Carborundum Australia Pty Ltd
J. I. Case (Aust.) Pty Ltd
*Caterpillar of Australia Pty Ltd
Champion Spark Plug Co. (Aust.) Pty Ltd
Chrysler Australia Ltd
*Coca-Cola Export Corporation
Colgate-Palmolive Pty Ltd
Comalco Industries Pty Ltd
Consolidated Pneumatic Tool Co. (Aust.) Pty Ltd
Corning Glass Works
Cummins Diesel Australia
Dowd Associates Pty Ltd
Ducon Industries Ltd
F.M.C. (Aust.) Ltd
Fenner Dodge (Aust.) Pty Ltd
Fischer and Porter Pty Ltd
*Ford Motor Co. of Australia Pty Ltd
Formfit of Australia Ltd
Fruehauf Trailers (Australasia) Pty Ltd

* Supported the project financially.

General Motors-Holden's Pty Ltd
Gilbert and Barker Manufacturing Co. (Aust.) Pty Ltd
*Gillette (Aust.) Pty Ltd
B. F. Goodrich-C.S.R. Chemicals Pty Ltd
H. J. Heinz Co. Pty Ltd
Hercules Powder Co. (Aust.) Pty Ltd
Hoover (Aust.) Pty Ltd
Hunter Douglas Ltd
IBM Australia Pty Ltd
*International Harvester Co. of Australia Pty Ltd
*Jantzen (Aust.) Ltd
Johnson and Johnson Pty Ltd
Joy Manufacturing Co. Pty Ltd
James N. Kirby Manufacturing Pty Ltd
Kodak (Australasia) Pty Ltd
Le Tourneau-Westinghouse Pty Ltd
Eli Lilly (Aust.) Pty Ltd
Lindberg Engineering Co. (Aust.) Pty Ltd
Lovable Brassiere Co. (Aust.) Pty Ltd
Lubrizol International S.A.
*McCulloch of Australia Pty Ltd
Chas. McDonald-Mead Johnson Pty Ltd
Metters-Clow Pty Ltd
*Mobil Oil Australia Pty Ltd
*Monsanto Chemicals (Aust.) Ltd
*Mount Isa Mines Ltd
Nabisco Pty Ltd
Nuodex (Aust.) Pty Ltd
Oppenheimer Casing Co. of Australia Pty Ltd
Outboard Marine Australia Pty Ltd

Parke, Davis and Company
Parker-Eversharp (Aust.) Pty Ltd
Parsons General Foods Pty Ltd
Pepsi-Cola Co. of Australia Pty Ltd
Pepsi-Cola Metropolitan Bottling Co. Inc.
*Pfizer Corporation
*Rheem Australia Industries Pty Ltd
Robertshaw Controls (Aust.) Pty Ltd
Ronson Pty Ltd
St Regis-Williams Pty Ltd
Schrader-Scovill Co. Pty Ltd
Scripto Pens of Australia Pty Ltd
Sheffield Corporation of Australia Pty Ltd
Singer Industries Pty Ltd
Smith Kline and French Laboratories (Aust.) Ltd
Sporting Arms Ltd
*Standard Telephones and Cables Pty Ltd
Steerings Pty Ltd
Sterling Pharmaceuticals Pty Ltd
G. H. Stuart Pty Ltd
Swift Australian Co. (Pty) Ltd
Taylor Instrument Cos. of Australia Pty Ltd
Texas Instruments Australia Ltd
U.K. Optical Bausch and Lomb Pty Ltd
Unbrako (Aust.) Pty Ltd
*Union Carbide Australia Ltd
Vick Products (Pty) Ltd
Vickers-Detroit Hydraulics Pty Ltd
Wallace and Tiernan Pty Ltd
White Wings Pty Ltd
Wiltshire File Co. Pty Ltd

* Supported the project financially.

Bibliography

(A) ARTICLES, BOOKS, THESES

Abramovitz, M. 1952. Economics of Growth. In B. F. Haley (ed.), *A Survey of Contemporary Economics*. Homewood, Ill.

Arndt, H. W. 1954. A Suggestion for Simplifying the Theory of International Capital Movements. *Economia Internazionale* VII, 469-79.

——— 1955. External Economies in Economic Growth. *Economic Record* XXXI, 192-214.

——— 1957. Overseas Borrowing—the New Model. *Economic Record* XXXIII, 247-61.

———, and Sherk, D. R. 1959. Export Franchises of Australian Companies with Overseas Affiliations. *Economic Record* XXXV, 239-42.

Australian British Trade Association 1964. *United Kingdom Investment in Australian Industry: Précis of Submissions to the Committee of Economic Enquiry*. Melbourne.

Australian Chemical Industry Council 1964. *Industrial Chemicals and Synthetic Resins*, I and II. Public evidence submitted to the Australian Tariff Board.

Australian Joint Committee for Productivity Group Promotion 1963. *Group News* 7.

Australian Petroleum Information Bureau 1962. *Oil and Australia, 1962*. [n.p.]

Avramovic, D., and Gulhati, R. 1958. *Debt Servicing Capacity and Postwar Growth in International Indebtedness*. Baltimore.

Ball, R. J. 1962. Capital Imports and Economic Development: Paradoxy or Orthodoxy? *Kyklos* XV, 610-23.

Balogh, T. 1945. Some Theoretical Problems of Post-War Foreign Investment Policy. *Oxford Economic Papers* 7, 93-110.

———, and Streeten, P. P. 1960. Domestic versus Foreign Investment. *Bulletin of the Oxford University Institute of Statistics* 22, 213-24.

Bank of New South Wales 1961. *Establishing a Business in Australia*. Sydney.

Barlow, E. R. 1953. *Management of Foreign Manufacturing Subsidiaries*. Boston.

———, and Wender, I. T. 1955. *Foreign Investment and Taxation*. Englewood Cliffs.

Bastow, S. H. 1964. Research in the Manufacturing Industry in Australia. Paper presented to the annual conference of the Australian Institute of Engineers, Canberra (mimeographed).

Behrman, J. N. 1962a. Foreign Associates and their Financing. In R. F. Mikesell (ed.), *U.S. Private and Government Investment Abroad*. Eugene, Oregon.

——— 1962b. Foreign Investment and the Transfer of Knowledge and Skills. Ibid.

——— 1962c. Economic Effects of Private Direct Investment. Ibid.

Bennett, F. N. 1961. The Pattern and Significance of United States Direct Investments in Australia. (B.Ec. (Hons.) thesis, University of Sydney.)

Berrill, K. E. 1963. Foreign Capital and Take-Off. In W. W. Rostow (ed.), *The Economics of Take-Off into Sustained Growth: Proceedings of a Conference held by the International Economic Association*. London.

Blainey, G. 1960. *Mines in the Spinifex: The Story of Mount Isa Mines*. Sydney.
―――― 1964. Technology in Australian History. *Business Archives and History* IV, 117-37.

Bloomfield, A. I. 1950. *Capital Imports and the American Balance of Payments 1934-39*. Chicago.

Blyth, C. D., and Carty, E. B. 1956. Non-Resident Ownership of Canadian Industry. *Canadian Journal of Economics and Political Science* XXII, 449-60.

Brash, D. T. 1964. *New Zealand's Debt Servicing Capacity*. Christchurch.

Brecher, I., and Reisman, S. S. 1957. *Canada-United States Economic Relations*. Ottawa (Royal Commission on Canada's Economic Prospects).

Brewster, jr, K. 1960. *Law and United States Business in Canada*. Washington (National Planning Association (U.S.A.) and Private Planning Association of Canada).

Bushnell, J. A. 1961. *Australian Company Mergers, 1946-1959*. Melbourne.

Cairncross, A. K. 1953. *Home and Foreign Investment 1870-1913*. Cambridge.
―――― 1962. *Factors in Economic Development*. London.

Caves, R. E. 1960. *Trade and Economic Structure: Models and Methods*. Cambridge, Mass.

Chakravarty, S. 1961. A Structural Study of International Capital Movement. *Economia Internazionale* XIV, 377-404.

Commerce Clearing House, Inc. 1962. *Revenue Act of 1962 with explanation*. Chicago.

Corden, W. M. 1963. The Tariff. In A. Hunter (ed.), *The Economics of Australian Industry*. Melbourne.

Domar, E. D. 1950. The Effect of Foreign Investment on the Balance of Payments. *American Economic Review* XL, 805-26.

Donovan, F. P. 1959. Australia. In W. G. Friedmann and R. C. Pugh (eds.), *Legal Aspects of Foreign Investment*. London.

Dunning, J. H. 1958. *American Investment in British Manufacturing Industry*. London.
―――― 1964. Capital Movements in the 20th Century. *Lloyds Bank Review* 72, 17-42.

Encel, S. 1961. Financing Scientific Research in Australia. *Science*, 28 July 1961, 260-6.

Fanno, M. 1939. *Normal and Abnormal International Capital Transfers*. Minneapolis.

Finch, D. 1951-2. Investment Service of Under-developed Countries. *I.M.F. Staff Papers* II, 60-85.

Ford Motor Company of Australia Pty Ltd 1950. *Strong Grows the Future: Ford's 25 Years in Australia*. [n.p.]

Forster, C. 1964. *Industrial Development in Australia 1920-1930*. Canberra.

Friedmann, W. G., and Kalmanoff, G. (eds.) 1961. *Joint International Business Ventures*. New York.

Gates, T. R., and Linden, F. 1961. *Costs and Competition: American Experience Abroad*. New York (National Industrial Conference Board).

General Motors-Holden's Pty Ltd 1962a. *Behind the Millionth*. Melbourne.
―――― 1962b. *1962 Annual Report*.

Goodyear Tyre & Rubber Co. (Aust.) Ltd 1952. *The First Twenty-Five Years: Goodyear Celebrates its Silver Anniversary of Manufacturing in Australia, 1927-1952*. Sydney.
―――― 1961. *Annual Report 1961*.

Gordon, L., and Grommers, E. L. 1962. *United States Manufacturing Investment in Brazil: The Impact of Brazilian Government Policies 1946-1960.* Boston.

Gott, K. D. 1965. Open for Business. *Australian,* 4 March 1965, 9.

Grant, J. McB. 1963. The Petroleum Industry. In A. Hunter (ed.), *The Economics of Australian Industry.* Melbourne.

Guth, W. 1963. *Capital Exports to Less Developed Countries.* Dordrecht, Holland.

Hall, A. R. 1963. *The London Capital Market and Australia 1870-1914.* Canberra.

Hampton, P. 1963. Foreign Investment and the Theory of Economic Growth, examined within the framework of Canadian Economic Development. (Ph.D. thesis, University of Ottawa.)

Harrod, R. F. 1963. Desirable International Movements of Capital in Relation to Growth of Borrowers and Lenders and Growth of Markets. In R. Harrod and D. Hague (eds.), *International Trade Theory in a Developing World: Proceedings of a Conference held by the International Economic Association.* London.

Hartnett, L. J., as told to Veitch, J. 1964. *Big Wheels and Little Wheels.* Melbourne.

Heckscher, E. 1919. The Effect of Foreign Trade on the Distribution of Income. *Ekonomisk Tidskrift* XXI (reprinted in *Readings in the Theory of International Trade,* London, 1950).

Hinshaw, R. 1946. Foreign Investment and American Employment. *American Economic Review, Papers and Proceedings* XXXVI, 661-71.

Hocking, D. M. 1955. The Contribution of Overseas Companies to Australia's Post-war Industrial Development. Paper presented to Section G, Australian and New Zealand Association for the Advancement of Science, Melbourne (mimeographed).

—— 1958. Research—the Economic Implications. *Journal of the Australian Institute of Metals* 3, no. 1, 23-30.

Hogan, W. P. 1961. Economic Aspects of the Chemical Industry. *Proceedings of the Royal Australian Chemical Institute* 28, 431-44.

—— 1962. The Impact of the Foreign Sector on Industrial Structure. Paper presented to Section G, Australian and New Zealand Association for the Advancement of Science, Sydney (mimeographed).

—— 1965. British Manufacturing Subsidiaries in Australia and Export Franchises. Paper presented to the Economic Society of Australia and New Zealand, New South Wales Branch, Sept. 1965 (mimeographed).

Horner, D. T. 1962. U.S. Direct Investments in the Post-War Period. Economic Monograph No. 241 of the Economic Society of Australia and New Zealand, New South Wales Branch.

Hunter, A. 1961. Restrictive Practices and Monopolies in Australia. *Economic Record* XXXVII, 25-52.

—— 1963. 'Relative Mildness' of Barwick Proposals. *Sydney Morning Herald,* 18 February 1963, 2.

——, and Webb, L. R. 1963. The Chemical Industry. In A. Hunter (ed.), *The Economics of Australian Industry.* Melbourne.

Hunter, J. M. 1953. Long-term Foreign Investment and Under-developed Countries. *Journal of Political Economy* LXI, 15-24.

Hutton, J. 1964. An Anatomy of Manufacturing Industry. Paper presented to Section G, Australian and New Zealand Association for the Advancement of Science, Canberra (mimeographed).

Ingram, J. C. 1957. Growth in Capacity and Canada's Balance of Payments. *American Economic Review* XLVII, 93-104.

Islam, N. 1960. *Foreign Capital and Economic Development: Japan, India and Canada.* Tokyo.

Jasay, A. E. 1960. The Social Choice Between Home and Overseas Investment. *Economic Journal* LXX, 105-13.

Kahn, A. E. 1951. Investment Criteria in Development Programs. *Quarterly Journal of Economics* LXV, 38-61.

Karmel, P. H., and Brunt, Maureen 1962. *The Structure of the Australian Economy.* Melbourne.

Kemp, M. C. 1962a. Foreign Investment and the National Advantage. *Economic Record* XXXVIII, 56-62.

———— 1962b. The Benefits and Costs of Private Investment from Abroad: Comment. *Economic Record* XXXVIII, 108-10.

Keynes, J. M. 1924. Foreign Investment and National Advantage. *The Nation and the Athenaeum*, 9 August 1924, 584-7.

Kindleberger, C. P. 1956. *The Terms of Trade: A European Case Study.* New York.

———— 1958a. *Economic Development.* New York.

———— 1958b. *International Economics* (2nd ed.). Homewood, Ill.

———— 1963. *International Economics* (3rd ed.). Homewood, Ill.

Knapp, J. 1957. Capital Exports and Growth. *Economic Journal* LXVII, 432-44.

Kraft Holdings Ltd 1962. *1962 Annual Report.*

Lary, H. B. 1946. The Domestic Effects of Foreign Investment. *American Economic Review, Papers and Proceedings* XXXVI, 672-86.

Lewis, Cleona, and Schlotterbeck, K. T. 1938. *America's Stake in International Investments.* Washington.

Lindeman, J., and Armstrong, D. 1960. *Policies and Practices of United States Subsidiaries in Canada.* Washington (National Planning Association (U.S.A.) and Private Planning Association of Canada).

Lovell, Enid Baird 1958, 1959. *Foreign Licensing Agreements*, 2 vols. New York (National Industrial Conference Board).

MacDougall, G. D. A. 1960. The Benefits and Costs of Private Investment from Abroad: A Theoretical Approach. *Economic Record* XXXVI, 13-35.

Machlup, F. 1943. *International Trade and the National Income Multiplier.* Philadelphia.

Manufacturing Industries Advisory Council 1960. *Oversea Investment in Australia.* [n.p.]

Marsh, D. B. 1951. *World Trade and Investment.* New York.

Marshall, H., Southard, jr, F. A., and Taylor, K. W. 1936. *Canadian-American Industry: A Study in International Investment.* New Haven.

Maxcy, G. 1963. The Motor Industry. In A. Hunter (ed.), *The Economics of Australian Industry.* Melbourne.

Meade, J. E. 1951, 1955. *The Theory of International Economic Policy*, 2 vols. London.

Meier, G. M. 1953. Economic Development and the Transfer Mechanism: Canada, 1895-1913. *Canadian Journal of Economics and Political Science* XIX, 1-19.

———— 1963. *International Trade and Development.* New York.

————, and Baldwin, R. E. 1957. *Economic Development.* New York.

Metzler, L. A. 1942. The Transfer Problem Reconsidered. *Journal of Political Economy* L, 397-414.

——— 1948. The Theory of International Trade. In H. S. Ellis (ed.), *A Survey of Contemporary Economics.* Homewood, Ill.

Mikesell, R. F. (ed.) 1962. *U.S. Private and Government Investment Abroad.* Eugene, Oregon.

Mill, John Stuart 1848. *Principles of Political Economy.* Boston.

Mundell, R. A. 1957. International Trade and Factor Mobility. *American Economic Review* XLVII, 321-35.

Murphy, J. C. 1960. International Investment and the National Interest. *Southern Economic Journal* XXVII, 11-17.

Myrdal, G. 1956. *An International Economy: Problems and Prospects.* New York.

Nurkse, R. 1953. *Problems of Capital Formation in Underdeveloped Countries.* Oxford.

——— 1961. International Trade Theory and Development Policy. In H. S. Ellis and H. C. Wallich (eds.), *Economic Development for Latin America: Proceedings of a Conference held by the International Economic Association.* London.

Ohlin, B. 1933. *Interregional and International Trade.* Cambridge, Mass.

Pazos, F. 1961. Private versus Public Foreign Investment in Under-developed Areas. In H. S. Ellis and H. C. Wallich (eds.), *Economic Development for Latin America: Proceedings of a Conference held by the International Economic Association.* London.

Penrose, Edith Tilton 1956. Foreign Investment and the Growth of the Firm. *Economic Journal* LXVI, 220-35.

Perkins, J. O. N. 1960. Some Fallacies about Overseas Borrowing. *Australian Quarterly* XXXII, no. 2, 74-88.

Phelps, D. M. 1936. *Migration of Industry to South America.* New York.

Philipps, E. A. 1960. American Direct Investments in West German Manufacturing Industries, 1945 to 1959. *Current Economic Comment* 22, no. 2, 29-44.

Polak, J. J. 1943. Balance of Payments Problems of Countries Reconstructing with the Help of Foreign Loans. *Quarterly Journal of Economics* LVII, 208-40.

Reitsma, A. J. 1960. *Trade Protection in Australia.* Leiden.

Robinson, H. J. 1961. *The Motivation and Flow of Private Foreign Investment.* Menlo Park, Cal. (Stanford Research Institute).

Rosenberg, W. 1961. Capital Imports and Growth—The Case of New Zealand—Foreign Investment in New Zealand, 1840-1958. *Economic Journal* LXXI, 93-113.

Rosenstein-Rodan, P. N. 1943. Problems of Industrialization of Eastern and South-Eastern Europe. *Economic Journal* LIII, 202-11.

Sadie, J. L. 1958. Foreign Capital in South Africa: II—Its Burden. *Finance and Trade Review* III, no. 1, 67-79.

Safarian, A. E. 1964. The Exports of American-owned Enterprises in Canada. *American Economic Review, Papers and Proceedings* LIV, 449-58.

Salant, W. S. 1950. The Domestic Effects of Capital Export under the Point Four Program. *American Economic Review, Papers and Proceedings* XL, 495-510.

Samuelson, P. A. 1948. International Trade and the Equalisation of Factor Prices. *Economic Journal* LVIII, 163-84.

——— 1949. International Factor-Price Equalisation Once Again. *Economic Journal* LIX, 181-97.

Singer, H. W. 1950. The Distribution of Gains Between Investing and Borrowing Countries. *American Economic Review, Papers and Proceedings* XL, 473-85.

Snider, D. A. 1964. The Case for Capital Controls to Relieve the U.S. Balance of Payments. *American Economic Review* LIV, 346-58.

Southard, jr, F. A. 1931. *American Industry in Europe*. Boston.

Sylos-Labini, P. 1962. *Oligopoly and Technical Progress*. Cambridge, Mass.

Thomson, E. J. 1962. Oversea Investment—the Lengthening Shadow. Economic Monograph No. 242 of the Economic Society of Australia and New Zealand, New South Wales Branch.

Viner, J. 1924. *Canada's Balance of International Indebtedness 1900-1913*. Cambridge, Mass.

—— 1937. *Studies in the Theory of International Trade*. New York.

—— 1962. Relative Abundance of the Factors and International Trade. *Indian Economic Journal* IX, 274-88.

Wheelwright, E. L. 1963. Overseas Investment in Australia. In A. Hunter (ed.), *The Economics of Australian Industry*. Melbourne.

Williams, B. R. 1962. *Industrial Research and Economic Growth in Australia: The 30th Joseph Fisher Lecture in Commerce*. Adelaide.

Williams, J. H. 1929. The Theory of International Trade Reconsidered. *Economic Journal* XXXIX, 195-209.

Wilson, R. 1931. *Capital Imports and the Terms of Trade*. Melbourne.

Zeidler, D. R. 1961. Some Research and Development Possibilities. *Proceedings of the Royal Australian Chemical Institute* 28, 452-67.

(B)   OFFICIAL PUBLICATIONS

Australia

Commonwealth Bureau of Census and Statistics
- 1960-3.   *Registrations of New Motor Vehicles, Australia.*
- 1964.   *Secondary Industries: Part I. Factory and Building Operations, 1961-62.*
- 1965a.   *Australian National Accounts: National Income and Expenditure 1948-49 to 1963-64.*
- 1965b.   *Annual Bulletin of Oversea Investment: Australia 1963-64.*

Commonwealth Parliament
- 1962.   Income Tax and Social Services Contribution Assessment Act 1936-1962.
- 1963-4.   *Parliamentary Debates* H. of R. 39-41 (New Series).

Commonwealth Treasury
- 1960.   *Overseas Investment in Australia.*
- 1965a.   *Supplement to the Treasury Information Bulletin: Private Overseas Investment in Australia.*
- 1965b.   *The Australian Economy 1965.*

Reserve Bank of Australia
- 1965.   *Statistical Bulletin: Company Supplement, February 1965.*

Tariff Board and related authorities
(i) Tariff Board Reports:
- 1927.   *Storage Batteries.*
- 1935a.   *Motor Body Panels.*
- 1935b.   *Pneumatic Rubber Tyres and Tubes for Motor Vehicles.*
- 1937.   *Motor Vehicles.*
- 1940.   *Files, Being Hand Tools of Trade—Tariff Item 219(c).*
- 1953.   *Files.*

1955a.	*Covered Cable and Covered Wire classifiable under Tariff Item 181 (A) (1) (a).*
1955b.	*Tractors.*
1957.	*Automotive Industry.*
1959a.	*Petroleum Refining Industry.*
1959b.	*Abrasive Cloths and Papers.*
1960a.	*Chlorination Regulators and Controllers.*
1960b.	*Cathode Ray Tubes and Parts Thereof.*
1960c.	*Roll Film Box Type Cameras.*
1961a.	*Refined Petroleum Products.*
1961b.	*Work Trucks, Mechanically Propelled.*
1961c.	*Vacuum Cleaners and Floor Polishers.*
1962a.	*Citric Acid, Tartaric Acid and Cream of Tartar.*
1962b.	*Aluminium and Aluminium Alloys.*
1962c.	*Abrasives.*
1962d.	*Paper Cones, Bobbins, Tubes, etc.*
1962e.	*Snap Fasteners and Eyelets.*
1962f.	*Glass Fibre and Glass Fibre Products.*
1962g.	*Precision Ground Tapered Roller Bearings.*
1962h.	*Styrene Monomers, Polymers and Copolymers.*
1962i.	*Electric Shavers.*
1962j.	*Synthetic Rubber.*
1962k.	*Capacitors.*
1963a.	*Iron and Steel Chain.*
1963b.	*Portable Electric Hand Tools.*
1963c.	*Vinyl Chloride Polymers and Copolymers.*
1963d.	*Knives with Forged Stainless Steel Blades.*
1964a.	*Aluminium Ingots, etc.*
1964b.	*Fluorocarbons.*
1964c.	*Caterpillar Tractor-Scrapers (By-Law).*
1964d.	*Glass Envelopes for Cathode Ray Tubes.*
1965.	*Crude Oil.*

(ii) Other reports:

1906.	*Royal Commission on Customs and Excise Tariffs, Minutes of Evidence VI.*
1914.	*Inter-State Commission of Australia. Tariff Investigation: Miscellaneous Group VI. Report.*

Trade, Department of

1959.	*Canadian Investment in Australian Manufacturing Industry.*
1960a.	*The Australian Pharmaceutical Products Industry.*
1960b.	*British Manufacturers in Australia.*
1962.	*Directory of United States Investment in Australian Manufacturing Industry, 1962.*

New Zealand

Health, Department of

1963.	*Report of the Special Committee on Pharmaceutical Benefits.*

United States

Commerce, Department of

1930.	*American Direct Investments in Foreign Countries.*
1938.	*American Direct Investments in Foreign Countries—1936.*

Y

1953.   *Factors Limiting U.S. Investment Abroad.*

1956.   *Investment in Australia: Basic Information for United States Businessmen.*

1960.   *U.S. Business Investments in Foreign Countries.*

1963a.   *Establishing a Business in Australia.* An *Overseas Business Report* prepared by Deane M. Black.

1963b.   *Balance of Payments Statistical Supplement.* Revised Edition.

1964.   *Survey of Current Business* 44, nos. 8 and 12.

Treasury Department

1947.   *Census of American-Owned Assets in Foreign Countries.*

Index to Companies

General Index